Organizing
Dissent

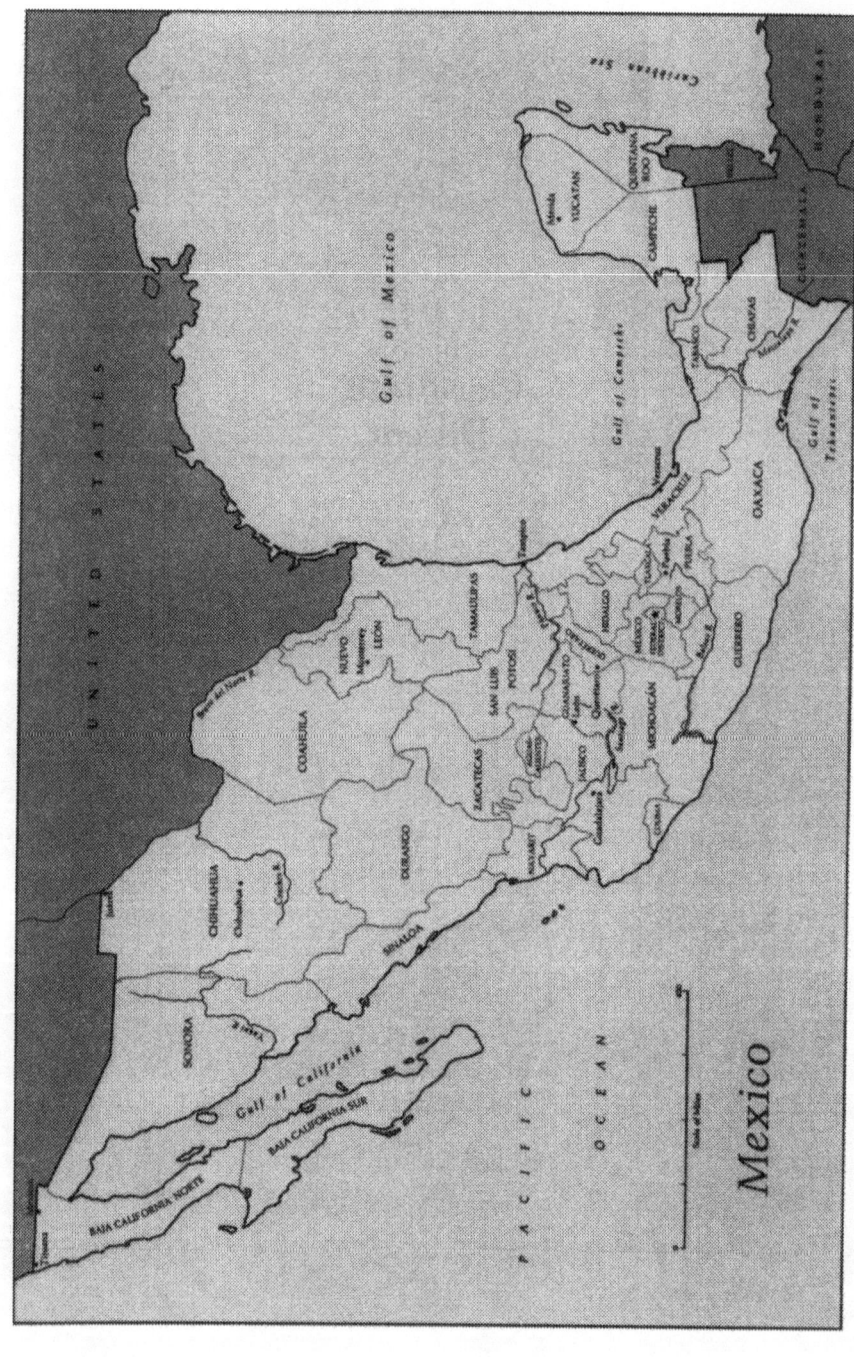

Maria Lorena Cook

Organizing Dissent

Unions, the State,
and the
Democratic Teachers'
Movement in Mexico

The Pennsylvania State University Press
University Park, Pennsylvania

Library of Congress Cataloging-in-Publication Data

Cook, Maria Lorena.
   Organizing dissent : unions, the state, and the Democratic Teachers' Movement in Mexico / Maria Lorena Cook.
      p.   cm.
   Includes bibliographical references and index.
   ISBN 0-271-01560-8 (cloth : alk. paper)
   ISBN 0-271-01561-6 (pbk. : alk. paper)
   1. Teachers' unions—Mexico—History.   2. Teachers—Mexico—Political activity—History.   3. Social movements—Mexico—History.
   I. Title.
LB2844.53.M6C66   1996
331.88'113711'0972—dc20   95-26109
                                                                  CIP

Copyright © 1996 The Pennsylvania State University
All rights reserved
Printed in the United States of America
Published by The Pennsylvania State University Press,
University Park, PA 16802-1003

It is the policy of The Pennsylvania State University Press to use acid-free paper for the first printing of all clothbound books. Publications on uncoated stock satisfy the minimum requirements of American National Standard for Information Sciences—Permanence of Paper for Printed Library Materials, ANSI Z39.48—1992.

FRONTISPIECE: Map of Mexico. Courtesy of the Center for U.S.–Mexican Studies, University of California, San Diego.

Contents

List of Tables and Diagrams	vii
List of Illustrations	ix
Acknowledgments	xi
Acronyms	xiii
1. Introduction	1
2. Social Movements in Authoritarian Environments: A Political Process Approach	27
3. Conflict and Alliance in State-Union Relations	59
4. Emergence of the National Teachers' Movement: A Regional Comparison	105
5. Oaxaca and Chiapas: Dilemmas of Legality	183
6. Sustaining the Movement: Democracy as Survival Strategy	216
7. Resurgence of National Mobilization	266
8. Conclusion	290
Appendix A: SNTE Leaders, Education Ministers, and Interior Ministers, 1976–1994	315
Appendix B: Chronology of the Democratic Teachers' Movement	316
Bibliography	321
Index	345

List of Tables and Diagrams

Table 3.1. Political office held by secretaries-general of the
   SNTE, 1949–1995   65–66

Table 4.1. Teachers by education level and by state: Chiapas,
   Guerrero, Morelos, Oaxaca, and Mexico, 1978–1987   146

Diagram 3.1. Chain of authority between central and state levels
   within the Public Education Ministry, before and after 1978
   deconcentration   91

Diagram 6.1. Organizational structure of union local, SNTE   218

Diagram 6.2. Statutory and nonstatutory organizations in Local 22,
   Oaxaca, 1982–89   220

List of Illustrations

Frontispiece: Map of Mexico. Courtesy of the Center for U.S.–Mexican Studies, University of California, San Diego

The following illustrations are on pages 174–82.

1. CNTE march, Oaxaca contingent, Mexico City, 1980 (photo by Jorge Acevedo)
2. CNTE rally in front of Education Ministry, Mexico City, 1981 (photo by Jorge Acevedo)
3. Morelos teachers' caravan-march to Mexico City, 1980 (photo by Jorge Acevedo)
4. Parents march in support of teachers, Valle de México, 1981 (photo by Jorge Acevedo)
5. Misael Núñez Acosta's funeral, 1981 (photo by Jorge Acevedo)
6. *Plantón* in Mexico City, 1981 (photo by Jorge Acevedo)
7. Audience at the public "political trial" of Vanguardia Revolucionaria, Oaxaca, 1985 (photo by the author)
8. SNTE labor goons, Mexico City, May Day March, 1983 (photo by Jorge Acevedo)
9. Raised fists and a minute of silence for murdered teachers' movement activists, Oaxaca, 1985 (photo by the author)
10. Oaxacan teachers' "silent march" for union electoral congress, Mexico City, 1986. Sign reads "Only One Way: Democracy" (photo by Jorge Acevedo)
11. CNTE rally in downtown Mexico City, 1989 (photo by Tomás Martínez for Cuartoscuro)

To my mother,
Fernanda Galván Vargas
and
To the memory of my father,
Charles Rudolph Cook

Acknowledgments

Sitting down to acknowledge the numerous individuals and institutions that helped to make this book possible is a daunting task. In reviewing the lists of names I am reminded not only of the generosity of many people but also of the highs and lows that inevitably mark any major intellectual project, but especially one's first. Of special importance during the earliest stages of this study were David Collier, Alex Saragoza, and D. Paul Thomas, all of whom provided guidance for the dissertation at the University of California, Berkeley. David Collier has remained an important source of encouragement throughout the book project. In addition, Ruth Berins Collier and Andrés Jiménez helped to cultivate my interest in Mexican politics. The Center for Latin American Studies at the University of California, Berkeley, provided support for an initial research trip to Mexico. Subsequent field research was funded by the Inter-American Foundation and through a Chancellor's Postdoctoral Fellowship from the University of California, San Diego.

Several individuals deserve special recognition for their generosity during my various research trips to Mexico in the 1980s and early 1990s: Alberto Arnaut Salgado, María de la Luz Arriaga, Jaime Moisés Bailón, René Bejarano, María Amparo Casar, Santiago Cortez, Rosa Albina Garavito, Enrique de la Garza, Carlos Heredia, Luis Hernández Navarro, Patricio Hernández, Samael Hernández, Víctor Raúl Martínez, Luis Méndez, Francisco Pérez Arce, Gisela Salinas, Víctor Solís, and Juan Luis Toledo. I am also grateful to Jorge Acevedo, who provided many of the photographs for this book. In addition to facilitating important contacts and intellectual exchange, the following friends and colleagues kept my spirits up during the field research: Hugo Aboites, Alejandro Alvarez, Miguel Díaz-Barriga, Jonathan Fox, Concepción Núñez Miranda, Keith Pezzoli, Susan Street, and Carol Zabin.

I am also indebted to the many very courageous people I encountered during my research, those who provided the experience and material for this study. Clearly this book would have been impossible without them. As most of these individuals were promised anonymity, their names cannot be mentioned here.

I only hope they will know who they are and will consider this book some small repayment for their generosity and trust. I am likewise grateful for the confidence and assistance of those government officials who did not have to help me but chose to do so anyway, and who were also guaranteed anonymity.

A number of individuals and institutions provided critical support as I was writing and revising this book. Support for writing the dissertation on which this book was based was granted in the form of a Visiting Research Fellowship at the Center for U.S.-Mexican Studies at the University of California, San Diego, directed by Wayne Cornelius. Later periods of revision were made possible by a Chancellor's Postdoctoral Fellowship in the Political Science Department of the University of California, San Diego, under the guidance of Peter H. Smith. During my time in San Diego many colleagues, but especially Vivienne Bennett, Luin Goldring, Neil Harvey, Kevin J. Middlebrook, and Keith Pezzoli, provided key criticism and feedback on parts of the research project. I have also been fortunate to have the support of my colleagues at the New York State School of Industrial and Labor Relations, Cornell University, where I completed the final revisions for this book. In particular, I have appreciated the support and advice of Cletus Daniel, Harry C. Katz, and Risa Lieberwitz, and of Cornell colleagues Alejandro Covarrubias, Cathy Schneider, and Sidney Tarrow. I am also grateful to María Jesús Encinas for help with the diagrams for this book, and to Sandy Thatcher, director of Penn State Press, and Cherene Holland, managing editor, whose patient prodding helped bring this book to completion.

Those who read and commented on parts or all of the manuscript at different stages in its development deserve special mention. I have benefited from the extensive comments and insightful criticism of the following people on parts of the manuscript: Vivienne Bennett, Jonathan Fox, Luin Goldring, Paul Haber, David Meyer, and Yemile Mizrahi. I have also been fortunate to have friends and colleagues willing to take on the task of reading and commenting on the entire manuscript: Hugo Aboites, Alejandro Alvarez, David Collier, John D. French, Kevin J. Middlebrook, Peter H. Smith, Susan Street, and Sidney Tarrow.

Special thanks also go to my sister, Pamela Cook Galván, for her faith, to Petiso, for not caring, and to Ronnie Earnest, who, with patience and humor, was there throughout. This book is dedicated to my mother, Fernanda Galván Vargas, and to the memory of my father, Charles Rudolph Cook, whose belief in the power of education got me this far, and whose lessons about dignity and perseverance have oriented my life and work.

Acronyms

ANOCP	Asamblea Nacional Obrero Campesino Popular (National Worker-Peasant-Popular Assembly)
ATE	Alianza Trabajadores de la Educación (Education Workers' Alliance)
CCL	Consejo Central de Lucha (Central Council of Struggle)
CCLMM	Consejo Central de Lucha del Magisterio Morelense (Central Council of Struggle of Morelos Teachers)
CCLMVM	Consejo Central de Lucha Magisterial del Valle de México (Central Council of Teachers' Struggle of the Valley of Mexico)
CED	Comité Ejecutivo Delegacional (Delegation Executive Committee)
CEN	Comité Ejecutivo Nacional (National Executive Committee)
CES	Comité Ejecutivo Seccional (Local Executive Committee)
CIOAC	Central Independiente de Obreros Agrícolas y Campesinos (Independent Central of Farm Workers and Peasants)
CNC	Confederación Nacional Campesina (National Peasant Confederation)
CNOP	Confederación Nacional de Organizaciones Populares (National Confederation of Popular Organizations)
CNPA	Coordinadora Nacional "Plan de Ayala" (National "Plan of Ayala" Coordinating Committee)
CNTE	Coordinadora Nacional de Trabajadores de la Educación (National Coordinating Committee of Education Workers)
COCEI	Coalición Obrero Campesino Estudiantil del Istmo (Worker-Peasant-Student Coalition of the Isthmus)
COCEO	Coalición Obrero Campesino Estudiantil de Oaxaca (Worker-Peasant-Student Coalition of Oaxaca)
CODEMA	Corriente Democrática Magisterial (Democratic Current of Teachers)

CONAMUP	Coordinadora Nacional del Movimiento Urbano Popular (National Coordinating Committee of the Urban Popular Movement)
COSDE	Corriente Sindical Democrática (Democratic Union Current)
COSID	Corriente Sindical Independiente y Democrática (Independent and Democratic Union Current)
COSINA	Coordinadora Sindical Nacional (National Union Coordinating Committee)
CROM	Confederación Regional Obrera Mexicana (Mexican Regional Labor Confederation)
CT	Congreso del Trabajo (Labor Congress)
CTM	Confederación de Trabajadores de México (Confederation of Mexican Workers)
ETA	Escuela Técnica Agropecuaria (Agricultural Technical School)
EZLN	Ejército Zapatista de Liberación Nacional (Zapatista National Liberation Army)
FMIN	Frente Magisterial Independiente Nacional (National Independent Teachers' Front)
FNDSCAC	Frente Nacional de Defensa del Salario Contra la Austeridad y la Carestía (National Front in Defense of Wages Against Austerity and the High Cost of Living)
FNOC	Frente Nacional de Organizaciones y Ciudadanos (National Front of Organizations and Citizens)
FRTECH	Frente Reivindicador de Trabajadores de la Educación en Chiapas (Front for the Demands of Education Workers in Chiapas)
FSTSE	Federación de Sindicatos de Trabajadores al Servicio del Estado (Federation of Public Service Workers' Unions)
IIISEO	Instituto de Investigación e Integración Social del Estado de Oaxaca (Social Integration and Research Institute of Oaxaca)
INAH	Instituto Nacional de Antropología e Historia (National Institute of Anthropology and History)
ISSSTE	Instituto de Seguridad y Servicios Sociales de los Trabajadores del Estado (Institute of Social Security and Services for State Employees)
LFTSE	Ley Federal de los Trabajadores al Servicio del Estado (Federal Law of Public Service Workers)
LP	Línea Proletaria (Proletarian Line)

Acronyms

MDM	Maestros Democráticos de Morelos (Democratic Teachers of Morelos)
MDM	Movimiento Democrático del Magisterio (Democratic Teachers' Movement)
MRM	Movimiento Revolucionario del Magisterio (Revolutionary Teachers' Movement)
NAFTA	North American Free Trade Agreement (Tratado de Libre Comercio de América del Norte)
OIR-LM	Organización de Izquierda Revolucionaria—Línea de Masas (Revolutionary Left Organization—Mass Line)
ORTE	Organización Revolucionaria de Trabajadores de la Educación (Revolutionary Organization of Education Workers)
PAN	Partido Acción Nacional (National Action Party)
PEMEX	Petróleos Mexicanos (Mexican Petroleum Company)
PRD	Partido de la Revolución Democrática (Party of the Democratic Revolution)
PRI	Partido Revolucionario Institucional (Institutional Revolutionary Party)
PRM	Partido de la Revolución Mexicana (Party of the Mexican Revolution)
PRONASOL	Programa Nacional de Solidaridad (National Solidarity Program)
PRT	Partido Revolucionario de los Trabajadores (Revolutionary Workers' Party)
PSUM	Partido Socialista Unificado de México (Unified Socialist Party of Mexico)
SCEP	Servicios Coordinados de Educación Pública (Coordinated Public Education Services)
SEP	Secretaría de Educación Pública (Ministry of Public Education)
SHCP	Secretaría de Hacienda y Crédito Público (Ministry of Finance)
SNTE	Sindicato Nacional de Trabajadores de la Educación (National Union of Education Workers)
SPP	Secretaría de Programación y Presupuesto (Ministry of Programming and the Budget)
UNAM	Universidad Nacional Autónoma de México (National Autonomous University of Mexico)
UNORCA	Unión Nacional de Organizaciones Regionales Campesinas

	Autónomas (National Union of Autonomous Regional Peasant Organizations)
UPN	Universidad Pedagógica Nacional (National Pedagogical University)
USED	Unidad de Servicios Educativos a Descentralizar (Unit of Educational Services to be Decentralized)
UTE	Unión de Trabajadores de la Educación (Education Workers Union)

1
Introduction

This book is about how popular social movements emerge and survive in authoritarian regimes and what their presence means for political and social change. The 1970s and 1980s saw the rise of social movements (urban neighborhood organizations, independent peasant and labor movements, environmental, women's, and human rights organizations) under authoritarian governments throughout Latin America. In 1989 the world watched in surprise as popular mobilizations in Eastern Europe helped topple one communist regime after another. The presence and apparent strength of social movements in authoritarian contexts challenged social science research, which had largely focused on the range of movements that emerged in the 1960s and 1970s in the United States or on the "postmaterialist" appearance of social movements in Western Europe—that is, on movements in advanced industrial democracies. What was missing was an explanation for why and how movements emerged in poorer countries with authoritarian governments, and an understanding of how this different political environment shaped their organization, strategies, and what they were able to achieve.

This study of the Mexican teachers' movement contributes to an emerging literature on Latin American social movements that has begun to address some of these questions.[1] The dissident teachers' movement was a rank-and-file movement for union democracy that emerged *within* Mexico's (and Latin America's) largest single trade union, the Sindicato Nacional de Trabajadores de la Educación (National Union of Education Workers, SNTE).[2] With approximately 600,000 members at the start of the movement in 1979, a decade later the teachers' union boasted a membership of over one million.[3] In addition, the union comprised over 40 percent of all public service employees organized in the Federación de Sindicatos de Trabajadores al Servicio del Estado (Federation of Public Service Workers' Unions, FSTSE) and was one of the most important members of the Confederación Nacional de Organizaciones Populares (National Confederation of Popular Organizations, CNOP), a sector of the ruling Partido Revolucionario Institucional (Institutional Revolutionary Party, PRI), and of the umbrella Congreso del Trabajo (Labor Congress). The teachers' union played an important role in the political system: the union was key in mobilizing voters for the PRI, and its members carried out important logistical support for PRI electoral campaigns. Union leaders also occupied positions on the national committee of the PRI, in the congress, and as directors of important state agencies.

---

1. See, for example, Eckstein 1989, Escobar and Alvarez 1992, Foweraker and Craig 1990, Jelín 1990, Alvarez 1990, Brysk 1994, Maybury-Lewis 1994, Schneider 1995.

2. The SNTE organizes nonmanagement and some lower-level administrative employees of the Ministry of Public Education: practically all public preschool, primary, and secondary schoolteachers, some higher education teachers, including all teaching college faculty, academic employees of institutes, research centers, and museums, and all technical, manual, and clerical personnel at these schools and facilities. In the 1980s the union had fifty-five locals, most of them of workers employed in the federal system, but also some locals of teachers under the jurisdiction of state governments, "federalized" locals (mixed state and federal), and one local of private school employees.

3. Estimates of union membership vary and must be taken with caution. Union officials tend to exaggerate their numbers. At the same time, data on the number of teaching positions are not a reliable indicator of union membership, as the number of positions tends to exceed the number of teachers (many teachers occupy more than one position [*Los Angeles Times*, April 18, 1989; *Ovaciones*, January 9, 1983]). In a 1982 internal document the Secretaría de Educación Pública (Ministry of Public Education, SEP) claimed it handled paychecks for more than 675,000 teaching and administrative employees, who occupied more than 1,250,000 positions (SEP n.d.). A 1983 estimate claims 768,000 teachers occupied 1,020,000 positions (*Ovaciones*, January 9, 1983). The dissident movement (CNTE) in 1982 claimed the union's membership was 600,000 (Pérez Arce, de la Garza, and Hernández 1982:63). Likely estimates of union membership by 1990 are in the range

Introduction

In 1979 dissident teachers belonging to the SNTE joined in an effort to democratize the teachers' union and push for higher wages, forming the Coordinadora Nacional de Trabajadores de la Educación (National Coordinating Committee of Education Workers, CNTE).[4] In the early 1980s the CNTE counted among its supporters between 100,000–150,000 members, as much as 16 to 25 percent of the union membership.[5] Within four years of its emergence the dissident teachers' movement managed to obtain official recognition of electoral victories in three union locals in southeastern Mexico.[6] Against strong opposition by government and union officials, the movement was able to defend these victories for several years. During this period dissident teachers established alternative practices and organizations that were broadly participatory and democratic in character; they formed contacts with other popular movements at national and regional levels; they questioned the union's long-standing relationship with Mexico's ruling party; and they challenged the government's austerity policies, reflected in the dramatically declining wages of schoolteachers and a reduced government contribution to public education.

In 1989 new demonstrations for union democracy and wage increases involving half a million teachers brought down the head of the union and one of Mexico's most notorious labor bosses, Carlos Jonguitud Barrios. Although President Carlos Salinas de Gortari (1988–94) imposed a new union leader, the democratic teachers' movement was able to obtain a stronger presence within the union and able to exert a greater degree of influence on the union leadership than ever before. The decade-long persistence of this democratic movement was unprecedented within both the teachers' union and the Mexican labor movement, and generally rare among popular movements in Mexico. The teachers'

---

of 800,000–1,000,000 members. Still, the SNTE remains by far the largest union in Mexico and most likely in all of Latin America (Greenfield and Maram 1987).

4. The dissident teachers' CNTE was not a separate union but a democratic movement *within* the official union, the SNTE. See Chapters 3 and 4 on the logic of forming currents within unions as opposed to parallel, independent unions in Mexico.

5. See Pérez Arce, de la Garza, and Hernández 1982:63. After a decline in the mid-1980s, the dissident ranks grew again in both absolute and proportional terms during mobilizations in 1989. Approximately 500,000 teachers were said to have been on strike in early 1989. The number of members located in contingents identified with the CNTE after 1989 probably stabilized at around 300,000, or approximately 30 percent of the union.

6. These included two locals of federal jurisdiction teachers, one in Chiapas (Local 7) and one in Oaxaca (Local 22), and one local of state jurisdiction teachers in Chiapas (Local 40). This study concentrates on the first two locals of federal jurisdiction teachers, as conditions for state teachers were somewhat different and information on them is more scarce. Not all states had teachers employed by the state government; Oaxaca, for example, had only the one union local of federal jurisdiction teachers.

movement's size, persistence, and success stood out in a country that, while perhaps not as repressive as many of its neighbors under military rule, was nonetheless renowned for its ability to coopt, control, and repress dissent.[7]

The existence of social movements under authoritarian environments raises two key questions, both of which are addressed in this book: How do oppositional social movements manage to emerge in authoritarian environments, contexts in which repression is generally more likely than in democratic regimes? What enables these movements to *survive* in such environments? A central puzzle in the case of the teachers' union was how a national dissident rank-and-file movement managed to emerge within Mexico's largest "official" union, one that enjoyed close ties with the authoritarian regime and that had managed to contain previous expressions of dissent among its ranks. Moreover, what explained the ability of two regional movements in particular—those in the southern states of Oaxaca and Chiapas—to obtain official recognition and sustain themselves as dissident movements for most of the 1980s, in spite of open hostility by the government and union leadership?

The key argument in this book is that the *timing* of the emergence of the teachers' movement can best be understood by the presence of conflict between major actors in the movement's immediate environment—namely, the state and union leadership—which in turn provided the movement with some protection from repression and opportunity for mobilization. Specifically, political conflict between teachers' union officials and the Education Ministry over educational and administrative reforms created an opening in the political arena that facilitated the emergence of the movement and its consolidation in some regions. After the dissident movement had emerged, and after the political opening created by the state-union conflict had disappeared, other elements— such as internal organization and the movement's mobilization strategy— became more important for understanding the movement's ability to survive. I argue in particular that the *democratic* organization of some regional contingents of the movement was an especially important factor in sustaining these movements. It is the interaction between the movement's organizational resources and strategy and *changes in the political environment* that offers the best understanding of the movement's development. As Eisinger has noted, the manner in which groups behave "is not simply a function of the resources they command but of the openings, weak spots, barriers, and resources of the political system itself" (Eisinger 1973:12).

---

7. On tactics employed by the state against dissident groups see, among others, Anderson and Cockroft 1972, and Stevens 1974.

Introduction

This study of the teachers' movement in Mexico makes several contributions in two key areas: 1) the comparative study of social movements, and 2) the analysis of political change in Mexico.[8] Studies of social movements frequently attribute the emergence of movements to broad structural changes or to exceptional periods of regime change. Yet movements also appear and persist under more "stable" political environments. Understanding how and why movements emerge under "everyday conditions" in stable authoritarian regimes, for example, is important for understanding how movements themselves contribute to periods of exceptionalism or regime change. In this study I draw on a "political process" approach to examine the more sectoral or intermediate, as opposed to national, political openings that may occur in the environments of movements. This focus on more immediate openings can help us to understand how oppositional social movements may occur in otherwise "closed" national political environments. The teachers' movement is an example of a movement that emerged under such conditions. It therefore provides a good empirical context in which to examine how movements emerge and survive in authoritarian environments.

The political process approach is largely drawn from studies of social movements in advanced industrial democracies and has not yet been applied widely

8. There are a number of accounts and studies of the teachers' movement in Mexico. Many of these were produced by the teachers themselves in small collections or pamphlets and are too numerous to list here; some of these are included in the bibliography. Important collections of documents can be found in Peláez 1980, Hernández 1981, and Hernández and Pérez Arce 1982. An excellent collection of interviews with movement leaders carried out by several people close to the movement can be found in *Testimonios* 1987. A two-volume, comprehensive history that includes a detailed chronological account of the emergence of the national movement, based largely on newspaper sources, is Salinas and Imaz 1984. A good article-length account of the emergence of the movement is Arriaga 1981; another is Luna Jurado 1977 on dissidence in a union local in Chihuahua. The first English-language account of the movement appeared in Hernández 1986b. Studies of the official teachers' union are scarce: Peláez 1984a and Espinosa 1982 offer solid historical accounts of the union's development; Arnaut Salgado's (1989a) work is excellent on the internal politics of the union. Susan Street has written on the impact of the democratic teachers' movement on the bureaucratic reform of the public education ministry during 1978–82 (1983, 1984, 1992a). Also see her review of the literature on education policy and teachers from 1970–90 (1992b), and her research on democracy and education inside the Chiapas movement (1994). A recent book-length study of the teachers' movement between 1977–87, focusing on the Chiapas movement, can be found in Foweraker 1993.

My study of the teachers' movement differs from the preceding studies in its scope (the study encompasses the emergence of the movement in the late 1970s through the resurgence of national mobilization in 1989 and changes in the early 1990s), in its comparative regional focus (the study compares six regional movements during 1979–82 and two regions, Oaxaca and Chiapas, subsequently), in its detailing of internal organization and the importance of internal democracy for the movement, and in its explicit framing of the teachers' movement in the context of the social movements literature, especially the literature on "political process."

to Latin America or to other developing regions or authoritarian regimes. In examining Latin American social movements, many scholars have tended to adopt another theoretical strand, the European-inspired "new social movements" approach, which has emphasized such issues as identity and autonomy in the construction of social movements. The political process approach, in contrast, places more emphasis on strategy and organization and the interaction of the movement with its political environment.[9] In particular, the political process perspective stresses the importance of "political opportunities" that appear in the environment in order to understand why movements emerge when and where they do, and how they develop subsequently.

The application of this approach to a more authoritarian context is especially fruitful for understanding how an oppositional movement may emerge and survive in circumstances where movements are typically more readily repressed or, as has often been the case in Mexico, coopted.[10] In other words, given that authoritarian states by definition "discourage popular politics" (Tarrow 1994:92), what must be explained is how movements survive *in spite of* this "discouragement" and what conditions obtain in an authoritarian environment that provide opportunities for movement emergence and mobilization—what prevents characteristic forms of repression from being carried out? Answers to these questions are to be found, I believe, in the political environments of movements, in the resources that movements command and mobilize, and in the interaction between the two. Given that the type of political opportunities that facilitate movement mobilization have typically been drawn from cases of industrial democracies, moreover, application of the political process approach to an authoritarian context also enhances our understanding of the way in which differences in political regime may affect the emergence, internal life, development, and impact of social movements.

Once a movement emerges, how is it able to sustain itself, especially in the midst of a hostile environment? This is an especially important question in the case of authoritarian environments because, even though collective action and protest may understandably emerge in response to an authoritarian regime or closed conditions, a more puzzling issue is how a movement is able to persist under such conditions. Here I argue that the *type of organization* a movement

---

9. These have often been counterposed as "identity-centered" approaches, on the one hand, and "strategy-centered" approaches, on the other. Yet increasingly, the emphases of these two perspectives are being combined in social movement studies (see Escobar and Alvarez 1992, Klandermans and Tarrow 1988). A more detailed discussion of the new social movements and the political process approaches can be found in Chapter 2.

10. A fuller discussion of Mexican authoritarianism appears later in this chapter.

adopts matters, both for understanding a movement's survival and its potential impact. The social movements literature recognizes that there are persistent challenges to the organizational stability of movements, such as cooptation, oligarchy, and the loss of member support (McAdam 1982). A key issue, then, in those movements that manage to sustain themselves, is how they construct their organizations so as to manage these challenges while pursuing their objectives in the larger political environment. Moreover, how is organization linked to strategy—what features of a movement's internal organization best support a strategy of confrontation or of negotiation? Finally, a study of movement organization is also a study of practices, and thus of means. What lasting difference does the means a movement employs make for the participants and for broader social change? These issues have received little explicit treatment in Latin America or in the context of authoritarian regimes. Moreover, empirical studies of the organizational characteristics of social movements have generally been scarce (Klandermans 1989:2).[11] This study, therefore, addresses an important gap in the literature on social movements in general and on Latin American movements in particular by its emphasis on the organizational characteristics of the teachers' movement.

I argue specifically that the creation of a strongly democratic and participatory internal organization by some regional contingents of the teachers' movement was key in enabling them to sustain themselves against government and union leadership attacks. This study reveals that it was not only possible to create organizational democracy in circumstances where it had not existed before and in the midst of an authoritarian environment but that democracy was also an *effective* form of organization for the specific time and political context in which the movement operated. This study also suggests that the participatory internal organization of some contingents of the teachers' movement aided their tactic of recurrent mobilizations, which was itself made necessary by the closed environment in which the teachers found themselves. Finally, I argue that whether a movement establishes democratic practices or not matters for how much the participants themselves are changed by their experience in the movement, for the possibility of the movement's recurrence, and for the broader process of democratization in civil society.

By focusing on the internal organization of the movement throughout its development, this book also contributes to a greater understanding of the "everyday life" of social movements. In contrast to many movement studies, it

---

11. See Klandermans 1989 for a volume that examines social movement organizations in several European countries and the United States.

does not focus primarily or solely on instances of collective action, on the public manifestations of a movement's existence. Instead it reviews what happens "in between" the massive public demonstrations, strikes, and building occupations that makes these actions possible. This does not necessarily mean that in this case resistance should be understood primarily in terms of the "everyday forms" it may take.[12] It does recognize, however, that most collective action is not spontaneous and that participation does not derive automatically from membership. Thus, what happens inside a movement—when it is not in the public eye—is crucial.

This study also offers a comparative assessment of the emergence of six regional contingents of the teachers' movement in order to understand why some regional movements were successful at meeting their goals and why others were not. Such comparative inquiries have been rare thus far in the literature on Latin American movements, which has tended to focus on single case studies.[13] This regional comparison of the movements' emergence allows us to assess the role played by strategy, organization, ideology, and environment in determining the differential outcomes of the six regional movements. The answer suggested here is that those regional contingents that pursued more legalistic and less confrontational approaches and that had an extensive network of grass-roots organization and participation were more successful in meeting their initial goals of authorized local elections than were those regional contingents that were concerned with "ideological purity," that adopted more confrontational tactics, and that had a weaker organizational network at the grass roots.

Finally, through its focus on the changing political environment of teachers, this study also explores what happens to a movement when that environment shifts and the movement finds itself operating in a more open political context. In the 1980s and 1990s, under the new democratic regimes in Latin America, many popular movements appear to have lost the organizational cohesion and strength they developed under authoritarianism. Similarly in Mexico, a relative political opening for the teachers' movement after 1989 presented a range of new challenges and dilemmas for the movement and in some sense threatened its very existence. Without going so far as to claim that Mexico's political system after 1989 had become democratic, this case tends to support initial findings about the demobilization and even marginalization of popular movements under new democracies, findings that raise important questions about the

---

12. The originator of this concept of "everyday forms of resistance" is James C. Scott; see Scott 1985.
13. For exceptions see Schneider 1995 and Maybury-Lewis 1994.

role of movements in the consolidation or further deepening of democracy in Latin America.

A second major area to which this study of the Mexican teachers' movement contributes is that of political change in Mexico. The teachers' struggle for union democracy took place within an "official" union—a union with historically close ties to the state and formally incorporated into the PRI through the party's "popular" sector.[14] Scholars have often attributed Mexico's political stability to the state's incorporation of major labor organizations through the party. Thus, the emergence of a large democratic movement (one that explicitly rejected union-party ties) at the core of the largest of these official unions called into question the continued viability of the Mexican state's mechanisms for controlling labor. In particular, the teachers' movement represented a breakdown in union officials' ability to control labor dissent and channel worker demands. Was this breakdown symptomatic of the unraveling of Mexico's corporatist political system, and did it portend the disintegration of the stability that had been associated with it? Dissident union movements were not new in Mexico, and independent popular organizations existed in other sectors. But in contrast to movements that emerged outside of the party and at the margins of core political and social institutions, the very existence of the teachers' movement—within one of the most traditional of official unions and among the state's own employees—reflected a crack in the system itself, a loss of control at its center.

Because of the centrality of official unions to the Mexican regime, important changes within these unions or in their relations with the state also imply significant changes in the character of the regime itself: in its social bases and in state-society relations. The labor movement has rarely been treated as the initiator of such changes, however. A central reason for this is that most academic studies have tended to explain the development of the Mexican labor movement primarily in terms of state controls over labor.[15] State controls on

---

14. The National Confederation of Popular Organizations was restructured in early 1991 to include territorial as well as organizational representation, and its name was changed to UNE, Ciudadanos en Movimiento (Citizens in Motion). By 1993 its composition and name were altered once again, to Frente Nacional de Organizaciones y Ciudadanos (National Front of Organizations and Citizens, FNOC). The national teachers' union formally withdrew from the CNOP (and thus from the PRI) during its February 1991 congress, but it retained a close relationship with the Salinas administration and many of its leaders remained active in the PRI.

15. Kevin J. Middlebrook has referred to this as the "state-centered" approach and argues that it is inadequate for understanding the evolution of the Mexican labor movement, requiring the addition of a "society-centered" perspective as well; see Middlebrook 1995: chap. 1. Ruth Berins Collier and David Collier (1991) also support a less state-centered approach in arguing for the centrality of the labor movement in shaping regime dynamics throughout Latin America.

union registration, strikes, and dissident movements have been largely effective at obtaining labor's acquiescence, especially during economic hard times. But an emphasis on state control tends to render unions as homogeneous entities, blurring any distinction between union leaders and rank-and-file members. In this context rank-and-file workers have typically been portrayed as passive followers of union leaders' decisions or helpless victims of their actions. Even under authoritarian corporatist regimes, however, the support or resistance of union members is a key determinant of union leaders' bargaining strength in their relations with the state. Once one accepts that unions under authoritarian regimes also shape relations with the state, and do not merely react to state actions, then the role of rank-and-file members takes on greater theoretical, as well as practical, significance.

This study takes as its central focus the three-way relationship between union leaders, the state, and rank-and-file union members. In this way, I argue, we are able to understand not only how a dissident movement manages to emerge, but we are also able to understand better the behavior of trade union leaderships, especially their relations with the state. By incorporating the interests and actions of rank-and-file workers into an analysis of state-union relations, these relations between the Mexican state and official unions appear much more conflictual and dynamic than many previous studies would have us believe.[16] This view of Mexican state-union relations ultimately yields a better explanation of why the state cannot always achieve what it sets out to do.[17] The point is that the process of political change and reform is shaped by the *interaction* of state and societal responses, even in a country with as powerful a state as Mexico's, and that the presence of social movements may be key in enabling or constraining the actions of elites. Indeed, it may be that social movements are more politically effective in authoritarian regimes (where political parties are nonexistent or else severely constrained) than in formal democracies, where party competition and elections offer channels for the organization of interests and the expression of dissent.

---

16. See Roxborough's (1984) critical discussion of the "standard account" of the history of state-labor relations in Mexico.

17. For instance, the reform-oriented administration of Carlos Salinas de Gortari (1988–94) was less successful in attaining the desired restructuring of the PRI than the restructuring of the economy, in part because of the successful resistance of the organized labor sector (see Tim Golden, "Mexico's Political 'Dinosaurs' Aren't Fossils Yet," *New York Times*, April 2, 1993, p. A4). In the case of the teachers the union had long been successful at stalling government efforts to decentralize public education, a move that implied the weakening of the national leadership of the union in favor of its locals. The reemergence of a dissident movement in the union in 1989 enabled the government to remove the union leadership and proceed with its reform plans.

Introduction

The centrality of the labor movement to the evolution of Mexico's postrevolutionary regime makes the study of conflict within "official" unions key to understanding the changing relationship between the state and society in Mexico. Since organized labor has been one of the main supporters of the authoritarian regime in this century, the democratization of "official" unions raises the question of whether these would continue to act as a regime ally or seek alternative alliances, key issues for the larger problem of regime democratization. Studying the limits and successes of cases such as the teachers' movement, therefore, tells us much about the prospects for union democracy in Mexico and about the likely impact of union democratization on relations between organized labor and the state.

Authoritarianism in Mexico

In the 1970s and 1980s it became the convention among scholars to refer to Mexico's regime as authoritarian, in spite of the widespread recognition that the Mexican case differed in significant ways from the bureaucratic-authoritarian regimes that had emerged during the 1960s and 1970s in other parts of Latin America.[18] What qualified Mexico as authoritarian was the fact that electoral competition was suppressed through the use of electoral fraud, restrictions on opposition party electoral participation, and control of the electoral process by the PRI (a party that had dominated the political system since 1929); that the state limited both political pluralism and political mobilization outside of the corporatist structure of the party; and that repression (as well as coercion and cooptation) were used by the state against challengers to the party's hegemony and to the established leaderships of mass organizations allied with the party. Some authors have identified additional distinctive features of the Mexican political system as critical in sustaining Mexican authoritarianism. These include Mexico's strong presidentialism, including the president's power to name his successor, and the lack of clear separation between the ruling party and the government, which takes on special significance during elections (Garrido 1989, Meyer 1989).

18. In contrast, in the 1950s and 1960s most scholars viewed Mexico as a "developing" or "one-party" democracy. For a summary of both views see Purcell 1977. The treatments of Mexico as an authoritarian regime are numerous: for examples see the essays in Reyna and Weinert 1977, and Collier 1979. An exception is Levy and Székely (1985:150), who prefer to view Mexico as a "hybrid" regime consisting of both pluralist and authoritarian elements.

At the same time, Mexico's differences with other authoritarian regimes in Latin America were many, leading some to characterize the regime as a case of "soft" or "semi" authoritarianism. Among these differences were the fact that Mexico had been ruled by a civilian government for most of the twentieth century and that, in contrast to much of the rest of Latin America, Mexico's history was characterized by a remarkable political stability. In addition, the extent of repression in Mexico was rarely as severe as that of such countries as Chile or Argentina under military rule. The Mexican regime was more adept at coopting dissenters, and repression was often applied selectively, in contrast to the state terrorism practiced by other authoritarian regimes. Perhaps more important, key sectors of the working and popular classes were incorporated politically into the Mexican system through the ruling party. These mass actors were critical in supporting and helping to legitimate the Mexican regime, and while they were dependent on the state in important ways, they also derived considerable benefit from the relationship. The incorporation of mass actors in this way was possible because the Mexican authoritarian regime had been forged out of the Mexican Revolution, which afforded postrevolutionary governments significant symbolic capital and enabled the regime to rely on popular, nationalist, and revolutionary appeals to consolidate its ties with key social actors.[19]

Recent scholarly views on the nature of the Mexican regime have seen it as undergoing a process of ongoing, incremental, and "irreversible" transition toward greater political liberalization and, possibly, democracy, although some scholars have also begun to see this process as perhaps more discontinuous and compartmentalized.[20] In particular, although a greater number of electoral reforms were implemented under President Carlos Salinas de Gortari (1988–94), it was widely recognized that political liberalization did not keep pace with the liberalization of the economy during his term and, moreover, that the scope of liberalization was limited and its pace deliberately slowed by the administration. Similarly, greater electoral competition in Mexico during the 1990s coincided with the maintenance and, in some cases, the strengthening of state controls over nonelectoral forms of mass participation, especially, but not exclusively, with regard to unions.[21] Others have pointed to the lack of a clear

19. Based on the key role of mass actors in supporting the Mexican regime, Middlebrook (1995) has made a convincing case for viewing Mexico as possessing a distinct type of *postrevolutionary* authoritarian regime, whose broad features were shared by other postrevolutionary regimes such as those in the Soviet Union and Sandinista Nicaragua.
20. See Cornelius, Gentleman, and Smith 1989: chap. 1; Alcocer 1994; Loaeza 1994; and Cook, Middlebrook, and Molinar 1994: chap. 1.
21. See de la Garza Toledo 1994; Cook, Middlebrook, and Molinar 1994:46.

Introduction

separation between the party and state bureaucracy and the lack of stronger limits on presidential authority as lingering obstacles to democratization (Whitehead 1994).

In spite of Mexico's differences with other authoritarian regimes and recent liberalization measures, the Mexican regime can be viewed as possessing important elements of authoritarianism throughout much of this century, including the 1970s and 1980s, the period in which this study is based (Meyer 1977). From the perspective of Mexican popular movements, moreover, there may be more of a basis of comparison with other authoritarian governments than a focus on the differences might suggest. Even if one acknowledges the importance of mass actors to the legitimacy and consolidation of the postrevolutionary regime in Mexico, this feature typically did not make the Mexican state more tolerant of popular mobilization outside of the sectors it recognized and the channels it cultivated. Indeed, the emergence of independent and autonomous popular movements in Mexico threatened in a fundamental sense the core character of the postrevolutionary regime, and such movements were combated. As José Luis Reyna has noted, autonomous political mobilization was "the Achilles' heel of the system" (1977:164). Despite Mexico's less harsh brand of authoritarianism, then, independent popular movements have commonly had to confront strong resistance, including repression.

There is also much more heterogeneity among authoritarian regimes than the label reveals. Even among the authoritarian regimes of South America, for instance, there were important differences: the Brazilian military regime between 1964–85 tolerated some popular mobilization in the late 1970s, culminating in the creation of a new, independent grass-roots political party, the Workers' Party, and it retained some formal fixtures of democratic government (congress, political parties) throughout its rule, while the Chilean (1973–89) and Argentine (1976–83) military regimes were generally more repressive (Keck 1992). Under the Peruvian military dictatorship of General Juan Velasco Alvarado (1968–75), meanwhile, both labor and the left were able to expand (Stephens 1983). A review of these cases reveals that even those countries ruled by the military exhibited a range of degrees of opening and closure, both over time and with respect to particular sectors.[22]

---

22. This was especially true with regard to the labor movement. In spite of the repression of labor and the persecution of trade union leaders in the early years of military rule, in most of these countries labor's importance for economic activity meant that the authoritarian governments had to forge some kind of relationship with the labor movement, which in turn provided some limited room for negotiation (Valenzuela 1989, Barrera and Valenzuela 1986, Keck 1992, Pozzi 1988). For a sectorally differentiated approach see also Valenzuela's (1989) comparative discussion of authoritarian governments' differential treatment of labor and political parties.

For purposes of this analysis the important question is, What features did Mexico and other Latin American authoritarian regimes share that set these regimes apart from most democracies? Although all states can be viewed as possessing these features to a greater or lesser degree, in general the following elements will be *missing* or *limited* in authoritarian regimes, with important implications for social movements.

1. *An electoral-representative system.* Among the most important features of democratic regimes is the presence of an electoral-representative system that serves to structure political participation and channel discontent and that provides equality of opportunity for contenders in electoral contests. The absence, weakness, or illegitimacy of such a structure is a defining feature of authoritarian systems. It also means that dissident movements must express their discontent through other, usually noninstitutionalized channels, and that political parties, insofar as they exist at all, are typically weak or at least limited in their ability to serve as conduits for popular demands. This increases the likelihood that movements that emerge in authoritarian contexts will not seek the resolution of their problems in alliances with parties nor in voting but rather in direct negotiations with the state.[23]

2. *Citizenship rights.* A second important feature of democratic regimes that is usually limited in authoritarian systems is the effective guarantee of citizenship rights, such as the freedom of speech, the right of association, and protection from arbitrary state action. The availability of such rights makes it more possible in democratic regimes for social movements to mobilize, use the media to gain sympathy or draw supporters, and develop alliances with other groups. Restrictions on such rights, on the other hand, limit the ability of movements to develop these resources.

3. *Pluralism and tolerance of mobilization.* Political controls on association and mass participation are likely to be more extensive under authoritarian regimes. Authoritarian regimes are less likely to tolerate or ignore the presence of independent social movements, since such movements typically have as their goal social or political change that poses a fundamental challenge to the

---

23. To the degree that electoral competition increases, as in Mexico during the 1980s and 1990s, the possibilities for movements to form alliances with political parties also increase. See the next section and the discussion of popular movements under the Salinas administration in Chapter 7.

stability and contours of the regime.²⁴ The response to such movements in authoritarian regimes is more likely to take the form of repression than in most democracies.

The degree to which the foregoing elements are present nationally and in a movement's immediate environment will determine the range of actions possible for movements and the likely responses they will face.

Popular Movements and Political Liberalization in Mexico

Although Mexico's regime retained important authoritarian features throughout the 1970s and 1980s, a slow process of political liberalization has been taking place in Mexico since at least the early 1970s. The last quarter century in Mexico has also been one of significant mobilization by independent popular groups, in spite of important constraints on their activities and the persistence of repression. The impact of these movements on the political liberalization process has been important, if not always direct. This section briefly examines the trajectory of independent and autonomous movements in Mexico and their relationship to political change.

In the 1970s political reform in Mexico was initiated largely in response to the delegitimation and political crisis that followed the 1968 massacre of protesting university students in Mexico City.²⁵ In response to this crisis President Luis Echeverría Alvarez (1970–76) initiated a "democratic opening" that included lowering the voting age, recruiting recent university graduates into the administration, and tolerating independent movements in labor, among the urban poor, and in the countryside (Camacho 1984:62–63). In 1977 a reform of the electoral laws eased restrictions on opposition political parties in order to facilitate their registration and participation in elections.²⁶ The 1977 political reform was conceived in part in response to the proliferation of leftist organizations and parties that were operating outside of the country's

---

24. As Tarrow notes, "while authoritarian states systematically repress collective action, the absence of regular channels for the expression of opinion turns even moderate dissenters into opponents of the regime, forcing them to pose the problem of regime overturn as the condition for reform" (1994:94).
25. On the 1968 student movement see, among others, Zermeño 1978, Poniatowska 1971, and *Nexos*, no. 121 (January 1988).
26. On the 1977 political reform see Middlebrook 1986.

political institutions in the 1970s (Rodríguez Araujo 1979:49). It was also seen by government officials as an alternative approach to the economic instability and growing strength of the left than that taken by the military regimes of Latin American countries during this same period.[27] The 1977 political reform represented Mexico's attempt to travel down a liberalizing rather than a more authoritarian path.

The Mexican student movement and the government's repression of it in 1968 was a watershed event, one that shaped both subsequent political organizing by the left and government proposals for political reform. The student movement directly influenced later pressures for democratization and social change by generating activists and leaders who moved into other arenas of civil society.[28] In the early seventies many students moved to poor urban settlements and to the countryside to begin political organizing. Some joined the urban and rural guerrilla movements active at the time. Student activists and organizers formed many of the radical leftist political organizations that operated among labor unions, peasant organizations, and in poor urban neighborhoods. Some of these organizations would later develop into political parties and help to shape the terms of debate over electoral participation and left unity that would become a central part of the electoral landscape in the late 1970s and 1980s.

The labor movement was among the arenas touched by the student activism of the period, in spite of the fact that official unions and workers in general remained on the sidelines during the 1968 student protests, and some union leaders went so far as to applaud the repressive actions of the government. In the early 1970s Mexico nevertheless witnessed a labor insurgency whose key demands were for union democracy and autonomy from political parties and official labor confederations. This labor insurgency was influenced by a number of factors: the existence of industrial communities that generalized worker demands and experiences, legal advisors that helped unions break away from larger confederations, and the organizing efforts of students and political activists (San Juan 1983). At the same time, worker dissent was prompted by an economic recession in 1971 and by changes in the production process and in the organization of work in such sectors as the automobile industry (Middlebrook 1995:228–32).[29] This democratic labor movement encompassed a range of industries and services (including autos, steel, mining, railroads, telephones,

27. See the speeches by Jesús Reyes Heroles, interior minister, in Comisión Federal Electoral 1979:x–xii; 186–87.
28. See Pérez Arce 1990; Carr 1991:135; and Bennett 1992.
29. On the sources of union democracy in the automobile industry see also Middlebrook 1989, and Roxborough 1984.

university workers) and reached its peak with the Democratic Tendency movement of the electrical workers in the mid-1970s.[30] Although the Democratic Tendency was repressed by 1976, some democratic locals and independent unions that had formed in this earlier period remained active in the second half of the decade, and new dissident movements emerged within public sector unions (San Juan 1984:120).

In the late 1970s several important independent unions and dissident currents made a decision to work within official organizations such as the Labor Congress rather than remain outside of the institutions that incorporated the majority of Mexican workers, a position that was facilitated by a more open policy toward independent unions on the part of the CTM and the Labor Congress.[31] This decision paralleled another much-debated position taken by leftist political parties to participate in elections under the provisions of the new electoral reform law of 1977.[32] At the same time, a number of political organizations of the left rejected electoral politics and opted for the construction of independent and autonomous nonparty sectoral organizations. These organizations, called "coordinadoras" (coordinating committees or networks), consisted of loose national networks of autonomous regional organizations.[33] The Coordinadora Nacional de Trabajadores de la Educación, the organization encompassing democratic teachers within the SNTE, was formed in 1979, as was the Coordinadora Nacional "Plan de Ayala" (National "Plan of Ayala" Coordinating Committee, CNPA), an organization of peasants and small farmers. Another organization, the Coordinadora Nacional del Movimiento Urbano Popular (National Coordinating Committee of the Urban Popular Movement, CONAMUP), was formed in 1981.[34]

In the beginning the coordinadoras represented an alternative approach to democratization that complemented but rarely overlapped with the electoral focus of the political parties (especially the former Communist Party, organized

---

30. There is a vast literature on the labor insurgency of the 1970s in Mexico. For accounts of this period see, among others, Basurto 1983, Bizberg 1983, Camacho 1984, Alvarez 1987, Trejo Delarbre 1984 and 1990, and de la Garza Toledo 1991. On the Democratic Tendency see Gómez Tagle and Miquet 1976, Gómez Tagle 1980, Trejo Delarbre 1978, and Cuéllar Vázquez 1986.

31. San Juan 1984:115–16; Trejo Delarbre 1984:72; Bizberg 1984:186–87.

32. See Rodríguez Araujo 1979 on the discussion among political parties of whether or not to take advantage of the provisions of the political reform.

33. On the origins of the coordinadoras see Prieto 1986 and Moguel 1987.

34. A coordinating committee of unions (Coordinadora Sindical Nacional, COSINA) was also formed about this time, but it never acquired the stability of the coordinating committees in other sectors. This may have reflected traditional difficulties with forming alliances among labor unions in Mexico and the special constraints on trade union mobilization relative to other kinds of organizations. On the CONAMUP see Hernández S. 1987.

with other left parties and currents as the Unified Socialist Party of Mexico, PSUM, in 1981). This alternative approach rejected a strategy of "targeting the state" and consisted instead of creating pockets of autonomous and democratic organization in *society* that could respond to the basic needs of members. The sector of the left involved in the coordinadoras believed that a focus on elections would channel scarce resources away from the task of organization into frustrating and often fruitless electoral struggles in which the rules of the game were still defined by the government and the PRI. Another reason for the coordinadoras's approach to electoral politics stemmed from the fact that so many different political currents were involved in these organizations. Electoral participation could easily cause divisions within the coordinadoras as different political groups competed for a social base within the same organization (Tamayo 1990). Electoral politics interfered with organizational cohesion, which was crucial for survival and for winning demands.

The economic backdrop to this period of popular sector organizing was, significantly, not the economic crisis but the 1979–81 oil boom. The high expectations for economic growth and recovery generated by the discovery of vast oil reserves led to a flurry of wage demands from both independent and official unions. The latter in particular pressed for increased wages, benefits, and subsidies as recompense for their restraint during the 1976–77 recession (Bizberg 1984:183, 186). Other sectors—represented by the coordinadoras—also mobilized in this period to press demands, although political factors in the late 1970s may have been just as important, if not more so, in explaining the timing of the formation of these new organizations. The political reform forced nonparty sectors of the left to define themselves with respect to electoral participation and where to concentrate their organizing activities. The appearance of left opposition parties in congress after 1979 as a result of the political reform was also at least partly responsible for the renewed political activism of the Labor Congress, the CTM, and the bloc of labor deputies in congress.[35]

The increased possibilities for electoral participation offered by the political reform eventually changed many popular organizations' attitudes toward participation. Regional popular organizations with extensive local support—such as the Coalición Obrero Campesino Estudiantil del Istmo in Oaxaca (Worker-Peasant-Student Coalition of the Isthmus, COCEI)—formed alliances with left parties in order to compete in local elections. Municipal elections and state and

---

35. See the document "Manifiesto a la Nación" by the bloc of labor representatives in the Chamber of Deputies; parts are reprinted in *Excélsior*, October 30, 1979. Also see Casar 1982 for a study of the legislation proposed by the labor bloc in congress during the 1979–82 legislature.

Introduction

federal lower-house congressional elections (if not yet elections for president, senators, and state governors) became contested terrain for the first time.[36] Members of popular organizations who were simultaneously members of political parties or regional political organizations involved in electoral politics began to participate in these contests, seeing them as opportunities to address the needs and demands of local communities, to expand their organizations, and to establish alternatives to the PRI.

By the mid-1980s much labor and popular sector activism had given way to protests over electoral fraud, especially in the north of the country where the conservative opposition Partido Acción Nacional (National Action Party, PAN) was strong. Urban popular organizing also surged after the devastation wrought in Mexico City by the earthquakes in 1985 (Tamayo 1990, Ramírez Saiz 1990). Labor, by contrast, was immobilized by dramatic wage decline, unemployment, industrial restructuring, and government repression of strikes throughout the economically troubled decade.[37] By this time the coordinadora "model" of organization (collective leadership; decentralized organization consisting of regional groups with tactical autonomy; autonomy from parties and rejection of electoral participation) also came to be overshadowed in some cases by the appearance of other types of popular organizations.[38] These organizations were typically more open to electoral participation and/or had more explicit party ties; some had a more vertical leadership structure. Their relative successes implicitly challenged the continued effectiveness of the coordinadora model.

In 1988, capping six years of economic crisis, opposition candidate Cuauhtémoc Cárdenas's presidential election campaign managed to mobilize a surprising number of citizens and members of popular organizations and the left. The electoral campaign gave rise in 1989 to a new political party of the left, the Partido de la Revolución Democrática (Party of the Democratic Revolution,

---

36. On opposition participation in municipal elections see Alvarado 1987, López Monjardín 1986, Martínez Assad 1985, Fox and Hernández 1992, Rodríguez and Ward 1995. On the COCEI see Rubin 1987 and 1990.

37. For a discussion of the impact of 1980s developments on the independent labor currents that emerged in the 1970s see Cook 1991.

38. Examples of other kinds of organizations that became important in the mid-1980s include the Unión Nacional de Organizaciones Regionales Campesinas Autónomas (National Union of Autonomous Regional Peasant Organizations, UNORCA) and the Central Independiente de Obreros Agrícolas y Campesinos (Independent Central of Farm Workers and Peasants, CIOAC) in the rural sector, and the Asamblea de Barrios in Mexico City among urban popular movements (see Fox and Gordillo 1989, Harvey 1990, Bennett 1992, Haber 1994). In the 1980s the union movement still had not produced a successful alternative to the coordinadoras, which were being touted by some as a promising focus for political opposition movements (see de la Garza Toledo 1991 and Carr 1991).

PRD). As Mexico moved into the 1990s, electoral contests would take on even greater importance as the focal points of conflict. Popular pressures continued to force government officials to reform electoral laws, and the PANista opposition achieved important electoral victories in gubernatorial elections in Baja California, Chihuahua, and Guanajuato.[39] For their part popular organizations would increasingly find themselves struggling to reconcile the often conflicting demands of electoral participation with meeting the everyday needs of their members, causing tensions that in turn produced important divisions between several popular organizations and the PRD (Haber 1994). By the time President Salinas named his successor to the presidency in November 1993, the administration appeared to have succeeded in isolating and demobilizing popular movements in its efforts to marginalize the PRD and push ahead with economic reform.

A number of developments near the end of Salinas's term, however, underscored the continuing role of popular pressures in political liberalization.[40] First, the January 1994 uprising of the Zapatista National Liberation Army brought the question of democratic political reform back onto the national agenda, giving rise to an expanded public debate on the issue and leading to a more extensive round of electoral reform. Second, although the passage of the North American Free Trade Agreement was widely recognized as a victory for Salinas and his program of neoliberal economic reform, vigorous opposition to NAFTA by labor unions and other citizens' organizations in the United States and Canada had led to an expansion of cross-border contacts and alliances and to greater awareness of Mexican politics in general by residents of these countries (Thorup 1991). Third, the international attention generated by the Chiapas uprising and by the debate over NAFTA led to heightened international scrutiny of presidential elections in August 1994. Moreover, the electoral process was closely monitored by several nongovernmental groups, including a Mexican nonpartisan citizens' association, the Civic Alliance, that has since served as a watchdog organization on a range of issues, including the peace negotiations in Chiapas, state elections, and the objectivity of the media.

As one of the largest and most active of the coordinadoras, the teachers'

---

39. Other gubernatorial election results in Guanajuato and San Luis Potosí in 1991 were challenged by the PAN, which led President Salinas to name interim governors. The leftist PRD did not obtain a similar response by the government when it contested electoral results in Michoacán and Tabasco, revealing the Salinas administration's dual strategy for dealing with the political party opposition.

40. For further discussion of these points see Cook, Middlebrook, and Molinar 1994, and Chapter 7 in this volume.

movement in the CNTE was key among the movements pressuring for democratization that emerged out of Mexican civil society in the 1970s and the 1980s. Far from an isolated instance, the movement of dissident teachers drew from earlier political struggles and at the same time fed into popular mobilizations in other sectors. Labor unions, neighborhood associations, peasant movements, students, and others played a role in generating demands and pressures for democratization, while at the same time forging a more democratic political culture through the creation of independent, autonomous, and representative organizations in civil society. The actions of such popular sector groups remain important for understanding the shape that the Mexican liberalization process will take in the future.

Teachers and Social Change

Teachers were not unique in challenging the authoritarian and corporatist features of the Mexican political system. But the special role teachers play in society tends to set them apart from other categories of workers. For instance, teachers play a unique role in transmitting a society's dominant cultural values and norms to its school-age children (Segovia 1975). In many societies, and particularly in less developed countries, this critical task grants the teacher substantial influence and authority in his or her community, even when the profession itself is undervalued and poorly paid. Their role in teaching the children of workers and the poor also places teachers in positions of considerable influence should they choose to act as a force for social change. In countries as diverse as Peru and Japan, for instance, teachers have been closely tied to movements for social and political change (Duke 1973, Angell 1980).

At the same time, however, teachers can be hesitant to challenge a system that offers them higher status and a channel of social mobility. Teachers are often considered middle class and, as a result, may be unwilling to share the interests of, or forge alliances with, workers and the poor. This gap may prove especially wide for working-class teachers who seek to use their new status to distance themselves from their class background. The relationship of teachers to social change is therefore often quite tenuous, and teachers may often find themselves in an ambivalent position. Their profession and status may make them part of the middle class, yet they possess a stronger potential than other professions to become radical. They are considered professionals, yet they are often thrust into economic circumstances resembling those of blue-collar workers.

The ambivalent role of teachers in social change has been especially evident throughout Mexican history. Teachers have played important roles as either the subverters or staunch defenders of the status quo. Teachers transmitted the positivist values of the Porfiriato in the late nineteenth century *and* advanced the cause of peasants and workers in the Mexican Revolution; teachers supported the government's agrarian reform and socialist education in the thirties *and* mobilized electoral support for the PRI in subsequent decades.[41] Some of Mexico's greatest statesmen, as well as its guerrilla leaders, were linked to the profession.[42]

In Mexico the rural and urban poor have traditionally regarded teaching as one of the most important channels of social mobility for their children. Teachers in Mexico therefore tend to come from the peasantry, urban working class, or lower-middle class.[43] This has reinforced the dual, almost contradictory, nature of teachers as a social group in Mexico. On the one hand, education is seen as a privilege rather than a right, and the teaching profession is regarded as a springboard toward higher economic and social status, and even toward political office. On the other hand, teachers are transformed by their presence in some of the poorest and most remote regions in the country and by their daily, firsthand encounter with the injustices suffered by the poor. At the same time, they are thrust into positions of leadership in the community and oftentimes into direct and violent conflict with local political bosses. The teacher in rural Mexico is the community's contact with the outside world. In this capacity he or she can either perpetuate the system or promote significant reform or even radical social change.

---

41. There are a number of historical sources on teachers and education in Mexico. On education policy during the Porfiriato and through the 1920s see Vaughan 1982; on education in the 1920s and 1930s see Raby 1974; on teachers' unionization during the 1930s and 1940s see Britton 1979; on the history of teachers' unionization through the 1980s see Peláez 1984a and Espinosa 1982; on socialist education during the 1930s and 1940s see Guevara Niebla 1985. On the historical role of women in education see Galván 1985 and Salinas Sánchez 1990.

42. These include, for example, Vicente Lombardo Toledano, a major figure in the Mexican left and the labor movement (in both the CTM and the SNTE), a key organizer of the Partido de la Revolución Mexicana (Party of the Mexican Revolution, PRM), the precursor to the PRI, and founder of the Partido Popular (Popular Party, later the Popular Socialist Party, PPS). Teachers Lucio Cabañas and Genaro Vázquez became guerrilla leaders in the state of Guerrero during the 1960s and early 1970s.

43. Indeed, the teaching profession in Mexico differs from that in other parts of Latin America in that it has a heavy representation of males as rank-and-file teachers and it serves as more of an alternative for employment and social mobility for the peasantry than for the middle class (Morales-Gómez and Torres 1990:52). Indigenous education is also an important component of education in Mexico, and most teachers involved in this field are themselves from indigenous groups.

The teaching profession also attracts a large number of women in Mexico, as in many other countries. Indeed, the teaching degree has served as the most common educational degree for urban and rural women workers (Cortina 1986:2). Approximately 60 percent of the teachers' union is made up of women, with a larger percentage of women teachers in urban regions and a lower one in the poorer, rural states (Salinas Sánchez 1990:85). Women also tend to be concentrated in preschool and primary school education, whereas men tend to dominate in secondary and higher education, in administrative positions, and in the bilingual indigenous education field. In spite of the large presence of women in the union, men have overwhelmingly dominated leadership positions within the union at both local and national levels, and women's influence on the leadership of the union and on the direction of the teachers' movement has been relatively circumscribed.[44] Yet events in the 1980s may have begun to change this. The economic crisis forced many women to retain their teaching jobs whereas before they might have left them after marriage. The experience of the teachers' movement itself also brought women to the forefront of their local union organizations in such places as Oaxaca and Mexico City.

Since its formation in 1943, the Mexican teachers' union has also played a crucial role in supporting the government and the Partido Revolucionario Institucional. Union leaders have held positions in federal and state administration and in popularly elected posts of the PRI. The close ties between union leaders and the official party have also been reflected historically in the use of the union to organize votes and support for PRI electoral campaigns. The tremendous size, extension, and cultural significance of the teachers' union continue to grant it an unusually important role in national politics. This importance of the union in political, ideological, and numerical terms has led twentieth-century Mexican governments to enlist teachers as political allies and to try to curb the expressions of dissent that emerged from them.

The special position of teachers in poor and remote areas throughout the country and the political centrality of their union meant that the goals and actions of the teachers' movement had political and social implications and consequences that extended beyond their organization. Nationally, movement

44. There have been important exceptions, however. The secretary-general of the SNTE after Jonguitud's fall in 1989 was a woman, Elba Esther Gordillo Morales. After the mobilizations of 1989 a number of women were elected to the leadership of Local 9 of Mexico City, which had an 80 percent female membership in the areas of preschool and primary education. By 1989 the leadership of Local 22 in Oaxaca also included a greater number of women. For more on women's involvement in the teachers' movement, including a discussion of some of the reasons why women's influence in the movement may have been limited, see Chapter 6. For studies that focus on women in the teachers' union see Cortina 1985 and 1986, Núñez Miranda 1990, Salinas Sánchez 1990.

teachers challenged both the Mexican government's economic austerity policies and their union's long-standing political relationship with the government party. At the local level, dissident teachers broke with clientelistic ties to national union and government officials and created largely autonomous union organizations that forced administrators to abide by teachers' collective decisions concerning their jobs and workplaces. Ambitious local union officials, displaced in those areas where the dissident teachers' movement emerged most strongly, lost their support base and often their political careers, and local PRI politicians could no longer rely on teachers' networks for local electoral campaigns. The success of the dissident teachers' movement in some regions of the country upset the regional balance of power and threatened, where it did not sever, previous ties with state and federal government, party, and union officials. In short, the teachers' movement threatened those state-party-union linkages at the heart of Mexico's corporatist political system.

The implications of the teachers' movement also spread "horizontally." For teachers in the dissident movement democratizing the union meant adopting democratic decision making in local union organizations, schools, and workplaces, as well as creating the opportunity to compete for leadership positions within the union. Teachers in the movement were also engaged in a struggle to redefine relations between themselves and their communities. A movement for an "alternative," indigenous, and democratic education grew out of the teachers' initial quest for higher wages and union democracy. Teachers' involvement in the democratic movement also led many to become active in local community struggles, particularly in peasant organizing in some of the most impoverished and oppressive rural regions of Mexico. And at the national level, as described above, teachers played a central role in a broader movement of popular organizations for democratization and social change.

Organization of the Study

This study analyzes the case of a "successful" social movement under an authoritarian regime. It seeks to understand how a national dissident teachers' movement (composed of several regional movements) was able to emerge from within Mexico's largest "official" union and how the movement was able to survive for years in the face of ongoing hostility from government and union officials. The conceptual framework I use throughout the book is developed in

Introduction

Chapter 2. As noted earlier, this framework draws upon a "political process" approach to the study of social movements. The chapters that follow analyze the emergence and development of the movement in light of the interaction between the internal resources of the movement (strategy, organization, leadership, alliances) and openings or closings in its political environment.

Chapter 3 addresses how it was possible for the movement to emerge within the context of the teachers' union, particularly given the history of repression of most dissident labor movements in Mexico and given the close historical ties between the union, the ruling party, and the government. It reviews the origins and historical development of the teachers' union as an official union that came to play a central role in the political system and as the central environment of rank-and-file teachers. An important dimension of this environment is the union's relationship with the government and, in particular, with the Education Ministry. In this chapter I analyze the main sources of strain and conflict between these two major actors in the teachers' immediate environment, which help to explain why the movement emerged nationally when it did.

In Chapter 4 I offer a comparative analysis of six regional teachers' movements as they emerged in Chiapas, Oaxaca, Guerrero, Morelos, Hidalgo, and the state of Mexico between 1979–82. Only two of these regional movements, those in Oaxaca and Chiapas, managed to win official recognition of their local leadership selected in democratic elections, a goal shared but not achieved by all contingents of the movement. Why two regional movements managed to obtain their initial goals while four other key regions did not is the core question I address in this chapter. I explore this by comparing regional political conditions, treatment by government and union officials, and organization, strategy, and tactics in each of the six regional movements.

The analysis then proceeds to the study of the two successful regional cases: the movements in Oaxaca and Chiapas. What were the advantages and the constraints of their "legal" status and of the legal strategies they pursued? How did their legality affect their ability to withstand renewed attacks on the movements? In Chapter 5 I trace the development of these two movements through the 1980s. Here I analyze important shifts in their national and regional political environments. This includes a resolution of the earlier conflict between union and government officials, which in turn translated into politically more closed and difficult environments for these movements. The implications of this shift in the environment for the movements are explored through their protracted campaigns to renew their local leaderships via elections authorized by the national union leadership. This chapter also evaluates the legal strategy pursued by these movements in light of their accomplishments, the limitations and dilemmas they faced, and the ways in which the movements confronted these limitations and dilemmas.

How did the movements' legal status affect their internal resources: their organization, mobilizational capacity, the relationship between leaders and members, their tactics and strategies? As they occupied the union locals in Oaxaca and Chiapas, the teachers' movements developed novel forms of organization and decision making and strove to expand member participation and increase leadership accountability. Chapter 6 pays special attention to the "inner life" of these regional movements and shows how they drew upon these internal resources in order to survive. In particular I argue that the movements' adoption of *democratic* organization and procedures was aimed at combating specific problems of organizational stability and of consolidation of the movement that grew more difficult with an increasingly hostile external environment. This chapter therefore offers a rare detailed examination of the internal organization of the movement and of the role democracy can play in sustaining social movements.

In the aftermath of the controversial presidential elections of 1988, the national political environment again shifted for the teachers' movement, and the first months of 1989 saw a nationwide mobilization of teachers that succeeded in ousting the union boss. Chapter 7 looks at the roots of this movement and what it was able to achieve and analyzes the implications for popular movements and democracy in Mexico of changes in the national political environment under President Carlos Salinas de Gortari. Finally, the concluding chapter evaluates the impact of the teachers' movement on national politics and civil society in Mexico and assesses the implications of this study and of this approach for the comparative study of social movements.

2

Social Movements in Authoritarian Environments

A Political Process Approach

Since the 1960s the study of political protest and social movements has generated several different theoretical approaches.[1] The "resource-mobilization" approach gained popularity in the United States in the 1970s, where it focused mainly on the internal organizational life of movements and on the ways in which movement organizations mobilized resources for their emergence and survival.[2] The resource-mobilization approach saw protest as rational, collective, and politically defined behavior, and as such it represented a decisive break with

---

1. The literature has referred variously to the phenomena studied in these approaches as social movements, political protest, insurgency, popular movements, and collective behavior. Social movements are often defined in broad terms, such as in this definition by Tilly: "an organized, sustained, self-conscious challenge to existing authorities" (1984:304, cited in Tarrow 1989a:17). Here I use social movements, protest movements, and dissident movements interchangeably both because I believe that these last two categories are contained within this definition of social movements and because I consider the case in this study to be an example of all three.

2. For examples of this approach see the work of Zald and McCarthy 1979, and Oberschall 1973.

the psychological and individual-centered theories of collective action that had preceded it.[3] Yet critics claimed that resource-mobilization theorists tended not to distinguish between social movements and formalized interest groups, that the perspective was "too microscopic," that it still tended to neglect the connection between collective action and institutional politics, and that it failed to acknowledge the political capabilities of movements' mass base.[4]

A second major approach to develop in the 1970s and 1980s came out of Europe and has been referred to as the "new social movements" perspective. Proponents of this perspective linked the appearance of new social movements in Western Europe to "contradictions" in advanced capitalism and saw social movements as a reflection of the decline of political parties' abilities to adequately represent citizen interests in the areas of the environment, women's and gay rights, and in other issues related to the "quality of life" (Offe 1987, Berger 1979).[5] Other developments in the new social movements literature included a focus on the cultural innovations represented by social movements and on the construction of movements' "collective identities" (Touraine 1981 and 1985, Melucci 1989).

In Latin America social movements began to attract the attention of analysts in the 1980s when nonparty popular movements and organizations emerged under authoritarian regimes in Brazil, Argentina, and Chile.[6] Many of these movements not only mobilized for basic demands but often posed a direct challenge to the regimes. Many scholars of Latin American social movements adopted the emphases of the new social movements approach, in particular its focus on autonomy, identity, and meaning.[7] This perspective has yielded a rich array of studies, which have in turn contributed much to our understanding of the internal processes of social movements and their impact on the democratiza-

3. See, for example, Kornhauser 1959, Davies 1962, and Gurr 1970.
4. McAdam 1982:25, 29; Morris and Herring 1987:157; Tarrow 1988:425–26; Tarrow 1991:14.
5. The classic "new social movements" include the student movement, the environmental movement, the women's movement, and the peace movement (Klandermans and Tarrow 1988:18–22). Latin Americanists have expanded the use of this approach to other kinds of movements as well. See, for example, Brysk's use of the approach for the human rights movement in Argentina (Brysk 1994) and the essays in Escobar and Alvarez 1992.
6. Here there is a vast literature. For studies published in English see, for example, Mainwaring 1985 and 1987, Slater 1985, Eckstein 1989, Munck 1989, Alvarez 1990, Jelín 1990, Escobar and Alvarez 1992, Maybury-Lewis 1994, Brysk 1994, Schneider 1995. On Mexico see Foweraker and Craig 1990, and Foweraker 1993. For a review of the literature on Latin American social movements see Escobar and Alvarez 1992: chap. 1.
7. See the essays in the volume edited by Slater 1985. Also see Munck 1990 and Escobar 1992. For an effort to bridge the new social movements and resource-mobilization approaches in the study of Latin American movements see Escobar and Alvarez 1992.

tion of daily life. Yet the new social movements approach has also come under attack for being too "globally conceived," for focusing on the economic and social macrostructure at the expense of politics, and for neglecting the forms that collective action takes among social movements (Tarrow 1988:423-24; Tarrow 1991:14). Some Latin Americanist scholars have also criticized this perspective for its claim that these social movements represent "new" phenomena, for underemphasizing Latin American social movements' role as political actors, and for attempting to transfer a model derived from advanced capitalist countries to Latin America.[8]

A third approach to the study of social movements, and the one that I adopt in this study, has been called the "political process" approach.[9] This approach has grown out of some analysts' frustration with the narrow focus of the resource-mobilization perspective and the excessively broad focus of the new social movements perspective (Tarrow 1991:14).[10] While there is still a great deal of diversity within the political process perspective, it differs from these other two approaches in the following ways: 1) it pays much more attention to political variables in the movement's external environment and to the ways in which these political variables shape the emergence and development of the movement; 2) it is concerned with the entire development of a social movement, from its emergence, through the various phases of its development, to its decline (McAdam 1982:36); and 3) it is concerned with the political impact of social movements (Tarrow 1989b).[11]

The political process perspective explicitly addresses the relationship between the emergence, development, and decline of social movements and their political surroundings. It asks how and why movements do what they do, given the constraints and opportunities present in their political environments. In this approach, then, environmental factors—especially the shape and location of political opportunities—are considered key in mediating between a discon-

---

8. For criticism of some new social movement theorists' claims of novelty see Boschi 1984 and Knight 1990. For criticism of the application of the new social movements model to Latin America see Davis 1989:226-27; Hellman 1992:52-53; Foweraker 1993:179-80; and Haber 1996.

9. Morris and Herring 1987 include this approach within their survey of the resource-mobilization perspective, while McAdam 1982 makes a case for political process as a distinct approach.

10. Those working from within the political process perspective include: Piven and Cloward 1979, Tilly 1978, Jenkins and Perrow 1977, Kitschelt 1986, McAdam 1982, Katzenstein and Mueller 1987, Costain 1992, and Tarrow 1983, 1989a, and 1994. For applications of this approach to Latin America see Alvarez 1990, Brockett 1991, Canel 1992, and Schneider 1995.

11. Tarrow (1988:428) makes a further claim that the political process "model" includes basic agreement on such concepts as "political opportunity structure," "social movement sector," and "cycles of protest."

tented group and its ability to protest and organize as a movement. At the same time, a movement's successful interaction with its environment depends on its ability to mobilize a range of political resources and to manage internal and external threats to the movement's existence, drawing the analyst's focus not only to the environments of movements but to their internal organization, leadership, strategies, tactics, and alliances. For McAdam (1982:39–40), one of the first analysts to refer explicitly to a "political process model," this model "rests on the assumption that social movements are an ongoing product of the favorable interplay of *both* [environmental factors and factors internal to the movement]. . . . Movements develop in response to an ongoing process of interaction between movement groups and the larger sociopolitical environment they seek to change."[12]

Like the resource-mobilization and new social movements perspectives, the political process approach developed out of cases of protest and social movements in advanced industrial democracies. For this reason the political process approach tends to define political opportunities in terms of specific political variables that commonly occur in these countries (e.g., institutional access, electoral realignments). There have been relatively few attempts to determine whether these same, or other, conditions provide opportunities for collective action in alternative contexts, such as in the newly democratizing or authoritarian states of Latin America and the rest of the developing world. Yet, given the political process approach's analytical focus on movements' interaction with their environment, and thus on contingent political relationships, the approach can be usefully applied in diverse political and economic contexts.[13] Undertaking this effort to understand how political opportunities emerge outside of the developed world presents at least two important advantages: comparative study may prevent the confusion of specific conditions within industrial democracies with general indicators of political opportunity; and the focus on political contexts may reveal much about important differences and similarities in the organization, demands, tactics, strategies, and outcomes of social movements in developing versus developed, authoritarian versus democratic states.

12. In some respects the political process approach reflects an attempt to combine elements from the resource-mobilization and new social movements perspective while maintaining a focus on the link between collective action and politics. For example, the concept of a social movement sector came out of the resource-mobilization school (see McCarthy and Zald 1977). Increased attention to ideology, perception, collective identity, and culture—elements that come out of the new social movements approach—has also become integrated into the political process perspective. See Tarrow 1988:428; and Tarrow 1994.

13. See Tarrow's suggestion that social scientists apply the approach to the emerging economies and political systems of Eastern Europe (Tarrow 1991).

The dissident teachers' movement's emergence and survival within Mexico's largest "official" trade union and within a relatively stable authoritarian regime make it a good case in which to study how opportunities for protest movements may be generated in authoritarian contexts. The political process approach also provides the most appropriate basis for examining the central question of this study: How was a dissident democratic movement able to emerge and survive within this context of an "official" union in an authoritarian regime? To answer this question, one must look to the appearance of rare opportunities in the movement's environment, as well as to the ways in which the union and political context shaped the movement's organization, demands, tactics, and strategy. In this study I argue that the emergence of the democratic teachers' movement within Mexico's authoritarian environment is a product of the *interaction* between changes in the movement's immediate political environment and resources internal to the movement, in particular the type of organization and the strategies it adopts. Both this focus and my attention to how this interaction occurs during the different phases in the development of the movement are consistent with the political process approach.

In other areas, such as understanding how movements sustain themselves, the political process literature has not developed a framework so much as it has raised specific issues and questions.[14] Thus, while I share many of the emphases of the political process approach, I have had to adapt some elements of this approach to fit the Mexican context. I have also had to build upon this literature to make sense of some elements that are inadequately covered by the political process approach. This is the case with some questions concerning organization and internal democracy, for instance, but also with such issues as the collective identity of the movement, the importance of autonomy, and the effects of movement participation on the members themselves. In this way I also adopt some of the emphases of the new social movements perspective, following a more general trend toward greater synthesis of these two approaches (Klandermans and Tarrow 1988). The result is the analytic framework presented in the following pages. However, the political process perspective provides the guiding questions and in some cases the conceptual lens through which to view the central concerns of this study: How did the *authoritarian* features of the movement's environment shape its emergence, development, ability to survive, and internal organization and strategies, and how did the movement mobilize resources to act within this authoritarian context?

---

14. Among the authors from this perspective who appear most concerned with this question of sustainability are Piven and Cloward 1979, Eisinger 1973, Lipsky 1968, and McAdam 1982.

This chapter introduces several of the conceptual issues and questions that guide the argument presented in this book. The first section criticizes the way in which the concept of corporatism (specifically with regard to state-labor relations) has been used in the Mexican case in particular and tries to recast our understanding of state-labor relations as a more dynamic, interactive, yet also more conflict-ridden set of relations. This discussion sets the stage for the second section, which examines the concept of political space and political opportunities for action by movements and suggests ways in which political opportunities may occur in authoritarian systems. A movement's ability to sustain itself is the problem addressed in the third section, where the issues of internal organization and democracy are seen to be crucial. Finally, the chapter concludes with a discussion of how to assess the political impact of social movements; in particular, what is the relationship between social movements and democracy?

Corporatism as "Unstable Equilibrium"

The political process approach is primarily concerned with an environmental explanation of the emergence of social movements. This section devotes special attention to the concept of corporatism because it is a key element of the political environment in the Mexican political system and in state-labor relations more generally. This is also an appropriate starting point because the way in which scholars have traditionally viewed Mexican corporatism has made it more difficult to make sense of sustained dissident movements, particularly when these have occurred at the center of corporatist institutional arrangements. This section attempts to understand in theoretical terms how dissident movements may emerge within trade unions linked to the state through corporatist arrangements.

Among the most-cited characterizations of corporatism is Philippe Schmitter's, who defined it as

> [a] system of interest representation in which the constituent units are organized into a limited number of singular, compulsory, noncompetitive, hierarchically ordered and functionally differentiated categories, recognized or licensed (if not created) by the state and granted a deliberate representational monopoly within their respective categories in exchange for observing certain controls on their selection of leaders and articulation of demands and supports. (Schmitter 1974:93–94)

From the 1940s until recently Mexico generally fit this ideal-type, with its "official" political party composed of three sectors: the labor, peasant, and popular sectors, each dominated by large confederations.[15] Moreover, the stability of Mexico's political system was often attributed to this party structure, in which sectors of society had representation within the party and consequently a stake in the regime. The standard treatment of Mexican corporatism saw it as involving an "exchange" that further sustained the system's stability. Sector leaders were appointed to positions in public administration and became party candidates in federal, state, and municipal elections. In exchange, sectoral organizations controlled the demands of their members, co-opted or repressed internal dissent, and mobilized their organizations in massive demonstrations of support for the party and the regime, especially during electoral campaigns.

The characterization of the Mexican political system as corporatist has been useful in distinguishing the Mexican case from other Latin American regimes. However, this classification has worked better as an explanation of political stability than in helping us to understand why and how change occurs within corporatist political systems. Neither does the extensive literature on corporatism in Latin America provide us with the theoretical tools to understand change; most analysts have instead engaged in the task of identifying corporatism or classifying varieties of corporatism.[16] As a result, change within corporat-

15. The PRI has gone through several evolutions since its founding. President Calles formed the Partido Nacional Revolucionario (National Revolutionary Party, PNR) in 1929, in 1938 President Cárdenas restructured the party with four sectors and renamed it the Partido de la Revolución Mexicana (Party of the Mexican Revolution, PRM), and in 1946 the party acquired its current name and the particular corporative structure (labor, peasant, and popular sectors) it retained through the 1980s. The major sectoral confederations within the party from 1946 through 1991 were the Confederación Nacional Campesina (National Peasant Confederation, CNC), the Confederación Nacional de Organizaciones Populares (National Confederation of Popular Organizations, CNOP), and the Confederación de Trabajadores de México (Confederation of Mexican Workers, CTM). After 1991, and especially after 1993, the PRI became organized around a new set of sectoral and territorial bodies (see Cook, Middlebrook, and Molinar 1994:24, n. 31).

16. See Schmitter 1974 for a classification of corporatist systems as state corporatist (Latin America) or societal corporatist (Western Europe). In his book on state and society in Peru Stepan builds on Schmitter's state corporatist category to distinguish between inclusionary and exclusionary systems based on predominant policy directions, however, and not regimes. Here Mexico falls within the categories of "state corporatism" and "inclusionary corporatism" (see Stepan 1978: chap. 3, esp. pp. 91–98). In Collier and Collier 1977 and 1979 the authors disaggregate the concept of corporatism by examining specific mechanisms used to structure the representation of subordinate group interests, and thus arrive at a basis for analyzing and comparing different systems of group representation. They argue, correctly I believe, that the concept of corporatism "appears to miss much of the give-and-take of politics" (1979:967). Even here, however, the ultimate objective is one of classification of different "types" of corporatism: "Once one has considered these important issues of corporative structure, however, it is essential to analyze the relationships of economic and

ist political systems has been difficult to understand theoretically, particularly in Mexico—traditionally one of the most politically stable regimes in the region—where the use of the corporatist label to denote and explain this political stability has often impeded an understanding of how Mexico's political system has evolved.[17]

The frequent focal point for this discussion of corporatism in Mexico has been the relations between organized labor and the state. Labor's economic position and its more militant history made it the most important sector of the party, and by most accounts it was largely labor's incorporation by the official party that has accounted for the Mexican labor movement's quiescence in the face of recent economic crises, for the relative lack of internal protest, and for labor leaders' continued support of the PRI. But this standard picture of state-labor relations in Mexico has been less effective in helping us to determine where changes in the state-union relationship were likely to occur. Instead of concentrating on the stabilizing features of this relationship, it might be useful to think of the exchange between unions and the state as one based on an "unstable equilibrium."[18] This perspective has the merit of forcing the analyst to look for built-in "pressure points,"[19] and therefore to identify potential areas and directions of change.

From this unstable equilibrium perspective the instability in the state-union relationship is based on the potentially contradictory demands put to the state and unions as they negotiate the terms of their relationship. Among the potentially contradictory tasks of state elites are those of securing economic conditions for capital accumulation and maintaining political legitimacy. For trade union leaders the pressure to represent their members is in constant tension with their interest in meeting the conditions placed on them by the state, which may involve restricting the demands of workers.[20] This situation is

---

political power that are ratified or consolidated through these structures to use differences in these relationships *as a basis for identifying different varieties of corporatism*" (1977:505–6; emphasis mine).

17. For a critique of this tradition see Cornelius, Gentleman, and Smith (1989:1–2), who state that the scholarly literature on Mexico has generally depicted the Mexican political system to be in some kind of stasis, yet contrary to this "the Mexican political system has been undergoing a constant process of transition ever since its consolidation in the 1930s." For a similar critique see Purcell and Purcell 1980:194. Rubin (1990) and Davis (1994) both question traditional treatments of Mexican corporatism and suggest that regional and local politics operate with considerably more autonomy than is usually acknowledged and may in turn influence the course of national politics.

18. Jessop (1982) borrows the phrase "unstable equilibrium of compromise" from Gramsci.

19. Foweraker (1989:112) uses this term.

20. The common yet increasingly challenged notion that union organizations are necessarily oligarchic has generally obscured the need to examine the different ways in which union leaders represent their members. The need for union leaders to represent their members at least minimally

not unique to corporatist regimes. However, in countries where labor's dependence on the state is high, such as under state corporatist regimes, labor's commitments and obligations to the state are likely to take on greater importance than in systems where labor is more autonomous.

This orientation of union leaders to the state may generate tensions within "official" labor unions. Official unions are those to which the state grants competitive advantage over other labor organizations through such supports as monetary subsidies, the indirect or direct repression of rival unions or of dissident groups within these unions, and sometimes partial authority for formulating or implementing aspects of public policy, as well as access to the decision-making centers of the state (Keeler 1981:185–88). The favored status that some labor organizations obtain gives the leadership of these organizations powerful incentives to act on interests that differ from those of their members. According to Offe (1981:137–38), attributing this status to labor organizations means that "the organization has resources to spend that do *not* flow from the willingness of members to contribute to a common objective; it has commitments to honor that are the price for political subsidy and hence are irreducible to the membership level." The tensions produced by union leaders' contradictory commitments are, in turn, likely to generate a gap between the actions and interests of union leaders and those of union members.

Political subsidy of unions is not the only condition that can generate this gap. As Pizzorno (1978:281) has pointed out, a union's long-term interests may lead it to conflict with the members it represents. Unions may moderate their wage demands according to leaders' calculations of long-term interest versus short-term gains, where the long-term interests are understood as political power to obtain benefits in the future (Pizzorno 1978:283–85). Both the long-term strategy of the union leadership and the state's political subsidy of unions combine to produce a breakdown of representation, in which workers no longer identify with the long-term interests of the union and therefore no longer perceive that their leaders adequately represent them. This difference in the way that interests are perceived by leaders and members may account at least in part for the emergence of discontent and even of new groups ("new collective identities") with claims for alternative representation (Pizzorno 1978). In this way tensions inherent to the exchange relationship between official unions and

---

must figure into leaders' strategic calculations in their bargaining with the state. The membership represents both the potential strength of the union leadership and a constraint on union leaders' actions. This tension has broader implications for the state's capacity to mediate popular forces through "incorporated" union leaders who contain demands, demobilize, and repress these forces.

the state can produce dissident groups that emerge to challenge the structure of representation within the union.

In addition, the Latin American economic crises during the 1980s and the central role of economic scarcity in the demands of labor and popular movements in developing countries make it important to discuss how economic conditions may intervene in the formation of dissidence and organized movements within unions. At the most basic level, poor economic conditions or economic crises constrain a union leadership's ability to represent member demands for wage increases. Economic crises may also affect the stability of state-union relations, particularly if leaders cannot deliver benefits to members or if they cannot control member demands.

The link between economic conditions and union protest, however, is not necessarily a direct one. The effects of worsening economic conditions are complex and may generate several different responses. For instance, a generalized crisis may lead workers to contain their demands in the belief that no one can make economic gains, or high unemployment during periods of crisis may lead workers to limit protest for fear of losing their jobs. By the same token, an economic downturn that affects sectors differentially could lead to a sense of *relative* loss that might in turn spark a more militant reaction among workers. Stronger unions may also win some economic concessions for their members, or the state's inability to concede economic gains may be compensated by concessions in other areas, such as nonwage benefits. Along these same lines, the state may grant unions greater access or influence that would in turn increase unions' ability to enhance future bargaining power in exchange for the short-term restriction of wage demands and protest. These concessions could take the form of greater union control over some aspects of public policy, greater political representation within the government or party, and state tolerance of union corruption or of internal repression to maintain control within the organization. However, the nature of these concessions would likely tend to strengthen union leadership control over dissidence, increase corruption, and widen the gap between union leaders and members—all factors that can compound member discontent down the road.

This brief discussion raises two points about the role of economic conditions in the formation of dissident groups. First, poor economic conditions may damage a union's ability to represent its members without engendering a militant worker response; they may generate discontent without the more obvious manifestations of that discontent. Second, economic conditions may contribute to a crisis of representation, but they are not sufficient for explaining the emergence of organized dissidence within unions. The emergence of dissident movements calls for a focus on other features of the movement's environment.

The Emergence of Dissident Movements

Although differences between the goals of union leaders and members can help to explain the emergence of dissidence within organizations, divergent interests or goals are not sufficient for explaining why dissident *movements* emerge. Nor do conditions or attributes that may be important to the formation of the new group's identity—gender, ethnicity, or traditions of protest—or the nature of the grievances themselves necessarily answer why opposition emerges *where* and *when* it does, particularly when given similar conditions elsewhere and at other times.[21] For this we must look to the political environment of the dissident movement.

The Political Environment

Consideration of a movement's political environment is one of the characteristics that distinguishes a political process approach from other approaches. Eisinger (1973:11) defined political environment as "a generic term used variously in the literature of political science to refer to, among other things, aspects of formal political structure, the climate of governmental responsiveness, social structure, and social stability." The political environment of a movement determines what forms of protest will be more effective, what alliances are possible, what strategies may be employed, and likely elite responses to the movement (Piven and Cloward 1979, Kitschelt 1986, Eisinger 1973).[22] Other authors have used the phrase "political opportunity structure" to refer to a similar set of environmental variables.[23] Both of these concepts must be disaggregated to be useful. Still, they call attention to the idea that changes in the environment constrain and enable movements in important ways. As Eisinger put it:

21. This point is made by Fox (1992a).
22. Piven and Cloward (1979:14–23) refer to this as a movement's "institutional location" and argue among other things that it determines a movement's disruptive capacity, its most potent weapon.
23. For a review of this literature see Tarrow 1988 and 1989b, Morris and Herring 1987.

[e]lements in the environment impose certain constraints on political activity or open avenues for it. The manner in which individuals and groups in the political system behave, then, is not simply a function of the resources they command but of the openings, weak spots, barriers, and resources of the political system itself. There is, in this sense, interaction, or linkage, between the environment, understood in terms of the notion of a structure of political opportunities, and political behavior. (Eisinger 1973:12)

Authors seeking to explain different aspects of protest movements have operationalized the political environment or "opportunity structure" in different ways. In a comparative study of antinuclear movements in Europe and the United States that focused on national political institutions, Kitschelt (1986) identified political regimes as strong or weak with respect to their degree of openness to protest movement demands and their capacity to implement policies. Eisinger (1973:25) looked in turn at the relationship between the incidence and intensity of protest activity and the degree of openness of urban institutions, agencies, and officials, concluding that "protest is often necessary to communicate discontent in a closed system," whereas "discontent . . . may be expressed more easily through conventional political strategies in an open system." For Jenkins and Perrow (1977:249) the salient environment in their comparative study of farm worker movements consisted of the institutions and groups with which the movements most frequently had to interact: the government and a coalition of liberal support organizations. The authors attribute the success of the United Farm Workers' movement in the 1960s to changes in the political environment rather than to characteristics of the movement's social base or organization. For these authors the movement succeeded when there was "a combination of sustained outside support and disunity and/or tolerance on the part of political elites" (Jenkins and Perrow 1977:249–51).

Throughout his recent work Tarrow has drawn on these and other studies in order to categorize the conditions under which political opportunities are likely to increase for a protesting group.[24] Synthesizing the existing literature, Tarrow includes the following: a) when there is (often newly created) access to institutional participation; b) when political (usually electoral) alignments are in disarray; c) when there are conflicts within the political elite; and d) when there are influential allies from within or outside the system (Tarrow

---

24. See Tarrow 1983, 1988, 1989a, 1989b, 1991, and 1994.

1994:85–89).[25] These conditions comprise elements of the "political opportunity structure" that tend to favor protest groups. These conditions may also occur in authoritarian regimes, but they may be expressed differently or occur with less frequency than in democratic contexts, with important implications for protest movements.

Before discussing political opportunities in authoritarian regimes, several modifications of the concept are in order. First, any study that analyzes the political environment of a movement should distinguish between different levels: the "systemic" or national political and economic environment, and the proximate environment of the movement (Tarrow 1989b). National conditions may be relevant for understanding why a wave of mobilization occurs but are typically less important for understanding the emergence and trajectory of a "single" social movement. In considering authoritarian contexts in particular, the existence of a national political opening (in the sense of general political instability or conflict within the national political elite) would almost always imply an exceptional situation of regime crisis. An opening in a movement's immediate political environment, on the other hand, could occur regardless of whether one exists in the larger sociopolitical environment. A focus on a movement's proximate environment can therefore prove essential when trying to explain the emergence of movements in authoritarian regimes where national political conditions are "closed."

Second, it may be fruitful to view political opportunities as political openings or spaces, understood as those periods during which opportunities for effective political action may be greater than ordinary. The concept of political space helps us to think not only of the existence of opportunities for effective political action, but to think of these as both temporally and spatially located. Political space usually opens up for limited periods of time and can be located in different sectors or at different levels (e.g., state or local versus national government).

The third modification that seems necessary is to define the specific functions that political opportunities or spaces fulfill for protest movements. Current notions of political opportunity tend to specify outcomes (such as increased bargaining leverage) rather than function. Alternatively, one can view the emergence of protest groups as dependent on the existence of some political space that not only raises expectations for the potential members of the group[26]

---

25. For a critique—from within the political process perspective—of the way in which the components of political opportunity structure have been identified see Brockett 1991:254.

26. Thus, political spaces have both a subjective and an objective dimension. A political space can open after some event that catalyzes existing discontent, usually an event that changes the way potential members of the new group view authority. See Piven and Cloward 1979:3–4 and McAdam

but also temporarily ensures that organization and mobilization will be possible by facilitating access to power holders and/or providing protection from repression.[27] Thus, the "function" that political opportunities or spaces perform is the provision of access and/or protection from repression.

These two conditions of political spaces are also relevant for protest groups in democracies, where institutionalized access predominates (as opposed to the more limited forms of *non*institutionalized access that may be possible under authoritarian regimes). However, securing some protection from repression is an especially crucial issue in the case of authoritarian regimes, where mobilization, disruption, or the radicalization of tactics—factors that can compel elites to respond or attract supporters in democratic contexts—are more likely to invite quick (and often violent) repression. For this reason political conditions that lessen the likelihood of repression against a movement are generally both more limited under authoritarian regimes than in democratic regimes and critical for movement emergence.

What, then, are the conditions that best facilitate access and protection from repression in authoritarian contexts—that is, in contexts with limited institutional access, limited political pluralism, and low tolerance of political opposition?

1. *Elite tolerance.* Elite tolerance replaces the "access to institutional participation" variable listed by Tarrow, but can be relevant for democratic regimes as well. The reason for replacing institutional access with tolerance is because the possibility of institutional access—understood as formal, sustained institutional participation—is more a defining characteristic of democratic regimes than it is of authoritarian regimes.[28] The key question here is, which conditions in the

---

1982:48–51 on the cognitive changes among group members that must take place in order for discontent to become transformed into collective action.

27. Fox (1992b) argues that "strategically located" democratic reformists in government provided some degree of protection from repression to democratic grass-roots movements in rural Mexico, thereby creating the political space for democratic social mobilization. Eisinger 1973, Tarrow 1989b, and Brockett 1991 have also seen the relative absence of repression to be a crucial variable within the political opportunity structure. However, the absence of repression has usually been treated as an indicator of the existence of opportunities rather than as a *function* of particular developments in the political opportunity structure (e.g., conflict or disunity among elites).

28. This is not to say that movements in authoritarian regimes do not target institutions, nor that they do not gain access to power holders or adopt "legal-institutional" strategies. But a distinction should be made between institutional access (as in regular, formal participation in and/ or access to institutions of government) and institutional activity (as in strategies that target institutions or involve institutionalized activity—for example, legalized demonstrations, union elections, telegram campaigns. In Latin America, moreover, the opening of institutional access

political environment offer movements access to power holders and protection from repression when institutional access either does not exist or is severely limited?[29] Elites are likely to exhibit hostility toward protest movements in both democratic and authoritarian regimes. In both cases, however, elites may tolerate the dissident movement if their interests are served by it in some way. For example, elite interests may be served by the existence of a protest movement during a conflict within the political elite (see below) or against another group in society. Elite tolerance may be reflected in a willingness to negotiate or in the willingness to prevent others from repressing the movement. Tolerance at the highest levels generally affords the broadest type of protection.[30] In Mexico, for example, a president's tolerance for a particular dissident movement is usually reflected throughout federal and state government. However, elite tolerance of protest movements is rare and in any case short-lived. This is especially true in most authoritarian regimes, which are generally characterized by an absence of tolerance for protest and political opposition.

In authoritarian states the more restricted formal access of protest movements to government is also likely to affect the frequency and nature of protest. The comparative absence of institutional channels through which to press claims may lead to more disruptive and spontaneous protests that rely for their success on their ability to unite a large number of people. Moreover, street mobilizations and other direct action tactics are more likely to invite repression than actions that use institutional channels; indeed, these noninstitutional actions may be directly outlawed by an authoritarian regime. At the same time, the lack of formal access does not imply that there is no access. As Piven and Cloward pointed out, a movement's disruptive action may secure access to key elites. But reliance on this kind of *informal* access will mean that movements' primary means of pressing claims will probably remain direct action and mobilizations. Not only are these tactics more likely to invite repression, they are also hard to sustain. Working to sustain this ability to mobilize will imply attention to

---

to movements under new democracies has more often than not led to the demobilization of these movements.

29. There is also a question here as to whether we can continue to consider movements with institutional access social movements, as opposed to interest groups. See Schwartz and Paul 1992:221–22 on the differences between interest groups and social movements.

30. Events in Eastern Europe and the Soviet Union after 1989 testify to the importance of openings at the top for the organization of protest and demands for more reforms. Hobsbawm offers another relevant observation from his study of peasant land occupations in Peru (1974:138): "[I]f peasants do not have much concrete knowledge about the wider framework which encloses their little worlds, they are acutely conscious of the changes in that wider framework which appear to affect its indestructibility. If the power structure is firm and closed, they retreat into their usual posture of waiting. If it begins to open and shake, they prepare for action."

different elements of a movement's internal organization than would be the case in movements with formal access to government.

2. *Elections or leadership turnovers.* The instability of political alignments as reflected in elections is also usually listed as a key indicator of political opportunity.[31] In the United States, according to Piven and Cloward, the electoral-representative system is the principal structuring institution. They explain that "ordinarily defiance is first expressed in the voting booth simply because . . . people have been socialized within a political culture that defines voting as the mechanism through which political change can and should properly occur" (1979:15). In authoritarian regimes, however, elections either do not exist or, if they exist, they do not play this precise functional role in society nor in people's socialization. In Mexico, for example, where electoral fraud has traditionally persisted and opposition parties have faced restricted opportunities for effective electoral participation, elections have played a quite different and more limited role than in democratic regimes. Nonetheless, periods of leadership renewal and elections can still weigh in as consequential, potentially space-generating features of movement environments. For instance, elections can be important for the political opportunities they afford through the potential for elite disunity rather than for the chances they give movements to influence candidate selection or policy. Similarly, political elites may respond to protest during electoral periods not because of their efforts to gain political support but because how a political leader handles the protest movement can affect his or her chances for career advancement. Electoral periods may also be important because of the expectations they raise for dissident groups, who may see the possibility of increased access or allies in a newly elected leadership. In this case what is important is not the election *per se* but the fact that leadership is changing.

These elections or leadership turnovers may occur at the national level or in the movement's immediate environment, but the level and sector where the turnover occurs will have different implications for protest movements. In Mexico presidential elections in particular were relevant for protest movements because many popular organizations considered the presidential succession cycle (the period that begins several months before the announcement of the PRI presidential candidate and continues through the presidential elections) a favorable period in which to organize and demonstrate. This was because of the

---

31. Piven and Cloward (1979) have referred to electoral instability as providing important opportunities for collective action, and Shorter and Tilly (1974) have pointed to an association between strike waves and national elections in France.

perception that there would be a lesser likelihood of repression and a greater interest in resolving disputes, if only because political leaders might want to look as if they could handle disturbances with minimal disruption and political cost. Similarly, dissident labor groups in Mexico tended to mobilize during national union electoral conventions because union officials were regarded as more vulnerable during these times. Elsewhere, authoritarian regimes' efforts to legitimate their authority through elections have created fertile terrain for dissent because of the contradictions embodied in the attempt to legitimate authoritarian rule. This kind of electoral instability, however, represents an exceptional situation for most authoritarian regimes.

3. *External allies.* Most of the literature tends to assume the need for resources from upper- or middle-class allies for a protest movement to emerge successfully (Lipsky 1968, Jenkins and Perrow 1977, McAdam 1982). However, who these allies are and what they can offer to the movement is likely to vary significantly in authoritarian and democratic regimes. Social movements may be more likely to reach out to political parties (or vice versa) in systems where electoral politics are more competitive than in systems where the number or ideological range of parties is restricted or where parties have been eliminated altogether. Similarly, governmental elites or other upper-class groups may provide access and critical resources to a movement, but they also tend to impose constraints that could ultimately destroy the movement by forcing leaders to moderate demands and by introducing conflicts between the membership and movement leaders (McAdam 1982, Lipsky 1968). Lower-class or popular organization allies, on the other hand, may provide a crucial resource for the movement's mobilizations—solidarity—without obligating the movement to moderate its demands or tactics. In authoritarian regimes this distinction can be even more pronounced. While external "allies" in the form of upper-class or government mediators may be important for movements in authoritarian regimes, it is unlikely that under unexceptional conditions there would be individuals or groups with sufficient independent power to secure meaningful access to authorities or protection from repression for a movement. One exception to this in some authoritarian countries has been the Catholic Church.

4. *Elite conflict or disunity.* This may refer to a conflict or disunity within the regime, such as occurred in several authoritarian Latin American countries prior to their democratic transitions (O'Donnell and Schmitter 1986, Tarrow 1991). Or it may refer to a conflict or stalemate between actors in the movement's immediate environment, in which the movement is ignored or else

it is "manipulated" to the advantage of one of the actors in the conflict. This latter point is significant in that it recognizes that dissident movements can emerge even in contexts where conditions are unfavorable in the larger political environment. Unlike elite tolerance or the presence of external allies, elite conflict or disunity does not admit direct support or even recognition of the dissident movement. Therefore, even when the larger political environment is "closed," the disunity of elites (or of relevant authorities in the movement's immediate environment) may offer limited yet significant political space for dissident organization and activity.[32]

It is important to distinguish between different types of elite conflict, as these may differentially affect the strategies and tactics employed by dissident movements. Conflicts can be distinguished according to their cause, the level or sector where conflicts are expressed, and the mechanisms by which they are expressed. The cause of conflict can indicate how long the conflict is likely to last and whether a systemic crisis is present that may lead to more generalized instability. The level or sector where the conflict occurs is also important. Is the conflict relatively contained at elite levels? Or does it spill into the immediate environment of popular groups? Conflicts that occur at a national or central level may have repercussions at regional or lower hierarchical levels. For instance, conflicts between unions and state officials at the national level may also affect lower levels of union and state bureaucracies, particularly if these have a high degree of hierarchy and centralization. At lower levels of the hierarchy this higher-level conflict can be directly experienced and exploited by members of the organization or rank-and-file movement. In general, the higher the level at which the space has opened, the broader the umbrella of protection and the more favorable the conjuncture for advancement toward the movement's goals. The lower the level, the greater the likelihood that favorable conditions in the environment will be short-lived and the gains more difficult to obtain and defend. Finally, conflict may be expressed in a number of ways. For example, among rank-and-file workers elite conflict may be expressed as policy change, mobilization of workers, leadership changes within union locals, or more tolerance of protest on the part of local government officials. Thus, the causes and location of conflict and the specific ways in which conflict is expressed can tell us much about the boundaries of protest and the resources that are then made available to the dissident movement. I turn now to a

---

32. This discussion is thus concerned with a more "middle-range" understanding of social movement behavior and with movements in nonexceptional and noncrisis situations. Contrast this with the literature on revolutions or even the discussion of "protest cycles" within the political process model (see Tarrow 1994: chap. 9).

particular type of conflict relevant for this study, that between the state and "official" labor unions.

State-Labor Conflict

An important political space may be opened for dissident union members in the case of conflict between the union leadership and the state. In the situation of unstable equilibrium described above, the potential for state-union conflict is always present. An additional source of conflict between unions and the state may come from the conflicting political loyalties of state officials and union leaders. In Mexico, for example, union leaders' interests may be shaped by their allegiance to political *camarillas* (patron-client career networks), which can cut across the government bureaucracy and the sectors comprising the party. Political competition between *camarillas*—especially in the period prior to presidential elections—may better explain tensions between union leaders and government officials than the existence of contentious issues that pertain strictly to the labor arena.[33] Because of the role union leaders have traditionally played in Mexico's official party, moreover, government-labor conflicts often take on a more political dimension and thus have the potential to reach beyond specific sectors.

Conflict between unions and the state may be expressed by reducing the number of political candidates selected from the labor organization, by reducing the number of union members appointed to government positions, by implementing policies and reforms that limit the prerogatives of the union leadership or adversely affect the livelihood of the membership, and by tolerating internal dissent or encouraging interunion competition. For its part the union may threaten to strike or it may withdraw its support by refusing to comply with government policies, by abstaining during elections, or by voting for the opposition. These responses to the state's restrictions of the union's sphere of influence involve the mobilization of union members. Union leaders need to appeal to their mass membership and gain their support if they wish to change members' voting behavior, demonstrate against unpopular policies, or strike. During such times dissident rank-and-file members have a greater potential

---

33. These *camarillas* are based on personal and professional loyalties and are formed by individuals for political advancement and survival (Camp 1980:468–69). In Mexico recruitment and career advancement through *camarillas* are not limited to the political system but extend to the universities and private sector as well (p. 472), and, I would add, to labor organizations.

bargaining leverage than normal vis-à-vis both union officials and state authorities.

Sustaining Dissident Movements

Analysts who subscribe to the political process perspective have distinguished between those conditions necessary for the emergence of a protest movement and those conditions involved in sustaining a movement through its subsequent phases (McAdam 1982, Tarrow 1989b). While protest may erupt given the existence of discontent, changes in leadership, and favorable conditions in the environment, it is widely recognized that building and sustaining an organization out of that protest is a far more difficult task. How is discontent transformed into a social movement: How do leaders organize dissent? How does a movement remain oppositional and survive? In great part the answer lies in the nature of the organization the movement constructs and in the way the movement organization interacts with its political environment.

Recent literature on protest movements has seen organization to be a central variable, yet it has paid little attention to the *kind* of organization found in successful movements.[34] Moreover, since movements tend to grow out of preexisting organizations, the problems of how membership and participation in the movement are sustained have been given relatively little attention (McAdam 1982:44–46; Morris and Herring 1987:168).[35] To understand the development and particularly the *persistence* of social movements, however, organization must be studied as a problematic phenomenon. To admit that organizational forms vary and that there are, to some extent, choices regarding these forms is also to assign insurgent leaders the capacity for strategic thinking and action within the parameters defined by their environments.

---

34. As Klandermans notes, "Despite the concentration on [social movement organizations, SMOs] over the last decade, literature on them *as organizations* is still scarce. In particular, empirical studies of the organizational characteristics of SMOs are lacking" (1989:2; emphasis in original). See the Klandermans 1989 volume, however, for essays that begin to explore organizational aspects of movements and for a framework for the study of movement organizations.

35. For instance, McAdam (1982:46) asserts that existing organizations "already rest on a solid structure of solidary incentives which insurgents have, in effect, appropriated by defining movement participation as synonymous with organizational membership. Accordingly, the myriad of incentives that have heretofore served as the motive force for participation in the group are now simply transferred to the movement. Thus, insurgents have been spared the difficult task of inducing participation through the provision of new incentives of either a solidary or material nature."

Success and the Question of Autonomy

The literature on social movements has not been clear about what is considered a "successful" movement. Analysts' differences on what constitutes success depend on what they consider important: survival, social change, recognition, etc. (Tarrow 1989b). The definition may also depend on the political environment in which the movement finds itself. "Mere" survival may be significant in some political contexts; it may even produce political or social consequences that transcend the initial goals of the dissident group. Also, must a movement only be considered successful if it attains its stated goals? What if only some of its goals are met? What if a movement achieves complete institutionalization and ceases to exist as a movement? Has it been successful?[36]

Two markers appear in the literature that may help us in determining a movement's success: the movement's ability to gain recognition or *acceptance* by elites as the legitimate representative of the group (which does not necessarily imply institutional status), and its ability to gain benefits—*new advantages*—for its members (Gamson 1990:28–29). If we also distinguish social movements from other types of movements by their goal of social or political change, a third indicator becomes relevant: the movement's ability to retain its autonomy.[37] Autonomy is defined here simply as the organization's ability to make internal decisions without external interference. An organization can become more or less autonomous, in the sense that some internal decisions can be affected by outside forces while others are not, and this degree of autonomy may vary over time (Fox 1992b:28). Loss of autonomy would be reflected in the loss of organizational integrity: the massive defection of members, the disappearance of decision-making structures and mechanisms, or the absorption of the movement by existing institutions. A movement's effort to sustain its autonomy should not be confused with an interest in remaining isolated from presiding

---

36. On the measurement of success and a discussion of outcomes see Gamson 1990: chap. 3. For the development of an initial approach to the conceptualization of social movement effects see Rucht 1992. Rucht distinguishes between internal and external effects of the movement and includes as internal effects the impact of movement activities on the movement itself and on its members.

37. Latin American social movements have been especially concerned with the issue of autonomy from the state and political parties. This may stem in part from the pervasive role of the state in Latin America (which is the principal referent for most movements), and from the clientelism and instrumentalism that have often characterized relations between parties and popular movements. See the discussion on autonomy in Alvarez and Escobar 1992:321–23; also Munck 1990:26–27. But see Hellman 1992 for a critique of researchers' emphasis on autonomy in the study of social movements.

institutions.[38] Most social movements in Latin America have pursued both autonomy (from the pervasive intervention of the state or control by political parties) and linkage with institutions of the state (recognition, access, and, in some cases, formal participation).[39]

A movement may obtain some of its demands but lose its autonomy in the process; it would then lose its capacity to continue to press for social or political change. In some instances, however, a movement's loss of autonomy can be the result of its success: the movement's dissolution or absorption by an institution or political party is consistent with the goals of the movement and may actually further them (Rucht 1992, Hellman 1992). In other cases a movement's loss of autonomy may indicate its failure. While it is important not to equate the loss of autonomy automatically with failure, it is also important to be able to view the maintenance of autonomy as a sign of movement success, particularly in especially hostile political environments. In this sense a movement that fails to meet its members' demands in a given period need not be labeled a failure if the movement has managed to sustain its ability to make its own decisions relating to the organization. The problem is that the failure to gain benefits for members can erode membership support for the movement and threaten its autonomy in that fashion. *This danger is lessened to some degree if autonomy is itself viewed as a desirable goal, and thus a gain, by members of the movement.*[40] If a movement's ability to maintain its autonomy is considered crucial, then it makes sense to talk of a successful movement as one that has been able to survive organizationally as a movement.[41]

Challenges to Organizational Stability

Studies of protest and social movements have indicated that movements face a number of pitfalls to organizational stability. In an argument that echoed Robert

---

38. This identification of autonomy and isolation is made by Foweraker (1993:145–46). For a critique of this position see also Chinchilla 1992:47.

39. The teachers' movement in Mexico, for example, staunchly defended the autonomy of the union locals it had won while at the same time seeking to consolidate its place within the union and vis-à-vis the Education Ministry. This strategy was consistent, even as it presented tensions for the movement.

40. Indeed, for many Latin American social movements autonomy "is at once a core movement value and a shrewd political strategy" (Alvarez and Escobar 1992:322).

41. The question of autonomy may be especially important for movements in authoritarian regimes because what is at stake for the movement is maintaining a protected arena where the movement or group can exist until the political environment changes to permit a more open strategic activity between the movement and other groups or institutions. It is the lack of such

Michels's findings on organizational democracy, Piven and Cloward suggested that the constraints of formal organization tend to bureaucratize a movement, moderate its demands, and distance leaders from members. Similarly, McAdam pointed to oligarchization, cooptation, and the dissolution of indigenous (membership) support as strong tendencies that ultimately destroy a social movement's effectiveness. These tendencies are further strengthened by a movement's reliance on "external support linkages," usually middle- and upper-class allies, which add a degree of external control over movement goals and actions and threaten to coopt the movement. The dissolution of membership support is also seen as "a virtually inevitable by-product of the establishment of external support links . . . as insurgents increasingly seek to cultivate ties to outside groups, their indigenous links are likely to grow weaker" (McAdam 1982:55).

Lipsky also referred to the tensions that "protest leaders" must manage if the organization is to survive. In the first place, leaders must successfully manage tensions with their own organizational base. Protest organization members limit the kinds of activities the group may engage in and the flexibility of the leadership in its dealings with external allies (Lipsky 1968:1,149). Other tensions occur in the relationship between leaders and the media, external allies or "third parties," and "target groups," or those at whom protest is aimed. Lipsky concludes that,

> [a]n estimation of the limits to protest efficacy . . . can be gained by recognizing the problems encountered by protest leaders who somehow must balance the conflicting maintenance needs of four groups in the protest process. . . . Even in an environment which is relatively favorable to specific protest goals, the tensions which must be embraced by protest leadership may ultimately overwhelm protest activity. (Lipsky 1968:1,157)

Unlike Jenkins and Perrow (1977), who see external allies as central to movement success, both Lipsky and McAdam see the need to secure resources (from external groups) as in conflict or at least in tension with the cohesion of the movement organization. Lipsky (1968:1,157–58) concludes that "long run success will depend upon the acquisition of stable political resources which do not rely for their use on third parties." Similarly, McAdam (1982:56) suggests that "should insurgents manage somehow to avoid [the dissolution of indigenous

---

protected spaces in authoritarian regimes, as opposed to democracies, that may account for Latin American social movements' emphases on autonomy and researchers' attention to identity (internal processes) rather than political impact in their study of these movements.

support] while maintaining an adequate flow of resources the movement is likely to endure."

The successful (i.e., surviving) movement is therefore one that manages to negotiate the tensions and pressures that tend to befall movements and avoid cooptation, oligarchy, and the loss of member support. How, then, do movements generate the resources they need to sustain their struggles without becoming dependent on outside groups (without losing their autonomy)? Can the necessary resources be generated independently of these external groups, as Lipsky suggests? How do movement organizations avoid oligarchy and cooptation? While the literature has successfully identified the tensions and dilemmas that are likely to strike movement organizations, it has focused largely on "external" pressures and less on the specific ways that organizational resources can be maneuvered to counteract these pressures.[42] A study of how a protest movement sustains itself is therefore the study of how the movement's internal organization develops and changes to deal with these pressures.

Mobilization, Organization, and Group Solidarity

One of the most important political resources that a movement possesses is its ability to mobilize, disrupt activities, and force elites to respond (Piven and Cloward 1979, Tarrow 1989b).[43] Movements must be able to mobilize members and supporters to successfully carry out protest by noninstitutional means. This mobilizational capacity of a movement depends in turn on a combination of leadership, organization, and group solidarity (Tarrow 1989b). The principal problem for movements is how to sustain the elements that give the movement mobilizational capacity while maneuvering through both internal and external challenges.

To understand this question we need to look at the relationship between leadership, organization, and group solidarity and determine how these relate to a movement's ability to mobilize. For instance, the ability to mobilize requires member support and participation, and a basic agreement on goals and the tactics and strategy employed to pursue them. The main danger is a loss of "solidarity" or cohesion—a weakening of ties between members and leaders—

---

42. This question has been more thoroughly explored by scholars looking at union democracy. See for example Lipset, Trow, and Coleman 1956; Edelstein and Warner 1976; Hemingway 1978; and Wolfe 1985.

43. In contrast, powerful elites have a variety of political and economic resources at hand and have less need of a large organization to press their demands. See Offe and Wiesenthal 1980.

that could cripple the movement's mobilizational capacity and its bargaining strength vis-à-vis authorities. What features of a movement's organization and leadership may best sustain group solidarity? Two issues are crucial in this regard: how leaders are made accountable to members of the organization, and how membership participation is structured.[44] Closer attention to these dimensions will return our focus to the type of organization that will be likely to strengthen a movement's chances of survival.

A leadership that is made accountable to the organization membership has a better chance of withstanding external pressures to compromise the movement's goals and a better chance of sustaining membership support than one that is relatively free to act unilaterally, without the prospect of having to account for its actions to the membership. Leaders may be responsive to their members in the absence of mechanisms to ensure accountability, but such a scenario is unlikely to prevail in view of the strains on movement organizations mentioned above. While the existence of fair and regular elections is the most obvious indicator of accountable leadership, elections may not be a good measure of participation and accountability in authoritarian environments or in social movements with less formal organization.[45] In these cases, then, what mechanisms does the movement organization adopt to secure accountable leadership? In the absence of formal elections, how are leaders selected? May members remove leaders who fail in their tasks? Are there committees or groups that oversee the actions of elected leaders in between electoral contests? Are there channels available to the membership to denounce abuses of power, and are there examples of the effective use of these channels?

Member participation can take many forms: voting, a physical presence during mobilizations, or decision making on important issues. What forms of member participation enable the movement to engage in repeated mobilizations? To what extent do members decide on strategies and demands, whether to negotiate or mobilize, or on the selection of their leaders? A high degree of member participation in decision making may strengthen leadership account-

---

44. For example, Fox (1992a) highlights the importance of member participation in group decision making and leadership accountability in determining the degree to which organizations are representative of their members. The crucial factor in representative organizations, he finds, is the existence of intermediate instances of participation that both sustain forms of direct participation in decision making and provide oversight and other functions that hold leaders accountable.

45. In this study, for example, regular elections in the dissident locals were prevented by national union officials, yet other mechanisms to ensure leader accountability came into play, and new forms of participation in decision making, not necessarily in voting of union leaders, were created. A focus on elections as the sole indicator of democracy in union settings has also been criticized by some analysts (see for example Hemingway 1978).

ability and stave off cooptation and oligarchy.[46] Where are major decisions affecting the organization taken? How are decisions made at each of the levels of the organization? What measures does the organization leadership take to increase member participation? How does the organization deal with members who refuse to participate?

How member participation and leadership accountability are structured within an organization are centrally important to a movement organization's ability to avoid both cooptation and oligarchy. Two other issues that relate to the question of what kind of organization may enhance a movement's sustainability have to do with the way that organizations manage relations with external allies and the goals, strategies, and tactics that the organization adopts. Whereas external allies have been regarded in the literature as crucial for movement success, they are also seen as responsible for generating tensions between leaders and the membership. These tensions may lead to a loss of support and/or cooptation. How do different types of organizations manage these tensions? What precise resources do different kinds of external allies offer, do they necessarily create internal tensions, and can the organization secure needed resources without falling prey to the demands of outside groups? Upper-class allies, for instance, may prove more threatening to the movement, while lower-class allies may prove less threatening to the organization but also less effective for achieving certain kinds of gains. Furthermore, how does an organization decide on goals and the strategies and tactics to be followed, and how does the type of organization, as well as the political environment, constrain these choices? How does the adoption of particular strategies and tactics shape the development of the movement organization?

These questions touch on a problem that remains neglected in the literature on social movements: that of the relationship between particular strategies and tactics and types of organization. For instance, a movement that needs to mobilize its membership repeatedly in order to obtain responses to its demands will most likely need to rely on more fluid forms of communication and more informal internal networks than a movement with a greater degree of institutional access and a less compelling need for frequent mobilization. How, then, do movement leaders and participants construct their organizations so as to accommodate these different requirements and constraints?

---

46. In later chapters this study will examine the specific ways in which member participation counterbalanced the centralization of power in the leadership of the locals. See also Gouldner 1955, Coleman 1956, Hemingway 1978, and Wolfe 1985, among others, on this point. Also see Sabel 1981 on competition between factions within unions as a curb on oligarchy.

Organization and Democracy

The literature has varied widely in suggesting what forms of organization prove most effective for social movements. Some authors have argued for centralized organization and bureaucracy, others for decentralization.[47] Similarly, scholars have differed with regard to the existence and importance of democracy in social movements. Many authors have been skeptical about both the likelihood and effectiveness of organizational democracy, while others have pointed to "direct democracy" as one of the defining features of "new" social movements.[48] Yet few studies of recent social movements have focused in a detailed way on the internal organization and internal practices of social movements (Craig 1990:284). The overwhelming concern in most social movement studies has been with the impact of movements on their environments and whether or not they are "successful" in achieving their goals (the external effects of movements), or else with the way movements shape group identity and transform the consciousness of members (the internal effects), without necessarily examining the way decisions are made or how the group is organized. The extent to which "democratization" is deemed important is most often considered in this sense of a movement's impact on its institutional environment, the political system, or civil society. In these cases it is usually either assumed that movements are themselves democratic or else the issue is simply not considered.[49] More precise definition as to what constitutes "democratic" movements is rare; often participation, mobilization, or autonomy are taken as signs of the existence of internal democracy, or democracy is defined in terms of outcomes rather than process: "In a social movement setting, democracy exists insofar as the actions taken reflect the collective (or majority) will of the rank and file" (Rosenthal and Schwartz 1989:46). This may obscure the extent to which members are actually involved in decision making, as opposed to leaders who are able to "represent" the interests of their members. Thus, the notion of democracy in

---

47. See Michels 1959 and Gamson 1990, on the greater effectiveness of centralized organization; see Tarrow 1994 and Alvarez and Escobar 1992 on the greater effectiveness of loosely coordinated decentralized movements. Other authors talk about the strong tendency toward centralization and bureaucratization in movement organizations but do not necessarily consider these more effective (see Piven and Cloward 1979).

48. See, for example, Michels's classic discussion of the "iron law of oligarchy" (Michels 1959). See Klandermans and Tarrow 1988:7 on direct democracy as a feature of new social movements.

49. Evans and Boyte go even further in suggesting that "conventional social-science approaches to the study of social movements normally assume that there is no analytical difference between democratic and nondemocratic movements, and thus manage to obliterate the issue [of democratic participation]" (1992:194).

social movements is often either ignored, treated with a high dose of skepticism as to its feasibility, or regarded with a naive romanticism that leads one to equate movements that aim to change aspects of society with movements that operate democratically.

Several factors are likely responsible for the relative inattention to organizational forms and internal democracy in the study of Latin American social movements. The first is that, given the strong influence of the new social movements approach on the study of Latin American movements, many may simply accept this perspective's contention that direct democracy is an important feature of new movements.[50] Conversely, for those who believe that Latin American social movements are primarily engaged in struggles for material demands and institutional access, internal democracy may be seen as irrelevant or ineffective; what matters is the efficacy of the movement in obtaining these goals. From this perspective, egalitarianism, consensus decision making, and participation—the internal democratic *process* of movements—are concerns primarily of the middle-class, postmaterialist movements that emphasize personal transformation and liberation and not of poor people's movements. Finally, the emergence of *democratic* social movements may be seen as more difficult in authoritarian political environments or in societies that lack a democratic civic tradition at the national level. Movements that emerge within an authoritarian (or paternalistic, or clientelistic) political culture will lack models or traditions to draw from in forging their own internal organizational life and are therefore more likely to reproduce the traditional leader-member relationships that exist in their surroundings.

A smaller group of scholars has looked at the role that democratic internal organization plays in movements that pursue democratic goals. Evans and Boyte argue that the existence of "free spaces"—"public places in the community . . . in which people are able to learn a new self-respect, a deeper and more assertive group identity, public skills, and values of cooperation and civic virtue"—are crucial in originating and sustaining the bases of democratic social movements and key to the revitalization of democracy at large. It is in these spaces that people acquire "the capacities and experiences that make democratic movements possible" (1992:viii, ix). Rosenthal and Schwartz argue that direct democracy is essential to the growth and vitality of movements: in particular, democracy helps to develop and sustain group unity and coordination

---

50. Some scholars, however, have criticized this assumption of the new social movements school in their own research. See Brysk 1994, Burdick 1992, Chinchilla 1992, and MacRae 1992.

(1989:37). Schwartz and Paul sustain that internally democratic movements are more capable of strategic reorientation, and thus of survival, when faced with the possibility of failure than are organizations with constrained internal democracy (1992:218–19). Studies of formal organizations such as trade unions have typically shown more interest in the issue of internal democracy. Lipset, Trow, and Coleman (1956) asked the basic question, "What makes democracy work in labor unions and other organizations?" and found that democracy (understood as absence of oligarchy, or alternance in power) within the International Typographical Union was sustained through the institutionalization of a "two-party system" based in turn on informal subgroups (the "occupational community") within the union. This concern with the existence and sustainability of democracy within representative organizations derived from a larger belief that the presence of democratic organizations in society contributed directly to sustaining democracy within society as a whole. In most recent studies of social movements, however, internal democracy has come to be seen as unrealistic, ineffective, or irrelevant rather than as *functional* to social movement survival and success.

In this study of the Mexican teachers' movement I argue not only that democracy was present in the more successful regions of the movement but that *democratic internal organization played an important role in sustaining the social movement.*[51] Democracy in this case involved both direct and representative forms of democracy, multiple instances where collective decision making could take place, the establishment of formal procedures and norms for decision making and participation in assemblies, and mechanisms to increase the accountability of leaders to the membership. Democracy became a *functional strategy* for the survival of the movement by helping to forge unity within the movement, by strengthening its mobilizational capacity, by reducing the likelihood of cooptation, and by transforming individual participants' perceptions and capacities. While democracy was by no means a perfect strategy, it did help to address fundamental problems of internal organization that can afflict social movements, particularly those in hostile environments.

Whether organizational democracy is also key to the survival of other

---

51. As noted above, democracy within the teachers' movement was not measured exclusively by elections for top leadership posts nor by turnover in the local union leadership but rather by changes in internal procedures and the creation of new organizational instances that greatly expanded effective decision making on a range of matters within the organization. Elections were also a component of this new organization: both representative and direct forms of democracy operated within the locals won by the CNTE. See Chapter 4 and especially Chapter 6 for a detailed discussion of the internal organization of the movements.

movements can only be discerned through case studies that focus on this dimension of social movements. Nonetheless, internal democracy typically involves the presence of mechanisms to ensure leadership accountability and membership participation in decision making, two elements identified above as central to group solidarity and to a movement's capacity to sustain mobilizations. Different components of democratic practice within an organization, then, can address specific problems ("fatal tendencies") that commonly afflict movement organizations. In this way internal democracy can serve the goal of organizational stability, and thus of movement survival.

The Political Impact of Social Movements

Many studies of social movements have taken as a partial measure of movements' success their ability to influence public policy (Piven and Cloward 1979, Kitschelt 1986). Tarrow in particular has devoted a considerable amount of attention to the relationship between cycles of protest and reform cycles in Italy (Tarrow 1989a). Similarly, scholars of new social movements in Western Europe saw social movements as raising "quality-of-life" issues that had been ignored by governments and political parties. Many of these issues eventually found their way into mainstream politics through policy changes, revised party platforms, or even through the creation of new political parties. According to Mainwaring and Viola (1984), social movements in Europe assumed the role of "invigorating" those democracies by expanding political agendas and the terms of debate, even when these movements regarded themselves as largely unconcerned with politics.

Social movements in authoritarian Latin American countries have often had to take on a more self-consciously political role. Many Latin American social movements have challenged authoritarian political regimes directly and played central roles in their countries' transitions to democracy (O'Donnell, Schmitter, and Whitehead 1986). After these countries underwent democratic transitions, however, political parties rather than social movements became the primary political actors and often developed complicated and conflictual relationships with social movements (Mainwaring 1988, Schneider 1992, Alvarez and Escobar 1992). Even in this context social movements continue to challenge and question the nature of the "minimalist" democracies evolving in these societies by raising popular concerns long relegated by authoritarian governments and often by demanding a radicalization or "deepening" of the democracies that replaced them (Mainwaring and Viola 1984).

In spite of the strong presence of social movements in Latin America during the democratic transitions of the 1980s, the precise relationship between social movements and *regime* democratization remains unclear. Some authors have criticized analysts' tendency to exaggerate the political efficacy of recent social movements in Latin America (Mainwaring and Viola 1984). Others have argued, following the new social movements perspective, that the contribution of Latin American social movements has come in the cultural arena: social movements represent new identities, establish new practices and new ways of relating, and enhance individual lives as much or more than they effect policy change or shape political practices (Escobar and Alvarez 1992:4).

Although it is perhaps easier to speak of the "political efficacy" of social movements if one is studying a wave of mobilization than studying a single social movement, it is still important to understand the ways in which a movement may affect, not just policy and political change, but movement participants, the surrounding environment and community, and other social movements and popular organizations. The specific ways in which movements affect their environments needs more research. For instance, how does the way in which a movement is organized affect the environment of that movement? This is an important issue to which the study of social movements may contribute: What effects do the means adopted by a movement have, not only on the end goals of the movement, but in the larger environment? In this study, for instance, the democratic organization of the teachers' movement—the teachers' concern with the means as well as the ends—was important not only for the movement's ability to sustain itself but also for the broader issue of democratization in the community, within the union, and even at the level of national politics. Thus, while it may be true that, as Alvarez and Escobar (1992:326) suggest, "[a]t the most basic level, social movements must be seen as crucial forces in the democratization of authoritarian social relations," the means by which this democratization takes place may be crucial for successful social transformation.[52] Attention to the internal organization of contemporary social movements makes it possible to examine and call into question what Munck (1990:37) has described as "the logic that sees it possible to achieve democracy through nondemocratic means."

52. For example, Evans and Boyte point to the importance of social movements as "schools for democracy," which "offer broad opportunitites for the acquisition and development of basic skills of public life. People learn to speak in public, run meetings, analyze problems and their sources, write leaflets, and so forth—the sorts of skills that are essential to sustaining democracy" (1992:192).

Another issue central to this study and to the general literature on social movements is the way in which a movement's environment—in this case an authoritarian political environment—may foster and even sustain the democratic internal organization and goals of a movement. For instance, an authoritarian environment may act as a negative referent; organization members who lack democratic models may intuitively seek out practices that are the direct opposite of those traditionally practiced in the environments they aim to change. This not only leaves room for creativity on the part of the members of a movement but also makes it possible for democratic movements to emerge in contexts where a democratic political culture has been weak. An authoritarian environment may also help to sustain a social movement by reinforcing the movement's democratic collective identity—group solidarity may result because what is opposed is defined with such clarity. These features of democratic social movements under authoritarian regimes may help to explain the difficulties that arise when movements find themselves under newly democratized regimes: the negative referent disappears, new actors (especially political parties) appear, the cohesion of the group is likely to be threatened and its role questioned.

Under authoritarianism the social movement is most likely to contribute to democratization in a way that is important but more difficult to measure than through policy output or electoral outcomes: by altering people's expectations of what is possible, by forcing issues of political change onto the agenda, by teaching people to question authority, by instilling new values and practices, by training new leaders, by serving as an example to other movements, by teaching ordinary people to "do politics" in their communities.[53] The experience of a successful social movement leaves behind people who are more politically aware, more independent, more used to bargaining with power. In short, social movements can contribute to the creation of a more democratic political culture in the midst of an otherwise authoritarian environment. While this development does not guarantee regime democratization, its implications for processes of political liberalization are important. These implications, as well as the other issues raised in this chapter, will be explored more fully in later chapters of this book.

---

53. This point echoes one suggested by Escobar and Alvarez (1992:7), in which they caution against disregarding "minor" forms of resistance and their "less visible effects at the levels of culture and everyday life" because they may not lead to "the fulfillment of sizeable demands or important structural transformations." See also their discussion on pp. 325–29.

3
Conflict and Alliance in State-Union Relations

> ¡Vanguardia asesina, el PRI te patrocina!
> Vanguardia, assassin, the PRI is your sponsor!
> —Chanted by dissident teachers during marches

The history of the Sindicato Nacional de Trabajadores de la Educación (National Union of Education Workers, SNTE) reflects the formation and consolidation of a classic "official" union, one that came to support the regime and was overseen by an oligarchic leadership that suppressed the more militant demands of dissidents within its ranks. In this way the trajectory of the SNTE came to parallel that of other "official" labor organizations among industrial workers, in particular, the Confederación de Trabajadores de México (Confederation of Mexican Workers, CTM). The consolidation of the union as an "official" organization involved a process that spanned decades, from its conflictive beginnings in the 1930s and 1940s through the relative stability of the 1960s. Rather than signal the unequivocal domination of the union by the state, however, this process reflected the bargaining and exchange that came to characterize the Mexican regime's relationship with most major unions. The state-union relationship was based on an "unstable equilibrium" in which the negotiation of the exchange of subsidies, political support, and influence was constantly renewed.

Despite the strongly progovernment character of the SNTE since the 1940s, the nature of the relationship allowed for tensions between the union and state officials to persist. The very characteristics of "official" unionism—especially union leaders' ties to government officials and limited accountability to rank-and-file members—also produced strong tensions *within* the union. The conflict between the government and the teachers' union can be understood in terms of the contradictory roles the union played, first as an important source of political support for the regime, and, second, as a large and powerful organization that by 1979 represented over half a million employees of the Secretaría de Educación Pública (Ministry of Public Education, SEP). The union mobilized its members in support of the political system in exchange for concessions in the form of political appointments for its leaders and, increasingly, control over the careers of education employees. In essence, the government's reliance on labor organizations such as the teachers' union for political legitimation and electoral support came into conflict with the administration of a crucial arena under state jurisdiction—public education in a large, complex, and developing nation. By the late 1970s the state's efforts to reform public education brought it into confrontation with the union, whose political power and social influence the Mexican state had itself helped to create.

The main argument of this chapter is that such conflict between union leaders and the government, given the existence of widespread discontent among union members, helped to provide some political space nationally for dissident teachers as they mobilized in states throughout the country between 1979–81. State-union conflict served the emerging dissident movement in two key ways: first, it occupied SNTE leaders in their battle with education officials, thus preventing union officials from directing their full attention and resources to stopping the grass-roots movement; and, second, government officials, intent on curbing the power and autonomy of SNTE leaders in order to push through education reforms, saw the emergence of the dissident movement as an opportunity to further weaken national union officials. Both of these developments helped provide some access to authorities and limited protection from repression for protesting teachers. This is not to deny the importance of the movement's ability to organize and mobilize, nor did it reflect an expanded elite tolerance for protest movements. Rather, this case illustrates the role that state-union conflict can play in providing political opportunities to dissident groups within "official" unions in Mexico, and reflects the way in which internal dissident movements can themselves affect the bargaining relationship between state and union.

Origins and Consolidation of an "Official" Union

The historical development of the national teachers' union parallels that of other "official" unions and labor organizations in Mexico.[1] Three main characteristics that define the development of official labor organizations in Mexico were also evident in the case of the teachers: 1) the eventual unification—directly supported by the state—of disparate organizations, political currents, and ideologies under a single national organization during the 1930s and early 1940s; 2) the purging of more moderate and radical tendencies of the left in the late 1940s; 3) rank-and-file challenges to the national leadership and repression of the dissident movement in the late 1950s; and 4) the increased political importance and involvement of the union on behalf of the PRI, declining pluralism within the union, and a generally stronger alliance with the state during the 1960s and early 1970s. At the same time, the history of the teachers' union reveals the importance and continuation of factional conflicts within the union—in spite of the virtual elimination of groups tied to opposition parties and left-wing ideologies by the early 1950s—and of the links between these factions and political groups within the government. Thus, while the story of the teachers' union is to some degree the story of the "taming" of the union by the state, the case also reveals internal tensions, conflicts, and competition for power that help to explain the emergence of dissident currents within the union as well as state officials' repeated efforts to both use and attempt to control the considerable power of the largest union in Mexico.

The Formation of the SNTE

During the first two decades of the twentieth century teachers' organizations were mostly regionally based; it was not until the late 1920s and the 1930s that

---

1. On "official" unions and their relationship with the state in postrevolutionary Mexico see Middlebrook 1995.

there were more efforts to unite teachers in a single national organization.[2] Several forces were especially important in unifying the teachers. Vicente Lombardo Toledano (a Marxist intellectual and labor leader) played a major role in these efforts, first as education secretary for the Confederación Regional Obrera Mexicana (Mexican Regional Labor Confederation, CROM) and later as the first secretary-general of the CTM (1936–41).[3] The Mexican Communist Party also began to fight for unification of the labor movement in this period, and was an important force behind the development of several teachers' organizations in the 1920s and 1930s. A third force pushing for unification at this time was the government, especially that of President Lázaro Cárdenas (1934–40), who also oversaw the formation of the Confederación Nacional Campesina (National Peasant Confederation, CNC) in 1935 and of the CTM in 1936.[4]

Government efforts to form a single national teachers' union during the 1930s met with resistance, and competition between rival confederations was strong throughout this period.[5] Although under Cárdenas's urging several "Unity Congresses" were held, each of these failed due to continuing conflict between rival groups, in particular, between the communists and the CTM faction led by Lombardo Toledano, a struggle that paralleled one taking place within the newly formed CTM (Peláez 1984a:22, Raby 1974:75).[6] In the end Cárdenas was unable to oversee the creation of a single national teachers' organization during his presidency, and the task fell to President Manuel Avila Camacho (1940–46), who named General Octavio Véjar Vásquez, an anticommunist and antiunionist, to the post of education minister. This shift to the right in the Education Ministry reflected a generally more conservative stance with respect to the state's relationship with the labor movement. Influenced by Mexico's formal entrance into World War II and a campaign of "national unity," the early 1940s were marked by wage restraint and important

---

2. Under Lombardo Toledano the Mexican Regional Labor Confederation organized many regional teachers' organizations during its growth and consolidation in the twenties (Espinosa 1982:67). On education in Mexico during the 1920s see Vaughan 1982 and Galván 1985.

3. On Vicente Lombardo Toledano's role in the labor movement see Chassen de López 1977.

4. On Cárdenas and the labor movement see Córdova 1974; Anguiano 1975; Collier and Collier 1991: chap. 5; and Middlebrook 1995: chap. 3. Cárdenas implemented a national program of "socialist education" and enlisted teachers' support for his reformist project; see Guevara Niebla 1985 and Raby 1974.

5. For a more detailed discussion of these efforts to form a single national union see Espinosa 1982, Raby 1974, Peláez 1984a, and Cook 1990a.

6. For a discussion of this struggle for the leadership of the CTM see Collier and Collier 1991: chap. 5; Middlebrook 1995:90–92.

legal and political controls on labor, as well as a commitment to industrial growth.[7]

Under Véjar Vásquez the government undertook firm measures to seize control of the teachers' unions by attempting to unify them under a progovernment leadership and by trying to keep them organizationally separate from other sectors of the labor movement.[8] Yet several unification congresses broke down as conflict between communists and CTM factions over the leadership and direction of the new organization continued. With the intervention of President Avila Camacho, the competing federations signed a unity pact in 1942, yet the conflict among them persisted, and it was not until Avila Camacho removed Véjar Vásquez as education minister and replaced him with the writer, diplomat, and independent Jaime Torres Bodet that another unification congress could be called. This one, held on December 30, 1943, finally produced the SNTE.[9]

The first few years after the SNTE's formation were characterized by internal power struggles led by the different factions that had founded the union. Several debates fueled these factional struggles. A key issue was the question of the union's relationship to the government and whether the new union should participate in politics through the government's Partido de la Revolución Mexicana (Party of the Mexican Revolution, PRM) or through a new party of its own creation. Although the union eventually decided to join the PRM, factional conflicts between supporters of the union's secretary-general, Luis Chávez Orozco, of Lombardo Toledano, and of the interior minister (and the government's presidential candidate), Miguel Alemán, persisted. Fed up with

---

7. The CTM and other labor confederations signed no-strike pledges in the 1942 labor unity pact and again in 1945 under the Industrial Worker Pact. Meanwhile, real wages fell dramatically throughout the decade. Between 1940 and 1950 the real minimum wage fell 44 percent (Middlebrook 1995:214). Teachers' wages fell even further in this period (see Aboites 1984).

Changes in the federal labor law in 1943 were in the direction of greater control over labor, including restrictions on the right to strike and facilitation of dismissal. In addition, in 1941 the federal penal code was revised to include the crime of "social dissolution." This provision was initially designed to curtail the activities of Axis agents, but it was used later as grounds to arrest and imprison dissidents, including the leader of a national railroad workers' strike in 1959 (Middlebrook 1995:366, n. 15). Threat of arrest under the crime of social dissolution was also used against dissidents within the teachers' union in 1958.

8. In 1938 the Statute of Workers at the Service of the State stipulated that teachers could not belong to worker or peasant organizations and incorporated teachers into the "bureaucracy" by way of obligatory membership in the Federation of Public Service Workers' Unions. Yet of the existing teachers' federations before 1943, one was affiliated with the CTM and another with the CNC (Loyo Brambila 1979:16; Peláez 1984a).

9. Several factions tried to break up this congress as well, but the intervention of Miguel Alemán, the interior minister (and later president), finally brought the congress to a successful conclusion (Peláez 1984a:33–37).

the ongoing struggle within the SNTE, and especially with the conservatism of Lombardo and his allies, Chávez Orozco resigned in 1945.[10] The subsequent reorganization of the entire national executive committee of the union under the leadership of a *lombardista* was a defeat for left forces within the union. Between 1945 and 1949 another series of power struggles in the leadership of the union took place, during which the "officialist" group allied with President Miguel Alemán (1946–52) gained the upper hand. By the end of the decade most leftist factions and groups within the union had been forced out, and *lombardismo* (and efforts to ally the union with Lombardo's Partido Popular [Popular Party], formed in 1948) had lost out to the union leadership's increasingly open commitment to the PRI, which was formed in 1946 (Espinosa 1982:73–74; Peláez 1984a:46, 52–53).[11]

Consolidation of the Modern SNTE: The Tenure of Jesús Robles Martínez

The election of Jesús Robles Martínez as secretary-general of the SNTE in 1949 marked the beginning of the consolidation of the modern SNTE. Although regular turnover of the national executive committee would take place and factional conflict would continue, Robles Martínez and his allies would dominate the leadership of the union for most of two decades. Robles Martínez blamed the poor conditions for teachers and problems in the union on the ideological conflicts that had been raging within the SNTE. He called for greater central control over union local governments in the states and put an end to the decision-making autonomy of locals and delegations, a holdover from the days when regional organizations were stronger than the center. The new leadership was also much more integrated into national politics and did not question its union's affiliation with or support for the government; involvement in the SNTE leadership came to be seen as a stepping stone on the way to political office (Peláez 1984a:59–60; Espinosa 1982:76, 78; see Table 3.1).

Nonetheless, opposition groups continued to challenge the national leadership of the union, although without success. The most important of these challenges came from groups of teachers identified with political organizations

---

10. Chávez Orozco criticized Lombardo's calls for restraint on wage demands and strikes during this period on the grounds of "national unity" (see ibid., pp. 42–43).

11. Lombardo Toledano had himself been expelled from the CTM in 1948, as were the communists. For a discussion of the exclusion of the left from the labor movement in this period see Collier and Collier 1991:408–16.

and parties that opposed the PRI. One of these was led by supporters of General Miguel Henríquez Guzmán, a popular opposition candidate for the presidency in 1952, and headed by former secretary-general Chávez Orozco. The most significant threat during this period, however, came in the early 1950s from teachers affiliated with the Partido Popular, the opposition party formed by Lombardo Toledano in 1948 (Peláez 1984a:60–61). Still, the SNTE leadership maintained its loyalty to the regime and took pains to distance itself from those who continued to advocate that the union should play an oppositional role to the government (Espinosa 1982:77). To underscore this position, the union's national council agreed to support the presidential candidacy of Adolfo Ruíz Cortines in the 1952 elections.

Table 3.1. Political office held by secretaries-general of the SNTE, 1949–1995

SNTE Secretary-General	Political Office[1]
Jesús Robles Martínez 1949–52	Federal Deputy, Colima, 1952–55
	Federal Senator, Colima, 1964–65
	Secretary-General, FSTSE, 1964–65
	Director-General, BANOBRAS, 1965–76
Manuel Sánchez Vite 1952–55	Federal Deputy, Hidalgo, 1955–58
	Federal Senator, Hidalgo, 1964–69
	Governor of Hidalgo, 1969–70; 1972–75
	President, CEN of PRI, 1970–72
Enrique W. Sánchez 1955–58	Federal Deputy, Durango, 1958–61
	Federal Deputy, Durango, 1964–67
Alfonso Lozano Bernal 1958–61	n.d.[2]
Enrique Olivares Santana[3]	State Deputy, Aguascalientes, 1950–53
	Federal Deputy, Aguascalientes, 1958–61
	Governor of Aguascalientes, 1962–68
	Secretary-General, CEN of PRI, 1968–70
	Federal Senator, Aguascalientes, 1970–76
	Secretary of Political Action, CEN of PRI, 1972–74
	Director-General, BANOBRAS, 1976–79
	Interior Minister, 1979–82
	Ambassador to Cuba, 1985
Alberto Larios Gaytán 1961–64	Secretary of Political Action, CNOP, 1961–65
	Member, National Council, PRI, 1964–65
Edgar Robledo Santiago 1964–67	Federal Deputy, Chiapas, 1967–70
	Secretary-General, FSTSE, 1968–70
	President, Labor Congress, 1970
	Federal Senator, Chiapas, 1970, 1975–76
	Director, ISSSTE, 1970–75
Félix Vallejo Martínez 1967–71	n.d.
Carlos Olmos Sánchez 1971–72	President, Labor Congress, 1971–72

Eloy Benavides Salinas 1972–74	n.d.
Carlos Jonguitud Barrios 1974–77	Secretary of Organization, CEN of PRI, 1970–72
	President, Labor Congress, 1976
	Federal Senator, San Luis Potosí, 1976–77
	Director, ISSSTE, 1976–78
	Secretary of Social Action, CEN of PRI, 1976
	Governor, San Luis Potosí, 1979–85
	Federal Senator, San Luis Potosí, 1988–91
José Luis Andrade Ibarra 1977–80	Federal Deputy, Baja California Sur, 1979–82
	Secretary of Social Action, CEN of PRI, 1979–80
	President, Labor Congress, 1979–80
	Secretary International Affairs, CEN of PRI, 1981
Ramón Martínez Martín 1980–83	Secretary of Social Action, CEN of PRI, 1981–82
	Federal Senator, Jalisco, 1982–88
Alberto Miranda Castro 1983–86	Federal Deputy, Baja California Sur, 1982–85
Antonio Jaimes Aguilar 1986–89	Secretary of Social Action, CEN of PRI, 1986–88
José Refugio Araujo del Angel 1989	Federal Deputy, San Luis Potosí, 1979–82
Elba Esther Gordillo Morales 1989–95	Federal Deputy, State of Mexico, 1979–82
	Subsecretary of Organization, CEN of PRI, 1984
	Federal Deputy, Federal District, 1985–88

Source: Compiled from Camp 1995, and Zazueta and de la Peña 1984.
[1] Includes top positions in national labor organizations, such as FSTSE and Labor Congress.
[2] n.d. = no data available.
[3] Enrique Olivares Santana was Secretry of Organization of the SNTE national executive committee under Enrique W. Sánchez; his ascension to the post of secretary-general was blocked by groups linked to Jesús Robles Martínez and Manuel Sánchez Vite (Camp 1995:515–16).

The final defeat of the left and of Lombardo's forces signaled an important change within the union. The nature of the cleavages within the union had changed from conflict between factions with ideological or programmatic differences to conflict stemming from loyalties to different personal networks within the government and the ruling party. This was a significant shift. It meant that questions over such issues as union political autonomy and internal structure had been settled for the most part and that future conflict would turn on competition for power within the union and for influence through the "official" party. Robles Martínez's long reign over the union leadership, for example, was temporarily broken in 1955–58, when an opposing faction headed by Enrique W. Sánchez took over the national executive committee. This conflict in the leadership of the union would coincide with, and in some ways facilitate, the emergence of an important opposition movement within a Mexico City union local in 1956.

The 1956–1960 Dissident Movement

The dissident rank-and-file movement that emerged within Local 9 (primary schoolteachers) in Mexico City mounted the most significant challenge to national control of union locals since the 1940s.[12] Its importance was even more pronounced because the movement emerged in Mexico City, and thus near the center of political control, both in terms of the union and the nation; because the local in which the movement took shape had been headed by a former secretary-general of the SNTE, Manuel Sánchez Vite (1952–55), and was an important power base for unionists aspiring to head the national union; and because the movement arose at a time of significant protest by other unions, especially railroad, oil, and telegraph workers, in a surge of labor militancy and conflict that paralleled that of the late 1940s.[13] The dissident movement of Local 9 also gave rise to one of the most important political currents in the opposition movement within the union. This current, called the Movimiento Revolucionario del Magisterio (Revolutionary Teachers' Movement, MRM) and linked to the Mexican Communist Party, was an important precursor to the nationwide dissident movement that emerged in the late 1970s and 1980s, and would play an important role in that movement, serving as a bridge between one generation of dissidents and the next.[14]

The dissident movement in Local 9 began in July 1956 with member dissatisfaction over wages and over the local committee's failure to negotiate an increase. The discontent carried over into the next committee elections, which were won by the leader of the dissident faction, Othón Salazar Ramírez. The national executive committee of the union refused to recognize the new leadership, and in 1957 the Federal Conciliation and Arbitration Board ruled in favor of the national committee's decision to intervene in the leadership of Local 9. Although the dissident movement was temporarily subdued, the conflict was renewed the following year when police repressed a demonstration. Dissident teachers of Local 9 stopped work and camped out in the central patio of the Education Ministry building, forcing education authorities to negotiate (Loyo Brambila 1979:42, Espinosa 1982:80–81). Eventually, President Ruíz Cortines (1952–58) announced that the government would increase wages and agreed to carry out a study to determine the further wage needs of teachers.

The conflict in Local 9 was only the most visible expression of broader discontent within the national teachers' union. A number of factors contributed to this discontent. Real wages had declined significantly between 1940 and

12. Reflecting conflicts in the SNTE leadership, during the late 1940s several states had union locals in which two different leadership groups battled for official recognition by the national executive commitee (Peláez 1984a:46).
13. For more on these industrial union conflicts in the 1940s, known as the *charrazos*, see Roxborough 1986, Durand Ponte 1984, and Middlebrook 1995: chap. 4.
14. For additional information on the 1956–60 teachers' movement and the origins of the MRM see Loyo Brambila 1979, Peláez 1984a, Ontiveros Balcázar 1986 and 1992, and Luis Hernández Navarro, "Entrevista a Rubelio Fernández," *Testimonios* 1987:131–38.

1955.[15] The status of schoolteachers had also eroded in this period, as evidenced by the growing proportion of women in the profession and by the fact that teachers increasingly came to regard teaching as supplementary work rather than as their profession. Regional protests in teachers' locals throughout the country in 1955–56 reflected some of these concerns and foreshadowed the Mexico City movement. Yet these protests remained uncoordinated, and in the end only Local 9 emerged as an organized movement. The emergence of the movement in Local 9 was further facilitated by factional conflict within the SNTE, which hindered the national executive committee from responding quickly to the dissident movement (Loyo Brambila 1979:18, 35–37).

When it came time for new local elections in August 1958, two electoral congresses were held in Local 9: one by the national executive committee and the other by the MRM, which again elected Othón Salazar as secretary-general. Faced with continued instability in the union local, the government threatened to adopt harsher tactics. Othón Salazar was detained during a march convened by the MRM in September, and the next day officials announced that dissident leaders would be charged with the crime of "social dissolution."[16] In response, the MRM threatened a series of strikes. The Interior Ministry finally intervened in negotiations between the national executive committee and the MRM, and got union leaders to agree to a new election in order to determine the composition of Local 9's executive committee.

This time the MRM candidate won overwhelmingly, and the new executive committee headed by the MRM was allowed to take power (Loyo Brambila 1979:97–98). Yet tensions between national officials of the union and Local 9's dissident executive committee continued to escalate. The local's decision not to participate in the May 1 Workers' Day march became the pretext for the national executive committee to expel its leadership in May 1960.[17] Local 9 teachers responded with a strike and a series of actions that met with both administrative and physical repression throughout the three months of the strike's duration, carried out in a political environment generally unfavorable to

---

15. According to Aboites (1984:71), teachers' real wages diminished 50 percent and 60 percent (for urban primary and rural teachers, respectively) between 1940 and 1945. Wages remained at these levels until 1955, when they gradually began to increase to reach 1940 levels again in 1960.

16. See note 7 earlier in this chapter for an explanation of social dissolution.

17. Local 9 members pushed for greater distance from the government in the wake of the government's repressive actions against labor movements in the late 1950s. This repression shaped the local's decision not to participate in the official Workers' Day march on May 1 (Loyo Brambila 1979:100, 103).

dissident movements—during the preceding year the government had repressed the democratic movement in the railroad workers' union, jailing its leaders.[18]

Indeed, the turbulent political context contributed to the movement's demise in Local 9. While teachers were challenging national control over their union local in Mexico City, leaders were also being challenged in other unions of strategic importance to the country, such as the railroad, telegraph, and oil workers' unions. Given this context, government officials perceived the dissident teachers' movement to be more threatening than might be the case at other times. Feeding this perception was the MRM's alliance with the telegraph workers and other unions belonging to the Federation of Public Service Workers' Unions and its "mutual assistance pact" with the besieged railroad workers (Loyo Brambila 1979:68–70). Other important factors included the MRM's links to the Mexican Communist Party and the recent revolution in Cuba, which emboldened dissident labor movements in Mexico and increased their perceived threat to the regime.[19]

The experience of the MRM is interesting for the parallels and differences it exhibits with the dissident movement that was to emerge twenty years later. As with the more recent movement, the 1950s movement formed in response to declining real wages and dissatisfaction with antidemocratic practices in the union local. Although the discontent was reflected throughout the country, the movement emerged only among primary schoolteachers in Mexico City, whereas the 1979–80 movement was more of a national phenomenon. The movement in Mexico City also emerged in the context of factional politics in the leadership of the national union, which may partly help to explain why it got as far as it did.[20] The MRM also pursued a strategy of trying to win spaces

18. For a discussion of the conflict between the government and the railroad workers' union in the late 1950s see Stevens 1974: chap. 4, and Alonso 1972.

19. According to Loyo Brambila, the dissident teachers' movement in Local 9 also committed important tactical errors. On several occasions the movement had adopted uncompromising, "all-or-nothing" positions in order to obtain recognition of the MRM. The emphasis the movement placed on recognition and not just on economic demands may have contributed to a waning of participation and support within the movement itself. Loyo Brambila suggests that the movement's demise was due in part to the leaders' overestimation of their own strength and importance, which led them to employ similar tactics under very different and often less favorable conditions. She notes, for example, that "the teachers erroneously perceived the election of [the MRM slate] as a simple and direct effect of their militancy" (Loyo Brambila 1979:60–64, 84, 104).

20. Sorting out the factional tensions of the period is complicated and made more so by the limited information in available sources. Nonetheless, it seems that factional rivalries were present between Robles Martínez (whose principal support base was in Local 10, among secondary teachers and the National Polytechnic Institute in Mexico City) and Sánchez Vite (former secretary-general of Local 9 and of the SNTE). Yet both were allied with the political group of Miguel Alemán, and both had their differences with Enrique W. Sánchez, who became head of the union from 1955–58

within the established structures of the union, yet it adopted some of the "extralegal" organizational forms (such as strike committees and mass congresses) that would be used by contingents of the CNTE years later. However, decision making within the movement also rested heavily with the executive leadership, and particularly with the charismatic Othón Salazar. Later movements would be based on more collective forms of leadership and on a greater incorporation of the membership in decision making. Repression by the government and by the union was also more brutal and direct in the late 1950s, and as a result people became radicalized more quickly. As one activist of the period put it, "With us there was neither dialogue nor negotiation, only beatings [*garrotazos*]."[21]

The MRM continued its struggle, but in greater isolation. Many of its members faced repression. Nonetheless, and in spite of continued obstruction by national union leaders, the MRM retained its presence within the local. It participated in the 1964 local electoral congress and managed to place four of its members on the executive committee, including one representative on the national executive committee. However, the MRM's decision to accept positions on union committees with its opponents forced divisions within the ranks of the opposition, eventually giving rise to a number of leftist organizations within the teachers' movement that were critical of the communist party line and that would become active in the movement of the 1970s and 1980s (Peláez 1984a:136).

Renewed Stability: The Remaining Years of the Roblesmartinistas

The 1960s were generally a period of economic growth, increasing real wages, low inflation, and the enactment of important labor legislation.[22] It was also a period of significant growth for the federal primary and secondary school system,

---

and who was allied with the group of President Ruiz Cortines. The conflict over Local 9 was interpreted by some as an effort by Enrique Sánchez's group to undermine Manuel Sánchez Vite, who had just become a PRI federal deputy for the state of Hidalgo. When Robles Martínez's supporters regained control of the union leadership in 1958, they also made sure to remove Sánchez Vite's followers from Local 9 so as to allow the MRM to occupy the leadership. Conflicts among authorities (between the government and the national union leadership) were also involved in the emergence of the CNTE in the late 1970s.

21. Hernández Navarro, "Entrevista a Rubelio Fernández," p. 136.

22. The government of President Adolfo López Mateos (1958–64) established the National Minimum Wage Commission, profit-sharing laws, and Section B of Article 123 of the Constitution, which regulated public sector employees, along with many other important reforms affecting labor (see Casar and Márquez 1983:247).

and, uncoincidentally, a period of growth and relative stability in the union.[23] The number of schools and students increased in urban areas, thereby increasing teacher mobility from the countryside to the cities, and with this the chances for advancement within the administration and union bureaucracy. Increased opportunities for upward mobility, together with a stable national economy, allowed the union to sustain relatively tranquil relations with its members and with the SEP. According to Arnaut Salgado (1986:193), "The SNTE, besides increasing its membership at an accelerated rate and with minimal effort, could claim among the union's achievements many of the benefits that accrued to teachers due simply to the expansion of the system."

Robles Martínez remained the power behind the throne in the SNTE, despite continued efforts from within the union to curb his influence. Meanwhile, many union leaders obtained important government and political appointments. For example, Enrique Olivares Santana, who had occupied a seat on the national executive committee during previous union governments, was named PRI gubernatorial candidate to the state of Aguascalientes in 1962, and Jesús Robles Martínez became secretary-general of the FSTSE. In addition, several union officials became PRI candidates for the federal senate and Chamber of Deputies. At the end of 1963 the union began to participate actively in PRI candidate Gustavo Díaz Ordaz's presidential campaign. This close relationship between the party, the government, and the union leadership was further reflected in the union's support for the regime on the occasion of the Tlatelolco massacre of university students in 1968, in which Education Minister Agustín Yáñez praised the SNTE for its restraint.[24]

The "Coup" of September 22, 1972

In spite of relative stability within the union throughout most of the 1960s, the early 1970s saw renewed factional conflict within the union. The expression of

---

23. Between 1958 and 1964 preschool, primary, and secondary public school enrollment grew a total of 6.91 percent. Between 1964 and 1970 the total *annual* rate of growth for all levels was 6.16 percent (Latapí 1980:96). The total number of students for all levels increased from 6 million to 11.4 million between 1960 and 1970; the total number of teachers increased from 147,000 to approximately 320,000 in the same period; the number of schools increased from 36,400 to 53,700 (Aboites 1984:76).

24. The harsh repression of the student movement in 1968 nevertheless divided the teachers' union. Some of this polarization was reflected in the refusal of the MRM members of the national executive committee, as well as of the local committee leaders in Mexico City, Chihuahua, and other states, to sign a public announcement pledging their support to the PRI presidential candidate, Luis Echeverría Alvarez, who had been interior minister during the repression (Peláez 1984a:146).

this conflict took a form that was reminiscent of leadership struggles in other unions but unprecedented thus far in the case of the teachers' union. On September 22, 1972, thirteen members of the national executive committee of the SNTE led a "coup" against the secretary-general, Carlos Olmos Sánchez, and his supporters, members of the *roblesmartinista* faction. The instigators of the coup took the executive committee offices by force, removed Olmos Sánchez as head of the national executive committee, and then informed local union leaders of their actions. The plotters used as a pretext Olmos's acceptance of a government offer to increase wages and to change the way teachers were paid without consulting the national executive committee and the membership. However, discontent with the continued dominance of the *roblesmartinista* faction had already become evident throughout the union; opposition forces had emerged in a number of states by 1971 but had either rejected participation in the union congress that selected Olmos Sánchez or were blocked from participating by national union officials (Peláez 1984a:150).

Other national executive committee members and local union officials made public their support of the "coup" soon after, among them Carlos Jonguitud Barrios, who was both head of Local 9 in Mexico City and head of the National Vigilance Committee of the national union.[25] In this latter capacity Jonguitud Barrios had approved the removal of Olmos Sánchez two days after it occurred. There was some resistance to the leadership takeover, particularly by members of Local 9, who protested the role their secretary-general had played in the plot.[26] Meanwhile, supporters of Olmos Sánchez had occupied the union offices of locals in Mexico City and in the state of Mexico and refused to leave until the government arbitration board settled the conflict. However, the Federal Conciliation and Arbitration Board ruled in favor of the new national executive committee on September 30. Olmos Sánchez's efforts to contest the decision and to denounce the illegality of the measures taken against him proved futile (Espinosa 1982:94).

The movement against Olmos Sánchez and his followers had been orches-

---

25. The National Vigilance Committee was an especially powerful organ of the union. Its members had the ability to suspend a local or delegation-level committee, expel members, suspend rights of membership, and apply sanctions against members who "undertake divisive actions or *actions which could endanger the unity and integrity of the SNTE*" (Article 250 of the SNTE statutes; emphasis added). In this way any attempt to challenge the union leadership's authority or any move to increase internal democracy could be interpreted as a treacherous act and subject to punishment by the Vigilance Committee (see de la Garza Toledo 1982).

26. Among other things, delegation-level union officers from Local 9 argued that Jonguitud Barrios had violated an article of the union's statutes which stated that no one could hold two positions in the union simultaneously.

trated by members of the union leadership, but also from within government circles in an effort to break the *roblesmartinistas*'s hold on the union. In this way the coup action went beyond a power struggle between two factions in the leadership of the union.[27] The action was backed by a president that had openly declared support for the emergence of new leaders within the Mexican labor movement in the context of a "democratic opening" (Peláez 1984a:155–57). Couched in terms of a renewed commitment to union democracy, this support was best understood as an effort by President Luis Echeverría Alvarez (1970–76) to curb the autonomy and power of old labor bosses and to create new bases of support for his administration among important sectors of labor.[28] The support of the government to the new leadership within the SNTE during the first half of the 1970s would give new meaning to the historic alliance between the union and the state.

Conflict and Alliance in State-SNTE Relations
Vanguardia Revolucionaria and the New State Alliance (1972–1976)

By the union's tenth national congress in 1974 Carlos Jonguitud Barrios had positioned himself to become secretary-general of the union. Jonguitud Barrios's tenure at the head of the union began another lengthy period of domination of the SNTE by a single labor boss and his allies. Later that year Jonguitud founded an internal organization that would act as a vehicle for him to maintain his influence over the leadership of the union for the next fifteen years. This organization, called Vanguardia Revolucionaria (Revolutionary Vanguard), served several pragmatic aims: it became a recruiting arm for the new leadership; through the use of populist and nationalist rhetoric it staked out an important

---

27. The "democratic opening" was reflected in a series of political reform initiatives taken by President Luis Echeverría Alvarez that aimed to distance himself and his government from the violent repression of the 1968 student movement, when he was interior minister. Within the labor arena this democractic opening took the form of tolerating some dissident movements within unions and of granting legal recognition to independent unions. For assessments of the impact of Echeverría's democratic opening on labor in the 1970s see de la Garza Toledo 1991; Middlebrook 1989 and 1995:223–24; and Camacho 1984.

28. The new union leadership was in fact far from democratic. Immediately after the September coup the new national executive committee purged its enemies, decertifying eighteen local committees that had been loyal to the previous faction (Peláez 1984a:160–61).

political role for the union that coincided with Echeverría's Third-World and revolutionary-nationalist discourse; and it provided a way for Jonguitud to remain in control of the union even though he could not be reelected as secretary-general: Jonguitud was made president-for-life of Vanguardia. Technically, the leadership of Vanguardia Revolucionaria was separate from the union's national executive committee, but the organization became identified with the union leadership itself rather than as simply another political current within the union (Hernández 1982:50). This identification was not difficult to obtain given the control that Jonguitud continued to wield over the leadership of the SNTE even after he stepped down as its secretary-general after his three-year term was over in 1977.

The formation of Vanguardia Revolucionaria also represented an effort by Jonguitud and his allies to imbue the union with a mystique and cohesive ideology that it had lacked under the *roblesmartinista* umbrella (Peláez 1984a:166). Vanguardia Revolucionaria developed its own anthem, which was sung at union meetings, as well as its own emblem, which appeared alongside the SNTE logo on union letterhead and publications.[29] The names of the main news organs of the union were also changed to recall the coup event ("Vanguardia Revolucionaria" and "22 de Septiembre"), and commemorative ceremonies, to which the president was invited, were held every year on September 22.

The formation of Vanguardia Revolucionaria and the rise of Jonguitud Barrios to the top position in the union coincided with an increased intolerance for the presence of diverse ideological and political factions within the union and with a move toward greater centralization of decision making and power within the national executive committee of the union.[30] Prior to this time various factions had coexisted, if uneasily, within the union, especially at the regional level, and dissident factions such as the MRM had managed to gain representation on the national executive committee. The establishment of Vanguardia, however, signaled the new leadership's attempt to consolidate its hold over the union through "ideological intolerance and the marginalization or exclusion of all pluralism" (Reséndiz 1992:9). This stance led the MRM, for instance, to

29. The Vanguardia anthem was later parodied by the CNTE, which invented new and less flattering words to the song. Members of the opposition CNTE also sang at their meetings: they adopted the Popular Unity song of the Allende period in Chile—"Venceremos"—and changed some of the words to reflect the situation of the teachers' struggle in Mexico.

30. There was also a move to concentrate authority even more within the secretary-general position of the national executive committee. For instance, changes were made to render the National Vigilance Committee—a powerful union committee once headed by Jonguitud—subordinate to the secretary-general (Alberto Arnaut 1989a, cited in Reséndiz 1992:9, n. 7).

change its strategy of trying to win positions within the union apparatus to instead creating a parallel and independent current of unionism that "would do what the union does not—voice the demands of the teachers" (Peláez 1984a:160–61). The new union leadership organized under Vanguardia Revolucionaria, therefore, blended an outwardly progressive political stance (through revolutionary-nationalist ideology and populist rhetoric) with tighter political controls within the union and less tolerance for competing ideological or political factions and internal dissent.

President Echeverría's support of the new SNTE leadership was evident from the very beginning. The ties between some of the authors of the coup within the SNTE and Echeverría stemmed from when Echeverría was the *oficial mayor* (central administrator) of the SEP between 1954–57. The decision of the Federal Conciliation and Arbitration Board to declare the change in leadership legitimate and the public recognition by key government and party officials that soon followed evidenced the government's involvement in the leadership change. During the remainder of Echeverría's presidential term, the SNTE did all it could to link its public image even more closely to the president. One brightly colored drawing reproduced on the cover of the September 1974 issue of the union magazine *Magisterio* shows President Echeverría backed by a throng of workers and peasants, pointing an accusatory finger at a mass of darkened, cowering figures, who are labeled "usurers" and "servants of transnational companies" and depicted harboring jewels and bags of money.[31] Another cover from March 1974 shows Echeverría, again backed by the masses of the "Third World" bathed in a golden light, confronting darkened figures identified as "Rich Nations."[32]

Government support for the union translated into further economic, material, and institutional concessions throughout the remainder of Echeverría's term.[33] The number of teaching and administrative positions increased by over 60 percent between 1970 and 1977, from 331,669 to 528,835 (Morales-Gómez and Torres 1990:75). Although the expansion of the education system was significant in this period, not all of these positions corresponded directly to the growth in the number of teachers. Many additional job assignments went to

---

31. *Magisterio*, Publicación del Sindicato Nacional de Trabajadores de la Educación vol. 15, no. 146 (September 1974).
32. Ibid., vol. 14, no. 142 (March 1974).
33. Among the concessions that directly benefited the union membership was the implementation of a new wage structure that permitted annual direct and indirect wage increases. Among the indirect increases was a substantial hike in the five-year bonus granted with seniority, an additional wage supplement for professional materials and transportation, and increased assistance for those pursuing advanced degrees (Peláez 1984a:166).

teachers who already had a position, in order to buy them off or as payment for loyalty (thus allowing them to collect more than one salary). Job assignments were also "sold" to union members. The massive creation of *doble plazas* in this period reflected increased corruption within the union and the SEP and expanded union control over the hiring and placement of teachers and administrative personnel.[34] The government's concessions to the union, the union's increasing wealth, and its control over the distribution of jobs helped to consolidate Vanguardia's hold over rank-and-file teachers.[35] The government's expanded education budget under Echeverría, "together with a good quantity of material concessions such as houses, automobiles, loans, and flexibility regarding attendance on the job, gave [Vanguardia] the material base with which to maintain the consensus of important sectors of rank-and-file teachers" (Hernández 1982:48–49).[36]

Jonguitud also used the enormous resources of the teachers' union for self-promotion and to raise the organization's political profile to a degree unprecedented in the history of the union (Greaves 1980:91, Peláez 1984a:166).[37] He converted the union into an even more important electoral machine for the PRI and argued that an alliance with the government was essential in order for the union to be able to launch its own political candidates:

> We can't fight with the Interior Minister because he is the one who holds the political helm of the country and we need to launch teachers as councilmen, as municipal presidents, as local deputies, as federal deputies; and if we burn our bridge to the one who has the helm, well, frankly, how are we going to launch our fellow union members [into politics]? Are we going to let them launch themselves and seek out other channels and forge commitments with [other] politicians or groups . . . because the organization can't help them? (Cited in Peláez 1984a:167)

---

34. The generation of *doble plazas* refers to the creation of job positions that were to be distributed to those who already held full-time jobs as SEP employees, thus enabling employees to collect salaries from more than one position. In 1983, for example, the union reportedly handled 1,020,000 positions for a total of 768,000 teachers (Fernando Ríos Parra, *Ovaciones*, January 9, 1983, p. 3).

35. Besides receiving membership dues through an automatic dues checkoff from SEP employee paychecks, the union also owned an impressive array of stores, hotels, and recreation centers, as well as its own press.

36. Education expenditures as a percentage of the federal budget in Mexico increased from 7.1 percent in 1965 to 9.8 percent in 1970 to 11.9 percent in 1975 (Tilak 1989:134).

37. Jonguitud's efforts on behalf of the union and of presidential candidate José López Portillo did not go unrewarded: Jonguitud became governor of the state of San Luis Potosí from 1979–85. For other political posts held by Jonguitud see Table 3.1.

Thus, under President Echeverría, Jonguitud received the support he needed from the state in order for Vanguardia Revolucionaria to become consolidated in the leadership of the union. Although union prohibitions against reelection forbade Jonguitud from reoccupying the secretary-general position, subsequent SNTE leaders would be handpicked by Jonguitud. Internally, the availability of material resources secured the loyalty of mid-level union officers to Vanguardia and obtained the acquiescence of the majority of union members, who had largely observed the leadership conflict in 1972 from the sidelines. Externally—as a player in the political system—the union became active in international educational fora, reaffirmed its involvement in the PRI's electoral campaigns, and energetically pursued political office for its members. In exchange, the SNTE offered political support to the government and control over its members. The forces that came to dominate the SNTE after 1972 had secured a new alliance with the state.

The Environment of Teachers: SNTE and SEP as Structuring Institutions

In order to understand the hold union officials had over their members and the root causes of the discontent that gave shape to the dissident movements of the late 1970s, one needs to look at the arrangement of power in the immediate, everyday environment of teachers, at their places of employment and in their careers, and at the structure of power within the union. The institutions in which people are located give shape to their demands, organization, identification as a collectivity, and strategic opportunities for defiance: "[P]eople experience deprivation and oppression within a concrete setting, not as the end product of large and abstract processes" (Piven and Cloward 1979:20). For Mexican teachers the two defining institutions in their daily work lives were their employer, the Ministry of Public Education, and the union. Teachers were primarily concerned with matters that affected their daily working conditions, their economic well-being, and their opportunities for professional advancement. The way in which these matters were handled and the groups and individuals who decided these issues would become the chief targets of protesting teachers in the late 1970s and early 1980s.

Teaching was an attractive profession for many Mexicans—especially women, members of indigenous groups, and those from poor and working-class backgrounds—for a variety of reasons. Besides offering a channel of social mobility for those from poor families or rural areas and providing an "acceptable" career for women, those who were trained to become teachers were guaranteed a job by the government at the end of their studies.[38] Given the consistently high rates of population growth in Mexico and the continuing if incomplete efforts to extend primary education to all children throughout the country, teaching was one of the few professions that continued to expand, even in the years of economic crisis and budget cutbacks. In contrast to the situation of many other workers, especially other public sector workers, teachers were not likely to face unemployment.

Teaching also offered a channel of social and professional mobility. For those of rural origin it meant the possibility eventually of working in an urban area, thereby increasing one's income, status, quality of life, and professional opportunities. For many, teaching offered the possibility of advancement through the profession through continuous training and self-improvement via summer courses, advanced degrees, and other means often subsidized by the state. Within the schools, teachers sought to improve their circumstances by obtaining an easier class assignment, transferring to a "better" school, or securing favored committee assignments, all of which implied a good relationship with the school director or zone supervisor. Meanwhile, the appointment of school directors and supervisors was strongly influenced by the union, to the point that teachers came to identify the supervisor with the union.[39] Those who occupied these positions could then move over into the SEP administration at the state level as federal director of education for a particular educational level, with the most important position—because of the number of people and resources it oversaw—being that of federal director of primary education. These administrative positions at the state level of the SEP offered the opportunity in turn for further advancement within the federal bureaucracy or to the national executive committee of the union. Similarly, a position on the executive committee of the union local could serve as a springboard into state government, to a high-level position in the local PRI, into education administration as a zone supervisor, on to the national executive committee of the union, or into political office as a municipal president or a federal deputy.

It is important to stress that administrative positions in the federal educational bureaucracy in the states were open to and indeed dominated by union members in spite of their "management" status. Indeed, these administrative posts were regarded as one of the "prizes" that the union could offer to its

---

38. Union membership was also automatic upon securing a position in the SEP. Union dues were discounted directly from members' paychecks.
39. Sandoval 1986, cited in Street 1992a:70–71.

members; these positions were incorporated into the hierarchy of positions (*escalafón*) that teachers could aspire to by moving up through the system.[40] These were also obviously positions of great power from the point of view of rank-and-file teachers. School directors, zone supervisors, and federal directors of education together controlled the most fundamental aspects of teachers' daily working lives and of their professional careers. Since their appointment typically required the approval of the union, this system elicited the loyalty of administrators to the union rather than to the SEP (Street 1992a:116). Moreover, after Vanguardia's ascent to the leadership of the SNTE, the active involvement of supervisors in union activities (for example, as union congress delegates or in organizing slates for delegation-level executive committees within the local) intensified (Arnaut 1989b:4).

The fact that the union controlled most of these administrative positions in the states also explains the tremendous power that the SNTE—in particular, the dominant factions in the union—wielded over its members. Whether or not a teacher's request for transfer to another school was granted, whether a teacher was promoted, and whether he or she obtained a loan or subsidized housing all depended on these administrators, and, by extension, on the approval of the union. The system encouraged all types of corruption and cronyism and made it easier to control dissidents by making their lives difficult: by transferring them to less desirable and distant schools, by denying their requests for transfers, by refusing to promote them, and by giving them heavy workloads, odious committee assignments, and little support. Given the extent of the control the administrators had over teachers' work lives, efforts to complain or resist often had a high cost. Being branded as a rebel (*revoltoso*) or a "communist" often meant that the teacher would be subjected to these methods of bureaucratic harassment (Street 1992a:72). Women in particular were especially vulnerable to administrator's demands for sexual favors in exchange for granting administrative and job-related requests. (When the dissident movement did finally emerge, it concentrated on changing these practices and demanding respect for teachers and for their rights; ending the practice of sexual harassment of female teachers was one of the central banners of the movement.) Those who continued to dissent in this environment usually had to give up the possibility of being at the

---

40. With the rapid expansion of the educational system in the 1960s these administrative positions came increasingly to be decided by appointment (via "*comisiones*"), which increased the influence of the union in deciding who would occupy the positions. The position would be formally incorporated later into the hierarchy of positions available through seniority, at which point the initial appointment was typically confirmed (Arnaut 1989b).

"best" schools, of gaining more pay, and of advancing through the hierarchy of the profession, assuming they were not simply sent out of the state or fired.

Under the leadership of Vanguardia Revolucionaria the union's greater degree of embeddedness in the state-level bureaucracy of the SEP, and especially its control over supervisory appointments, coincided with increased restrictions on the internal life of the union (meetings, elections). Union locals enjoyed relatively little autonomy with respect to the national leadership of the SNTE, and within the locals themselves decision making was typically heavily centralized in the local executive committee. Although union statutes contemplated the holding of delegation-level assemblies, these had to be approved by the local executive committee, and in practice such meetings were rarely convened. In addition, the national executive committee of the SNTE authorized all electoral congresses at the local level, controlled the distribution of finances to the local (each local received from the national committee a percentage of members' dues that were automatically deducted from teachers' paychecks and accrued directly to the national committee),[41] and held important powers of intervention at local and delegation assemblies. Union statutes also allowed union officials to suspend or expel workers for "disloyalty, lack of discipline, and treason," and for activities said to "threaten the unity and integrity of the union," charges used to control the activities of union dissidents (de la Garza Toledo 1982:40–43).

Their institutional location as public sector workers also imposed organizational constraints on Mexican schoolteachers. Labor regulations governing public sector workers in Mexico are different from those governing private sector employees and are located in a separate section (*Apartado B*) of Article 123 of the Mexican Constitution. While legal restrictions on strikes are strong in the case of both Apartado A and Apartado B workers, constraints on public sector workers are far more stringent, making these extremely difficult to carry out in practice and extremely rare.[42] Workers in Apartado B unions are also not regulated by collective bargaining contracts as are workers in the private sector, who are permitted to enter into such agreements by the Ley Federal del Trabajo

---

41. The amount that union locals received was not a fixed percentage but fluctuated depending on the "needs" of the local. In practice, this meant that the national committee could withold funds from the local for reasons of political control (see de la Garza Toledo 1982:42).

42. This means it is impossible to rely on strike data as an indication of conflict among workers who are regulated under Apartado B, since only official strikes and petitions are recorded by the government. For information on legislation regulating private sector strikes see Middlebrook 1995:67–69. On legislation governing public sector strikes see Zapata 1987:55.

(Federal Labor Law, LFT). Instead, workers in the public sector are regulated by the Ley Federal de los Trabajadores al Servicio del Estado (Federal Law of Public Service Workers, LFTSE), which stipulates that each government department, ministry, or agency establish General Conditions of Employment (*condiciones generales de trabajo*, CGT) for its employees in "consultation" with the respective union. As of the mid-1980s there was an increasing tendency toward standardizing these conditions across the federal bureaucracy, and both job classifications and salary levels were centrally determined by the Secretaría de Programación y Presupuesto (Ministry of Programming and the Budget, SPP). These laws and institutions governing public sector employees also determined the target of workers' complaints: economic matters had to be taken up with the SPP, conditions of employment with the head of the government agency, department, or ministry in question, and issues relating to social security to the Instituto de Seguridad y Servicios Sociales de los Trabajadores del Estado (Institute of Social Security and Services for State Employees, ISSSTE) (Zapata 1987:29, 50).

These conditions meant unions of public employees could not formally negotiate their employment conditions. In the case of the teachers, it also meant that when changes were implemented, they were rarely negotiated with SEP employees. As a result changes in employment conditions as well as changes in education policy (affecting teacher training and accreditation, compulsory education requirements, textbooks, etc.) almost always produced conflict with the union and discontent among the rank-and-file. In this way all policy changes had the potential of generating conflict and disrupting public education. Moreover, the tendency for a large proportion of the central SEP bureaucracy to be replaced every six years (or more frequently, if the education minister was replaced) and the introduction of new programs and reforms each time exacerbated the potential for conflict.[43]

Government regulations concerning union formation also meant that dissatisfied employees did not in reality have the option of organizing independently of

---

43. This phenomenon is captured well by González-Paredes and Turner, who write: "Like all branches of the administration in Mexico, SEP suffers from sexennial dislocations. Although the PRI has been the party of government since the Revolution, each six years the new President appoints his own men and women to key positions. The hierarchy of SEP is deeply affected by these political appointments, which can extend a considerable way down the hierarchy. While each six-year period may be marked by striking and frequently imaginative initiatives in adult education or programmes for the indigenous peoples of Mexico, the planning process lacks the continuity which one would expect from such a long period of single-party rule" (1990:243-44).

the SNTE.[44] Although there was no explicit legislation preventing a group of workers from contesting the title held by the union, by law only one union of government ministry employees could be recognized by the government. While this did not technically prevent employees from trying to form an independent union, it did mean that in order to be able to function legally as a union they would have to gain government recognition, an unlikely proposition given the close and functional relationship between SNTE leaders and most administrations and the anticorporatist politics implied by most independent union movements. Moreover, legal and practical restrictions on workers' ability to carry out officially recognized strikes in the public sector meant that workers would have to express their discontent via other means: wildcat strikes or work stoppages (*paros*), sit-ins, encampments, marches, building occupations, rallies, and hunger strikes.

The Union as Obstacle: Sources of Conflict in State-SNTE Relations (1976–1982)

Relations between the government and the SNTE under President José López Portillo (1976–82) differed markedly from those under the previous administration. A number of developments affected both teachers and the Education Ministry in this period in ways that would contribute to increasing the friction between the government and the union and between leaders and the rank-and-file within the union.[45] The 1976 balance-of-payments crisis and subsequent austerity measures adopted by the government (including a series of wage ceilings [*topes salariales*]) meant that for most workers real wages began their long-term decline during this administration (Casar and Márquez 1983:252).[46] Government budget cuts and wage erosion hit the public sector particularly hard during this period, especially in the health and education sectors (Bizberg 1984: 173–75, 177).[47] Teachers' real wages fell throughout López Portillo's

---

44. Nonetheless, dissident teachers organized in the CNTE debated long and hard as to whether they would try to form an independent union or an independent current within the union. See Chapter 4 for more on this debate.

45. For an analysis of the sources of conflict between the SEP and the SNTE between 1978–88 see also Reséndiz 1992.

46. Real minimum wages fell by 19.6 percent between 1976 and 1979 (Middlebrook 1995:214–15; table 6.1).

47. Public expenditure on education as a percentage of GNP in Mexico was 2.5 in 1970, 3.8 in 1975, 3 in 1980, and 1.6 in 1984 (Tilak 1989:131).

term, reversing slightly only during 1980–81, at the height of the dissident movement's protests.[48]

Sectors of the labor movement tried to resist these austerity measures. However, the government reacted strongly against those unions that tried to break the wage ceilings during a 1977 strike wave, and it intervened in labor conflicts against independent unions and opposition currents within unions (Bizberg 1984:170). Whereas in the early 1970s increased militancy among independent unions had led directly to wage increases that in some cases (e.g., automobiles and rubber) were higher than the national average, under López Portillo the efforts of the more independent unions to gain more for their members were blocked despite their militancy during this period. "Official" labor unions in private firms, however, were able to move successfully against the wage ceilings in 1979–80, as did the dissident teachers in the CNTE, the only independent group to do so (Bizberg 1984:174–79, 183–84). The second half of the 1970s also saw a wave of dissident unionism within public sector unions (San Juan 1984).[49] However, most of these dissident currents were repressed, defeated, or otherwise contained by the early 1980s. In this way the López Portillo administration moved away from the previous administration's early support for independent labor movements but continued the rapprochement with the official labor movement that Echeverría had taken up during the second half of his term. Meanwhile, the unions that made up the "official" Labor Congress struggled to maintain labor's voice in national economic and social policy. They became more militant in response to wage erosion and austerity and more flexible in their alliances toward independent unions, they developed a series of economic proposals within the Labor Congress, they became more active as a labor bloc within the Chamber of Deputies, and they opened up the Labor Congress to independent unions and even supported some of these in their struggles.[50]

The discovery of substantial oil reserves by the mid-1970s and the oil and debt economic boom that ensued (1978–81) had several consequences for the

---

48. Morales-Gómez and Torres 1990:74–76 and Aboites 1984. Between 1976 and 1982/83 the annual rate of growth for student enrollment at all levels of nonuniversity education was 6.6 percent. The annual growth rate for number of teachers during the same period was 9.7 percent.

49. For instance, dissident currents emerged among workers in government agencies (INFONAVIT), government ministries (Agrarian Reform, Agriculture and Water Resources, Education, Health, Commerce and Industrial Promotion, Fisheries), among city employees (Mexico City subway workers), and among bank workers.

50. On the actions of the Labor Congress and the CTM in this period see Bizberg 1984:186–87, San Juan 1984:115–16, Trejo Delarbre 1984:72, and Casar 1982. For an overview of this period see Cook 1990a and 1991.

labor movement. Many official unions, which had demonstrated earlier restraint, began to demand and secure increases in wages and benefits. The government's differential treatment of official and independent unions in this matter helped to undermine the fragile alliance that had begun to form between these two sectors within the Labor Congress. However, the growth of the economy, the expansion of urban employment, and the widely held view that oil revenues would bring unprecedented growth rates in coming years also contributed to raise expectations among workers.[51] Rising expectations set off by the boom, together with wage erosion and continued maintenance of the wage ceilings, helped to stir discontent among workers.[52]

The end of the 1970s also saw important organizational efforts taking place outside of the labor movement. The most significant independent popular organizations to emerge in this period were the coordinadoras in the rural sector (Coordinadora Nacional Plan de Ayala, National "Plan of Ayala" Coordinating Committee, CNPA, 1979), among the urban poor (Coordinadora Nacional del Movimiento Urbano Popular, National Coordinating Committee of the Urban Popular Movement, CONAMUP, 1981), and among teachers (Coordinadora Nacional de Trabajadores de la Educación, National Coordinating Committee of Education Workers, CNTE, 1979). The emergence of these networks was the product of several factors, including the prior existence of regional organizations and movements that had developed throughout the decade across the country, the diffusion of organizational, strategic, and tactical ideas across these sectors, and the political conditions of the time. Significant here was the adoption of the political reform in 1977–78, which eased requirements for electoral participation by opposition parties and established a system of proportional representation in the Chamber of Deputies of congress. The electoral reform stirred much debate among sectors of the political party and social left as to the costs and benefits of participation in elections. The founding of the coordinadoras, therefore, reflected the choice of a sector of the left to reject the electoral path and pursue instead the construction of autonomous organizational networks among the masses as the more efficacious and enduring way to effect social and political change.

It was in this context—of declining wages, increasing inflation, and expand-

---

51. Total GDP grew at an annual average of 8.4 percent, total investment increased by 16.2 percent a year, and urban employment expanded at 5.7 percent a year between 1978 and 1981 (Lustig 1992:20).

52. Inflation was also an important factor in this period: annual rates of inflation for 1979, 1980, 1981, and 1982 were, respectively, 18.2, 26.3, 28, and 56.9 percent (Middlebrook 1995:215). This contrasted with the single-digit rates throughout the 1960s and early 1970s (until 1973).

ing employment; of budget cutbacks, administrative reform, and oil money; of both growing discontent among the rank-and-file and heightened activism by the official labor movement—that tensions between the SNTE and the Education Ministry began to develop. The sources of government-union conflict in this period could be seen as "structural" in the sense that they were rooted in the education union's immense political power and influence, accumulated over the decades under the encouragement and support of the state itself. Since the union's formation state elites had been engaged in a process of building a union that could provide them with powerful political support. The union as political legitimator of the party/state, however, had exacted a cost in terms of the government's ability to control education—an arena that was supposedly under state jurisdiction. In particular, the union's embeddedness in the SEP bureaucracy and its control over the hiring, placement, and mobility of SEP employees stood in the way of the government's ability to gain greater control over the administration of the educational system. With the adoption of austerity policies in the mid-1970s the government was also forced to reform unwieldy government bureaucracies. The teachers' union—or rather, the entrenched leadership of the union—stood in the way of the needed reform. Under López Portillo SNTE-government relations therefore moved away from the populism that had characterized the alliance in the first half of the decade to a more "technocratic" relationship in which teachers were viewed as obstacles to modernization. The dominance within the SEP of a technocratic faction reinforced this change in the relationship.

Friction between the government and the union in this period would be expressed in several ways. Although the SNTE had little power to influence public policies at their formulation, it could obstruct their implementation. The union could do this by refusing to cooperate ("boycotting" public policies), by allying with high-level SEP officials who might be sympathetic to the union, and by pressing for political influence through positions for union members in government, the party, and the state bureaucracy, thus gaining the capacity to wield political influence through the placement of allies in high-level positions. The SEP's technocratic plans for reforming the professional development of teachers and for carrying out the administrative reform of the educational system were to be imposed without any compromise with the union, yet in fact these reforms were obstructed by the union and compromised at the implementation stage. For its part the SEP would try to undercut the union's influence by attempting to gain control over the professional development of teachers, by devising additional requirements for accreditation, by removing SEP officials that sympathized with the union, and by attempting to fracture union power with the administrative deconcentration of the Education Ministry (Pescador and Torres 1985:27, 30).[53]

The central struggle between the Education Ministry and the teachers' union was reflected in a number of policies pursued by the López Portillo administration: the formation of the Universidad Pedagógica Nacional (National Pedagogical University, UPN), the "modernization" of teacher training, and the administrative deconcentration of the SEP. The specific ways in which conflict between the government and the union was expressed in each of these instances had different implications for rank-and-file teachers, and ultimately for the opposition movement that would emerge within the union. For instance, although the struggle over the formation of the UPN reflected deep differences between government technocrats and unionists, the conflict was relatively contained within the institution based in Mexico City. The conflict over requirements for accreditation and changes in teacher training was managed in a similar way—through protest and pressure by national union officials with government officials. Conflicts over these policy issues were symptomatic of a deeper political struggle by the government to regain control over public education and its employees. Each of these government reforms contributed to an overall climate of tension and conflict between the Education Ministry and the union, which would form the backdrop against which the dissident teachers' movement would emerge.

The administrative deconcentration of the SEP, however, was the policy innovation that would have the greatest impact on the union and its members. In contrast to the formation of the UPN and reform of the requirements for teacher training, issues that, while important, were fought out in arenas far removed from most rank-and-file teachers, the deconcentration had three characteristics that, when taken together, had an important effect on teachers: (1) it affected the entire country and therefore all union members at once; (2) it disrupted the balance of power between the union and the SEP at the regional level without providing a strong and consolidated substitute authority in the state SEP delegations; and (3) it forced union leaders to turn to the mobilization of their members to resist the reform rather than fall back on more traditional

53. Deconcentration was the first phase in the planned decentralization of public education in Mexico. Deconcentration refers to the delegation of authority to a lower level of an agency (within the SEP), whereas decentralization refers to the transfer of responsibility and resources for education from the federal government to state governments. For an excellent analysis of the deconcentration of the SEP and its effects on the union see Street 1983, 1984, and 1992. On education decentralization see Pescador and Torres 1985, Martínez Assad and Ziccardi 1988, and Noriega Chávez 1992. For a discussion of deconcentration in areas other than education in Mexico see Bailey 1994:102–3, and Rodríguez 1987 and n.d.

forms of elite pressure and bargaining. In this way SEP-SNTE conflict was displaced from the narrow arena of high-level negotiations and transferred to the states: to the immediate environment of rank-and-file teachers. In those states where teachers were mobilized by local union officials in order to resist the deconcentration, such mobilization unleashed movements that later escaped leaders' control. Also important from the perspective of the dissident movement was that the climate of SEP-SNTE conflict, and especially the battle over the deconcentration, would generate political openings for the dissidents as the government sought to further weaken the position and power of the national union leadership in an effort to push through its reform plans.

Each of these sources of conflict and their implications for the emergence of the national dissident teachers' movement are examined below.

1. *The National Pedagogical University.* The formation of the National Pedagogical University in 1978 reflected the widely divergent projects of two groups—the union, on one side, and the technocrats in the SEP, on the other—and contributed to the climate of conflict.[54] The UPN was a postgraduate teachers' college whose creation had been a demand of the SNTE's since 1975. The demand was taken up by President López Portillo, and a joint commission was formed to develop proposals for the university. The projects offered by the SNTE and the SEP proved to be very different. The subsequent development of the university was shaped by this difference and by the confrontations and negotiations it generated. The SNTE proposal, for example, called for a large university system to be directed by a high-ranking union official, with branches in all states and an open admissions policy. In contrast, the SEP called for a much smaller, regulated, and elitist university program unconnected to the existing normal school system.[55] The normal schools were controlled by the union; thus, the UPN reflected the government's attempt to bypass this traditional bastion of union influence and to gain greater control over teachers' professional training and development.[56]

---

54. Although the changing composition of the elite was already evident in the Echeverría administration, under López Portillo the technocrats were clearly dominant in several ministries. In the Education Ministry the technocratic faction gained control in 1978 under the direction of Fernando Solana Morales, who replaced Porfirio Muñóz Ledo, the former labor minister who was bitterly opposed by the union and forced to resign in 1977.
55. For more details on the differences between these two projects see Pescador and Torres 1985:20–21.
56. The differences between graduates of teacher-training colleges ("normalistas") and technocrats trained in universities also typically extended to the socioeconomic background of individuals in each group. Normalistas were often from humble, generally rural, origins, and their main channel

In the end few elements of the SNTE's original proposal for the UPN were actually implemented. At the same time, many of the SEP's initial expectations were also frustrated due to the stalemate produced by SNTE resistance and the simultaneous struggle against SNTE officials by dissident members in the UPN's union delegations. The result was a hybrid institution that fell short of everyone's expectations and that reflected the three-way conflict between the CNTE, SNTE, and SEP that was beginning to occur on a national scale (Kovacs 1983, 1990; Pescador and Torres 1985:31,37–39). However, because the conflict was contained within the UPN, it did not play the catalytic role in the emergence of the dissident movement that the government's more far-reaching deconcentration plan did.

2. *Education policy reform.* The union and government also differed on educational policy beyond the UPN. The SNTE criticized SEP study programs and curriculum planning for being developed without consulting educators and for not taking into account Mexican culture and history. The union also criticized the SEP's system of educational planning for being more concerned with supervision and administration of the plans than with whether or not they actually worked (Pescador and Torres 1985:24). Similarly, the government's deconcentration plans were attacked because they were devised and managed by young professionals (engineers, economists, and lawyers) who were unfamiliar with the practical aspects of teaching and were disconnected from the normal school traditions.[57] Finally, there were conflicts over the education and training of the nation's teachers, as exemplified in the controversy over the form and content of the UPN. The SEP's tone was critical of the teachers and emphasized the need to "modernize" and professionalize the educator while excluding teachers from any participation in the decisions that would affect them (Pescador and Torres 1985:26). While most rank-and-file teachers shared

---

for upward mobility has traditionally been the SEP. The technocrats often come from the rural upper-middle or urban middle class, and receive university degrees in law, engineering, or business administration. Part of the tension between these groups derives from the fact that, increasingly, top positions in the SEP have been going to the latter rather than the former group (Morales-Gómez and Torres 1990:78).

57. The fundamental issue behind these tensions had to do with the union's (and in particular, Vanguardia's) resistance to efforts to curb or undermine its power over teachers, within the bureaucracy of the SEP and in the political system. As a consequence this conflict occurred at two levels: between the "fixed" personnel of the SEP and those who filled top positions and came in with each new presidential administration, and between education professionals and those from other professions who not only made incursions in the SEP but also in other areas of the political system (the "technocrats"). In addition, the deconcentration helped to extend these tensions and their expression throughout the country (Arnaut 1989b:7–8).

these views of the government's educational policies, they also saw the conflict as a power struggle between their *charro* leaders and the government over issues about which they had never been consulted. In this way controversial reforms in education policy did not trigger the grass-roots national protests that were to emerge, yet they did contribute to an overall climate of tension between union leaders and education officials.

3. *Deconcentration.* The administrative deconcentration of the SEP, decreed in March 1978, fell within the administrative reform plans of the López Portillo government (Street 1992a:86).[58] The deconcentration was spearheaded by the technocratic current in the government that rose to dominance in the SEP under López Portillo with Education Minister Fernando Solana Morales. Among the stated objectives of the deconcentration program was to modernize the educational system (educational planning and administration) by substituting technical criteria for personalist or patrimonialist criteria in the allocation and distribution of resources within the jurisdiction of the SEP. In the management of SEP employees, the application of technical criteria meant the rational assignment of job positions—the elimination of double and triple assignments per employee, the dismissal of those who collected paychecks without working (known as "*aviadores*" or "flyers"),[59] and of other anomalies—and the effort to modernize the training and "mentality" of teachers (Street 1984:18).

The 1978 administrative deconcentration of the SEP changed the structure and hierarchy by which authority, information, and the designation of resources flowed between the SEP's administrative apparatus in the states and the center (see Diagram 3.1). Prior to 1978, head offices (*direcciones generales*) for each educational level (e.g., primary, secondary, preschool) oversaw resource allocation in the states. Each general director presided over a chain of command that included the federal directors, zone supervisors, and school directors in the states (Street 1984:18). The general directors received information on schools and teachers directly from this chain and received their budgets directly from the *oficialía mayor* of the SEP, a "patrimonialist" stronghold.[60] Over the years

---

58. An earlier attempt to deconcentrate had occurred in 1973 under President Echeverría; this was regarded as a modest and incomplete effort that ended up merely facilitating some administrative work in regions throughout the country but not in changing the structure of authority within the SEP (see Street 1992a:85).

59. The term *aviador* or "flyer" was used colloquially to refer to employees who only "touched down" at work in order to collect their paychecks.

60. The *oficialía mayor* was the central administrative department within each ministry; it was responsible for decisions relating to the ministry's relations with its employees and handled demands raised by the union. The *oficialía mayor* was equivalent to an under secretary position (*subsecretario*),

the union had successfully penetrated the SEP bureaucracy to the point where union allies occupied many key positions in the administration at both state and national levels. The task for the technocratic faction that occupied the Education Ministry after 1978 was to try to regain control of this administrative apparatus from the union and from its allies that extended all the way into the central administration of the SEP.

Solana tried to do this by establishing a single SEP delegation in each state and granting the newly established SEP delegates—the heads of these delegations—primary authority over the coordination of budgetary and personnel matters (for primary, secondary, and technical secondary levels) in each state, thereby attempting to undercut the unbridled power enjoyed by the general directors in the central SEP (Street 1984:15–16). While the deconcentration did not expressly do away with the position of the general directors, it tried to render their position ineffective by bypassing them and requiring federal directors to report directly to the delegate, who in turn reported directly to the education minister. In this way the deconcentration aimed to marginalize those bureaucrats sympathetic to the union, gain greater control over education administration in the states, and provide stronger links between the center and the regions.

The administrative deconcentration of the SEP had several important immediate consequences. First, the reform threatened the union's control over the appointment of teachers, school directors, and district supervisors, as well as many of the administrative positions in the state SEP bureaucracy. It consequently affected the very bases on which the union had built its power. As a result, the reform threw the education minister and state delegates into a "brutal confrontation with the union." In spite of their technical arguments for implementing the deconcentration plan, the technocratic group in the SEP also fully acknowledged the union's political aims and claimed to have anticipated the intensity of its resistance. According to a former SEP official, the SEP had undertaken a mission to "cut the octopus's [SNTE's] tentacles."[61] SEP officials spoke of the implementation of the deconcentration plan as a battle of wits, wills, and strategies—as in a chess game—where the SEP was obliged to keep "one move ahead of the union." Consequently, the deconcentration was

---

which means that he or she had direct access to the minister. The *oficialía mayor* also was the ministry's link with the Ministry of Programming and the Budget and the Ministry of Finance (Hacienda y Crédito Público). See Zapata 1987:28.

61. The quotes in this section are taken from interviews by the author with former high-level SEP officials in the López Portillo administration on August 25, 1987, and September 29, 1987, in Mexico City.

Conflict and Alliance in State-Union Relations

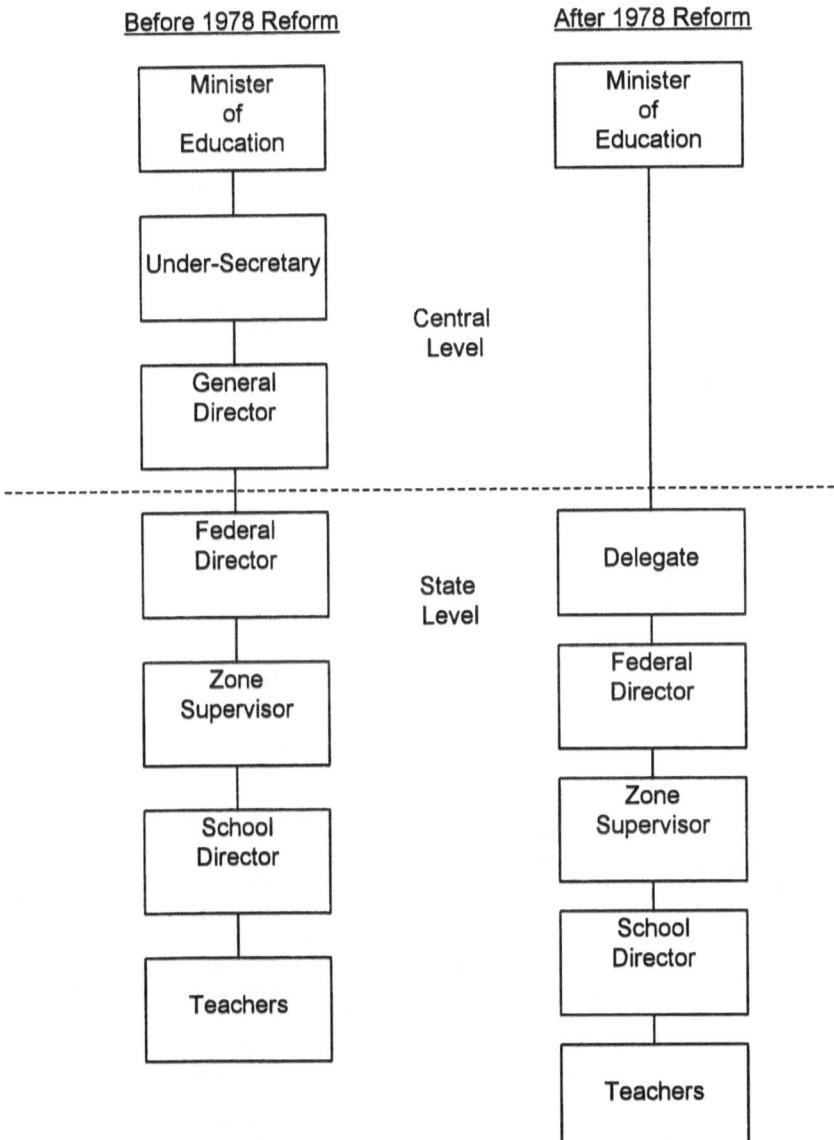

Diagram 3.1. Chain of authority between central and state levels within the Public Education Ministry, before and after 1978 administrative deconcentration

implemented suddenly, "by surprise," in order to prevent the union from organizing resistance at the outset (*"nos hacen una huelga"* ["they would strike on us"]).

SEP officials therefore "learned to deconcentrate by deconcentrating."[62] Solana appointed as SEP delegates in the states people in whom he had the strictest confidence and who responded directly to him. Delegates were sent surreptitiously to the states with little more than a letter of introduction for the state governor and a check for 50,000 pesos (approximately U.S.$2,200). Most arrived to find no office space or support services and hostility from state politicians and regional union leaders—one former official referred to these first delegates as "apostles."[63] SEP officials likened this period to a battle in which the delegations became the frontline. According to one SEP official, "When they [the union] finally reacted, they went against the delegates, because they had not had sufficient time to act against the head." What followed was "a cold war, which at times heated up, for example, when [the union] would take over the delegations."[64]

A second aim and consequence of the deconcentration was to alter the balance of power within the Public Education Ministry and, in particular, to marginalize those factions within the SEP bureaucracy that were identified with the union. The reform forced some of the head offices within the SEP where personal "fiefdoms" had been created to fall into line under the education minister.[65] Thus the deconcentration was not only an attack on the union, it

---

62. Attempts to maintain the element of surprise in order to avoid union resistance may have exacted the price of administrative efficiency (Prawda 1984:201–2). In Oaxaca, for example, the "deconcentrate-as-you-go" method adopted by the SEP worsened the already severe payments problem in the state. There were also complaints about deficient statistical information and methodology in recovering data on resources in the states, a lack of communication and coordination among delegation officials, and duplication of efforts (Hernández Ruiz and Velázquez García 1983:19, 31). Also see Street 1992a on the inefficiency and problems of the SEP delegations after deconcentration.

63. The conflict between the SEP and the SNTE that played itself out over the state delegations also tended to draw in the state governors, whose role became more important after the deconcentration.

64. The most conflictive delegations were those in which the dissident movement was strong: Mexico, Morelos, Hidalgo, Chiapas, Guerrero, and Oaxaca. According to a former SEP official, other conflictive areas included Zacatecas, Campeche, Baja California, Jalisco, Chihuahua, Michoacán, and Veracruz. High delegate turnover can but does not necessarily indicate conflictive zones. Between 1978 and 1982 the following states had the highest rates of delegate turnover: Chiapas (6), Zacatecas (5), Michoacán (5), Campeche (5), Morelos (4), Oaxaca (4), Guerrero (3), and Hidalgo (3) (Prawda 1984:209). For a discussion of the experience of SEP delegates in Chiapas see Street 1992a: chap. 4.

65. Interview with former SEP official, September 22, 1987, Mexico City.

also represented a factional struggle for dominance within the SEP (Street 1992a). Control over the planning, programming, and budgeting of education expenses in the states shifted from the head offices to the Undersecretariat of Educational Planning in the SEP, an office controlled by the technocratic faction. These changes resulted in the institutionalization of a "new centralization of planning": a more direct link between central and state (regional) levels, as well as a centralization of political power *within* the SEP (de los Reyes 1986; Street 1984:16).[66]

Third, the deconcentration increased the autonomy of union locals vis-à-vis the national executive committee of the union. In particular, after dissident movements occupied the union locals in Chiapas and Oaxaca in 1981 and 1982, these locals was able to influence the state-level SEP administration in ways that increased their own participation in determining the distribution of resources and improving the quality of services to teachers.[67] This was not necessarily an outcome the SEP preferred, as it meant that the union continued to "intervene" in the administration. In those states where the dissident teachers' movement dominated the local, for instance, the union still determined who would occupy the positions of zone supervisors and school directors, as well as how transfers and promotions would be decided. In areas where the traditional union factions remained strong, the functioning of the SEP delegations was shaped by the particular arrangements that could be "negotiated" between unionists and SEP bureaucrats in the delegation. In this way it was the regional balance of forces between the union and the SEP rather than any directives from the center that determined the outcome in the states.

In some instances this regional negotiation initially led the SEP to shift its focus from one of attempting to control what happened in the states to trying to provide better services to its employees (Street 1992a:132–33). This was especially the case in those states where the dissident movement was strong and clamored for changes. This focus on service provision implied a more direct relationship between the SEP and rank-and-file teachers, and generated competition with the union in the delivery of services to its members (Street 1984:19–20). A key issue, for instance, was the system of paycheck delivery to employees. Traditionally, checks had to be picked up in the state capital. The

---

66. For a discussion of the centralizing tendencies of decentralization as pursued by the Mexican government see Bailey 1994 and Dresser 1991, on the Salinas administration's National Solidarity Program (PRONASOL).

67. In Oaxaca, for example, the democratic teachers' movement helped to accelerate the deconcentration of services. This was reflected in the reform of the system of paycheck delivery to the work centers, for which Oaxaca was a pioneer.

state delegations devised a network of regional distribution centers that would not only deliver checks to teachers in municipalities throughout the state but make a variety of other services available as well. The administrative reform thus began to make direct resolution of employees' problems possible and weakened the role of the union representative as mediator.

SEP officials encountered strong resistance from the union in implementing the administrative deconcentration. Methods of resistance ranged from simple lack of cooperation to work stoppages and occupations of delegation offices in efforts to force out delegates appointed by the SEP. The federal directors especially resisted the changes imposed by the deconcentration. They were powerful under the old system: they controlled the mobility of personnel in the schools and in the school zones (Street 1992a:109–10). Many federal directors expressed their resistance to the new chain of command by continuing to authorize supervisors to carry out personnel changes without informing the delegations. The attempt to consolidate authority in the delegations was complicated by the fact that federal directors continued to receive some of their budget from the central administration of the SEP rather than through the delegations (Street 1992a:114). Key and lingering points of contention surrounding the deconcentration were whether the positions in the delegation would be union or management positions;[68] what the jurisdiction of the delegations would be and the extent to which this would conflict with the activities of the zone supervisors and federal directors in the states; who would control the distribution of resources and of job positions; and who would exercise real control over the delegation's activities (Reséndiz 1992:14).

This war between the SEP and the union being waged in the states coincided with and in some cases helped to spur mobilization among discontented rank-and-file members. In some areas national and local union leaders' calls for work stoppages, occupations, and other actions against the SEP delegates stimulated the mobilization of teachers who had other long-standing grievances and demands, such as wage increases, increases in the cost-of-living adjustments, and union democracy. For its part the dissident teachers' movement organized in the CNTE saw the conflict between the SNTE and the government as signaling a conjuncture that facilitated mobilization for the movement (CNTE 1980, cited in Street 1992a:127). Its recognition of these tensions within the

---

68. Prior to 1978 all positions in the states were union positions, linked to the *escalafón*; after 1978 a whole new set of positions were created that were reserved for managerial appointments (*puestos de confianza*) and therefore technically not subject to negotiation with the union (Street 1992a:140–41).

"political bureaucracy" helped to define its strategic approach toward government and union officials:

> As part of the political bureaucracy, *charrismo* has contradictions with other sectors of the political bureaucracy with different interests and projects. These contradictions, we know, are secondary. . . . Nonetheless, it is necessary that the movement know how to take advantage of these contradictions while not allowing itself to be used by anybody. At all times we must try not to confront simultaneously—as far as possible—both *charrismo* and the federal government. (Hernández and Pérez Arce 1982:208)

In late 1979 and early 1980 an additional administrative crisis contributed to the growing tensions between the SEP and the SNTE. In this period the SEP experienced serious delays in issuing paychecks to thousands of teachers.[69] SNTE leaders had another grievance to add to their fight against the deconcentration: teachers' protests were especially strong in the states of Jalisco, Aguascalientes, and Nayarit, and took place as well in Coahuila, Sinaloa, Sonora, and Zacatecas (Street 1992a:118–19). For the most part these protests were headed by members of Vanguardia Revolucionaria in the states as part of the union's battle against the SEP delegations and the deconcentration. In other states, such as Oaxaca, the emergence of the dissident movement coincided with the payments crisis. This issue eventually became a demand of the CNTE as well, although it took a back seat to other demands of wage increases, revision of the cost-of-living adjustments, and union democracy. While for SNTE leaders the payments issue was one more point of conflict between them and the SEP, and one that could be used in the larger struggle against the deconcentration, for dissident teachers in most regions the payments issue was one among several more important demands. Interestingly, the CNTE also did not adopt a position on the deconcentration throughout this period (Street 1992a:119–21, 126).

Ultimately, the SEP gave in to union pressure by removing unpopular delegates and "sharing power" in some delegations in order to secure a degree of stability. According to Street, "[s]ome delegates lost their jobs because they failed to recognize the importance of negotiating the distribution of positions with the union and with the federal director" (1992a:140–41). The need to secure the smooth functioning of the delegations thus forced SEP delegates to

---

69. A key problem was in matching paychecks with teachers who had moved to another school or district. In an internal study the SEP estimated that there were approximately 350,000 cases of such delays in early 1980 (SEP n.d.).

work out a *modus vivendi* with the federal directors of education in the states, which in turn implied limiting the original reform plans of the SEP. Stability in the delegation came to be built upon an implicit pact between the SEP and the union, in which the former would give up its efforts to control the assignment, transfer, and promotion of unionized employees in exchange for the union's tolerance of some of the new planning and programming activities of the SEP (Street 1992a:141–42). The SEP was forced to negotiate with the union its spheres of activity within the delegation, and in some cases a whole set of parallel structures were created that were filled by union members. In this way a reform among whose aims it was to weaken the union ended up strengthening it at the local level, especially as more positions were created within the SEP delegations that the union could use as a channel of social mobility to the federal bureaucracy (Pescador and Torres 1985:50–51, Street 1984:21). The deconcentration therefore revealed again the limits of state reform when confronted with union resistance.

The Dissident Teachers' Movement as a Source of Conflict

Although a more detailed discussion of the rise of the dissident teachers' movement will be undertaken in the next chapter, it is important to point out here the ways in which the emergence of the movement itself affected the relationship between the SNTE, the SEP, and other areas of the government. Some have argued that the union and Education Ministry joined forces as soon as the dissident movement emerged in an effort to stop it. While this issue perhaps cannot be fully resolved here, there is some evidence to indicate that the movement itself became a lingering source of conflict between the union and the government for some time. Moreover, each side tried to employ the movement as a tool in their struggle, while the movement advanced its own objectives.

The emergence of the dissident teachers' movement between 1979–80 called into question the ability of national union officials to speak for their membership and signaled the failure of the leadership to uphold their end of the exchange with the state: securing the quiescence of the union membership and limiting the demands of the rank-and-file. This evident failure to manage internal disruption in the union weakened the leadership's bargaining power vis-à-vis the government at a time when a number of contentious issues had made their way onto the union's agenda. For these reasons the union leadership reacted to the dissident movement by struggling to recover its damaged role as interlocutor of teachers with the state. It did this initially by becoming more "militant": by making demands, threatening to mobilize its supporters, and attacking the dissident movement. The government, for its part, appeared willing to capitalize on the emergence of the movement in order to further weaken the SNTE leadership, thereby facilitating the government's reform agenda. Moreover, that the government would take advantage of internal dissent as a way of trying to gain greater bargaining leverage over national union leaders was customary practice in Mexican state-union relations.

Due to the strength of the dissident protests, the SEP was forced to recognize the dissident movement and to address its demands for wage increases and cost-of-living adjustments, bypassing traditional forms of negotiation with national union officials. This and the gains made by the dissident movement throughout 1980 led SNTE officials to try repeatedly to disqualify the movement while attempting to maintain their authority to speak to the government for teachers. SNTE leaders clearly felt threatened by the dissident movement's ability to stage mass rallies and to attract the attention of the government. Yet they appeared even more threatened by the government's early refusal to adopt a hard line toward the mass movement. National union leaders railed against the dissidents at a national council meeting held in June 1980, after a large and successful CNTE protest in Mexico City. However, the interior minister, Enrique Olivares Santana, who attended the meeting's closing ceremony, refused to fan the flames by countering that "the demonstrations by the dissidents are in no way destabilizing to the country" (Peláez 1984a:187).[70]

The emergence of the dissident movement did indeed threaten the stability of the leadership: it generated turmoil within the union and revived old factional conflicts. Attendance at the SNTE's national congress in 1980 was greatly reduced due to the national executive committee's efforts to block the participation of democratic delegates sent from locals that had either participated in or had been influenced by the teachers' movement and the formation of the CNTE in late 1979. The political turmoil caused by the emergence of

70. Some observers and activists believed that Olivares Santana's role was crucial in leading government efforts to undermine the union's position vis-à-vis the government and the dissident movement. They suggest that the interior minister may have had a more personal interest in doing so; he had been a member of the union's national executive committee in the 1950s when the union was dominated by the *roblesmartinistas*, the faction Jonguitud and his allies later expelled from the leadership. However, Olivares Santana was on the executive committee when it was headed by Enrique W. Sánchez, who was a member of a rival faction in the union. Olivares Santana's rise to secretary-general of the SNTE was presumably blocked by the Robles Martínez group (Camp 1995:515–16).

the movement intensified the competition within local congresses and in the selection of delegates for the national congress as various factions tried to gain control; even the old *roblesmartinista* group tried to regain its foothold in the union (Peláez 1984a:179–80, 193). The renewed rank-and-file militancy evident in locals throughout the union led the new SNTE head, Ramón Martínez Martín,[71] to demand "substantial and permanent" wage increases and the reclassification of high cost-of-living zones—demands that had been raised by the dissident movement—in meetings with López Portillo and Education Minister Fernando Solana.[72] While the emergence of the movement was evidence that the official union leadership had failed to represent its workers, the SEP did not escape blame, either. Union officials tried hard to highlight the SEP's role in the political instability. The fact that in 1980 López Portillo felt obligated to apologize to the union for the payments crisis, and that the interior minister would have to intervene to help resolve the disputes, pointed to the dimensions of the conflict and to the SEP's inability to contain it (Peláez 1984a:189).

As the dissident movement grew throughout 1980 and 1981, the behavior of the union leadership became increasingly defensive; it lashed out at enemies inside and outside of the union. In particular, the union's attacks on the government grew stronger in 1981. In this year the national executive committee negotiated with the CNTE—under pressure from the Interior Ministry—to broaden local executive committees in Hidalgo, Guerrero, and Mexico State to make way for representation by the opposition. The national executive committee expressed its strong disapproval of the government's position in a paid press announcement on July 22 which charged that the payments problem had still not been resolved, that state governors had intervened in Chiapas and Morelos in favor of the dissident movement, and that former leaders such as Sánchez Vite, low-level SEP bureaucrats, and the majority of SEP delegates had intervened in the union's affairs. In additional reprisals officials expelled an MRM representative who was on the national executive committee and issued a strong statement criticizing the government's decentralization policies. Martínez Martín warned, "there are people who are trying to divide this organization and

---

71. Ramón Martínez Martín was Jonguitud's son-in-law, and some members of the teachers' movement believed his lack of skill and inability to run a tight ship went a long way toward explaining the initial advances of the movement. A related argument was that Jonguitud was himself too busy as governor of San Luis Potosí to keep close tabs on the union. These speculations are hard to confirm and, in any case, are inadequate for explaining the movement's emergence in this period.

72. The failure to specify the amount of increase in their demands was characteristic of Vanguardia and strongly criticized by the CNTE.

hand it over to the highest bidder, implementing . . . a return to past conditions" (Peláez 1984a:206–7). The union accompanied its defensive posture with stepped-up demands for greater influence in formulating education policy and in the control of the National Pedagogical University, a greater role in the appointment of SEP delegates in the states, more senate and deputy seats in congress, as well as the post of education minister in the next administration.

By 1981, but increasingly in 1982, the response of SNTE officials to the advancing dissident movement had turned violent, as vanguardistas in the states responded to movement actions. Violent incidents, in which people were wounded or killed, were recorded in Hidalgo, Morelos, and the state of Mexico. The union also continued to attack the government in newspaper announcements, such as this one by the executive committee of Local 9 in February 1982:

> We demand that officials of the SEP and its state delegates stop their partisan intervention, as they have been intervening in Oaxaca, Chiapas, Morelos, Puebla, Valle de México, Hidalgo, and Guerrero, in matters that pertain to teachers only. We demand that they respect the union's right of self-determination and abstain from supporting and promoting the dissidents with a variety of resources and access. (Cited in Peláez 1984a:210)

Days later the dissident members on the expanded local executive committees of Hidalgo and Mexico State were expelled in a special meeting of the union's national council. In this meeting union officials called again on the SEP authorities to "stop encouraging, promoting, and tolerating those who call themselves leaders, . . . cause problems and engage in blackmail with the needs of our comrades" (cited in Peláez 1984a:211). The union council called for the removal of Fernando Elías Calles, who was director of SEP delegations and chief negotiator for the Education Ministry in meetings with the CNTE. Fernando Elías Calles was removed, and SNTE secretary-general Ramón Martínez Martín was named the PRI's senatorial candidate for the state of Jalisco.

The attacks and counterattacks between the union and the government were the result not only of the handling of the teachers' movement but were also due, as we have seen, to an ongoing struggle over the terms of the deconcentration in the states. At the same time, 1982 was a presidential election year, and both the union's attacks on the Education Ministry as well as the initial concessions to the union can be understood in this light as well. The concessions to the union at the central level may well have corresponded to presidential orders to contain the conflict during a presidential succession year, in which the support and loyalty of the union were important. The role of the SNTE in supporting the new presidential candidate, Miguel de la Madrid Hurtado, was even more crucial considering the CTM's qualified support of the candidate (Zazueta and de la Peña 1983:115). Moreover, Education Minister Fernando Solana had himself been considered a possible presidential candidate; a successful bid for the presidency would have required, at a minimum, good relations with the union. In any case, his presidential aspirations made him vulnerable to the union's pressures.[73]

In this context it is likely that the dissident teachers' movement was a secondary consideration in the eventual rapprochement between the government and the SNTE. Moreover, some SEP officials admitted that the presence of the CNTE in the leadership of the locals did not necessarily run counter to their goals and objectives.[74] In some states the SEP was able to work with the dissident leaders of the union locals in advancing some aspects of their program, such as decentralizing the system of paycheck disbursement. One top official even acknowledged that the CNTE was easier to work with through the delegations than the vanguardistas had been.[75] Although eventually there was a rapprochement between the government, the SEP, and the SNTE, reflected at both national and regional levels, factors such as the instability in the delega-

---

73. Education officials believed that any education minister who wanted to become president, or advance politically, would have to have the support of the union (interviews with former SEP officials, August 25, 1987, and November 24, 1987, Mexico City). President Ernesto Zedillo Ponce de Leon's (1994–) experience as education minister may have been the exception that proves the rule: Zedillo headed the SEP during 1992–93, when a scandal broke out over the content of the new primary school history textbook and with the way in which the textbooks had been commissioned. The SNTE, led by Elba Esther Gordillo, refused to use them. Admittedly, however, Zedillo did not become the PRI presidential candidate by conventional means, but rather was nominated by Salinas after the assassination of the original candidate, Luis Donaldo Colosio, on March 23, 1994. On the textbook scandal see Maza 1992 and Terrazas 1993. On tensions between Zedillo and the SNTE while Zedillo was minister of education see Aguirre M. 1994.

74. The attitudes of different state delegates with respect to the emergence of the dissident movement varied, and some delegates had stronger political commitments or political pressures to conform to vanguardista demands. According to a former SEP official, the delegate in Chiapas reacted by trying to strengthen the vanguardistas when faced with a growing dissident movement (interview September 22, 1987). Another former SEP delegate reported that some delegates tried to argue that the SEP should deal with the CNTE in those cases where it was the majority; yet another delegate claimed that she applied technical criteria to problems as they came up and tried to remain objective, which led her to deal with both sides (interview September 8, 1987). A former high-ranking SEP official admitted that the CNTE's struggle was just in its opposition to an authoritarian and hegemonic faction within the union and in its upholding of local autonomy (interview November 24, 1987).

75. Interview with former SEP official, November 24, 1987, Mexico City.

tions and the union's effective resistance to the reform, the presidential aspirations of the education minister, and, later, the presidential succession were more likely central in explaining the government's and the SEP's concessions to the union.[76]

Conclusion

The incorporation of trade unions into the political system has often been regarded as key to the stability of the Mexican regime. Yet the history of the SNTE and of other official labor organizations in Mexico shows this process of incorporation as more drawn out and conflictive than has sometimes been portrayed. In the case of the teachers' union, the unification of the teachers in an organization that would come to support the PRI and the government was achieved through a process of factional struggle in which independent political positions and ideologies were defeated or expelled from the union. Over time the union leadership forged a stronger commitment to the government and the party, reflected in its support for PRI presidential candidates and its own launching of union leaders into politics through the party. Union currents sympathetic to other political positions were marginalized, and dissident movements were dealt with harshly, as shown in the case of the Mexico City movement in 1956–60. The SNTE also came to be dominated by a single faction from 1949 until a government-backed "coup" ousted the *roblesmartinistas* in 1972.

With the appearance of a new union leadership in 1972 and the formation of Vanguardia Revolucionaria, the relationship between the SNTE and the government grew closer. The educational system expanded, as did the union's membership and political and financial resources. Although there was some expression of dissent in locals throughout the country, by and large union members received steady wage and benefit increases in the first half of the decade. After 1976, however, several factors came together to generate discontent within the union: real wage decline combined with the high expectations generated by the discovery of oil reserves and with the relatively high inflation

---

76. For the two sides of this issue see Street (1992a), who argues that the emergence of the dissident movement forced a truce between the SEP and the union leadership, and Reséndiz (1992:15), who supports the argument made here that other factors were more important in the conciliation between the SNTE and the SEP. In the literature produced by the teachers' movement one also sees both positions.

that affected some regions of the country in this period. For many union members the unwillingness of their union leaders to take up their demands concerning wage increases and cost-of-living adjustments underscored the extent to which leaders had become more preoccupied with their political privileges than with their responsibility to the membership. It was in this context that many of the first mobilizations of the national dissident teachers' movement took place.

This growing discontent within the union coincided with increased tensions between the government and the SNTE. The teachers' union had become the largest and one of the most politically powerful unions in the country. The tensions in its relationship with the government derived from this power, especially from the union's expanding demand for material subsidies and increased political influence and institutional access in exchange for electoral support and containment of teachers' demands. In particular, the union's expanded influence over aspects of education administration and its control over the employment of SEP personnel came increasingly to conflict with government plans to reform the administration of education and to move gradually toward decentralization. But this conflict encompassed more than a struggle between the government and the union of public education employees over wages, benefits, and working conditions. It was a conflict that affected the work of government itself in an area of great political, social, and cultural importance—public education. It also played itself out at a broader national level due to the important national political influence the union wielded through its role in elections, in the party, in congress, and in numerous government agencies. Finally, the conflict between the teachers' union and the government epitomized and foreshadowed what would become a central issue in later years: increasing tensions within the regime between the technocrats, whose influence over the economy and politics was growing, and the more traditional politicians and trade union leaders (later referred to as the "dinosaurs").

Nonetheless, the conflict that took place between government officials and the leadership of the teachers' union in the late 1970s and into the early 1980s did not result in a national political opening in the sense of those elite divisions that precipitated regime transitions in other authoritarian regimes in South America (O'Donnell, Schmitter, and Whitehead 1986). Instead, the conflict was a sectoral one that, while it did not seriously affect national politics (this was not a "systemic crisis"), did have important implications for education workers throughout the country. At the same time, it is important to keep in mind that this conflict did not have predictable consequences for the dissident movement that was forming within the SNTE. For instance, it did not produce an obvious ally for the dissidents among government officials. As one document of the CNTE warned, the fact that differences exist between the government and union leaders "does not mean that the federal government or the Interior Ministry are our friends or allies of the teachers' movement" (Hernández and Pérez Arce 1982:198). Rather, the power struggle between union leaders and government officials provided a temporary opening or opportunity that the movement could take advantage of in order to advance. The movement could do so by acknowledging the existence of "contradictions in the state apparatus," by employing a careful strategy of confronting only one enemy at a time (thereby "allying" with and "neutralizing" the other), and by not overestimating its own strength and underestimating the strength of its government and union enemies (Hernández and Pérez Arce 1982:48, 208). For this reason the "contradictions" between the government and the union leadership that were being expressed at the time could not be regarded as permanent and the movement's gains could not be seen as irreversible. If it were to survive, the movement could not confuse tensions between powerful authorities in its immediate environment with a stable source of protection from repression and permanent institutional access.

As noted in this chapter, the particular ways in which conflict between the state and the union was expressed had different implications for rank-and-file teachers and for the opposition movement. While numerous conflicts played themselves out under the López Portillo administration, one of them in particular involved structural changes in the way education was administered in the states, which in turn disrupted and altered the balance of power between leaders of union locals, rank-and-file members, national union leaders, and education officials. The administrative deconcentration of education threatened to undermine the entrenched union networks in the states, disrupting union control over internal (state-level) labor markets, and in some instances mobilizing rank-and-file union members who then pressed for their own demands: wage increases, higher cost-of-living adjustments, timely payment of salaries, and union democracy. With the deconcentration issue the conflict between education and union officials thus spilled over into the immediate political environment of rank-and-file teachers, in contrast to other kinds of conflict—over education policy and control of the UPN—that remained relatively contained at the level of national bargaining among government and union officials.

While in some cases the deconcentration struggle was more directly responsible for the initial mobilizations of dissident teachers than in others, in all cases what was important were the strategic opportunities such a conflict between the union and the government generated for the dissidents. In the succession of conflicts over educational policy and administrative reform, the government had an interest in curbing the political power and influence of national teachers' union officials. This interest did not derive, clearly enough, from a desire to see the democratization of the union but rather from the desire to remove the key obstacle to the government's reform plans. In this context government officials saw the emergence of the dissident teachers' movement as an opportunity to exploit the divisions within the union and the weaknesses of the leadership that the movement's emergence revealed. However, failure to establish stability within the union and to contain the dissident movement not only reflected poorly on union leaders, it also revealed the SEP's inability to establish order in its own jurisdiction. There was no denying that the emergence of the dissident movement had much to do with SEP policy: low wages, inadequate cost-of-living adjustments, and delayed paychecks. The involvement of the more powerful Interior Ministry in the conflict signaled the failure of the SEP as well.

It was in this context of inter- and intrabureaucratic conflict that the dissident teachers' movement emerged. Yet teachers mobilized in this period not because they knew they would get a positive response from government officials but because they had managed to organize a large number of people around a particular set of demands. While this context of conflict among national government and union officials does not by itself explain the movement's emergence, it increased the teachers' chances of making significant gains with their mobilizations. Thus, it helps us to understand why the movement went as far as it did. The ways in which several regional movements of teachers emerged and mobilized in this context will be examined in the next chapter.

4

Emergence of the National Teachers' Movement

A Regional Comparison

> ¡País petrolero, maestros sin dinero!
> Oil-rich country, teachers with no money!
> — Teachers' march slogan during the oil boom

The national political and economic context by the late 1970s, when dissident regional teachers' movements began to emerge, presented several features that would prove significant to the movement. The oil boom and economic growth of the period raised expectations among all workers and contrasted sharply with the declining real wages and effects of budget cutbacks experienced by public sector employees. The context of the political reform spurred unification efforts among the left in sectors that declined to participate in elections as well as among the political parties. Among education workers the discontent generated by economic conditions and by the practices of Vanguardia Revolucionaria within the union coincided with a split in the alliance between the government and the union leadership. The conflict between authorities in the teachers' environment was expressed in a number of ways, but as I argued in the last chapter, it was the deconcentration that brought this conflict to rank-and-file teachers in the states. The split in the state-union alliance, then, afforded dissident teachers some room to maneuver and a greater degree of bargaining leverage than might be possible otherwise.

These conditions go a long way toward explaining why the movement emerged nationally when it did. Yet an understanding of why and how the movement emerged where it did requires a closer look at the regional level, especially at regional political conditions and at the leadership, organization, and tactics of the movements themselves. In this chapter I examine the emergence of the national teachers' movement as it took shape in six states between 1979–82: Oaxaca, Chiapas, Guerrero, Morelos, Hidalgo, and the state of Mexico.[1] The initial emergence of dissident regional movements in each of these states was due to the extensive organizing efforts of activists, aided by the diffusion of ideas and experiences from other regions in conflict, to divisions within the union locals in these states, and to widespread discontent over economic conditions. In addition, in each region there was a particular event or set of circumstances that "ignited" the movement, typically an event that underscored an injustice committed against the teachers or that highlighted the unwillingness of local union leaders to spearhead the demands of their membership.

Not all of these regional movements, however, were successful in obtaining the shared goal of holding democratic local elections. Regional differences—regional political conditions as well as the character of the regional movements—help to explain the differential ability of each contingent of the teachers' movement to obtain its goals and to survive. Regional political conditions played an important role in determining the outcome of the regional movements: the preexisting strength of vanguardistas and relations between local politicians and the different factions of the teachers' union affected the balance of forces in each region, and the responses of union officials and of local and national state authorities to these movements were also key. Other important differences occurred at the level of the movements themselves: their internal organization, tactics, and strategies, and the timing of their emergence.

This chapter will perform two tasks: (1) describe the emergence of the national teachers' movement as it took shape in six states between 1979 and 1982, and (2) examine some of the common features and key differences between the six main regions to erupt in protest in an effort to understand why

1. Although protests among teachers emerged in a number of states throughout Mexico, notably in Tabasco, Guanajuato, Michoacán, and Puebla, this chapter will discuss only the largest and most durable of these: Guerrero, Hidalgo, Morelos, Valle de México, Oaxaca, and Chiapas. For discussion of other cases see Salinas and Imaz 1984, Hernández 1981, Hernández and Pérez Arce 1982.

some regional movements managed to win official recognition and why others did not. The national context, and especially the context of conflict between the Education Ministry and the union, were laid out in the previous chapter. In this chapter I turn to the regional political environments and opportunities for mobilization that emerged within each region and to the internal resources (organization, tactics, strategy) each regional movement drew upon throughout the course of what can be called a "cycle of protest" of national scope within the teachers' union, if not in society at large.[2] The following section reviews some of the traditions of protest and various early influences that preceded the emergence of the national teachers' movement and that helped to shape its leadership.

Traditions of Social Protest

The dissident teachers' movement that emerged in the late 1970s drew from a number of social protest traditions both within the union and outside of it. While many of the movement's leaders were forged in the course of the movement, a great many brought to the CNTE prior experience with organization and struggle. Several generations of teachers fed their experiences into the emerging dissident movement: those who remembered the socialist education of the 1930s,[3] those with extensive experience in the rural normal schools, those who had participated in the Mexico City teachers' movement during the 1950s, and those who had participated in various dissident union currents throughout the country during the 1970s. Another great defining experience for the generation that formed and led the CNTE was the experience of 1968: the student movements in Mexico City and throughout the country and, indeed,

---

2. A "cycle of protest" is "a phase of heightened conflict and contention across the social system that includes: a rapid diffusion of collective action from more mobilized to less mobilized sectors; a quickened pace of innovation in the forms of contention; new or transformed collective action frames; a combination of organized and unorganized participation; and sequences of intensified interaction between challengers and authorities which can end in reform, repression and sometimes revolution." Important is the structure of the cycle: "the broadening of political opportunities by the early risers in the cycle, the externalities that lower the social transaction costs of contention for even weak actors, the high degree of interdependence among the actors in the cycle and the closure of political opportunities at its end" (Tarrow 1994:153–54).

3. For a discussion of the reform of Article 3 of the Constitution, which established a system of "socialist education" in Mexico, see Guevara Niebla 1985:9–16, and Raby 1974:44.

the world;[4] the repression and killing of students in Tlatelolco; and the subsequent political organizing among peasants, workers, and the urban poor. Few universities and normal schools escaped the heady politics of the time; many of those who would subsequently organize among teachers had participated in student politics, later in semiclandestine political groups and community and peasant organizing.

An especially important radicalizing influence for a generation of teachers that would find themselves in the movement was the rural teacher-training schools (*normales rurales*). Historically, teachers in rural areas were much more involved with their communities. During the period of socialist education and the expansion of the rural school network in the thirties, many of the teachers connected to these schools moved beyond traditional classroom tasks to teaching the communities about such matters as hygiene and agricultural techniques, and many also engaged in helping to organize peasant communities into cooperatives, *ejidos*, peasant leagues, and rural unions (Hernández 1988:14). In the 1960s and 1970s rural normal schools became centers of political activism.[5] In these schools (which were specifically targeted at the children of peasants), students from poor backgrounds had their first encounters with the political struggles of the 1960s, with *charrismo*,[6] and with student organization and government (SNTE. Sección 7. n.d.:4–5). Many of those who eventually became leaders in the teachers' movement graduated from rural normal schools.[7]

The struggles for democratic control of normal schools in cities and rural areas were precursors to the democratic battles fought in union locals during the late 1970s and early 1980s. Certain universities and teachers' colleges were especially influential in forging politicized graduates: leaders of the dissident teachers' movement in Chiapas had studied at the Macumatzá normal school in Tuxtla Gutiérrez; some leaders of Oaxaca's teachers' movement were involved in the university student protests at the Universidad Autónoma Benito Juárez in

---

4. On the student protest movements in regional universities throughout Mexico see de la Garza, Ejea, and Macás 1986.

5. Transcribed interviews with Consejo Central de Lucha, Chiapas, n.d., p. 1.

6. *Charrismo* roughly means labor union bossism and has typically been used in Mexico to refer to antidemocratic and corrupt union practices and union leaders who are linked to the government and the PRI.

7. Transcribed interviews with Consejo Central de Lucha, Chiapas, n.d., p. 2. In the late 1950s and early 1960s some movement leaders from Oaxaca and Chiapas had been affiliated with a student organization in the rural normal schools (Federación de Estudiantes Campesinos Socialistas de México, FECSM) that was headed by Lucio Cabañas, who later led a guerrilla movement in Guerrero.

Oaxaca in the early 1970s and in the normal school struggles of the 1960s and early to mid-1970s.[8] The Escuela Normal Superior of Mexico City had a strong radicalizing influence on student teachers and was the site of an important conflict in 1974–75; it also trained regional leaders who attended the school's summer courses until the closure of the main campus by the government in 1983.

In addition to the radicalizing experiences of the universities and normal schools in this period numerous conflicts were taking place within specific locals, delegations, and sectors of the teachers' union in the 1970s, prior to the formation of the CNTE. In the mid-1970s, for example, the delegation that encompassed the country's *telesecundarias* began to organize on behalf of the demands of that sector. One movement leader subsequently described this struggle as a key link between the teachers' movement of the 1950s in Mexico City and the CNTE.[9] The *telesecundarias* were a system of secondary schools, located mostly in rural areas, where one teacher taught all subjects at a particular grade level, and teaching was conducted with the aid of closed-circuit television monitors.[10] *Telesecundarias* teachers organized as a national bloc (Comisión Nacional de Maestros Coordinadores de Telesecundarias) in order to negotiate directly with the Education Ministry, and managed to organize students and parents around wage and job classification issues in the mid-1970s. By 1977–78, however, the *telesecundarias* movement declined, after their organization became subsumed under union locals in the states, effectively splitting the movement and making it more vulnerable to control by official leaders.[11]

Other important, though isolated, dissident organizing efforts in the mid-1970s included that of the federal union local in the state of Chihuahua, which experienced a significant if ultimately unsuccessful effort to democratize the local (Luna Jurado 1977). Efforts to democratize parts of the union local at the delegation level were also strong in Chiapas in the mid-1970s. A movement among teachers at agricultural technical high schools *(escuelas técnicas agropecuarias)* in Chiapas in 1977–78 was an important precursor to the statewide movement that would emerge the following year. It also produced a key part of

---

8. The most important normal school conflicts in Oaxaca occurred at the Centro Regional de Educación Normal (CREN) in 1966–69, at the Normal at Tuxtepec in 1976–78, and at the Normal in Tamazulapan in 1972–73.
9. Interview with former Valle movement leader, Mexico City, August 21, 1987.
10. According to González Paredes and Turner (1990:242), the SEP had started experimenting with *telesecundarias* in 1966 as a supplement to traditional schools, as "part of a general move to make secondary education 'open' and available to all who wanted it." Also see Solana 1982:86–87.
11. Interview with former Valle movement leader, Mexico City, August 21, 1987.

the leadership of the Chiapas movement (Foweraker 1993:33–36). The MRM also experienced somewhat of a resurgence in Mexico City locals in the early 1970s, and numerous other political groups and currents emerged among teachers at this time, many of them forming outside of and in direct response to the Mexican Communist Party line that dominated the MRM.

Another group whose presence and struggles had a strong influence on the emerging dissident teachers' movement was the indigenous bilingual teachers, especially in those states with large Indian populations: Oaxaca, Chiapas, and Guerrero. In 1988–89 the size of the indigenous population in Mexico was recorded at nearly seven and a half million people, of which two million spoke only their Indian language. Approximately half a million students were enrolled in indigenous education at the primary level during the 1988–89 academic year.[12] Oaxaca and Chiapas had by far the largest primary enrollments in indigenous education of any other state, with 127,234 and 122,333 students respectively, followed by Guerrero (60,233), Veracruz, Puebla, and Hidalgo.[13]

The roots of *indigenismo* and of bilingual education are to be found in the 1920s, when Education Minister José Vasconcelos implemented a vast network of schools in rural Indian communities (Raby 1974). In the decades that followed, teaching developed into a desirable profession for many members of indigenous ethnic groups, mostly young men, for whom teaching was a form of social mobility, a sign of status, and a means toward self-improvement and further education.

The experience of most indigenous communities in Mexico—and of the teachers who came out of these—was defined by poverty, conflicts over land, repression, and violence. Most indigenous teachers could not escape these conflicts; many became community leaders in struggles over land and in disputes with regional caciques, and many more became the targets of violence. Indigenous teachers nonetheless had tremendous advantages over other members of indigenous communities: they had a steady, if meager, salary; they spoke two languages; and they had some experience in dealing with bureaucracy and authority. At the same time, they received the lowest pay among education workers and labored under the worst conditions. If teachers were generally regarded as second-class professionals, one analyst has remarked, then bilingual teachers were certainly treated as if they were third-class (Hernández 1988:16).

Their adverse environment, together with the pressing needs of indigenous

---

12. Estados Unidos Mexicanos, Presidencia de la República, "Carlos Salinas de Gortari: Primer informe de gobierno" (Mexico City: Presidencia de la República, 1989), p. 172.
13. Ibid., p. 183.

children, led indigenous teachers to formulate early on strong demands for improvements in the conditions of their schools, greater assistance for student boarders in isolated communities, and teacher training. The relatively high level of attention paid to indigenous education by the Echeverría and López Portillo administrations during the 1970s also helped to buttress the organizations and demands of indigenous teachers. Many of these demands centered around the teachers' efforts to move out from under the jurisdiction of the Instituto Nacional Indigenista (National Institute for Indigenous Affairs, INI) to become part of the SEP.

The case of the Oaxacan bilingual teachers' struggle to become SEP employees is illustrative. Indigenous education in Oaxaca prior to 1978 was administered by the Instituto de Investigación e Integración Social del Estado de Oaxaca (Social Integration and Research Institute of Oaxaca, IIISEO), a training center for bilingual education established by the wife of Governor Víctor Bravo Ahuja in 1970. The IIISEO trained bilingual teachers, or *"promotores,"* to go into Indian communities to teach Spanish. Promoters' salaries were low, they received patronizing treatment, and they were marginalized by the union local. In April 1974 bilingual teachers formed the *Coalición de Promotores* in the course of a successful strike and occupation of the IIISEO to demand recognition of bilingual promoters' rights to benefits and to a *"plaza"* (position) as education workers under the SEP. The coalition finally won both recognition of their organization and their job classification as teachers under the SEP in 1978, after extensive mobilizing, including a takeover of SEP offices.[14] Bilingual teachers succeeded in pressuring the SEP to create a separate Office of Indigenous Education, under which the indigenous teachers' traditional organizational structures and forms of democratic selection of representatives would be respected.[15] In this way indigenous teachers won the right to benefit from the wage structures and working conditions that regulated other government education employees at the same time that they retained some autonomy over the form their organization took and in the democratic selection of both their representatives and of education officials in indigenous education.[16] Indigenous teachers also pushed hard for teacher education programs so as to improve their

---

14. Francisco Pérez Arce, "Entrevista a Fernando Soberanes," *Testimonios* 1987:33.

15. Once bilingual teachers technically became SEP employees, they also became members of the SNTE. They remained marginal to the union organization until the beginning of the dissident movement, however, due to the control of the *charros* over the union local and their efforts to obstruct the demands of the Coalición; see Coalición de Promotores Indígenas de Oaxaca, 1981.

16. Interview with advisor to the Coalición de Promotores Indígenas, Oaxaca, Oaxaca, June 14, 1990; also see Coalición de Promotores Indígenas de Oaxaca, 1981.

training levels and facilitate mobility through the system or to urban areas.[17] By the time the dissident teachers' movement began in the late 1970s, then, indigenous teachers in states such as Oaxaca had already been organized and mobilizing for years.

Aside from the various struggles taking place within the teachers' union, the late 1960s and early 1970s in Mexico was also a time of significant political activism. The Tlatelolco massacre of 1968 radicalized thousands of students, sending them into rural, shantytown, or factory organizing, or even into the guerrilla movements that emerged during this period. The ideology and strategies that led to this extensive political and community organizing reflected the multiple developments in the Mexican left at this time.[18] The 1970s was also a period of land occupations in the countryside and by migrants to urban areas: new, grass-roots organizations of peasant farmers and of the urban poor began to form outside of the tutelage of the official party. Workers, too, broke away from PRI-affiliated confederations and formed independent unions; the numerous struggles for union democracy in this period led observers to refer to the "labor insurgency" of the early 1970s.

The states in which the movement emerged most strongly were also sites of important regional political struggles. Regional grass-roots political organizations gained strength in states like Oaxaca, where a coalition of students, workers, and peasants (Coalición Obrero Campesino Estudiantil de Oaxaca, Worker-Peasant-Student Coalition of Oaxaca, COCEO) proved strong enough to force out the state governor in 1977 (Bustamante et al. 1984; Santibañez 1982).[19] Another regional organization in the Isthmus of Tehuantepec, the Coalición Obrero Campesino Estudiantil del Istmo (Worker-Peasant-Student Coalition of the Isthmus, COCEI), became strong enough to win municipal elections in Juchitán in 1981 in an alliance with the Mexican Communist Party. Both the COCEI and the Mexican Communist Party-MRM (which helped found the COCEO) contributed activists to the emerging teachers' movement in Oaxaca: the former in the form of rank-and-file teachers in delegations that had been organizing for years, and the latter in the form of

---

17. The lowest status positions in education were in indigenous education, and within this preschool and primary education were the lowest status jobs. Indigenous teachers thus tried to get out of indigenous education as soon as possible, and their demands for improved education and training reflected these efforts. (Interview with advisor to the Coalición de Promotores Indígenas, Oaxaca, Oaxaca, June 14, 1990.)

18. For a succinct history and description of the political currents and organizations of the left during this period see Moguel 1987.

19. On the student and popular movements of Oaxaca in the 1960s, 1970s, and 1980s see also Martínez Vásquez 1990.

small groups of activists concentrated in the central valleys of Oaxaca. In Chiapas one part of the leadership of the statewide movement came from the rural normal school Macumatzá in Tuxtla Gutiérrez, which had ties to former militants of Línea Proletaria, a maoist political current active in earlier industrial and urban struggles in the north and center of Mexico. As noted earlier, another important group, linked to the trotskyist party (Partido Revolucionario de los Trabajadores, Revolutionary Workers' Party, PRT) came out of the Agricultural-Technical School (ETA) movement in 1977–78.

In other states, such as Morelos, an important peasant movement and independent union movement, along with an extensive network of Christian base communities and a progressive archbishop, Sergio Méndez Arceo, prepared the terrain for the emergence of the teachers' movement. One of the leaders of the movement in this state, Víctor Ariel Bárcenas, came out of the Christian base communities. In the state of Mexico teachers were shaped by the struggles of industrial workers and of *colonos* (urban poor), as in Hidalgo, which was also the site of an important struggle for union democracy and better wages among miners. A key leader of the teachers' movement in this state, Roberto Meza, had been active in the urban popular movement. Guerrero had been the site of strong rural guerrilla movements, led by schoolteachers Lucio Cabañas and Genaro Vázquez, and remained an important area of peasant and indigenous movement activity, as did Chiapas.[20]

The Movement Emerges (June 1979–June 1980)

The democratic teachers' movement began to emerge in states throughout the country during 1979–80. The specific incidents or events that set off teachers' protests varied from case to case, although they often reflected common concerns among teachers. In many cases it was the manifest unwillingness of union leaders to take up the (mostly economic) demands of their members that prompted teachers to take matters into their own hands. Regional discontent and protest had existed before, but in the late 1970s and early 1980s these took on a national dimension.

The periodization depicted in this and the next two sections reflects the development of the movement during 1979–82, in which each phase is defined

20. Levels of socioeconomic development varied in the six states examined here. Oaxaca, Chiapas, Guerrero, and Hidalgo are among the poorest states in Mexico, while Morelos and the state of Mexico are typically ranked in the middle among thirty-one states and the Federal District.

by a core development or theme: the period between June 1979 and June 1980 is when most of the regional movements first emerged and the contours of a national movement began to take shape; it was also a period of significant advances, especially for the movements in the states of Oaxaca and Chiapas. During the second phase, July 1980–April 1981, a core objective among the regional contingents was securing new democratic elections in their regions; a third phase, from September 1981–April 1982, marks the slow decline of the national movement. This phase is characterized by increasing confrontation between regional movements and the SNTE, and by a growing gap between the Oaxaca and Chiapas movements and those in other states, the former which experience an initial success and the latter which suffer lasting defeats in this period.[21]

The six regional movements are divided here into two groups to facilitate the account of their emergence. The movements in Oaxaca and Chiapas share important features and are also the movements that manage to survive this initial period of emergence, whereas the movements in Valle de México and Hidalgo display more similarities among themselves and differences with the first two regions, and they are also the ones that in the end do not attain legal recognition. The movement in Morelos moves between these two camps: at the national level it is treated in a way similar to Chiapas and appears to have the regional strength to command this treatment, yet in the end it suffers the same outcome as the movements in Valle and Hidalgo.

Chiapas and Oaxaca

The birthplace of the national democratic teachers' movement was Chiapas. There, members of Local 7 of the SNTE became the first dissident group to secure the national union executive committee's backing in its demands for wage increases and changes in the regional cost-of-living supplements in September 1979. The relative success of this strike action, the Chiapas movement's efforts to reach out to teachers in other states, together with the presence of similar sources of discontent throughout the union membership helped to launch the Coordinadora Nacional de Trabajadores de la Educación (National Coordinating Committee of Education Workers, CNTE) in Chiapas in Decem-

21. Most of the writing on the teachers' movement adopts a different periodization of these years, based on five or six peak waves of mobilization led by different regional contingents of the CNTE. For a characteristic treatment see Paco Ignacio Taibo II, "Cuatro años de la CNTE: Entrevista con Luis Hernández," *Testimonios* 1987:124–28.

ber 1979. Later, the Chiapas movement would be the first to secure a democratic electoral victory in the union local in 1981. In the neighboring state of Oaxaca the dissident movement did not emerge until May 1980, later than some of the other regions. Yet the Oaxacan case was especially important for the development of the national democratic teachers' movement. Oaxacan teachers were the first of the many regional contingents to take their protest to Mexico City, the first to obtain the intervention of the Ministry of the Interior in resolving their dispute with the SNTE's national executive committee, and the first to obtain official recognition of their democratically elected executive commission, which replaced the "official" local executive committee. The very presence of the Oaxacans in the national capital, moreover, served to further embolden incipient dissident movements in neighboring areas, such as the Valle de México, Morelos, and Hidalgo. The movements in Oaxaca and Chiapas were the only ones to obtain official recognition of their democratically elected local executive committees in this period, and the relative success of both strongly influenced the central strategies adopted by the CNTE.

The origins of the national democratic teachers' movement can be found in the northern part of the state of Chiapas in 1978-79, at the height of the oil boom. This region was an oil-producing zone that bordered another state rich in oil, Tabasco. Residents of this area were affected by climbing prices, yet unlikely to gain access to jobs in the petroleum industry, which went to unionized migrants (Benjamin 1989:230). Teachers were among those affected by the high inflation rates in this area. Moreover, the regional supplements that were intended to complement teachers' salaries and offset cost-of-living differences had not been adjusted since 1956. Teachers began to press for an upward adjustment of the regional cost-of-living supplements, insisting that their region was now as expensive as the international border regions and major urban areas, where supplements to income were as much as 100 percent of the base wage.

The inflationary effects of the oil boom spread the discontent throughout the northern border region of Chiapas state. Teachers in the north set out in small groups, or "brigades," to carry information to the rest of the state in order to gather supporters behind their protest of economic conditions and in particular to push for an adjustment of the regional supplements. Finally, in May and June 1979 teachers in Chiapas managed to stop work for eighteen days. In response, the SNTE's executive committee sent a commission to Chiapas, and in an unprecedented move members of the commission signed a document committing the local and national executive committees to strike if by September 15, 1979, the SEP had not increased the cost-of-living supplements by 100 percent for all SEP personnel in Chiapas, retroactive to July 1979 (Salinas and Imaz 1984:47). Teachers in Chiapas said that members of the national commission signed the document in the belief that the protest movement would die down by September. But when the deadline came, the document became the noose around union officials' necks as teachers in Chiapas held national union leaders to their commitment.[22]

The strike of the Chiapas teachers began on September 16, 1979, and lasted twenty-nine days. Teachers began organizing *comités de lucha*, or struggle committees, at the delegation level of the union local, either dissolving the delegations or in open repudiation of their delegation leaders.[23] During this period eighty union members commissioned by the SNTE arrived in Chiapas in order to pressure the striking teachers into accepting an offer the SEP had made—an increase of $1,500 pesos per person for teachers in the oil-producing areas of Chiapas and Tabasco only, with no changes in the regional income supplements.[24] Protesting teachers decided to reject the SEP's offer and continue the strike until the supplement was increased. In the meantime the state SEP delegate began to pressure the strikers, threatening them with dismissals, suspension of pay, and other administrative sanctions for "abandoning" their jobs during the strike.[25]

In October thirty members from the recently formed dissident teachers' organization, the Consejo Central de Lucha, met with members of the national executive committee of the union, led then by José Luis Andrade Ibarra. In negotiations between the national executive committee and the CCL, the parties agreed to accept the SEP's proposal as a first step in negotiations for a larger base wage increase. In addition, the CCL managed to secure a guarantee that the repressive administrative measures taken against the strikers would be dropped, and it agreed to form part of a national executive committee-CCL commission that would study cost-of-living conditions in the region.

Although the decision to lift the strike after receiving only a partial response

22. Transcribed interviews with the Coordinadora del Centro, Chiapas, n.d., p. 6.
23. Teachers also began to raise the question of democratic union elections at this time. In response to the discrediting of the local union leadership and the turmoil in the region SNTE officials had replaced the committee with a new commission. The Consejo Central de Lucha (Central Council of Struggle, CCL) recognized this commission in the understanding that new elections would be forthcoming. At the same time, teachers responded to the administrative repression by the SEP delegate by occupying the delegation in October until the delegate was recalled (Foweraker 1993:41–42).
24. Salinas and Imaz 1984:47–48, Peláez 1980:11, SNTE-CNTE 1983.
25. For a more detailed account of the strike see Salinas and Imaz 1984:48–49, Peláez 1980:13, and Foweraker 1993:39–40.

to the movement's demands was heavily criticized within the movement, in general the results were viewed as positive.[26] The strikers had obtained the authorities' recognition of the CCL as the representative of Chiapas teachers and had committed the national executive committee of the union to taking up the demands of union members (Salinas and Imaz 1984:52–53). The protesting Chiapas teachers had also received strong showings of solidarity not only from other teachers but also from other sectors of the labor movement, peasants in the region, and the parents of the children they taught. Those teachers who had participated in the brigades that traveled throughout the country during this period had also sown seeds of discontent among teachers in a number of states, and new demands began to be raised by teachers in Tabasco and Guerrero and in teachers' colleges throughout the country.

This nationwide solidarity with striking teachers in Chiapas led to the founding of the National Coordinating Committee of Education Workers and Democratic Organizations in Tuxtla Gutiérrez, Chiapas, on December 17 and 18, 1979. The founding meeting of the CNTE brought together dissident union members from throughout the country to share experiences and join forces after what had been a year of burgeoning regional protest movements within the union. Hosting the meeting were the dissident teachers' organizations of Chiapas (both federal Local 7 and state Local 40) and Tabasco. Attending the meeting were dissident organizations from Guerrero, the Laguna region, the Polytechnic Institute in Mexico City, Puebla, the Valley of Toluca and the Valley of Mexico (both in the state of Mexico), Guanajuato, Monterrey, Michoacán, Querétaro, Yucatán, delegations of teachers from the *telesecundarias*, delegations of administrative and technical workers and academics from the National Institute of Anthropology and History, and numerous political organizations of teachers linked to various political parties and currents.[27] At this first meeting participants discussed whether to form an independent union or work to democratize the SNTE from within,[28] and they adopted several joint demands, calling for a 30 percent wage increase, an upward adjustment of the regional cost-of-living supplements, and for the formation of the CNTE in order to coordinate different regional movement actions and demands in the future.

26. The critics argued that the government had given them mere crumbs, not a substantive response to their demands. To others, however, it was becoming increasingly evident that the teachers could not hold out on strike much longer.
27. For a full list of participants see Pélaez 1980:39.
28. This debate on whether to work within the union or to establish a parallel organization is discussed in further detail below.

The strike and organization in Chiapas had therefore set an important precedent for movements in the rest of the country, and the founding of the CNTE would provide a national forum for the exchange of experiences and, increasingly, the coordination of actions and a growing consensus on strategy. Meanwhile, other regional movements continued to form, sparked by grievances shared with other teachers and specific regional developments.

In Oaxaca several elements converged that helped to set the stage for the emergence of the dissident movement. First, there was a turnover in the leadership of the local executive committee. In January 1980, during the electoral congress in Huajuapan, Oaxaca, Fernando Maldonado Robles was named secretary-general of the executive committee by local union boss Ernesto Aguilar Flores, when many regional leaders preferred another candidate. This action divided the local—especially affecting relations between the executive leadership and delegation leaders—and generated discontent among the majority of teachers. Second, there was a turnover within the PRI in Oaxaca, and Maldonado, the recently appointed secretary-general of the local, became head of the party as well.[29] Finally, there were a series of administrative problems, including a delay in the payment of teachers' salaries, which worsened with the administrative changes within the SEP as it underwent deconcentration. This particular issue heightened tensions between the SEP and the SNTE at both national and regional levels.

After the Huajuapan congress groups of teachers throughout the state began to organize to push economic demands and to protest the lack of democracy within the local. Teachers from delegations in the central valleys of Oaxaca distributed fliers noting their dissatisfaction with the undemocratic way in which the new secretary-general had been selected at the congress. Groups of teachers also began to organize in the Isthmus of Tehuantepec in favor of a regional work stoppage protesting the local committee's unwillingness to pressure the SEP to resolve the delayed paycheck problem. On the coast of Oaxaca many teachers also began to organize around these issues as well as to protest the punishment of delegation leaders who had called meetings to discuss these problems (Yescas and Zafra 1985:83–84).

During the first few months of 1980 the local executive committee began to mobilize in order to force the removal of the SEP delegate in Oaxaca, in the regional version of the nationwide "war" between the union and the SEP over

---

29. This appointment was made in a context of tension between the state government and union officials, which further weakened the latter's position when the movement finally emerged. One symptom of this friction was that newspapers in Oaxaca were relatively sympathetic to the dissidents once the movement emerged (Yescas and Zafra 1985:103).

deconcentration. Local union officials wanted to replace the SEP appointee with one of their own, a man who had been secretary-general of the local in 1977–80. In 1978 a work stoppage organized by local union leaders had succeeded in removing the SEP delegate. In a move that recalled that earlier action, secretary-general Maldonado called a meeting of delegation leaders, who called in turn for a work stoppage on May 6 to press for the removal of the SEP delegate. Dissident teachers, meanwhile, insisted that a demand for increased wages be included among the demands behind the work stoppage and disagreed with officials on the removal of the SEP delegate, interpreting this as merely a ploy by local officials to place one of their own in this position (Yescas and Zafra 1985:86–87).

In this context, in which local union officials were trying to enlist rank-and-file support in their battle against the SEP, the Workers' Day march of May 1, 1980, proved to be a watershed event for the teachers' movement of Oaxaca. Many teachers participated in the march in the state capital. However, police prevented teachers from reaching the central square after teachers had removed PRI banners and prevented trucks with PRI emblems from joining their contingent of the march.[30] Upon learning that rank-and-file members had taken control of the march, members of the executive committee, apparently fearful of the disgruntled marchers, barricaded themselves in the union building. Meanwhile, secretary-general Maldonado, in his capacity as president of the state committee of the PRI, oversaw the parade from his position on the balcony next to the state governor. For many teachers present at the march the police action, the cowardice of their leaders, and the latter's ties to the PRI made evident during the march were radicalizing events that helped to crystallize rank-and-file opinion against local union officials.

The movement grew rapidly after that moment, with some disagreement among different groups over how much to emphasize "political" demands (of union democracy). This disagreement stemmed from the fact that many delegation leaders, who found themselves among the dissidents, still entertained hopes of reconciliation with the local executive committee. Meanwhile, discontent over the payments crisis had already succeeded in spurring the formation of *comités de lucha* throughout the state. The day after the Workers' Day march more than 20,000 teachers in Oaxaca set out on an indefinite work stoppage to protest paycheck delays. On the first day of the strike about half of the delegations in the central valleys area of Oaxaca joined to create a "permanent assembly" that was similar to the CCLs that had been created by protesting

---

30. Francisco Abardía, "Entrevista a Pedro Martínez Noriega," in *Testimonios* 1987:22.

teachers in other states. Soon the rest of the delegations from the central valleys and delegations from other regions joined the protests for economic demands. On May 5 teachers formed a coordinating committee of *comités de lucha*, and on May 6 both Aguilar Flores and Maldonado were repudiated by teachers during an assembly when they refused to take up the additional demand of a wage increase that members called for. On May 8 the local executive committee asked dissident teachers to lift the strike but they refused, adding to the payments issue the demand for a wage increase.[31]

The work stoppage was successful in ousting the SEP delegate, but he was replaced by another SEP appointee—and not the union's choice. He immediately insisted that teachers return to work. However, teachers responded on May 10 with a "silent march," in which approximately 10,000 teachers (out of a state total of nearly 30,000) from the central valleys of Oaxaca participated. The silent march reflected the caution with which movement leaders proceeded in the early stages of the movement; the idea was that members could participate without feeling compelled to shout slogans or otherwise engage in behavior that might invite repression.[32] This caution also reflected the presence of a significant conservative tendency within the emerging movement. In particular, differences between movement activists and delegation leaders over the appropriateness of movement tactics were coming to light: the latter group resisted what it still considered to be "illegal" measures. This so-called "constitutionalist" wing, whose base was especially strong among delegation leaders from the Isthmus of Tehuantepec and the Mixteca regions of the state, also reportedly fought to prevent a total rejection of the local executive committee (Yescas and Zafra 1985:109–13).

As the month wore on, the dissident teachers' actions gathered momentum. On May 13 representatives from delegation executive committees rejected the entire local executive committee leadership (*comité ejecutivo seccional*, CES) during an "extraordinary plenary," which included all (238) but 8 delegations in the state.[33] Representatives named an executive commission in its place and drew up a list of demands emphasizing primarily economic issues: an increase in regional income supplements, a 60 percent wage increase, payment of overdue salaries, and a government response to the demands presented at the national SNTE congress earlier that year (Yescas and Zafra 1985:95). On May 19 the executive commission formed by the dissident teachers appealed to national

31. Peláez 1980:73–75; Yescas and Zafra 1985:94,105–6; Salinas and Imaz 1984:87–88.
32. Abardía, "Entrevista a Pedro Martínez Noriega," p. 23.
33. Peláez 1980:72, Yescas and Zafra 1985:94.

union officials to authorize new local elections. National officials, however, refused to recognize the commission or support its economic demands and instead threw all of their support behind Maldonado, the rejected secretary-general. The permanent assembly then organized a series of protests at the regional, state, and national levels.

On May 29 thousands of protesting Oaxacan teachers went to Mexico City to demand that national union officials take up their demands and recognize the commission. There they were joined by contingents from other regions, including Chiapas. The protesters waited outside of the SEP while the head of the national teachers' union met with Education Minister Fernando Solana. National union officials finally promised to recognize the commission and to authorize new local elections. In addition, Solana agreed to form a commission composed of representatives from the SEP, the union, and the Ministry of Programming and the Budget (Secretaría de Programación y Presupuesto, SPP) to study the economic needs of teachers. The teachers decided to remain outside the SEP, however, until they obtained a concrete response on the wage issue, and the next day Solana assured them that a wage increase would be granted, with the specific amount of the increase to be announced by June 6. The teachers then returned to Oaxaca, leaving their leaders to continue negotiations in Mexico City.[34]

Once public pressure had been removed from the negotiations, however, union officials and education authorities retreated on their promises. The wage increase studied by the SEP-SPP-SNTE commission did not come through by the promised date. Meanwhile, the SNTE retracted its original concessions and refused to recognize the Oaxaca executive commission. Under the auspices of the CNTE the teachers then resolved to organize a march in Mexico City and a twenty-four-hour work stoppage for June 9, in the belief that a national mobilization would force a firmer commitment from the SEP on the wage issue (Salinas and Imaz 1984:89–90).

On June 9, 1980, dissident teachers from Oaxaca again went to Mexico City. There they met with other teachers' contingents, including those from Morelos, Chiapas, Guerrero, Hidalgo, and Valle de México. After a march that drew as many as 70,000–100,000 protesters and supporters, 20,000 teachers set up camp in front of the SEP and SNTE offices for the second time in a month (Peláez 1980:78, Yescas and Zafra 1985:143–44, 148). After they had sat out in front of the buildings for twenty-four hours and the national executive committee had refused to negotiate the movement's economic demands, officials from the Ministry of the Interior intervened. SEP officials appeared willing to

34. Peláez 1980:75–76, Salinas and Imaz 1984:89, Yescas and Zafra 1985:121, 124–27.

negotiate a wage increase, but in an effort to avoid direct negotiations with the dissident CNTE the SEP insisted that the national executive committee of the union support the demand and participate in the negotiations. The under secretary of the Interior Ministry, Fernando Gutiérrez Barrios, then forced national union officials to the negotiating table.

At these negotiations with the commission from Oaxaca, national union representatives proposed that the executive commission for Local 22 of Oaxaca be reduced from twenty-seven teacher-selected members to thirteen, with seven members appointed by the national union and six elected by the dissidents. In an intervention that would prove very significant, Gutiérrez Barrios of the Interior Ministry rejected this proposal and stated that the national executive committee should get only the presidency of the commission. The dissident negotiating commission's first reaction was to reject the Interior Ministry proposal, partly from inexperience and partly because the proposal had not been discussed with the "permanent assembly" who was waiting outside in the streets of Mexico City. But the commission ultimately accepted the government's terms. The assembly selected the twelve members of the executive commission, which returned to meet with Interior Ministry officials the following day (Yescas and Zafra 1985:153–54, 158).[35]

The Oaxacan teachers had succeeded in getting the federal government and the national executive committee of the union to formally recognize the Oaxaca teachers' executive commission. After this victory, however, the protesters remaining in Mexico City were threatened with repression if they did not leave the streets within twenty-four hours. Many teachers did not want to leave the encampment outside of the union building and Education Ministry because they wanted more assurances that the national executive committee would abide by the agreements and that the government would satisfy their wage and other demands, but they ultimately moved out of the city center to the outskirts of the capital. Many teachers also felt that the negotiating team had not bargained effectively, and tensions with the leadership came to a head (Yescas and Zafra 1985:162–63,166–67).

Finally, on June 15 the SEP announced a wage increase of 22 percent, plus

---

35. National officials of the teachers' union responded immediately to this forced arrangement by threatening the government with a massive mobilization of their members, but the threat was not carried out. In an effort to claim as its own the demands raised by the dissident membership the executive committee of the union called a special meeting of its national council on June 12–13 to analyze some of the issues that had been at the head of the dissident teachers' demands in several states, such as the payments crisis and adjustments in the regional cost-of-living supplements, as well as to discuss the application of sanctions against the protesters (Yescas and Zafra 1985:161).

500 pesos per month for workers in the so-called marginal zones or poorest regions of the country. The increase was not made effective until August 15, and at that point the teachers would not be eligible for the wage increase normally granted to public sector employees on September 1. While this qualified the teachers' wage gain to some degree, the 22 percent increase broke the wage ceiling imposed by the López Portillo administration, and it was a victory won by the CNTE rather than by national union officials for all teachers nationwide. These gains therefore helped to validate the Oaxacan leaderships' efforts and to appease members at a critical moment when morale was low. After this announcement the work stoppage was lifted and teachers returned to Oaxaca.[36]

Guerrero, Morelos, Valle de México, and Hidalgo

Several other regional movements also emerged in the 1979–80 period. The movements in Guerrero, Morelos, Valle de México, and Hidalgo were among the strongest of these and were key players in the coordinated actions of the CNTE during the 1979–82 period. In the western state of Guerrero the teachers' movement also began during the fall of 1979, as in Chiapas. In the highland region of Guerrero known as "La Montaña" the firing of the director and several other popular officials of a special educational program sparked a protest in October 1979 that soon encompassed a range of demands of special concern to indigenous teachers and their communities as well as salary issues.[37] These included demands for more *albergues* (boarding schools for children from isolated rural communities), scholarships, clinics, and demands that registration fees and maximum age limits be dropped for secondary schools (because many students also worked, they tended to enter secondary school at a later age).[38] Union democracy was also a key demand early on, influenced by the communal traditions of Indian communities in the area and by the fact that most of the union delegations in the region were already run democratically. Because of this, the organization of the first work stoppage, agreement on a set of demands, and the formation of an early dissident organization—the Consejo Regional

36. Salinas and Imaz 1984:96, Equipo Pueblo 1985:6, Yescas and Zafra 1985:173.
37. Francisco Pérez Arce, "Entrevista a Fernando Jiménez del Consejo Sindical Regional de la Montaña," in *Testimonios* 1987:101. Eighty percent of the population in the forty-three municipalities of the region spoke one of four Indian dialects: nahuatl, mixteco, amuzgo, and tlapaneco.
38. Pérez Arce, "Entrevista a Fernando Jiménez," p. 102.

Sindical Magisterial de la Montaña de Guerrero—met with fewer initial obstacles than did similar efforts in other states.

The lack of response to the movement's demands led leaders of the Consejo to orchestrate a surprise takeover of SEP offices in the municipality of Tlapa in November 1979. The *plantón* (sit-in or encampment) was dislodged violently by police, and hundreds were injured. The teachers retreated to a local high school and holed up for several days, surrounded by police and living off supplies brought in by sympathetic peasants. Governor Rubén Figueroa of Guerrero threatened the protesters with repression if they did not accept the terms extended to them by the SEP, which finally stepped in to negotiate with the Consejo. Most of the "popular" demands with respect to the scholarships, registration fees, and age limits were met. A tripartite commission was also formed to study the issue of the wage increase and regional cost-of-living adjustments, but the union democracy issue went untouched.[39]

In early 1980 the dissident movement began to spread to other parts of Guerrero. Teachers from La Montaña organized brigades to travel throughout the state. Indigenous teachers were relied upon heavily for these tasks; to reach some of these communities required as much as two days of foot travel, and they were capable of covering villages in the isolated mountainous regions in a relatively short time. The other region in Guerrero besides La Montaña that began to organize actively at this time was the north, where the communist party had a strong influence among the teachers. Much of 1980 was spent on building a statewide organization and on regional coordination.

A second important regional movement to emerge in early 1980 was that of the state of Morelos, which borders the Federal District. As in Oaxaca, in Morelos a source of widespread discontent were the union local elections in January 1980, where regional delegates became upset over the imposition of union leaders from Mexico City and over the rotation of a small group of union members in committee positions (Treviño 1984:52–54). Members of a dissident group that had attended the founding of the CNTE the month before, the Maestros Democráticos de Morelos (Democratic Teachers of Morelos, MDM), began to organize among the disgruntled delegates.

However, the event that triggered the first large mobilization of what was to become the Consejo Central de Lucha del Magisterio Morelense (Central Council of Struggle of Morelos Teachers, CCLMM) occurred on March 7, 1980. A teacher had died while giving birth at an ISSSTE hospital in Morelos. Teachers were outraged at the poor service offered by ISSSTE hospitals and

---

39. Ibid., p. 104.

clinics, and angry with their union local committee because it had neglected to demand an explanation for the teacher's death at the hands of ISSSTE doctors.[40] This incident was a catalyst for the movement in two respects: it managed to draw a number of delegation heads into the protests, and the tactic of trying to get the local union officials to spearhead the protests had the effect of further delegitimating these leaders when they refused.[41] The following month dissident teachers in Morelos formed a CCL, following a pattern set by other states.

During the month of June 1980 the Morelos CCL followed the Oaxaca movement's lead in repudiating the local secretary-general and executive committee. As in Oaxaca the previous month, delegates named an executive commission to take the committee's place, but national union officials and the SEP refused to recognize the commission. In the meantime, the "official" executive committee of the Morelos local holed up in a nearby hotel as the summer vacation approached and the movement began to lose momentum (Treviño 1984:59, 63–65). In contrast to the Oaxacan case, efforts to secure recognition of Morelos's executive commission during the following months produced no results, although the CCL did manage to meet with the national union's secretary of organization and later with Ramón Martínez Martín, the secretary-general.

A third important contingent of the teachers' movement to emerge in this period did so just outside of Mexico City in the state of Mexico.[42] Here the emergence of the dissident movement was influenced by several factors. As in other states such as Oaxaca and Morelos, Local 36 in Valle de México also experienced a conflict-ridden electoral congress, this one in 1977. Dissident delegates were already present at this congress, where the secretary-general "won" with a minority of votes.[43] Conflicts between factions vying for power within the union local spread discontent throughout the membership, facilitating the task of teacher activists who began to organize throughout the state. In some communities school supervisors allowed dissident brigades in to agitate in

40. A popular slogan at the time, and one that reflected teachers' feelings about the inadequacy of the services they received in government hospitals, was ¡Si quieres morir, al ISSSTE debes ir! (If you want to die, you must go to the government hospital!).

41. Interview with leader of Morelos movement, Mexico City, June 28, 1990.

42. The state of Mexico has two locals of federal teachers, one covering the region in the Valley of Toluca and another in what is known as the Valley of Mexico, east of Mexico City. The latter, Local 36, was the most active in the teachers' movement.

43. Interview with former Valle leader, Mexico City, August 21, 1987. The secretary-general in this case was a woman, Elba Esther Gordillo, who in 1989 became head of the national teachers' union.

the schools because they saw the emerging dissident movement as a likely counterweight to the faction headed by Elba Esther Gordillo, the new secretary-general.[44]

In early 1979 political organizations and dissident delegation committees in the Valle de México formed an organization called the Bloque Reivindicador (Vindicative Bloc).[45] The Bloque, together with emerging *comités de lucha* and democratic delegations concentrated in and around the northern town of Ecatepec, sent brigades to schools throughout the region and sped the process of dissident organization.[46] Another regional organization, the Consejo Regional del Norte, was also based in the north where the movement was most active, and it too played an important role in disseminating the movement through brigades.[47] The actions of other dissident regions were also very influential in spreading the movement throughout the Valle. The Chiapas teachers' strike in late 1979 led Valle teachers to organize strike support committees; the brigades sent by the Chiapas and later the Oaxaca movements helped to spread the dissidents' demands. The presence of several thousand Oaxacan teachers in nearby Mexico City in May and June 1980 eased communication with dissenting regions and at the same time raised hopes regarding the possibilities of a similar protest movement in the state of Mexico (Pérez Arce 1988:69–70).

Against this backdrop a group of activists and representatives formed the Consejo Central de Lucha Magisterial del Valle de México (Central Council of Teacher's Struggle of the Valley of Mexico, CCLMVM) in June 1980 (Salinas and Imaz 1984:161).[48] According to one activist from the region, the CCL was formed prior to popular mobilization in the region in order to help the organization of the dissident movement. The Valle CCL drew up a list of demands calling for an increase in the base wage and the cost-of-living supplements, payment of overdue paychecks, democracy in naming union representatives, better service in the ISSSTE, and the creation of clinics, hospitals, child-care centers, and decent housing, among other demands.[49] This list was presented to SEP authorities in the state's capital city of Toluca on June

44. Francisco Pérez Arce, "Entrevista a Teodoro Palomino," in *Testimonios* 1987:63.
45. Interview with Valle leader, Mexico City, August 31, 1987.
46. Consejo Central de Lucha "Misael Núñez Acosta" 1982:8–9.
47. Pérez Arce, "Entrevista a Teodoro Palomino," p. 62.
48. The CCL in Valle was organized with two representatives per *comité de lucha*, which in turn was composed of delegation representatives and activists. There were also intermediate organizations called Consejos Regionales de Lucha (regional councils of struggle). Activists could participate in councils but could not vote.
49. Consejo Central de Lucha "Misael Núñez Acosta," p. 9; Salinas and Imaz 1984:162–63.

20, and authorities were given until September 17, after the summer vacation, to respond.

A surprise participant in the national democratic teachers' movement was a fourth contingent from Hidalgo, a state many in the movement considered impenetrable due to the interweaving of local cacique and union interests. On June 9, 1980, the day of the march organized in Mexico City by the CNTE, an effort by local union officials to get members to denounce the movements taking place in Oaxaca, Chiapas, and Guerrero and to reaffirm support for Martínez Martin, leader of the SNTE, backfired. Instead, a group of delegation secretaries present at the assembly in which this maneuver was taking place claimed the demands of the dissident movement as their own.[50] One week later Hidalgo teachers held their first protest march, ending in front of the union building where protesters called for the local executive committee to adopt a set of economic demands similar to those being voiced by other contingents of the movement at the time. In response, union officials ordered the building closed and placed armed guards at its entrance. As in other regions, the unwillingness of union officials to respond to the demands of union members made evident in this action fueled the growing dissident movement in this state (Hernández and Pérez Arce 1982:276–77).

The Struggle for Elections (July 1980–April 1981)

What had begun as a movement oriented around economic demands became increasingly intertwined with "political" goals—with the issue of representation and control of the union apparatus at the local level. Contingents of the teachers' movement pursued two different paths to obtain local control. The first, followed by movements such as Oaxaca, Chiapas, and Morelos, consisted of forming and then obtaining official recognition of executive commissions that would in turn push for authorized elections in which *democráticos* could compete fairly for executive committee posts. The second path, followed by Valle, Hidalgo, and eventually Morelos as well, was to elect executive committees among dissident delegates only or in a "mass congress," and then to function in effect as an officially recognized committee, to the extent that this was possible, while continuing to insist on official recognition. Both strategies

50. According to a movement leader in Hidalgo, many of these people who first participated in the movement later returned to Vanguardia (Ana Graciela Bedolla, "Entrevista a Roberto Meza," in *Testimonios* 1987:86).

rested ultimately on a tricky proposition: securing the official recognition of the national executive committee of the union, the sworn enemy of the dissident movement.

Both strategies also raised the issue of formal-legal status for the movement. Even while dissidents recognized the constraints of acting within the official union, they also recognized that any possibility of obtaining important gains for members depended on the movement being able to occupy formal positions of power within the union structure, with the legal authority to bargain, on a routine basis, with union and government officials. This, too, was what the democratization of the SNTE consisted of—winning elected positions on union local and national committees in order to create, from an oligarchic organization dominated by leadership interests, a representative trade union responsive to member needs and demands. Obtaining formal-legal status, with all its contradictions and limitations, through either of the two strategies thus became a central pursuit of all of these regional movements during this period.

Morelos, Guerrero, Hidalgo, and Valle de México

After the summer vacation in 1980, Morelos teachers continued to fight for official recognition of the executive commission they had elected in June. On September 10 the secretary-general of the SNTE, Ramón Martínez Martín, met in Cuernavaca with movement leaders during an assembly (in the presence of members) and signed a series of agreements, including a commitment to hold new elections.[51] He set a meeting for the following day, during which the CCL was to provide proof that the majority of teachers wanted to decertify Quintero Bahena, the union local secretary. Martínez Martín never showed up at that meeting. Later he denied ever having been in Cuernavaca and refused to acknowledge that he had signed an agreement. This action subsequently led the Morelos movement to adopt more radical measures.[52]

The Morelos CCL announced a strike for October 13, 1980. Their demands included a 30 percent wage increase, a 100 percent increase in the regional cost-of-living supplement, an end to SNTE threats and intimidation, more ISSSTE clinics, and recognition of the democratic commission. The Morelos CCL, claiming that it had a constitutional right to strike, took the novel step

---

51. Teachers at the assembly refused to let him go until he had signed; despite this pressure, Martínez Martín refused offers by the state attorney and by the chief of police to escort him out of the building.

52. Arriaga 1981:91, Salinas and Imaz 1984:118, Treviño 1984:71.

of filing a petition to strike through the local labor arbitration board.[53] The CNTE supported Morelos with a march and work stoppage on October 16. However, after receiving no response from either the SEP or the SNTE, the dissident teachers requested the governor's help in resolving the strike and in putting an end to the administrative sanctions and harassment by municipal officials. On November 3 the Morelos teachers walked from Cuernavaca to Mexico City—a journey that took two days—to join with other contingents of the CNTE in a march and *plantón* in front of the SEP and SNTE offices in Mexico City. Police set up barricades along the route in an attempt to block Morelos teachers from reaching the city center. Eventually, however, they reached the Zócalo, Mexico City's enormous central square, in an emotional encounter with other teachers' contingents who had been waiting for them.[54]

The national action on November 5, 1980, led to negotiations between the national executive committee and the CCLs of Chiapas and Morelos over the authorization of local elections, in the presence of officials from the Interior Ministry. Chiapas and Morelos were offered a package that included the formation of new executive commissions composed of seven national executive committee appointees and six dissident members. The national executive committee also agreed to authorize new elections within 120 days. Both contingents initially refused the package. Still on strike, the Morelos contingent was forced to return to its state, while the Chiapas contingent lifted the *plantón* and retreated to the Escuela Normal Superior. Eventually, and apparently under threats of repression, Chiapas signed an agreement with the national executive committee accepting the terms the latter had proposed (Hernández and Pérez Arce 1982:287). The Morelos CCL held out for two more weeks for economic demands and for recognition of its executive commission composed entirely of movement people. But in the end the Morelos movement was forced to lift its strike on November 24, after accepting the initial terms set by the national executive committee and signing an agreement in which the SEP committed itself to increasing the cost-of-living supplement (Treviño 1984:86, Salinas and Imaz 1984:143–44).

In the Valle de México, meanwhile, both the SEP and the local executive committee had refused to respond to the CCL's demands. Dissidents continued

---

53. The strike was declared illegal by state authorities. SNTE statutes did not allow for any local or group of union members to strike without national executive committee authorization and filing of the petition with labor authorities. The Morelos CCL's action was thus a direct challenge to both the union statutes and the restrictions on strikes that most public sector employees faced.

54. Arriaga 1981:91; Treviño 1984:71–72, 81; Salinas and Imaz 1984:136; Hernández and Pérez Arce 1982:286–89.

to organize throughout this period, but the Valle movement was still not as successful as other regions in backing up its demands with mobilizations.[55] Even though less than half of the school zones (60 out of 188) were represented at an assembly of the Valle movement in late October, members decided to initiate a series of actions in order to take advantage of the national mobilizations spearheaded by Chiapas and Morelos (Pérez Arce 1988:74–75). The first twenty-four hour work stoppage was held on October 28, 1980, with approximately 8,000 out of a total of 24,000 teachers from Valle Local 36 participating. On October 30 a forty-eight hour work stoppage was organized, in which approximately half of the union local members participated, and on November 4 teachers set out on an indefinite wildcat strike.[56] On November 13, 1980, over 12,000 teachers met in a "mass congress" at the National Autonomous University in Mexico City, where they flouted the union statutes by electing an unauthorized executive committee.[57]

Authorities continued to refuse negotiations with the Valle CCL. Union and local government officials began a strong campaign against them in the state of Mexico. After fifteen days on strike the Valle movement decided to step up the pressure with a *plantón*, but was forced to call off both under the threat of repression. With pressure from Interior Ministry officials, the CCL obtained only partial resolution of some economic demands and none of the political-union demands. However, the actions of the Morelos and Valle movements in this period did lead to a readjustment of the cost-of-living supplements, a concession that national union officials wanted to claim as the fruit of their efforts (Hernández and Pérez Arce 1982:295).

In Hidalgo the dissident movement formed its CCL in November 1980. By this time SEP authorities in the state were harassing and intimidating many activist teachers through firings, unsolicited transfers, demerits that would affect promotion, and other forms of administrative harassment. Local union officials also refused to represent the demands of the protesters to national union officials, and the press began an intensive campaign aimed at discrediting the emerging movement. Following Valle's lead, on December 3 the Hidalgo CCL

---

55. Consejo Central de Lucha "Misael Núñez Acosta," p. 10; Pérez Arce 1988:69, 71; Salinas and Imaz 1984:163. Some sources attribute this to the fact that a relatively small number of people had been involved in the formation of the CCL.

56. Consejo Central de Lucha "Misael Núñez Acosta," p. 12; Pérez Arce 1988:76.

57. Consejo Central de Lucha "Misael Núñez Acosta," pp. 12–13. The precedent for the mass congress had been set during the 1959 teachers' movement in Mexico City. Instead of electing congress delegates who would then select the executive committee, the procedure stipulated in the union statutes, the mass congress was open to all members of the local upon presentation of a work identification and last paycheck stub (Salinas and Imaz 1984:165).

also held a mass congress where it "decertified" the local executive committee and elected a new committee from the movement. This new committee immediately sought recognition from the SEP delegation in the state, a demand that the delegate ignored. Dissidents then began to organize throughout the state and to initiate contacts with other CCLs. After the Christmas holidays, on January 15, 1981, the CCL organized a statewide work stoppage and *plantón* in front of the governor's residence. The list of demands presented to the governor included requests for the removal of the federal director of primary education, a SEP post; the reinstatement of three local SEP officials who had been pressured out of office by local union officials; the reinstatement of teachers who had been fired due to their participation in the movement; and a commitment from the state government not to repress the protesters (Hernández and Pérez Arce 1982:279–80).

Three days later the teachers lifted their *plantón*, after reaching an agreement with the governor, the SEP delegate, and representatives of the national executive committee of the union. The agreement, forged just prior to state elections for governor and local legislative deputies, was surprisingly favorable to the CCL. It called for resolution of practically all of its demands within seventy-two hours, and SEP officials claimed that they would recognize the CCL via the formation of a commission composed of CCL representatives, representatives from the national executive committee of the union, and the state SEP delegate. According to the agreement, this commission (which would replace the committee elected in the mass congress) would have the authority to handle grievances, bypassing the local executive committee in Hidalgo. However, local union officials reacted swiftly and angrily by occupying the SEP delegation, the federal offices of primary education, and the normal school, and by calling for a work stoppage in order to force the government and SEP to abandon the agreement signed with the CCL. This pressure proved effective, as officials did not follow through on their commitments with the CCL.

By the beginning of 1981 the teachers' movements in Morelos, Chiapas, and Oaxaca all had officially recognized executive commissions. Valle, Hidalgo, and Guerrero continued to struggle for executive commissions recognized by national officials, even though Valle and Hidalgo had both elected local executive committees in mass congresses.

The CNTE played a more active role in coordinating the actions of the Guerrero, Valle, and Hidalgo movements in early 1981. A joint work stoppage, march, and *plantón* were organized for February 2. The Morelos movement also picked up again, and other contingents participated in solidarity work stoppages. Days before the national action, however, a prominent Valle leader, Misael

Núñez Acosta, was assassinated. "Misael," as he was known throughout the movement, was shot as he emerged from a meeting in the community of Tulpetlac, in the state of Mexico, the evening of January 30, 1981. A parent attending the meeting, Isidoro Dorantes, was also shot and killed, and another teacher, Darío Ayala, was wounded. The two assailants were picked up by police and, when questioned, claimed that an "advisor" to the national executive committee of the union had paid them to quiet the "agitator"; this advisor was never arrested.[58]

News of Misael's death swept the movement. Recently elected to Valle's democratic executive committee, Misael was an important figure in the teachers' movement and a natural leader who had participated alongside industrial workers and *colonos* in their struggles. His murder was viewed by all as a warning to the democratic movement. But Vanguardia had also given the movement a martyr: for the next decade Misael would serve as a reminder of the worst that Vanguardia was capable of, as well as a symbol of commitment to the teachers' movement and to the struggles of other popular classes. At the same time, Misael's murder cast a pall over the dissident teachers' organizations, especially in Valle, and frightened many activists, not to mention less experienced supporters of the movement. The assassination contributed to the movement's unraveling.

Just days after Misael's death thousands of teachers turned out for the CNTE march voicing demands that were far more political and antigovernment than in previous demonstrations (Salinas and Imaz 1984:183). After the march a joint committee of representatives from the Guerrero, Hidalgo, and Valle movements entered into intense negotiations with the SEP and SNTE. According to a movement leader present during the negotiations, these went on for twelve days, between fifteen and eighteen hours a day, with the SEP pressuring national union representatives to negotiate at every step.[59] Meanwhile, teachers in the streets organized marches, held meetings in front of the Cuban, Indian, and U.S. embassies, and met with President López Portillo's personal secretary (Salinas and Imaz 1984:209–10). The *plantón*, organized mainly by teachers from Guerrero and Hidalgo, was also sustained throughout this period. By participants' own accounts, it functioned as a "school of democracy": a classroom in organization, democratic decision making, and solidarity. In this general climate of repression after Misael's death, however, the *plantón* was soon

---

58. CNTE/Información Obrera, "Misael Núñez Acosta: Biografía de una lucha, relato de una infamia," 1981.

59. Pérez Arce, "Entrevista a Teodoro Palomino," p. 69.

dislodged violently by police. Protesters were herded onto buses and driven to the outskirts of Mexico City.

After they were dislodged from the *plantón*, the dissident teachers from Guerrero retreated to nearby Morelos rather than return to their own state. In Guerrero Governor Figueroa had issued an order to arrest all members of the CCL, and hundreds of teachers were being fired for their participation in the protests. Just days before, the governor had traveled with police to several schools in the city of Iguala, where striking teachers were standing guard. There the governor threatened and arrested a number of teachers, causing others to abandon some of the other schools (CCL del Magisterio de Guerrero 1985:22–23). The Guerrero teachers remained in Morelos for a week, housed in school buildings and fed by teachers from Morelos. Finally, Guerrero teachers decided to return to Mexico City via a "dignity march." According to one movement leader:

> We weren't prepared for a march, for so many days of physical exhaustion. What were we going to eat? Well, we ate what we could, practically all oranges. The march was very difficult; nonetheless, people responded. We began the march with about 8,000 people and kept growing. Finally most of us arrived, and all during the march negotiations were taking place.[60]

In negotiations with the Guerrero, Hidalgo, and Valle leaders the national executive committee agreed to negotiate economic and labor demands with the SEP and agreed to meet with the ISSSTE, but refused to recognize the new executive committee voted in by the mass congress held by the Valle CCL. Finally, the Hidalgo, Valle, and Guerrero movements accepted SEP and SNTE proposals to expand the executive committees of these locals to include five additional positions that would be occupied by the CCL.[61] Other agreements included lifting all types of repression, holding delegation assemblies in the three states to determine the legitimacy of the local executive committees, and a SEP commitment to adjust the regional cost-of-living supplement and to increase compensation for teachers who worked in the marginal zones.[62] On February 21 teachers returned to work.

Leaders of the Valle movement had at first resisted the national union

60. Pérez Arce, "Entrevista a Fernando Jiménez," p. 109.
61. Consejo Central de Lucha "Misael Núñez Acosta," pp. 12–13, 17.
62. Pérez Arce, "Entrevista a Fernando Jiménez," p. 109; Consejo Central de Lucha del Magisterio de Guerrero 1985:24.

committee's terms, provoking some internal divisions, but they were ultimately forced to accept the package offered them under the threat of ending talks and of layoffs for 13,000 workers.[63] A similar debate over whether or not to accept the five additional positions on the committee took place within the Guerrero movement, which finally accepted the idea of an expanded committee. Leaders of the Hidalgo CCL also faced some internal criticism but finally joined the Guerrero and Valle CCLs in accepting the conditions in order to halt the repression against their members, to obtain representatives on the committee who could negotiate with authorities in an official capacity, and because they wanted to save the membership's strength for future battles (CCL del Magisterio Hidalguense n.d.).

After the peak mobilizations in January and February of 1981 the national teachers' movement ebbed, and several regional movements entered a period of withdrawal marked by little participation in mobilizations. This was particularly true in Valle, where activists concentrated instead on internal organization. Valle's participation in the national actions had not been as strong as it had during the previous fall. Community support had also waned, and many members were disillusioned by the movement's limited success, in particular by the way in which the previous *plantón* had been lifted (Pérez Arce 1988:107). Only the most committed activists continued their participation.[64] At the same time, the new expanded executive committee was wracked by problems. Some handling of administrative work and grievances was possible with the expanded committee, but the official majority on the committee blocked dissident proposals to hold a referendum in order to determine its representativeness.[65] The Valle movement had also decided to use its representatives on the committee to confront the other, "official" members of the committee so as to maintain a level of "ideological purity." (Later documents of the CCL charged that this strategy was mistaken and led the movement to expend its efforts counterproductively.) In addition, the CCL, which was having its own internal difficulties, reportedly did not play a leadership role during this period, leaving the movement's representatives on the committee without a plan of action.[66]

In Hidalgo, meanwhile, the CCL held a second mass congress in order to elect the five members who would participate on the expanded executive committee. These five representatives signed an agreement whereby they con-

63. Consejo Central de Lucha "Misael Núñez Acosta," pp. 18, 23; interview with former Valle leader, Mexico City, August 21, 1987.
64. Consejo Central de Lucha "Misael Núñez Acosta," pp. 15–16.
65. Ibid., p. 32.
66. Ibid., pp. 23–24.

sented to resign if they did not act on behalf of the demands of the membership and the CCL. Their tasks were to try to unmask corruption by the other members of the committee and to fight for new elections. But the other members of the local executive committee refused to allow these five to take their positions, and in November 1981 members of the CCL took over union local headquarters in protest.

Chiapas, Morelos, and Oaxaca

Encouraged by the example of Oaxaca, which had obtained very favorable representation on the executive commission and the promise of authorized elections in the near future, the Chiapas CCL began to declare more forcefully the need to control the local. In June 1980 the CCL issued a press statement in which it recognized the futility of negotiations with union leaders in the executive commission and declared its need and willingness to "wrench" (*arrancar*) from the national executive committee what was rightfully theirs— the authorization of new local elections (Peláez 1980:24).[67] Until then, it argued, the CCL could not solve the everyday problems of teachers and was therefore of limited use to its members. As one movement leader indicated, "we began to feel the urgent need to legalize our strength" (SNTE. Sección 7. n.d.:16–17). Control over the handling and resolution of the teachers' concrete problems meant the chance to consolidate and extend the democratic movement. In Chiapas, then, as in other regions, the pursuit of economic and workplace demands led the movement toward the struggle for political control of the local.

As agreed, the SNTE issued a call for local elections in Morelos and Chiapas to be held March 6–7, 1981. Both movements were offered electoral congresses in exchange for their commitment to end mobilizations. This was a condition that the Morelos movement refused and that the Chiapas movement apparently accepted (Arriaga 1981:99). The Chiapas movement held its congress on the stated date; the Morelos congress was postponed to March 26–27.

In the weeks before the Chiapas congress, vanguardistas tried actively to recruit supporters in the state and to build opposition to the *democráticos* in preparation for the elections. As the congress date neared, the various political

67. The executive commission had been set up in Chiapas after the 1979 strike and was composed of a majority of national union appointees, plus four "democratic" members. Although it was intended to be temporary, teachers in Chiapas had to join national mobilizations in order to obtain authorization for new elections.

positions and ideological differences within the movement also became more defined.[68] Success in the local elections depended on being able to check vanguardistas' efforts to gain representation in the congress illegally: for instance, by manipulating the delegation assemblies in which delegates to the congress were elected and by negotiating for positions on the committee ahead of time. To this end supporters of the democratic movement held prior assemblies and a "precongress" in order to hammer out differences, forge agreements, and present a united front at the formal meetings stipulated by the statutes and presided over by national union representatives: the delegation assemblies and the congress. According to a document from the movement, "Events stipulated in the statutes [of the union] were held only in order to sanction our prior agreements and to avoid provocation by the *charros*" (SNTE. Sección 7. 1984a).

During these delegation assemblies 192 delegates were selected, including 12 "vanguardistas." Delegates from throughout the state then gathered at the union hall in Tuxtla Gutiérrez on March 6 for the "precongress," which in this case consisted of a CCL assembly at which the congress delegates were also present. They worked for the next two days, checking delegates' credentials, making sure every statutory requirement had been filled, writing position statements on various topics for approval by the assembly, and selecting the next executive committee. They finished at 3:00 A.M. on March 9, after having worked for thirty-four hours. The official congress was to start just eight hours later.

Later that morning, tired and nervous delegates gathered at the site of the congress to wait for the representatives from the national union committee to arrive in order to oversee the congress. What followed was a day of negotiations during which the national executive committee tried to get "proportional" representation on the local committee. The CCL held its ground and informed the Ministry of the Interior of the maneuvers; eventually the conditions imposed by the national executive committee were dropped and the congress could take place (Pérez Arce 1988:104–5).

The first officially authorized democratic congress of the national teachers' movement finally took place on March 9, 1981. The election of the new committee at the official congress was finally completed at 3:30 A.M. on March 10, 1981. Amid shouts and applause, delegates left the congress site and poured into the streets of Tuxtla Gutiérrez, where 2,000 teachers were awaiting the news. "We won!" they repeated over and over, in disbelief. Against all odds,

---

68. On the sources of these conflicts see Pérez Arce 1988:99–100.

the teachers in Chiapas had won the first statutory victory for the opposition movement. This marked the entrance of the movement into a new phase, that of formal recognition and legality.[69]

In Morelos, as in Chiapas, similar precongress efforts by national union officials to impose a committee made up in part of vanguardistas were rejected by the CCL. However, in contrast to Chiapas, teachers from the Morelos movement did not hold prior assemblies and a precongress, but went headlong into the officially sanctioned events. Even with the manipulation of delegation assemblies by national executive committee officials, CCL members nevertheless selected seventy-five delegates to attend the electoral congress to "vanguardia's" forty-eight. Officials then gave a time and date, March 26, but no location for the congress. On the day of the congress members of the CCL learned that the congress was being held without them, with the vanguardista delegates only, at a resort near Cuernavaca. Blocked from entering the resort, the teachers called the Interior Minister, who suggested they speak to the governor. The CCL requested the governor's intervention but received no response. Dissident teachers then began a series of protest actions: they staged a *plantón* in front of the state governor's mansion, began a hunger strike, took over radio stations, blocked highways, and requested the mediation of the interior minister. After twelve days of the hunger strike with no response, the strike and *plantón* were lifted. The delegates held an open-air congress in the central plaza, whereupon they elected their own executive committee.[70]

The new committee elected by movement delegates in Morelos (where there were now two committees) then set out to try to gain official recognition. The SEP delegate refused to get involved. Interior Ministry officials finally arranged a meeting with national executive committee representatives on April 28 in order to discuss the formation of a composite committee (part vanguardistas and part CCL). The Morelos CCL rejected the proposal because it was not willing to accept a minority position on the committee, claiming to have the support

69. Movement leaders had their own explanations for why the congress had been able to take place. Some remarked that it was a way to divide the national movement by resolving the demands of some regional contingents and not of others. Others commented that denying the congress in Chiapas at this point would make the national movement explode. Some in Chiapas explained the congress in terms of a complicated set of contextual factors: "mobilizations of teachers in Mexico City in February; the aspirations of the president of the executive commission in Chiapas to become secretary general of the SNTE; the presence of a SEP delegate who . . . was in charge of promoting the SEP's deconcentration program and of calming the situation among teachers in Chiapas . . . ; contradictions between Jonguitud and Juan Sabines [the governor of Chiapas], the Minister of Education, and the Minister of the Interior, perhaps due to political jockeying around the presidential succession" (Peralta Esteva et al. 1985:24; SNTE. Sección 7. 1984a).

70. Salinas and Imaz 1984:254–55, Treviño 1984:95–97, Pérez Arce 1988:120.

of the majority of delegates. Eventually, however, the CCL was forced to accept an Interior Ministry proposal to name eleven of its members to union commissions. These were not committee positions, and therefore CCL representatives would have no authority to process members' job requests and grievances, but they could technically participate in other executive committee tasks. Acceptance of these commissions, however, rendered the possibility of ever winning the executive committee in democratic elections even more distant. Moreover, after the strike vanguardistas had opened three offices in cities where the dissident presence was strongest in order to handle union members' paperwork and deal with problems. In this way they were able to co-opt movement supporters and divide delegations.[71]

In Oaxaca, meanwhile, the executive commission installed after the mobilizations in 1980 had been functioning as a de facto executive committee throughout the remainder of 1980 and 1981. The national executive committee appointee that headed the executive commission was relatively flexible and fairly powerless to oppose the rest of the commission, composed entirely of "democratic" members. Vanguardia Revolucionaria was also unorganized in Oaxaca, and the efforts of the executive commission's president to organize the vanguardista opposition did not bear fruit. As a result, according to movement leaders much was accomplished in the period prior to the electoral congress (which was finally held in February 1982). Due now to the "legality" of the movement, relations were established with the SEP, ISSSTE, and the state government. The payments problem was stabilized, officials attended to teachers' requests for transfers, the SEP hired personnel proposed by the union, medical services were improved, short-term loans were facilitated, and childcare centers were created. During this period the state government also often served as mediator and guarantor of the agreements.[72]

In spite of the movement's gains and greater access to authorities, however, it frequently resorted to mobilizations in order to pressure officials. The Oaxaca movement also continued to support other contingents of the teachers' movement as it worked to resolve local problems, and it tried to extend and consolidate the democratic movement in the state by creating new forms of organization and decision making. In fact, the delay in the congress date was reportedly due not only to the reticence of national officials but also to groups within the teachers' movement who wanted to strengthen their support base

71. Treviño 1984:99, 101–2; Consejo Central de Lucha Magisterial Morelense 1981:35.
72. Interview with Oaxaca local executive committee member, Oaxaca, February 1987.

prior to the elections by strengthening rank-and-file organizations or by forming a CCL within the union local.[73]

Although six of the strongest regional movements to emerge in this period had sought authorization for local elections, by the summer of 1981 the results were mixed. Chiapas was the only region to secure an electoral congress that managed to produce an executive committee composed entirely of movement supporters. Oaxaca's executive commission was dominated by movement activists and largely functioned as an official committee; for internal reasons, however, the Oaxacan teachers postponed their electoral congress until 1982. Morelos had followed Chiapas's cycle in large measure, securing authorization for a congress at about the same time. Yet in Morelos vanguardistas staged a spurious congress and sent the movement into a prolonged series of protests that ended with the movement accepting virtually powerless commissions on the "official" executive committee. Hidalgo, Valle, and Guerrero, the key protagonists of the January–February 1981 cycle of mobilizations, were each forced to settle for places on "expanded" committees. Yet when movement representatives moved to occupy their positions on the committees, they were blocked or marginalized by the other members. These results all took place, moreover, in the aftermath of the killing of one of the leaders of the Valle movement and amid ongoing administrative repression by the SEP in the states.

The Movement Winds Down (September 1981–April 1982)

This third phase in the development of the national teachers' movement was marked by a general decline in the ability of regional movements to organize effective national mobilizations and by a reduced ability to advance on "political" demands involving recognition and acceptance of movement representation

---

73. There was some discussion within the commission between more conservative and more radical forces on when to hold elections for a new executive committee. The national committee of the union had offered authorization of the congress to the Oaxacans at the same time as the Chiapas congress, but this date was rejected "because conditions were not right" for a victory that consisted of a majority of "democratic" forces. For their part the more conservative forces, who dominated the commission, wanted to push for an election as soon as possible in order to secure their presence on the new committee (interviews with Oaxaca local executive committee members, Mexico City, June 23–24, 1990; Organización Revolucionaria de los Trabajadores de la Educación 1982:2–3).

on union local committees. The exceptions were the Oaxaca and Chiapas movements. The Oaxaca movement managed to hold its electoral congress in February 1982, and in Chiapas the now official democratic executive committee was actively working to resolve local problems and to democratize union and workplace decision making. The other contingents were left to pursue earlier political as well as pressing economic and social demands with a dwindling base of support, growing internal factionalism, and the national movement's diminished capacity to provide an umbrella of protection for regional contingents in conflict.

Elections in Oaxaca

In Oaxaca local elections were finally held in February 1982. The national executive committee had resisted authorizing the elections, but the February 21–22 dates were set after a series of mobilizations, including a march called by the CNTE in Mexico City that drew over 70,000 people on January 29, 1982.[74] Oaxaca Governor Pedro Vásquez Colmenares also played an important role in pressuring the national executive committee to authorize the elections so as to keep peace in his state on the eve of the presidential candidate's campaign tour through the area.[75]

As in Chiapas, and in an effort to avoid the negative example of Morelos, the decision to hold a precongress was taken by the permanent assembly in order to avoid divisions and manipulation by national union officials at the congress. Delegation assemblies were held throughout Oaxaca in order to select delegates for the electoral congress; both preassemblies and formal assemblies (at which national executive committee representatives were present) were held.[76] At about 2:00 A.M. on the day that the formal congress was to be held (February 21), delegates at the precongress divided into groups representing the

74. At first national union officials also insisted on positions on the committee, but when the Oaxaca leaders refused, they retracted this condition (interviews with Oaxaca local executive committee members, Mexico City, June 24, 1990).
75. Organización Revolucionaria de los Trabajadores de la Educación 1982:4; SNTE. Sección 22. Comisión Ejecutiva n.d.:24.
76. Two categories of delegates were selected: "effective" delegates, with voice and vote; and "fraternal" delegates, with voice only. Effective delegates were chosen in delegation assemblies in the proportion of one delegate per every one hundred members or group over forty. Fraternal delegates were named by their delegations and by democratic organizations within the union invited by the executive commission (SNTE. Sección 22. Comisión Ejecutiva n.d.).

different regions in the state, each of which selected three candidates and their deputies. The local executive committee would be selected from this collection of regional candidates. The methods used to select candidates varied in these regional meetings, as did the degree of democracy in the methods chosen.[77] Each regional assembly determined the method it would use to elect the candidates; most opted for "multiple choice": listing as many candidates as nominated and then going through several rounds of voting to fill the available positions. The autonomy of the regional assemblies within the precongress allowed for inconsistent, and sometimes antidemocratic, criteria and procedures to appear. Some regional assemblies engaged in real discussion about the candidates, and in one, the indigenous region of the Sierra, care was taken not to nominate anyone who had already held a position on the executive commission. In contrast, members of the group from the Isthmus of Tehuantepec furthered candidates' names with little discussion.

The delegates then gathered between 5 and 6 A.M. to choose the next executive committee. The method proposed and accepted for election to the fourteen positions on the local committee called for the candidates with the most votes from each regional meeting to step to the front of the assembly. Delegates then voted on these candidates to select the first seven positions, then the next seven.[78] The final democratic slate included a PRI member in the second most important office on the committee, secretary of organization. Some delegates objected, but the candidate was allowed to remain both because he had been named by delegates from his region (the Isthmus) and because members feared that if they tried to exclude him national union officials would find a pretext to disavow the election results.[79] Delegates had also decided that people who had served on the executive commission could be reelected to the executive committee, and because of this several people, including the secretary-general, continued in the leadership. However, some of the political currents that had been trying to gain influence in the leadership (MRM and Línea Proletaria) did not win positions on the committee (SNTE. Sección 22. Comisión Ejecutiva n.d.:27). Although there were times when factional conflicts threatened to split the precongress, exhortations by rank-and-file representatives and some delegates to maintain unity helped keep them on course. As one leader later commented, "From that point on we guided ourselves in large

77. Ibid., p. 16.
78. Ibid., p. 18.
79. Fernández 1982:70; SNTE. Sección 22. Comisión Ejecutiva n.d.:20.

measure by the directions of the rank-and-file; that helped to reorient us and put the pre-congress back on track at the point when it was about to break down."[80]

On the day the congress was to be held, representatives from the national executive committee tried to bargain for positions on the executive committee, as they had done in Chiapas. Negotiations continued unsuccessfully into the following day, and it was not until 9:00 P.M. on February 22 that delegates were finally transported to the congress site. Then, two hours and ten minutes after it began, the congress was over—without incident, without vanguardista representation, and with the previously approved slate of candidates elected to Oaxaca's first democratic local executive committee.[81] In this way Oaxaca became the democratic teachers' movement's second electoral victory.

Guerrero, Morelos, Hidalgo, and Valle de México

While the democratic movements in Chiapas and Oaxaca had "conquered" their union locals, movements in the other states struggled to survive. After the wave of protests in early 1981 the Valle movement's ability to participate in national mobilizations diminished, and it resorted to spectacular actions in order to attract attention to its demands. In October 1981 movement supporters took over the federal office of primary education in Valle to protest the government's lack of response to earlier agreements.[82] While the occupation did not have the general support of the membership, which later created problems within the movement, it was viewed as a success in other respects in that it forced the government to respond. Laid-off teachers were reinstated in their jobs and their salaries were reactivated.[83]

For the Morelos CCL the remainder of 1981 was marked by efforts to revive the movement and attract former supporters by raising economic and job demands, initiating political and union education training for members, and joining with other popular movements in support of their demands. But internal divisions plagued the movement. In an assembly on November 28 the CCL accused the secretary-general elected during the mass congress of not consulting with or reporting to the membership. Although he secured a vote of confidence and continued at the head of the movement, in the end only a small group

80. Francisco Pérez Arce, "Entrevista a Fernando Soberanes," pp. 38–39.
81. SNTE. Sección 22. Comisión Ejecutiva n.d.:25.
82. Consejo Central de Lucha "Misael Núñez Acosta," p. 24.
83. Ibid., p. 27; Salinas and Imaz 1984:279.

continued to push the political-union demands after many of the economic and social demands had been addressed (Treviño 1984:101, 105–6).

In late 1981 and 1982 events began to take a more violent turn. In December 1981 an activist of the Morelos teachers' movement and of other movements in the state, Ezequiel Reyes Carrillo, was abducted and held in clandestine jails and tortured until his release in May 1982, after months of protests and appeals by his wife and the CNTE, and, finally, Amnesty International.[84] Hidalgo became the site of bloodshed on February 15, 1982. Dissident teachers who had occupied the union offices since November 1981 agreed to turn over the installations to the state government with the understanding that the governor would help to mediate the union conflict. A march of just over 1,000 teachers left the CCL headquarters in Pachuca and headed to the governor's mansion. There teachers held a meeting and approved an agreement that had been worked out with the governor's office. The teachers then proceeded to the vanguardista headquarters where they planned to hold another meeting. On the way they ran into an ambush of a group of men, later discovered to have ties to the official leadership, who began to fire on the marchers. Several people were wounded; two people died later in the hospital, one man linked to the *charro* camp, Odón Zaragosa, and the other, Pedro Palma, a teacher sympathetic to the movement.[85]

The violence in Hidalgo was immediately capitalized upon by vanguardistas and the local SEP, who, pointing the finger at the leaders of Hidalgo's CCL, referred to them as "a small group of teachers, supported by outsiders . . . provoking anarchy and violence."[86] Tensions were further heightened after the decision by the Valle and Morelos CCLs to occupy the state SEP delegations at around the same time as the Hidalgo incident. These decisions were criticized within the CNTE not only because they were not discussed in the CNTE but because they further increased tensions at a time when the Hidalgo matter had to be handled with care, so as not to unleash a wave of violent repression and lose what little ground the movements had gained up until that point. Both Valle and Morelos withdrew from the buildings they had taken, but the events during this period had a strong negative effect on relations between the CNTE and the government. Talks between the CNTE leadership and SEP and union officials were halted, and resolution of the problems in Valle, Morelos, and

---

84. Reyes Carrillo claimed that the repression he suffered was due to his involvement in other popular movements and to his close relationship with Misael, the Valle leader assassinated in January 1981 (*Testimonios* 1987:81–82).

85. Equipo Pueblo, CNTE, and Información Obrera, "La violencia charra," pp. 15–19.

86. *Unomásuno*, February 18, 1982, cited in Salinas and Imaz 1984:325–26.

Hidalgo was postponed (Salinas and Imaz 1984:327–28). Moreover, several days after the Hidalgo incident the SNTE's national council met in a special session to discuss strategies for dealing with the dissident movement. The council called for the removal of Fernando Elías Calles, the SEP's negotiator in the union conflict, and it expelled CCL representatives on the expanded executive committees of Hidalgo and Valle de México.

During the month of March 1982 the CNTE again organized a series of actions intended to force negotiations with the government and union officials, but authorities remained closed to the protesters. Relations between the union leadership and the government also appeared to be closer at this time. The union's demand to remove the chief negotiator for the SEP was met, and several key union leaders were promised seats in the Chamber of Deputies; Secretary-General Martínez Martín was made a senator. While the traditional CNTE contingents tried to participate in actions, there were few sparks of protest anywhere else in the country. In Hidalgo the SEP delegate refused to issue paychecks to protesting teachers. The SEP delegations in Morelos, Valle, and Guerrero did the same (Salinas and Imaz 1984:343–44). These measures were intended to warn the CNTE off its scheduled work stoppage on March 17. For its part the Morelos CCL responded by occupying the delegation offices and holding the delegate hostage until government officials promised to pay salaries on time.

The national work stoppage went forward on March 17, 1982; in some states teachers stopped work for twenty-four hours and in others for longer. On March 30 contingents from Hidalgo, Chiapas, Oaxaca, Guerrero, Valle, Morelos, and Mexico City locals held a march in Mexico City, totaling 25,000 teachers. At one point during the march the Valle contingent occupied the union building that housed the offices of several locals. This action changed the nature of the march; other contingents decided to show support for the occupation so as not to break ranks and moved in front of the occupied building, which police also surrounded. This action forced the national executive committee to negotiate with representatives from the Valle, Hidalgo, Morelos, and Chiapas contingents (the first three were still demanding that democratic elections be held). The SEP stayed out of the conflict, but Interior Ministry officials participated in the talks. The next day the occupiers of the union building were forcibly removed and placed on buses to the outskirts of the city.

Negotiations with national union officials continued. Finally, on April 2, 1982, representatives from the Hidalgo, Morelos, and Valle de México contingents signed an agreement in which they would each be allowed six positions on the local committees, expanding the total size of the local executive committees to nineteen, and a national union representative was to oversee the committees and "coordinate their work." The national executive committee also announced that electoral congresses would be scheduled in September for locals in Hidalgo, Morelos, and Valle, and that a bipartite commission formed by an equal number of representatives from each side would help to prepare the congresses (Salinas and Imaz 1984:364–65).

After this agreement was reached, union officials unleashed a campaign in these states to strengthen Vanguardia and bolster the existing local executive committees. In Valle and Morelos, moreover, local officials kept postponing the incorporation of the CCL's representatives into the committee. The summer vacation further weakened and dispersed the dissident forces of the CNTE, and by the fall the movements were too weak to mobilize on behalf of local elections, which national union officials did not authorize after all. This left only the Oaxaca and Chiapas movements with officially recognized executive committees. The rest of the contingents—Morelos, Valle, Hidalgo, and Guerrero—maintained a weak and sporadic presence in the CNTE but were incapable of raising the recognition issue again until the end of the decade, when the national movement experienced a comeback.

The National Coordinating Committee of Education Workers

The formation of the National Coordinating Committee of Education Workers in 1979 as the umbrella organization of dissident currents within the SNTE reflected the recognition that the regional movements emerging in various parts of the country shared conditions and demands, and that coordination among the movements would help each of them in their respective struggles. At the same time, the creation of the CNTE represented a coordinated effort to construct a national *democratic* movement that would challenge the methods, domination, and ideology of Vanguardia Revolucionaria in the union (Pérez Arce, de la Garza, and Hernández 1982:71). Rather than a centralized or bureaucratic organization, the CNTE was a loose network of regional dissident movements in state and federal locals of the SNTE; it represented the instance where the different regional movements came together. As a national organization, the CNTE played an important though not always consistent role in coordinating the different regional movements and succeeded in pulling to-

Table 4.1. Teachers by Education Level and by State: Chiapas, Guerrero, Morelos, Oaxaca, and Mexico, 1978–1987[1]

State	Level	1978–79	1979–80	1980–81	1981–82	1982–83	1983–84	1984–85	1985–86	1986–87
Chiapas	Preschool[2]	147	622	729	932	1,339	1,481	1,723	1,941	2,192
	Primary[3]	8,164	9,637	10,976	12,677	13,741	13,301	14,589	15,009	15,365
	Secondary	1,215	1,288	1,670	1,763	1,929	2,007	2,245	2,408	2,420
	TOTAL	9,526	11,547	13,375	15,372	17,009	16,789	18,557	19,358	19,977
Guerrero	Preschool	289	562	749	1,323	1,681	2,227	2,663	3,013	3,274
	Primary	9,717	10,037	11,252	12,690	13,434	14,143	14,232	14,812	15,911
	Secondary	1,940	2,858	3,345	4,116	3,915	4,223	3,989	5,220	5,595
	TOTAL	11,946	13,457	15,346	18,129	19,030	20,593	20,884	23,045	24,780
Morelos	Preschool	223	238	354	403	503	603	655	710	804
	Primary	4,236	4,052	4,385	4,690	5,628	5,183	5,887	5,924	5,889
	Secondary	1,547	1,863	2,146	2,537	2,868	3,137	3,252	3,598	3,674
	TOTAL	6,006	6,153	6,885	7,630	8,999	8,923	9,794	10,232	10,367
Oaxaca	Preschool	211	1,579	1,618	2,342	2,355	2,936	3,276	3,398	3,774
	Primary	14,491	15,360	16,228	17,362	18,262	18,763	19,179	19,354	18,970
	Secondary	2,565	2,836	3,270	3,612	4,182	4,222	4,543	4,682	4,296
	TOTAL	17,267	19,775	21,116	23,316	24,799	25,921	26,998	27,434	27,040
Mexico	Preschool	640	722	921	1,331	2,011	2,007	2,340	3,510	3,818
	Primary	17,200	18,300	20,255	21,564	21,661	23,175	22,778	24,218	24,902
	Secondary	4,363	5,938	6,599	7,065	8,085	9,726	9,696	10,969	11,871
	TOTAL	22,203	24,960	27,775	29,960	31,757	34,908	34,814	38,697	40,591

[1] Numbers are for teachers in preschool, primary, and secondary levels under federal jurisdiction only.
[2] Preschool includes kindergarten and Spanish for indigenous children (*castellanización*), which began in 1979–80.
[3] Primary includes general federal primary and bilingual and bicultural (indigenous) education.

SOURCE: Adapted from internal documents, Secretaría de Educación Pública, 1987.

gether joint negotiating committees and in gaining external recognition as the representative and voice of the dissident movement in the union.

The ideological and strategic differences that characterized the various CNTE contingents emerged in the course of efforts to define key elements of CNTE objectives, organization, political alliances, and strategy. Over time a minimal consensus concerning the organization's political alliances and central strategy was forged. CNTE participants agreed, for example, to maintain a position of autonomy with respect to political parties, to restrict the participation of parties and political currents inside the movement and the union, and to act as a democratic current within the union, working to occupy the union's formal structures through elections.

The decision to maintain autonomy with respect to political parties and to restrict the role of political organizations within the movement derived from several factors. One was the perception among teachers that many of their union's problems were due to their leaders' relationship with the government and the official party, which produced stronger leadership ties to the state and party than to union members. Thus autonomy from political parties would lessen the likelihood that leaders would forge political commitments outside of the movement and remove the possibility of political parties manipulating the movement for their own ends. The restrictions on participation by political groups was intended to solve the problem of internal factionalism. Rank-and-file teachers tended to be suspicious of political parties, and open party factionalism within the movement could turn away many supporters.[87] Party or political group competition within the CNTE would therefore destroy a crucial resource—the unity of the movement. Although the existence and importance to the movement of diverse political groups and activists within the CNTE was recognized, members of the CNTE tried to structure the incentives of participation within the organization so that the positions of those who had been elected as representatives by the membership would carry more weight. In this way activists could speak at CNTE assemblies and make proposals, but as political organizations they had only one vote, in contrast to the five votes granted to CCLs and member locals, and the three that *promotoras* (smaller dissident organizations in locals that were not yet able to form a CCL) were allowed. In a short time, and particularly in the more consolidated regions such as Oaxaca and Chiapas, a strong stigma came to be attached as well to political organiza-

---

87. Although the movement's national leaders were mostly people who had worked in various political organizations and parties of the left, the rank-and-file membership of the CNTE was, for the most part, "apolitical": unaffiliated or not active in political parties.

tions and parties within the movement, forcing members to speak not on behalf of political organizations but either as individual members or, more important, as representatives of schools, workplaces, and organizational instances within the union.

The decision to work as a current within the union rather than form an independent union was taken after determining that the dissident organization did not have enough support within the union to get away with an independent registration effort and that the government was unlikely to recognize an independent union of government employees. Because of legal restrictions for government employees, which only permitted one union per government ministry or agency, the CNTE would have to be able to amass a majority of members within the SNTE and win a representation election among the membership. This was not only technically difficult, but politically it was practically impossible (Hernández and Pérez Arce 1982:40–41).

The organizational structure of the CNTE proved to be more controversial. When the CNTE was formed, one other national coordinadora existed, the rural Coordinadora Nacional "Plan de Ayala" (National "Plan of Ayala" Coordinating Committee, CNPA). In 1981 an urban popular movement national coordinating committee (CONAMUP) would also form. The coordinadoras were decentralized networks of regionally based movements that retained their tactical autonomy; they were also nonbureaucratic and inclusive, with a diffuse leadership. These organizations shared other common features. For example, they all maintained group autonomy from political parties while permitting individual affiliation. Consequently, the coordinadoras steered clear of the national electoral struggles that were gaining strength after the political reform of 1977. The coordinadoras were widely viewed as key actors in a growing *social* as opposed to political party left, and were seen as grass-roots and independent alternatives to the top-down incorporation efforts of both leftist and official political parties.

Member organizations of the CNTE typically met monthly at different locations throughout the country. In between these meetings there was a more permanent commission formally composed of five representatives from each regional contingent. But rarely did the permanent commission or the CNTE, as a separate organizational entity, play a strong leadership role in defining the course of the movement. Instead the CNTE was guided by the regional autonomy of its member contingents, whose internal decision-making processes and tactical decisions were generally respected.

Some groups within the CNTE criticized this organizational looseness in the belief that the CNTE should play a stronger leadership role in directing the movement. Others, such as the representatives from the Bloc of Democratic Delegations (Local 11 in Mexico City) and the Chiapas movement, favored regional tactical autonomy and the "consolidation of smaller victories," and believed that the teachers' movement was not prepared to take on the SNTE leadership and the government head-on (Salinas and Imaz 1984:126–27). The decentralized strategy that won out within the CNTE tended to permit regional movements to negotiate directly and separately with the government and with union officials. Detractors of this position argued that this strategy facilitated authorities' efforts to divide and weaken the movement.[88]

The decision during many negotiations not to negotiate jointly but to do so separately was in a sense forced upon the regional movements by the government and national union officials. The threat of government repression often limited the "choices" of regional movements involved in negotiations. Still, some contingents felt that the CNTE was insufficiently committed to the idea of joint negotiations, preferring, as one dominant position argued, simply to "resolve the problem [at hand]:"

> What was fundamental in the struggle was to negotiate, that is, to resolve the problems we had; how to do this (jointly or separately) was secondary. Probably if we had maintained the position to negotiate as a whole, the repression would have been greater. Accepting to negotiate separately therefore resolved what was essential: solving the problem. (Hernández and Pérez Arce 1982:290)

Coordination was complicated by the fact that the needs and mobilization cycles of the various regional movements frequently did not coincide. This coordination was particularly difficult when the calculus proved unfavorable for a particular regional movement. The Chiapas movement, for example, was roundly criticized for abandoning other movements during key negotiations, accepting guarantees for its own survival rather than holding out for a joint solution to the movements' demands (Salinas and Imaz 1984:142–43, Arriaga 1981:99). But regional autonomy was the product of different regional conditions and different degrees of susceptibility to repression; to refuse to recognize this and insist on a greater centralization of decision making would probably have meant lack of rank-and-file support for critical mobilizations and, ultimately, defeat for the regional movements. Because mobilization was so important during this period, so was decentralization. In any case, tensions between

---

88. See Salinas and Imaz 1984, esp. pp. 127–30, for elaboration of this debate.

those who called for greater national coordination of the movement and those who privileged regional autonomy persisted. These tensions were fed by the fact that the political organizations with little developed membership that were also active in the CNTE were generally more critical of the so-called unilateral actions taken by regional leaders who were accountable to their mass membership.[89]

The decentralized organizational structure of the CNTE was also responsible for another characteristic that was heavily criticized by many of its members: its spontaneous and "conjunctural" nature and apparent inability to formulate any long-term strategy for the teachers' movement. The CNTE would spring to life during "mobilizational cycles"—periods of protest by one or more of its contingents—and the actions it supported would be largely determined by whichever contingents happened to dominate the protest cycle. This led at times to ad hoc support of spontaneous actions that might otherwise have been opposed by most contingents. At the same time, the spontaneous and massive character of the CNTE, the inability to predict when any of its member regions might erupt in protest, and the lack of a central leadership (the CNTE even lacked any physical headquarters) hindered authorities' efforts to co-opt the CNTE leadership and repress the national movement.[90] Salinas and Imaz captured the contradictory qualities of this position when they observed that "the CNTE's main strength is also its principal weakness": the heterogeneous character of the CNTE's mass support base also restricted its ability to function as a fully coherent national organization (Salinas and Imaz 1984:68–69).

National and Regional Strategies: Responses of Government and Union Officials

The responses of national and local government and union officials to the dissident teachers' movement headed by the CNTE were crucial in constraining

---

89. As some leaders from Oaxaca put it, CNTE leaders from Mexico City and Valle would come to Oaxaca "to scold us (*a regañarnos*) for our actions, claiming that we hurt the CNTE, when, in fact, we *are* the CNTE."

90. The organizational structure of the CNTE resembled that of movements elsewhere. According to Tarrow, "most effective forms of organization are based on autonomous and interdependent social networks linked by loosely coordinated mobilizing structures" (1994:136). Yet, such "loose mobilizing structures" as those represented in the coordinadora model of organization also "encourage a lack of coordination and discontinuity" (p. 149). At the time that the coordinadoras were formed, however, this type of organization at the *national* level was relatively new in Mexico.

or facilitating the actions and gains of the national movement and of the specific regional teachers' movement contingents. Government actors played a quite different role from national union officials, and state officials, while constrained by national authorities, were often influenced further by local political interests in their responses to the movement. National union officials, caught off guard by the initial mobilizations of teachers, tried to resist any concessions to dissident members. Seeing the mobilizations as a threat to their hold over the union, and fearful of government intervention, union officials tried simultaneously to discredit the dissident movement in the press, organize opposition to the movement in the states, mobilize their own ranks to prove their legitimacy, raise economic demands presented by the movement, and attack government "interference" in "union autonomy." To the extent that the national executive committee yielded to the movements' demands for local election timetables and interim commissions, it did so under direct pressure from the interior minister. Even when national union officials conceded on these political demands of the dissident regional movements, they did so only insofar as protesters were able to maintain pressure at a national level. Once the different regional movements returned to their states, national union officials invariably ignored earlier agreements or simply put them off using a variety of bureaucratic delaying tactics.

As presidential elections approached in mid-1982, the balance of forces began to turn in favor of national union officials. Union officials obtained a series of important political concessions at this time. The union successfully obtained the removal of Elías Calles, chief negotiator for the SEP, at the same time as union officials were named to seats in the federal congress. The interior minister withdrew from his mediating role, leaving union leaders and dissidents to resolve their conflicts, a situation that invariably left regional movements more vulnerable to the manipulations of union officials. The repression in Hidalgo and various occupations of SEP and union buildings by members of the CNTE also helped to unify the responses of government and union officials to the movement, even though the violence had come at the hands of vanguardistas.

Officials from the Ministry of the Interior were key governmental actors involved in the teachers' conflict. The national scope of the teachers' protests and the site of their mobilizations in the national capital, together with the refusal of union authorities to forge a compromise with their members, led the Interior Ministry to assume a mediating role. All of the political demands conceded in agreements were due to Interior Ministry officials' pressure on union officials. The ministry also pressured protesters by identifying "final offers" during negotiations and by threatening—and occasionally following through with—repression. That political solutions were discussed at all testified to the dissident movement's ability to exert strong disruptive pressure on the SEP and on union officials (movement leaders noted that the Interior Ministry intervened whenever their mobilizations had been strong). But the inability of the union to control the conflict and the nature of the tensions between the government and the union on the deconcentration issue also increased government resolve to end the conflict in a way that might prove costly to members of the SNTE leadership.

The federal government also became involved in the conflict because it was the government that was responsible for many of the economic grievances of the teachers' movement. Wage increases, regional cost-of-living adjustments, paycheck delays, clinics, housing, loans, and other job-related issues were all handled by the SEP or other government agencies such as the ISSSTE (the social security institute), and the Ministry of Programming and the Budget, which approved wage increases. The paycheck delays in particular were caused by bureaucratic inefficiency and confusion in the SEP (due to the administrative deconcentration). Because of this, the SEP tried to maintain a distinction between the teachers' economic and political demands, seeing some of the former as legitimate while portraying the latter as part of an intraunion conflict that had nothing to do with the SEP. Some sectors of government, however, saw the political demands of the CNTE as legitimate, and believed that representation of the teachers' opposition in the structures of union government would help to contain an otherwise explosive situation. In any case, the SEP's position during this period was complicated. The inability of the SEP to contain the conflict, and the perception by some that the SEP was responsible for it, weakened the political standing of top SEP officials within the government. Many of the conflicts that arose between the union, SEP officials, the Ministry of Programming and the Budget, and top officials of the Ministry of the Interior were no doubt also colored by interbureaucracy competition and political jockeying around the presidential succession. For instance, some government actions in this period seemed calculated to undermine Carlos Jonguitud Barrios, the head of Vanguardia, who was then governor of the state of San Luis Potosí and an aspirant to a cabinet position in the next administration.

As an employer and administrator of national public education, the SEP was interested in quelling the disturbances and getting teachers back to work. At the same time, the SEP was engaged in a complex battle with a powerful teachers' union whose intransigence taxed the government's administrative capabilities but whose political support was considered crucial to the regime as well as to individuals in the SEP interested in political careers. The lengthy parade of SEP delegates who moved through the state delegations in the most conflict-ridden areas, as well as their contrasting styles and often contradictory responses to the regional movements, reflected the SEP's conflictive and often ambivalent relationship with the union. This strained relationship proved beneficial to dissidents at times. But more often the tenor in the states was one of uncertainty, and whatever opportunities presented themselves to the dissident movements were fleeting. SEP delegates could act as local mediators in conflicts or they could use their position to repress protesters by withholding paychecks, transferring dissidents against their will, and firing them. Many delegates were either allied with vanguardistas from the union or in some other way compromised with local or national union officials. In some states where the dissident movement was strong, however, such as in Oaxaca and Chiapas, SEP delegates eventually found themselves forced to respond directly to dissident demands.

In spite of the government's occasionally favorable mediation, the tactics used by the government were mostly aimed at restricting the conflict to the regional rather than national level. To this end the federal government frequently tried to divide the different contingents engaged in protests and force them to accept different solutions. Given the enormous resources of the government, this was not generally difficult to do. The contingents of the CNTE, on the other hand, were often faced with dwindling resources, members' physical exhaustion, repression, and a commitment to regional autonomy that in most cases led them to look out for their own survival rather than for any "national" interest of the movement. Moreover, the timing of the dissident teachers' mobilizations was tightly constrained by the school calendar. National actions had to take place well before the Christmas, spring, or summer holidays, so as to be able to wrench a concession before vacations rendered the work stoppages meaningless and members' commitment to the actions untenable. There was, therefore, a rhythm or cycle the teachers' mobilizations followed that government and union officials could and did upset.

Another important set of government actors in the dissident teachers' mobilizations were the state governors. Governors could serve as vulnerable points of pressure or as valuable mediators: they were vulnerable to the disruption of education (and public order) in their states and could use their political influence to intervene with federal government officials in order to resolve conflicts. Similarly, within their states governors could pressure local education officials to attend to teachers' demands, offer protection to protesting teachers, or, conversely, send out police to break up demonstrations or occupations. Governors displayed a broad range of political styles, and their relations with the federal government could differ substantially, although all governors at the time belonged to the same party as the president and other top government officials. The closeness of a state governor's relationship with the president or other top federal officials would typically determine the effectiveness of his or her political influence and mediation. For instance, governors appointed by a previous president and riding out their terms under a new one generally wielded less political influence than those appointed by the sitting president (although all governors were subject to removal if the president saw fit to do so). At the same time, political competition between governors and the national leaders of the SNTE could encourage the former to mediate on behalf of the latter's opponents. The authorization of the 1981 Chiapas local union elections has been attributed in part to the tensions that existed between Jonguitud and the governor of Chiapas and top officials of the Interior and Education ministries.

Also key to governors' ability to play a mediating or facilitating role was the fact that most of the teachers involved in protests were under federal jurisdiction, and thus state government was often not a direct target of teacher protests and demands. The planned decentralization of the educational system was likely to shift the role of governors increasingly from potential mediators to targets of teacher protests, intensifying the conflicts between teachers and state governments and effectively "regionalizing" the protests. But in the early 1980s state governments were often on the sidelines of what was largely a federal government conflict with a national union.

The presence of "neutral" or sympathetic state governors generally benefited the dissident movements emerging at the beginning of the decade of the 1980s, as did a political transition in state government or the presence of an interim governor. In both Oaxaca and Chiapas the teachers' movements emerged during years in which a gubernatorial transfer of power took place. In Oaxaca the movement emerged during Pedro Vásquez Colmenares's (1980–85) gubernatorial campaign. General Eliseo Jiménez Ruiz, the interim governor of Oaxaca from 1977–80, did not intervene to quell the teachers' protests but rather sought to keep the peace after what had been an especially conflictive period in Oaxacan state politics. He replaced governor Manuel Zárate Aquino (1974–77), who had been forced to leave in March 1977 after a series of strikes, conflicts in the university, and calls by a coalition of popular organizations for him to step down (Basáñez and Martínez V. 1987:148–53). Because of the polarization in the state wrought by Zárate Aquino in the 1970s, and the strength of the teachers' movement in Oaxaca, Vásquez Colmenares often mediated in the teachers' conflict in ways that were beneficial to the movement.

The teachers' movement in Chiapas emerged in 1979, also a year of gubernatorial transfer of power. The new governor, Juan Sabines Gutiérrez (1979–82), was a political enemy of the former governor, Salomón González Blanco, whose chaotic last months in office left a power vacuum and culminated in the governor's resignation in November 1979 (Balboa and Reyes 1988:27). As a federal senator Sabines had offered to help bring together the parties in conflict during the first Chiapas teachers' strike of 1979, and thus he had already played a mediating role in the teachers' conflict prior to governing the state. According to a former leader of the Chiapas teachers' movement, relations with the governor were civil: "The governor at least never attacked us, never repressed us. . . . We always respected the governor in turn as the political authority in the state."[91] Despite this statement, the governments of Jorge de la Vega Domínguez (1976–78), Salomón González Blanco (1978–79), and Juan Sabines Gutiérrez (1979–82) have been singled out as representing the period of "bloody populism" in Chiapas politics. State spending for rural programs increased during these years, but so did rural protest and violent repression of protest (Benjamin 1989). Later, Governor Absalón Castellanos Domínguez (1982–88) would jail several teachers (including the author of the above quote) for participating in peasant protests. Even in a context of political repression, however, teachers were often too large, too organized, and too educated a group to be ignored or to suffer mass repression at the hands of state government. In Oaxaca and Chiapas, in particular, teachers were the only organization that could mobilize thousands of members, which gave them considerable bargaining power.

In other regions where the teachers' movement emerged, such as Morelos, Hidalgo, and Valle de México, state governments also played a neutral or facilitating role; often doing nothing was just as likely to facilitate protest as more deliberate intervention. Governor Armando León Bejarano (1976–82) of Morelos, for instance, was considered a weak governor unable to stand up to either the dissident teachers or the vanguardistas in his state. He often met with dissident teachers in order to avoid conflicts. The next governor of Morelos, however, intervened more actively, proposing that a committee be formed composed of dissidents and vanguardistas and presided over by a "neutral arbiter" named by the state.[92] State of Mexico governor Jorge Jiménez Cantú extended protection to the Valle movement and helped to resolve some demands. Governor Jiménez gave the Valle CCL a letter for state civil and judicial authorities asking them not to become involved in the union conflict.[93] In Hidalgo the state government tried to maintain a "neutral" position that

91. Luis Hernández, "Entrevista a Manuel Hernández," in *Testimonios* 1987:47.
92. Interview with Morelos movement leader, Mexico City, June 28, 1990.
93. Consejo Central de Lucha "Misael Núñez Acosta," pp. 18, 29. Also in interview with Valle movement leader, Mexico City, August 31, 1987.

would allow it to play a mediating role, and only intervened to contain the dissident movement as a last resort.[94] Governor Figueroa of Guerrero took the most active interest in the teachers' movement, albeit one with negative consequences. Figueroa intervened personally with local police and state education authorities to repress and fire protesting teachers. The harassment and lack of protections teachers suffered in Guerrero went a long way toward dissipating the strength of the movement in that state.

In most of the states where the dissident movement emerged Vanguardia Revolucionaria was not a strong force. Movement leaders in Oaxaca and Morelos admitted, for instance, that Vanguardia was not a strong organization in their states when the movements emerged, but union members were nonetheless required to sign a form stating that they were members of Vanguardia Revolucionaria.[95] Neither the membership nor much of the leadership identified with this organization created by Jonguitud in 1974, although many rank-and-file teachers initially respected what they perceived as the institutional legitimacy of Vanguardia and seemed to accept the "revolutionary-nationalist" ideology it upheld.[96] In some of these regions more than others, however, the national executive committee of the union was more aggressive and more successful in combating the dissident movement. How successful these efforts were seemed to depend on a number of factors: whether or not the dissidents comprised a large majority in the state, whether or not groups of local "vanguardistas" could be found to carry out acts of intimidation and violence, and whether or not local state and municipal officials took sides in the conflict. While in many cases local union leadership factions may not have identified with Vanguardia, they often did identify with local caciques or politicians who opposed the dissident teachers, or else they had ties to officials in the national bureaucracy of the union because of career networks and the possibilities for professional advancement such ties afforded.[97]

In many states where the movement emerged the membership did not come to identify Vanguardia as its opponent until much later. Instead members simply saw local union officials as their enemy. More important for many teachers was the fact that local union officials were often linked to local politicians or caciques. This was especially true in Hidalgo, where one movement leader

---

94. Bedolla, "Entrevista a Roberto Meza," p. 88.
95. Interviews with local union officials from Oaxaca and Mexico City, June 24, 1990; interview with Morelos movement leader, Mexico City, June 28, 1990. In the central valleys of Oaxaca many so-called vanguardistas turned and fled at the first signs of opposition. This was in contrast to those identified with the organization in the Isthmus, who were much stronger, and may explain in part why the Isthmus became the last region to join the dissident movement in Oaxaca (interview with Víctor Raul Martínez, Oaxaca, February 1987).
96. Bedolla, "Entrevista a Roberto Meza," p. 96.
97. Interview with movement leader from Morelos, Mexico City, June 28, 1990.

pointed out that class divisions between caciques and peasants were reproduced in the rural normal schools, where sons of caciques went on to occupy positions in the union hierarchy and the sons of peasants became "dissidents."[98] The violence that filtered into the teachers' movement in Hidalgo and other areas was therefore deeply rooted in local social conflict that preceded the creation of Vanguardia in the early 1970s. As evidence of this deep-seated antagonism, local union officials in Hidalgo frequently refused to honor commitments to the movement that national union officials (and vanguardistas) had made.[99] Similarly, in states such as Guerrero, Chiapas, and Oaxaca, the violence against local teachers was attributable not to the strength of Vanguardia *per se* but to the historical conflict between landowners and political bosses, on the one hand, and indigenous peasants and those who worked among them (teachers), on the other. Where ties to Vanguardia were strongest among local union officials was in the Valle de México and in Mexico City, locals that were traditionally under close control by the national union leadership.

National officials of the union tried to organize campaigns against the dissident movement in each of the states where it emerged. Before the congresses in Oaxaca and Chiapas, the national executive committee sent its people out to organize against the dissidents and to orchestrate a media campaign against them. These unionists commissioned by the national office then tried to meet with groups of dissident teachers to create divisions and force them to settle for deals offered by the SEP or the union. They also tried to co-opt individual leaders. In Valle officials eventually used corruption to co-opt former and potential dissidents: thousands of *doble plazas* were offered to local unionists, and the number of school districts nearly tripled in order to increase the number of directorships that could be distributed.[100] Morelos, Hidalgo, and Valle also saw the darker sides of such campaigns: two dead in a shoot-out in Hidalgo, two leaders abducted and tortured in Morelos,[101] and another leader murdered in Valle de México.

Organization, Strategies, and Tactics

The emergence and subsequent development of the national teachers' movement was burdened by powerful constraints: a hostile national union leadership,

98. Bedolla, "Entrevista a Roberto Meza," p. 88.
99. Ibid., p. 92.
100. Interview with Valle movement leader, Mexico City, August 31, 1987.
101. In June 1982 the former head of the dissident committee in Morelos was abducted by thugs linked to the union, raped, and tortured in a campaign to further terrorize that movement's activists.

the opposition of federal and state government officials, the overwhelming superiority of officials' resources, and a regional strategy of division and conquest. Some regional movements also had to contend with a more organized opposition to the dissidents in the states, repressive state governments, and the greater use of violence against them. Still, in order to emerge and survive, however briefly, these regional movements drew creatively from their internal resources—their capacity for organization and strategic action. That some regional movements were able to do so more effectively than others speaks not only to the different external constraints these movements faced but also to regional differences in organization and in strategic and tactical decisions.

Most contingents of the teachers' movement adopted similar forms of organization, at least outwardly. These were commonly called *comités de lucha* and Consejos Centrales de Lucha, and typically consisted of some form of representation at the school or workplace, a delegation-level organization, and a higher-level assembly or council that brought these representatives together. Such forms of organization were not contemplated in the union statutes and were thus considered "extralegal" forms of organization by union officials. For dissident teachers these nonstatutory forms of organization—most of which were roughly parallel to the statutory forms—enabled the movements to construct parallel "free spaces" where decision making and organization could take place without being hindered by union officials.[102] These alternative organizations thus also provided movement teachers with a relatively autonomous arena in which to prepare for winning seats on the statutory committees during authorized elections. In areas where the dissident movement was strong, such as Oaxaca and Chiapas, these parallel or alternative structures supplanted the statutory delegation executive committees, and eventually also the traditional forms of the local executive committees.

Dissident teachers formed Consejos Centrales de Lucha in most states where the movement emerged. The structure of the CCLs did not strictly correspond to any prior organizational forms with which the teachers had been involved, but teachers did draw from precedents within the Mexican labor movement, in particular from the striking railroad workers in the late 1950s and from the student movement in the 1960s (Taibo 1984:53). The first CCL was formed in Chiapas in 1979 as teachers prepared for their strike. The organization responded directly to the need for communication and coordination among regions within the state in the course of the statewide work stoppage.[103] The

---

102. The concept of "free spaces" was developed by Evans and Boyte (1992); see Chapter 2 for a discussion of this term.

103. Two members from each delegation, elected in delegation assembly, made up the CCL. One of these delegates to the CCL was "permanent" and would work on commissions, participate

dissident teachers felt it necessary to justify their creation of an extralegal union structure to their fellow teachers and the public, and they portrayed this effort as a response to the refusal of their local leaders to spearhead the demands of the majority of the membership, as evidenced by this excerpt published in a Mexico City newspaper:

> We think it necessary to explain to the nation's teachers why we have a *Consejo Central de Lucha* in Chiapas and not the statutory union structure. The teachers of Chiapas created this form of organization because of the incapacity of the local leaders, who refused to head a struggle that the majority of the membership had begun. In effect, in the absence of any political leadership that could orient and execute the agreements of the majority, the membership created its own organization in such a way as to avoid the pitfalls of union corruption that we have traditionally had to bear. (Cited in Peláez 1980:23)

Teachers in Chiapas set about to create an extensive network of these alternative organizations. In response to a need for greater communication between the CCL and the schools, *comités municipales de lucha*—municipal strike committees, joining together several delegations—were formed at the municipal level. Their tasks were to try to resolve regional problems, communicate regional needs to the central CCL, and, more important, ensure that vanguardistas not penetrate their ranks. This network of smaller committees also increased levels of communication among teachers at the school or workplace level. With the discussions that took place at the level of the *comités de lucha*, movement leaders "began to realize that [they] were resolving a central problem, which was the massive politicization of the people." Small assemblies at workplace, delegation, or *comité de lucha* levels were far more effective in increasing participation and encouraging discussion than were larger meetings. As one leader observed, ". . . [in the smaller assemblies] the most inhibited *compañero* gives his point of view" (SNTE. Sección 7. n.d.:15–16). Thus, the new organizational network dissident teachers created also began to help in the creation of a grass-roots movement where new practices—discussion, participation, and rank-and-file decision making—began to take shape in schools and union meetings.

The *comités de lucha* functioned as an intermediate organizational instance between teachers in their workplaces and the CCL, and brought base-level

---

in brigades, etc., and the other, "mobile" member was the link between the base at the delegation level and the CCL. See Hernández, "Entrevista a Manuel Hernández," p. 49.

agreements and opinions to the CCL. In those areas of the state where the delegation executive committees (*comité ejecutivo delegacional*, CED) had the support of the majority of teachers, the *comités* worked together with these delegation committees. In delegations considered to be nondemocratic the *comités* restricted delegation committee activities and functioned as a vehicle to bypass the committees. The exact composition of these *comités* varied from case to case within the state, but all served the purpose of increasing communication and the exchange of information and thus of extending and consolidating the dissident movement.

The Oaxaca dissidents did not organize into a CCL as did their neighbors from Chiapas. Instead they formed a "permanent assembly" composed of delegation leaders, which reflected the leading role played by dissident delegation officials in Oaxaca. The permanent assembly rejected the local executive committee and elected an executive commission for purposes of negotiating with the national executive committee. This commission—along with other organizational instances that developed later (including the executive committee)—reflected the movement's preferences for a regional distribution of representation, meaning that members believed that the different geographic and ethnic regions within the state should be represented in the union and movement leadership. This was due to the presence of strong regional and ethnic identities in Oaxaca, but perhaps even more it reflected the fact that two strong poles of organization had emerged within the Oaxaca movement—one among activists linked to the student movement in the 1960s and 1970s, concentrated in the central valleys, and another located in the Isthmus of Tehuantepec, where a strong opposition political organization, the COCEI, existed alongside a similarly strong PRI. The creation of a permanent assembly as opposed to a CCL also reflected the caution of delegation leaders participating in the movement. These leaders resisted forming an organization like Chiapas's, which so clearly stood outside of statutory boundaries. Those who pushed for a CCL were the younger activists and former student leaders with political experience but little formal union experience, who were behind the organizing around the first work stoppage.

In Oaxaca, Chiapas, Guerrero, and other states teachers also formed "brigades"—small teams of teachers who would travel throughout the state and the country to relay information about the movement. These brigades played a crucial role in the emergence of the movement by carrying information to the remotest villages and to other states, often setting off other dissident movements.[104] The work of the brigades helped to increase understanding of

---

104. In 1980 about eight hundred brigades were organized by members of the executive

the movement's goals and combated vanguardista attacks by increasing teachers' participation in the movement and building support for the movement in the community.

The regions where the teachers' movement became most consolidated all formed CCLs (or a permanent assembly, in the case of Oaxaca), but the consolidation of the membership organizations and the flow of information, opinions, and, ultimately, decisions from the membership to the "leadership" in the CCL varied from case to case. In time some movements' failure to obtain authorized elections, together with the larger presence of vanguardistas, and thus of resistance at the membership level, contributed to breaking down the organizational structure of the movement. Key to developing an effective network of rank-and-file committees and assemblies was leadership commitment to the task, and this also varied greatly from region to region, and even within a regional movement. In the Valle movement, for instance, there was frequent tension over the role to be played by movement activists as opposed to members with representation in the decision-making organs of the movement. Activists were important in organizing the movement but they generally were not bound to relay or follow the opinions of constituencies. Similarly, in Guerrero two competing ideas about leadership and organization clashed frequently in CCL assemblies. The first, represented by members linked to the Mexican Communist Party (after 1981 the Unified Socialist Party of Mexico, PSUM), was a more vanguard view of the role of leadership in the movement; decisions were taken by leaders, who had more information and understanding of specific situations, and then explained to the membership. The second was a more grass-roots view, adopted by members from the Montaña region, and held that rank-and-file members were both capable of making decisions and should be the ones to decide the course of their movement. From this perspective school and workplace committees and other rank-and-file based organizations where discussion and decision making could take place were crucial for the survival and development of the movement. Teachers from La Montaña worked to build these smaller organizations, while leaders linked to the vanguard perspective questioned this effort in CCL meetings.

In this sense the type of organization movement leaders constructed, as well as the kinds of strategies and tactics the movements would adopt, were clearly linked to leaders' ideas about the role of leadership and decision making. Among the six regional teachers' movements considered in this chapter those movements with a more grass-roots understanding of organization and decision

---

commission in Oaxaca (Yescas and Zafra 1985:97; interview with member of local executive committee, Oaxaca, February 1987).

making and a more extensive network of rank-and-file organization also tended to be more cautious and moderate in the tactics they adopted, in their strategy for obtaining legal-formal status through authorized elections, and in their relations with government and union officials. In contrast, those movements with a weaker network of rank-and-file organization and a more vanguardist perception of leadership (or with strong internal leadership divisions) adopted more confrontational and ideological positions in their relations with government and union officials, in the strategy they adopted in pursuit of the electoral congresses, and in some of the tactics they adopted.

The teachers' movements in both Oaxaca and Chiapas appeared to proceed more cautiously than those that emerged in Valle de México, Hidalgo, Morelos, or Guerrero. In Oaxaca the presence of people in formal union positions led the movement to stick relatively closely to statutory organizational forms and to assure state government and national officials that the movement did not seek to attack them or question their authority.[105] In Chiapas leaders followed a similarly restrained tack in pursuing political demands. Their caution in linking political and economic demands, moreover, reflected the desire of leaders not to alienate and overwhelm rank-and-file teachers who constituted the base of the mobilizations on which the movement relied to obtain its demands. In Oaxaca, however, the conflict-ridden local congress had eroded the legitimacy of the executive committee before the strike, shortening the time between the strike call and the call for local elections. The fact that the Chiapas movement had already emerged and organized its CCL was also an important factor that encouraged the organization of the dissidents in the neighboring state of Oaxaca. In both Oaxaca and Chiapas, however, the moderate and cautious approach had its strong detractors, and the position had to be forged out of factional conflict and debate within each of these movements.[106]

---

105. A note published in *Excélsior* (May 29, 1980, p. 36-A) by the executive commission in Oaxaca stated, "We want to make clear that our struggle only reflects our wage demands and is not politically motivated; therefore the membership of Local 22 of Oaxaca does not accept the meddling of any political party or group, from inside or outside of the teachers' organization, that tries to alter the objectives of our movement. We also consider it important to clarify before the National Executive Committee that we are not against them; on the contrary, we ask that they spearhead our movement, since the Local Executive Committee has neglected to do so" (reprinted in Peláez 1980:76). Yescas and Zafra (1985:110–11) also note that it became clear that there was a difference between movement activists and delegation leaders over the appropriateness of certain tactics of mobilization; the latter group resisted what it still considered to be illegal measures.

106. Another move that reflected some of the differences within the Oaxaca movement was the decision to formally join with the CNTE in October 1982, long after the Oaxaca movement had in fact participated with the CNTE in national marches and attended its meetings (Fernández Dorado 1982:89). This formal affiliation with the CNTE had been opposed by some forces within the

Emergence of the National Teachers' Movement

The leadership in both the Chiapas and Oaxaca movements was drawn from people representing diverse political backgrounds and styles, but in each case the executive committees came to be dominated by more moderate leaders. The Oaxaca leadership was especially diverse. It included members linked to the MRM, the PRI, the COCEI, and others with militancy in the movement but little explicit connection to political groups. Any clear political affiliation or ideology played a relatively smaller role in the dynamics of that movement. Yet the secretary-general, Pedro Martínez Noriega, was known as a moderate and a negotiator. In Chiapas the executive committee was dominated by members of the maoist political current Línea Proletaria, but it also included others of different political backgrounds and experiences. The Línea Proletaria philosophy consisted of a grass-roots and economicist approach that rank-and-file members responded to positively, at least in the early years of the movement. Members of Línea Proletaria were also relatively open to negotiations and compromise in their dealings with officials and favored a nonconfrontational strategy.

The strategy and tactical ideas of Línea Proletaria members not only came to dominate the Chiapas movement but also became very influential in the CNTE. However, the positions of Línea Proletaria would generate conflict with other political factions in the CNTE and within the Chiapas movement.[107] In the latter case conflict was especially strong with the group that came out of the ETA's struggle and was identified with the trotskyists; it saw itself competing with Línea Proletaria for the leadership and direction of the movement in the state. Nonetheless, the importance of decision making at the level of the CCL or permanent assembly in each of these movements helped temper the potential for divisiveness among the leadership. Although the discussion was often heated in these meetings and the disagreements sharp, the positions adopted by these movements were frequently the product of compromise and were driven by the common recognition that the movement must show unity to the outside world, particularly to its enemies. The slogan that summed up this position and that served as the watchwords of CCL and CNTE assemblies was "*Lucha ideológica, unidad táctica*" (ideological struggle, tactical unity).

Against the relatively restrained approach of the Oaxaca and Chiapas

---

movement who were linked with the PRI, as well as by some smaller groups on the left, who saw the CNTE as directed by "nonrevolutionary" opportunists. Much of the rank-and-file was also distrustful of the CNTE in the beginning, largely due to a demonization campaign orchestrated by union officials at the moment the CNTE was formed. For these reasons membership in the CNTE was only formalized after two years of internal discussion and a process of persuasion (Pérez Arce, "Entrevista a Fernando Soberanes," p. 39).

107. See Chapters 5 and 6 for a more extensive treatment of the role of political factions in the movements.

movements stood the more confrontational positions of the Valle, Hidalgo, and Morelos movements. In the cases of the Valle de México and Hidalgo movements, this more confrontational position may have been due to the movement's being led by a smaller and perhaps more ideologically cohesive core of activists. The Morelos movement may have been driven to more confrontational positions by the actions of national and local union officials, and divisions in the leadership could have lent more strength to supporters of more extreme positions. In all three of these movements leaders opted for more confrontational tactics, such as building takeovers (sometimes decided without consultation), and they initially rejected compromise solutions regarding elections. Later in the course of the Valle movement, for example, such building takeovers reflected the inability of the movement to mobilize a large number of supporters for an action and the need to employ dramatic tactics to call attention to the movement's demands. In addition, the Hidalgo and Valle movements went the route of the mass congresses and later found themselves fighting for official recognition under practically any terms. This was in contrast to the Oaxaca and Chiapas movements' more legalistic strategy of securing official recognition for their executive commissions from the outset. Morelos, which had started out on a path similar to that of Oaxaca and especially Chiapas, adopted the "parallel strategy" only after its electoral congress was thwarted by Vanguardia.

The leaders of the Valle, Hidalgo, and, to a lesser extent, the Morelos movements also appeared committed to a notion of ideological "purity" not shared by the movements in Oaxaca and Chiapas. This ideological purity was reflected in various ways, among them an overt disdain for the legality and institutionality authorities insisted upon, a lack of tolerance for rank-and-file members whose commitment to the movement was perceived as wavering or lukewarm, and an almost self-righteous rejection of compromise. For instance, Valle movement leaders with whom I spoke were particularly skeptical of arrangements in which the movement "shared power" with vanguardistas on executive commissions or committees. They stressed the danger in trying to change power relations from inside structures set up by the vanguardistas ("*no se puede minar fuerzas desde adentro,*" you can't undermine power from within), and claimed instead that the task was to construct alternative, independent bases of power. Those who participated in joint local committees, for instance, risked becoming co-opted and alienated from the membership, particularly since those who were less radical were typically the only ones allowed to take part in these arrangements. According to one leader from Valle, the notion that one should accept power-sharing arrangements derived from a problem in the way that some members conceived of the movement: the democratic teachers' movement should see itself as *the* alternative form of unionism, not merely as an opposition current within the SNTE struggling to obtain representation on legal committees.[108] This position led the Valle movement to argue initially that the CNTE should form a separate union rather than try to compete for positions within it, a stance that was rejected by the majority of the contingents. When the Valle CCL later accepted the additional positions on the executive committee that national union officials offered them, they justified their participation by maintaining their "independence." This meant that the CCL would use these positions on the committees as a forum for denunciation and would clash with the other *charro* members of the committee whenever possible as a way to elevate the consciousness of members.

The Morelos CCL also appeared to follow a strategy of confrontation: "Although today we do not have an officially recognized local committee . . . it has been shown that our policy of uncompromising confrontation with *charrismo* (without demobilizing or sacrificing demands) is a correct one" (CCL Magisterial Morelense 1981:33). In order to counter the efforts of national officials to weaken the Morelos movement, the CCL called for developing "a permanent campaign of harassment of *charrismo* and of the new SEP delegate (who has clearly placed himself on their side)" (CCL Magisterial Morelense 1981:38). This uncompromising policy where the *charros* were concerned translated into a type of witch-hunt against members who either had contact with the *institucionales* or who did not participate in the movement (Treviño 1984:178–79). In Valle, too, movement leaders had accused those guilty of lukewarm support for the movement of being *charros*, a practice that threw members in fact closer to the *charro* camp.[109] Leaders later admitted that the movement's reaction to those members who wavered or weakened in their support for the movement had been too harsh and had cost it supporters. This ideological position of some leaders also gave the impression that some movements were dominated by political parties and afflicted by political factionalism, which further alienated members. This was the case in Morelos, where some members felt that the movement was being used to advance the goals and political candidacies of opposition parties (Treviño 1984:174, 179). One former leader from Morelos explained that his suggestion that the movement become involved in supporting the opposition in local municipal elections met with strong resistance from PRI members within the union local.[110]

---

108. Interview with Valle movement leader, Mexico City, August 31, 1987.
109. Ibid.
110. Interview with Morelos movement leader, Mexico City, June 28, 1990.

While leaders of the Oaxaca and Chiapas movements tended to interpret all gains as at least partial victories, leaders from some of the other movements were critical of the types of advances made in which formal positions of power rather than "the strength of the masses" were used to negotiate with authorities. One leader from the Valle movement considered it important to distinguish between movement "conquests" and "concessions," and believed that there was such a thing as "negative gains"—gains won through special relationships with authorities that could therefore disappear at any point, leaving a movement vulnerable to demobilization and repression. According to this leader, some of the advances won by the Chiapas and Oaxaca movements, whose secretaries-general at one point or another had special access to state governors, fell into this category.[111] Movement leaders would become accustomed to looking to the state for concessions rather than to mass support for their conquests. This position came to embody the *gobiernista* (progovernment) critique frequently levied by factions within the CNTE against the Chiapas leadership in particular, and later also the Oaxaca leadership. One prominent CNTE leader who shared this view stated that it was better to be defeated, in circumstances where one knew oneself to be defeated, rather than to win a questionable victory by virtue of the authorities in which ideology remained murky.[112]

In Valle "ideological purity" led movement leaders to initially reject positions on the expanded executive committees, a stance viewed later as a tactical error that ultimately weakened the movement's bargaining position.[113] In Morelos, too, the CCL's policy of *"nada con los charros"* prevented its accepting a composite committee at a time when its lack of mobilizational capacity left it few options. But ideological purity did not always lead to purist results: these regional movements often found themselves later accepting the compromise positions they had initially rejected.

In contrast to the Chiapas and Oaxaca movements, the CCLs in Valle, Morelos, and Hidalgo tended to regard the CNTE's strategy of union democratization via a legal strategy of winning elections as, at best, a step in a process leading toward broader social change and, at worst, as a distraction that incorrectly involved movement resources in a useless struggle for legal recognition. As with Valle, leaders of the Morelos CCL stressed that their most important objective was not obtaining authorized elections or even the democratization of the union or the local but rather "the socialist transformation of

---

111. Interview with former Valle movement leader, Mexico City, August 21, 1987.
112. Ibid.
113. Interview with Valle movement leader, Mexico City, August 31, 1987.

Mexico" (CCL Magisterial Morelense 1981:33). In Hidalgo, also, leaders saw the democratic conquest of a local as "one of the channels for the general transformation of the country, and not an objective in itself."[114] According to a Hidalgo leader, the CNTE's emphasis on legal democratic victories had divided the movement and led the weaker regions to fight for goals that they were perhaps too weak to pursue in the first place. This tension between some leaders' commitments to national social transformation and others' more "reformist" expectations for the teachers' movement persisted within the CNTE. However, the relative success of the more reformist contingents raised the question of whether any movement for social change could survive without obtaining some advances—especially material gains—for its members, and whether such advances could be obtained (routinely, not just sporadically) in the absence of the bargaining authority afforded by legal-formal status.

The Valle, Morelos, and Hidalgo movements appeared more ideologically rigid than either of their counterparts in the southeast—all three had initially refused to accept composite commissions and had set up parallel committees. Both the Morelos and Valle movements were also internally divided and unforgiving of local members who were undefined in their support of the movement. Their political and ideological "clarity" came at the cost of membership support. While this support existed at the beginning, it waned with the growing politicization of the demands, the defeats, and the growing factionalism in the leadership of the movements. It should also be pointed out, however, that neither the Morelos, Valle, Hidalgo, or Guerrero movements appeared to have as many supporters within the local as did the Chiapas and Oaxaca movements. The difference between being able to draw 50 to 75 percent of the delegates and 90 percent was probably enough to indicate to union officials that they had a chance to defeat the movement.

This differential ability to sustain a mass base also points to important differences in the internal organization of these movements. The Valle, Hidalgo, and Morelos movements appeared to be based on more centralized decision making among a core of activists. The focus on consolidating more base-level and participatory forms of decision making, which might have moderated leaders' positions, did not seem as developed as in Chiapas and Oaxaca. For instance, leaders in Valle credited "obvious errors" to "the lack of information among the membership concerning what the leadership did."[115] In

114. Bedolla, "Entrevista a Roberto Meza," p. 92.
115. José Luis Sánchez, "Entrevista al Prof. Ezequiel Reyes Carrillo . . . ," in *Testimonios* 1987:82–83.

Morelos one young former activist claimed that the members never came to feel that the movement was theirs to defend; that instead they identified the movement with its leadership, which they believed had sold out the movement.[116] Similarly, in Guerrero the movement suffered from "a lack of mechanisms that allow the membership to be continuously informed about the progress of negotiations" (Hernández and Pérez Arce 1982:256–57, 265).[117] The Guerrero movement also did not manage to consolidate its organization throughout the state. It remained in essence a movement comprised of different regions in relative isolation. The organization of the Guerrero movement was also hindered by two very different political styles and forms of organization mentioned earlier, the vanguard model represented by the current linked to the communists and the "mass line" that called for greater rank-and-file participation and consultation with the membership.[118]

Conclusion

A number of factors contributed to the emergence of the national teachers' movement. Teachers throughout the country shared strong economic demands due to (1) a decline in real wages of teachers that began in 1976, (2) rising inflation and the existence of outdated cost-of-living supplements, (3) severe lags in issuing paychecks due to the deconcentration of the SEP, and (4) the fact that all of this was occurring in the context of an oil boom much lauded by the government. The presence of a core group of activists or leaders, many of them formed in the social and political struggles of the 1960s and 1970s, was also important to the movements in each state. These leaders in some instances were able to capitalize on the discontent that was building among teachers regarding the corrupt practices of state and national union officers: the acceptance of bribes and sexual favors for jobs and transfers, the use of favoritism in

116. Personal communication with former teacher movement activist from Morelos, Mexico City, November 1987.
117. In a candid act of "self-criticism" members of the CCL of La Montaña in Guerrero admitted that they had pushed the movement further than it was ready to go, leaving members vulnerable to repression, and that in doing so they had overestimated their own strength and underestimated that of their enemies. Similarly, they faulted themselves for falling back on the leadership of one person in communicating with the assembly, giving the impression to the membership that this was the *caudillo* of the movement, instead of encouraging a broader leadership; and for not allowing the members in the assembly a greater role in discussing proposals suggested by leaders. These were seen as "errors" due to lack of experience rather than the result of ideology (Hernández 1981:146–48).
118. Francisco Pérez Arce, "Entrevista a Fernando Jiménez" pp. 105–6; 109.

making appointments and resolving teachers' problems, and the lack of democracy within the union.

The presence of divisions among local union officials, usually expressed in conflictive local elections, provided regional political opportunities for the movements to emerge in some states. These divisions were a product of the lack of democracy that was characteristic of most union locals. Also important, however, was the fact that national union officials' frequent imposition of local union leaders generated resentment among regional leaders. Thus, these internal divisions and regional resentment of the "center" opened up a political space in some cases in which the opposition could organize. Finally, what was needed for a *mass* movement to develop was typically some event that fueled members' sense of injustice and/or served to delegitimate local union officials. This event is what would convince those who had never set out on strike or participated in political activities that they had no recourse left but to move into the streets, march to Mexico City, and set up a *plantón* in front of government buildings. This was the event that ignited the protests, the element that altered the *perceptions* of rank-and-file teachers. For the Oaxacans this event was the May Day march in 1980; for teachers from Morelos it was the death of a teacher at the ISSSTE hospital; for the teachers in the Montaña region of Guerrero it was the firing of several administrators that directed a social program for the indigenous population of the area; for teachers from Hidalgo it was the fact that union leaders barricaded themselves in the union hall and placed armed guards in front. In Chiapas it was the combination of inflation and low salaries in the oil-producing zone, and in Valle de México it was the actions of fellow teachers in other states: the strike in Chiapas, the events in Oaxaca, and the presence of thousands of protesting teachers nearby in Mexico City.

These conditions combined in most of the cases covered here to initiate the regional teachers' movements. In addition, several other elements appeared to be important in determining which of these regional movements were able to sustain themselves through the initial emergence of the movement in order to obtain legal-formal status.

1. *Cautious adoption of political (versus economic) demands.* In all six regional cases economic grievances were central to the emergence of the teachers' movements. Declining real wages, late paychecks, and insufficient cost-of-living supplements were issues close to the hearts of rank-and-file union members. In the minds of many teachers local union officials' unwillingness to spearhead these demands linked the issue of union democracy—the need to

replace existing local union leaders through new elections—to the satisfaction of these economic grievances. In Chiapas, however, movement leaders were cautious in drawing the links between economic and political goals for fear of frightening away supporters. In the Oaxacan case this link appeared relatively quickly, but the participation of delegation officials and close attention to statutory forms in the organization of the movement also gave the Oaxaca movement a comparatively moderate appearance. In other regional movements political demands were introduced from the beginning. In part this was due to the fact that the precedent had already been set by Oaxaca. Still, a focus on political demands in movements such as Valle's and Morelos's tended to narrow these movements' support base before this support had become consolidated in base-level organizations.

2. *Successful maintenance of a broad, inclusionary dissident coalition.* In each of these states core groups of activists emerged, many influenced by the 1968 student movement, the struggles of *normalistas* in the 1960s and 1970s, and social and political movements in their regions. While these core activist groups appeared crucial to the emergence of the movements, the most successful regional movements emerged in those areas where union officials also joined dissident activists. In Oaxaca, Valle, and Morelos, mid-level local union officials had expressed dissatisfaction with the selection of local leaders and with the way positions were distributed on the executive committees. In these regions the divisions among local union officials facilitated the emergence of an opposition movement. But not all regional movements were able to sustain this broader coalition after their emergence.

Developing an inclusionary dissident coalition involved incorporating a substantial percentage of former union officials (typically at the delegation level) into the movement as well as being able to sustain rank-and-file supporters. The most successful regional movements, Oaxaca and Chiapas, were able to sustain the overwhelming majority support necessary to combat their enemies. Maintaining a broad coalition called for an approach that did not alienate any of the elements of this heterogeneous alliance, requiring tolerance for diverse political positions and a willingness to compromise on tactics, strategies, and the definition of demands. One way to do this was to ensure that each faction developed a stake in the movement through an equal opportunity to participate in the decisions that were taken and a consensus on procedure—that is, through the construction of internal democracy.

3. *Ability to sustain a mass base of support within the movement.* The ability to sustain a mass base of support within the movement was crucial for

these movements' ability to obtain gains and defend them. The amount and strength of support any regional movement sustained also seemed to influence the way that national union and government officials dealt with the movement. Those that could consistently demonstrate strong majority support (through mobilizations and assemblies repudiating executive committees) were more likely to obtain concessions. Those with more limited support were vulnerable to officials' manipulations of delegation assemblies and congresses. The ability to sustain a mass base of support seemed to depend on incorporating members in setting demands and objectives, and on building an organization that treated members differently from the way they had been treated in the past. Mechanisms that ensured representation and leadership accountability to members and that incorporated rank-and-file members into the decision-making process were at the same time elements of movement *construction*—a way of instilling in members a sense of their "ownership" of the movement—that revolved around the education and politicization of rank-and-file teachers.

4. *Limited use of confrontational tactics; acceptance of "institutionality."* No single regional contingent of the teachers' movement was strong enough on its own to confront government and union officials head-on, and nationally the movement was too divided to do so. This called for a relatively moderate strategy aimed at avoiding a repressive response from union or government officials. Such a moderate strategy might involve addressing authorities respectfully and using nonideological language, using legal channels to voice demands before submitting to extralegal or illegal actions, and making use of legal and statutory instances of organization, appealing to these forms as a way to legitimate dissident movement claims. This more moderate approach also involved a more nuanced understanding of "the state." State and union officials' interests conflicted at times; under these circumstances the movement could appeal to the government to mediate in a conflict in a way that could benefit the movement. This use of legality and of state "allies" demanded a less confrontational approach and reflected an appreciation of the strategic role that formal institutions could play.[119]

5. *Weak local vanguardista presence and limited use of violence.* This was an "external" condition that movements could do little to affect. Those

---

119. In his study of rural trade unions under the military dictatorship in Brazil Biorn Maybury-Lewis argues similarly that unions which pursued progressive objectives were obliged to proceed cautiously, to recognize the importance of "cultivating allies who enjoyed respect in official circles," and to avoid needless provocation of power holders, eschewing "inflammatory rhetoric and any position remotely suggestive of communism" (1994:73).

movements that emerged in regions with a relatively weak vanguardista presence were more likely to have the opportunity to draw union officials into the dissident coalition. A strong vanguardista presence, or strong union officials' ties with local political interests, would complicate the dissident movement's efforts to sustain a broad inclusionary coalition. These factors would also increase the likelihood of violence against the movement. Oaxaca and Chiapas were areas where vanguardista ties were relatively weak and the violence employed against the movement was limited. In Valle, Morelos, Hidalgo, and Guerrero, on the other hand, vanguardista and/or local union-cacique interests were strong and the violence employed against dissident teachers was also much more intense.[120]

6. *Timing in the cycle of protest.*[121] The movements that emerged later, especially the Valle and Hidalgo movements, were at a distinct disadvantage with respect to those regional movements that emerged earlier. The gains of the Oaxaca movement were due in part to the fact that it was the first regional movement to mobilize nationally for recognition of its executive commission. Other regional movements then erupted onto the national scene, taking advantage of the cycle begun by Chiapas and Oaxaca. The regional movements of 1979 and the initial national mobilizations of 1980 had caught union and government officials off guard. In contrast, the events of 1980 altered union officials' plan of action vis-à-vis both the dissident movement and the state. National union officials were committed not to "lose" more locals, and they used their ample resources to defeat those regional movements that were relatively weak.

Given the complexity of these regional cases, it is difficult to separate out the relative importance of "external" factors from "internal" factors in determining the outcomes of these movements. Clearly, the movements in Guerrero, Morelos, Hidalgo, and Valle faced especially difficult conditions in their states. However, based on this comparative review, it also appears that a case can be made for the relative success of a more moderate and legalistic strategy (yet backed by mobilization) *and* for the importance of a broad-based network of rank-and-file organizations at the state level that participate in decision making

---

120. Sánchez, "Entrevista al Prof. Ezequiel Reyes Carrillo . . . ," p. 79.

121. The argument regarding protest cycles is that waves of mobilization may generate a favorable environment for other movements to emerge and decrease the relative importance of internal resources at the moment of their emergence. But because of these movements' organizational weakness, when the structure of opportunity changes, their "successes are usually brief and their outcomes sometimes tragic" (Tarrow 1994:8).

and support the movement. In fact, strong links with the rank-and-file and the latter's incorporation into decision making regarding when to mobilize, for example, helped to limit the chances that movement leaders would "ask that people do what they cannot do," thus ensuring that mobilizations were based on strength (Piven and Cloward 1979:22). Movements such as Valle, for example, were criticized by some in the CNTE for overestimating their strength in the face of the enemy and for overpoliticizing their demands. Advancing based on the strength of each regional movement was most possible when the leadership was closely tuned to the abilities and "spirit" (*ánimo*) of the membership. This in turn required an internal organization that facilitated strong communication between the leadership and members of the movement. Thus, regional movement leaders did what they could when they could do it: when rank-and-file teachers were willing to mobilize and when authorities were willing to negotiate. After political opportunities waned and mobilization ebbed, the relatively limited mass support of some movements and the divisions among the leadership revealed the initial organizational weaknesses of some of these movements.

The legal-formal status of the Chiapas and Oaxaca movements (after their electoral victories in 1981 and 1982, respectively) served to further separate them from other regional movements by altering their demands and the focus of their organizing and activism. Their electoral victories were sustained and defended over several years. These two cases provide us with a rare opportunity to examine what happens when a democratic movement succeeds in gaining power within an authoritarian environment, which is the subject of the next chapter.

Fig. 1. CNTE march, Oaxaca contingent, Mexico City, 1980 (photo by Jorge Acevedo)

Fig. 2. CNTE rally in front of Education Ministry, Mexico City, 1981 (photo by Jorge Acevedo)

Fig. 3. Morelos teachers' caravan-march to Mexico City, 1980 (photo by Jorge Acevedo)

Fig. 4. Parents march in support of teachers, Valle de México, 1981 (photo by Jorge Acevedo)

Fig. 5. Misael Núñez Acosta's funeral, 1981 (photo by Jorge Acevedo)

Fig. 6. *Plantón* in Mexico City, 1981 (photo by Jorge Acevedo)

Fig. 7. Audience at the public "political trial" of Vanguardia Revolucionaria, Oaxaca, 1985 (photo by the author)

Fig. 8. SNTE labor goons, Mexico City, May Day March, 1983 (photo by Jorge Acevedo)

Fig. 9. Raised fists and a minute of silence for murdered teachers' movement activists, Oaxaca, 1985 (photo by the author)

Emergence of the National Teachers' Movement

Fig. 10. Oaxacan teachers' "silent march" for union electoral congress, Mexico City, 1986. Sign reads "Only One Way: Democracy" (photo by Jorge Acevedo)

Fig. 11. CNTE rally in downtown Mexico City, 1989 (photo by Tomás Martínez for Cuartoscuro)

5

Oaxaca and Chiapas

Dilemmas of Legality

> *¡A Oaxaca no regreso, si no hay congreso!*
> *To Oaxaca I won't return, if there is no congress!*
> — Oaxaca teachers' chant

Through their formal occupation of the union locals the dissident teachers' movements in Oaxaca and Chiapas entered a period of legal standing that lasted for most of the 1980s in the case of Chiapas and for all of the decade in the case of Oaxaca. This newfound legal status for which all of the regional movements had fought so hard enabled movement leaders at the head of these locals to act as the official link between the teachers and the state governor, the federal offices of the SEP and the ISSSTE in the states, and the national executive committee of the union. Their legal-formal status gave the movements the ability to better meet the demands and needs of teachers, to extend and consolidate their democratic organization, and to establish a "new unionism" in their states.

At the same time, the legal status of the movements in Oaxaca and Chiapas presented them with a dilemma: maintaining their legality was important, yet it meant securing authorization for local elections from national union officials.

During the emergence of the national teachers' movement in 1979–80, this permission had been wrenched from the national union through massive national mobilizations, a context of conflict between the SEP and the union, and the intervention of the Interior Ministry. After 1983 and throughout most of the decade of the 1980s, however, the scenario would be quite different. Among the significant developments were a severe economic crisis that would last throughout the decade, harsher treatment of labor and dissident movements by the government, and an increasingly more conciliatory relationship between government education and union officials. This latter development in particular would generate a much more hostile environment for the dissident union locals, one that would lead them into prolonged battles for authorization of their electoral congresses. This chapter therefore examines two strands that are important to the story of the movements in this decade: it traces the major changes in the national and regional political contexts of the teachers; and it explores the implications of this more closed environment for the movements in Oaxaca and Chiapas, noting both the impressive achievements as well as the tremendous vulnerability that were a consequence of legal status in this particular political environment.

Changes in the Political Environment

The 1982 change in presidential administration under President Miguel de la Madrid Hurtado (1982–88) altered the context of SEP-SNTE relations and, consequently, conditions for the dissident movement. The new education minister, Jesús Reyes Heroles, still came into conflict with the teachers' union, this time over the government's new decentralization plan and over education policy, but he was also harsher on the dissident movement than the previous minister had been.[1] For instance, the new administration dealt a blow to the CNTE by decentralizing the Escuela Normal Superior in Mexico City (which had functioned as a CNTE training center) and closing its main campus in 1983. The government also took a hard line against protest of the government's austerity policies by the labor movement in June 1983.[2] The defeats suffered by the independent labor movement (including the CNTE) in the summer 1983 strike wave dampened union militancy for much of the rest of the term.

1. Street 1984:27; interview with member of the CNTE's Permanent Commission, Mexico City, August 18, 1987.
2. On the 1983 strike wave see Durand Ponte 1991 and Cook 1990a:60–61.

The government of de la Madrid also coincided with the beginning of a severe economic crisis in Mexico, characterized by high foreign indebtedness, strong fiscal austerity measures, and declining real wages. The crisis affected levels of activism and organization among workers in general, but especially among public sector employees, who were directly affected by budget cutbacks and by government layoffs in the mid-1980s.[3] At the same time, the lesser likelihood, under the crisis, of winning economic demands led many unions to change the nature of their demands and the ways in which these were formulated (for instance, strikes became less effective weapons in this new economic environment). The economic crisis marked the beginning of a period in which primary schoolteachers' real wages would fall by 63 percent between 1982–89, while the average minimum real wage declined nearly 62 percent in this same period.[4] While the situation of the economy generated discontent, it also reduced the amount of time teachers could devote to the movement as they were forced to seek additional income elsewhere. In some regions, such as Oaxaca, many teachers joined the migration northward to seek work in the United States.

Under de la Madrid tensions initially persisted between SNTE officials and the government as the administration proceeded in the decentralization of the education system. The decentralization—the transfer of funds, resources, and responsibility for education to state governments—was the next and final phase in the reform of the education administration system. The planned decentralization was, according to Pescador and Torres (1985:73), "the most ambitious exercise of educational planning attempted since 1921 [when the SEP was created], aimed at ending, once and for all, the confrontation between Vanguardia Revolucionaria and educational planners over national education policy." Nonetheless, the case of decentralization under de la Madrid again illustrates the degree to which the union could wield political power to stall and reshape reform. Continued union resistance to the decentralization plans and a general lack of political will in the SEP, particularly after 1985, would lead the

---

3. Although teacher employment continued to grow throughout this period, government spending on education declined by 29.6 percent between 1983–89. Lustig suggests that the reduction in education spending "primarily reflects the drop in real wages of education employees and investment in the sector. It also might reflect a cut in the availability of school materials and in the maintenance of existing facilities" (Lustig 1992:79, 83).

4. Wage information for primary schoolteachers is from Guzmán Ortiz and Vela Glez 1989:47. Information on minimum wage (real minimum wage for Mexico City) is from Middlebrook 1995:215, table 6.1. Wages to government employees declined by 57.1 percent between 1982–89 (Lustig 1992:68–69, table 3.2).

government to extend guarantees to the union that would help to block the full decentralization of education.

Both the dissident CNTE and SNTE officials generally agreed in their criticisms of the government's decentralization plans, the details of which were never made clear. The union persisted in the belief that the measure would strengthen union organizations in the states at the expense of the union as a whole. Decentralization represented a reversal of the union's struggle in the early part of the century to federalize education, to standardize work conditions, salaries, and benefit levels, and to have the content of education determined not by the states but by the federal government. It also threatened to give state governors more power, which could then be used for political ends, and state government control of education meant that the resources channeled to education would vary widely from state to state (*Punto Crítico* 1983:7). Both dissidents and officials in the leadership of the union feared that decentralization would fracture the union, dividing it into thirty-two unions, each with a different employer, the state government.[5] During the SNTE congress in February 1983 union leaders attacked the government's decentralization plan, warning that it "harmed the unitary structure of the union organization."[6]

The union also objected to other changes in education policy and curriculum that were being discussed under the de la Madrid administration. These included a requirement that applicants to normal schools have a secondary school degree[7] (which the union feared would limit access to a teaching career for the children of peasants and workers), and changes in the "basic cycle" of education from twelve to ten years.[8] These proposed measures formed part of

5. See Norma Brena Güereca, *El Heraldo*, January 19, 1983, p. 4: "Instead of one large organization there would be small unions that could be manipulated by the [state] governors."

6. Miguel Angel Ramírez, *El Día*, February 5, 1983, p. 2. At this congress, moreover, Alberto Miranda Castro, the new secretary-general of the union, insisted on a return to former administrative structures in the states: "We demand the disappearance of the SEP delegations in the states and in their place we propose the creation of Educational Head Offices [*Direcciones Generales de Educación*] and of offices for each one of the [educational] levels. . . . All of these appointments should come from the union membership and be occupied by teachers" (cited in Pescador and Torres 1985:49).

7. Prior to these reforms in 1983–84 teacher training in normal schools began at the secondary level. Since 1983–84 entry requirements and course requirements have been raised to bring them into line with other higher education establishments. While this policy change was aimed at improving the quality of teacher education, it was in tension with the constant shortage of teachers in Mexico. Although there has also been a move in Mexico toward training teachers in universities and higher education institutions rather than normal schools, during the 1980s the majority of teachers were still trained in normal schools (González Paredes and Turner 1990:244–45).

8. Education in Mexico consists of preschool (although this is not available everywhere in Mexico), primary school (through grade six), lower secondary (*media básica*, similar to junior high),

the so-called education revolution under Reyes Heroles, aimed at "increas[ing] the quality of education at all levels" (González Ruiz 1985:18). For its part the SNTE claimed not to oppose the decentralization *per se*, nor the "education revolution," but rather opposed "the arrogance, in the sense that decisions were being made behind the teachers' backs, ignoring their experience and their contributions."[9]

By the end of 1983, however, it appeared that a gentlemen's agreement with respect to the decentralization plans had been reached. In response to extensive union pressure the SEP eventually abandoned the original, more radical version of the decentralization plan for one that involved "a simple coordination of education services between the federation and the states" (Reséndiz 1992:15). In what was a certain victory for the union the SEP assured the union that the normative character of education would remain in the hands of the central SEP, that the structure of the SNTE would not be affected, that the rights and benefits of members would not be harmed, and that the union would retain its status as representative of SEP employees (de los Reyes 1986). Secretary-General Miranda Castro declared, "we unconditionally support the plan to decentralize education," due, he added, to the government's willingness to respect the participation of teachers, the structure of the union, and the rights of the workers.[10]

By 1983 SNTE leaders also had time to regroup after an especially conflictive period in which their authority had been undermined by both the dissident movement and the government (Hernández 1986b:69, Prieto 1986:79). Moreover, by 1983 the CNTE's battles were being fought regionally rather than nationally— Oaxaca and Chiapas already had their democratic executive committees; Morelos, Valle de México, Hidalgo, and Guerrero were greatly weakened by the end of 1982. The CNTE's last big mobilization at the national level had been during the June strike wave in 1983, and after this the regional movements withdrew to deal with local problems and to shore up their defenses. The pressure of a mass movement on the SNTE and on the government was gone.

The reduction of substantive conflict with the government by the end of 1983 released the national executive committee to focus on the dissident movements in the states. In their strategy to recover old losses and preempt new

---

and upper secondary (*bachillerato*, or high school). Until the Salinas administration (1988–94) education was compulsory through primary school. Under the Salinas government compulsory education was extended through the *media básica* level, or until age fourteen.

9. Cited in Martínez Assad and Ziccardi 1988:37.
10. Crescencio Cárdenas, *El Universal*, August 9, 1983, p. 9.

ones national union leaders sent top cadres to Oaxaca and Chiapas in order to organize opposition to the democratic locals. Prior to this, in 1982 the union had already begun to lash out at the dissident movement, taking advantage of the greater weaknesses of a decentralized movement to violate agreements for electoral congresses signed under pressure from the Interior Ministry with locals in Hidalgo, Morelos, and Valle de México. In spite of important setbacks for the regional movements during 1982, however, dissident union members were successful in obtaining representation on the national executive committee during the national SNTE congress in January–February 1983.[11] At this congress seventy-one democratic delegates present managed to negotiate with the national union leadership and gain two positions on the executive committee and three positions on auxiliary commissions.[12] This dissident victory and the relatively strong showing by the CNTE during the June 1983 strike wave further increased the national leadership's resolve to put an end to the movement and led in turn to a stepped-up effort in the states to "take back" the union.

An important consequence of the change in the presidential administration was political changes in some states as new state governors took their positions. In Chiapas General Absalón Castellanos Domínguez was named governor—the first military governor in the state since 1952. General Castellanos's appointment as governor (1982–88) coincided with the federal government's assessment of Chiapas as a security priority due to its strategic natural resources,[13] strong independent political movements, and its location—bordering a Central American civil war that had already spilled into Mexico by way of thousands of Guatemalan refugees (Aguayo Quezada 1987:3).[14] General Castellanos was a

---

11. In Guerrero dissidents gained some representation on the local executive committee and sent three delegates to the national congress. Local 11 of Mexico City also obtained representatives on the local executive committee and sent one delegate to the national congress.

12. Interviews with CNTE members revealed a sense that these positions on the committee had not been used to best advantage; some people believed the CNTE representatives on the committee should have used them to organize the movement, resolve problems for teachers, see to obtaining a headquarters for the movement, and so forth. Yet the representatives were accused of doing little and of not coordinating their activities with one another. After a time most of the representatives stopped going to the national committee offices. It was also noted, however, that CNTE representatives had been treated harshly by the rest of the committee; at one point they were barred from occupying their offices, and one representative was beaten (interviews with CNTE leaders, Mexico City, August 18 and August 21, 1987).

13. Chiapas was considered economically strategic because the state was the largest producer of electricity in the country and the second largest producer of petroleum (Aquayo Quezada 1987:5).

14. Conditions in Chiapas touched off a series of popular struggles in the seventies and eighties, especially among the peasantry. For an excellent analysis of the development of independent peasant organizations in Chiapas see Harvey 1990. In 1994 this tradition of popular struggle continued with the indigenous uprising of the Zapatista National Liberation Army (EZLN; see Harvey 1994).

member of the Chiapas landowning oligarchy that continued to dominate Chiapas politics. His appointment caused discontent among a more dynamic and emergent agroindustrial and commercial bourgeoisie and among younger members of the PRI, as well as among popular organizations in the state (Cruz 1982:37).

Under the new government Chiapas became the target of massive federal funding of projects and plans to develop the region, preserve resources, and connect the state with the rest of the country, a proposal also clearly related to the federal government's security concerns. Part of de la Madrid's National Development Plan, "Plan Chiapas" was budgeted at 300 million dollars. Even though many of the projects in the plan eventually failed because of corruption and a lack of coordination among government offices, the influx of resources deepened existing tensions between the governor and local political groups and disrupted indigenous communities in areas of highway or dam construction (Aguayo Quezada 1987:40–41).

The Castellanos government was an especially repressive one. Governor Castellanos looked the other way when paramilitary forces and municipal police were employed against peasants by local caciques and landowners. Over eight hundred Chiapanecans were allegedly assassinated during Castellanos's term, and his government was characterized by the Mexican Academy of Human Rights as one of the most corrupt and repressive state governments of the de la Madrid presidency (Benjamin 1989:240–41). Meanwhile, teachers' involvement in peasant and Indian communities brought them directly into conflict with local caciques, landowners, and the state government.

The changes at both the national level and in the states provided the vanguardistas with new incentives to squeeze the democratic movement. As noted, national union officials sent top cadres to Oaxaca and Chiapas in order to organize opposition to the movement. The national executive committee became noticeably more closed to the local's demands in Chiapas and orchestrated a major propaganda campaign against the Chiapas committee. The vanguardistas who had concentrated in the SEP delegation (now called USED) formed an organization, the FRTECH (Frente Reivindicador de Trabajadores de la Educación en Chiapas, Front for the Demands of Education Workers in Chiapas), as well as a parallel executive committee. According to movement leaders, these vanguardistas were aided in their organizational efforts by the national executive committee of the union, the CNC, and municipal presidents in the state.[15] Similarly, in the capital city of Oaxaca, on October 22, 1983,

15. SNTE. Sección 7. 1984a. The CNC was also known to participate in attacks against peasants; see Benjamin 1989:235.

vanguardistas occupied the union local but were forced out by the pressure of hundreds of teachers who surrounded the building and by the intervention of the state governor, Pedro Vásquez Colmenares, who sent in police. Several days later vanguardistas met near the Veracruz border and formed a committee (Comité Institucional), reportedly with financial support from the national union leadership, in an effort to take over executive functions and gain adherents, but they received little support from rank-and-file teachers in Oaxaca (SNTE. Sección 22. CES. n.d.). A conservative organization that local members identified as being linked to Vanguardia (FUSTEO) was also formed in January 1983.

An additional change in the de la Madrid cabinet had special significance for Mexican teachers. After Reyes Heroles's death from cancer in March 1985, Miguel González Avelar was appointed to head the SEP. González Avelar's tenure as education minister signaled a period of strong concessions to the union leadership and a partial rollback of many of the reforms initiated during the previous two administrations. The minister's interest in the presidential nomination especially weakened his resolve to delimit the power and activities of the union. In particular, the new education minister adopted a conciliatory position that enabled the union leadership to negotiate the appointment of directors of the state SEP delegations, now called Unidades de Servicios Educativos a Descentralizar (Units of Educational Services to be Decentralized, USED). The devolution of state-level SEP positions to union members that in fact had begun with Solana and continued with Reyes Heroles was accelerated under González Avelar (Reséndiz 1992).[16]

Other signs of government concessions to the union included dropping the phrase "education revolution," to which the union had so objected, and reinstating the SEP-SNTE "mixed commission" (for joint review of policies affecting the SEP and its employees). In addition, the decentralization ceased to be a major point of conflict between the union and the government. In spite of the SEP's signing of thirty decentralization agreements (*convenios*) with state governments by 1987, the full decentralization of the education system was stalled.[17] As of 1987 the union also continued to exert tremendous influence in

16. Interview with former SEP official, Mexico City, November 24, 1987. See also "Carta de la CNTE a Bartlett" in *La Jornada*, October 23, 1987, p. 2: "[T]he majority of Ministry positions have been turned over to them, so that almost all of the *Unidades de Servicios Educativos a Descentralizar* and the *Coordinaciones de Servicios Regionales* in the states are occupied by bureaucrats who belong to Vanguardia."

17. Interviews with former SEP officials, Mexico City, September 22, 1987, and November 24, 1987. These agreements were signed with state governments prior to the actual implementation of the decentralization as a statement of intent to decentralize. Agreements to decentralize education

the definition and assignment of jobs *(plazas)*, even though the number of positions was supposed to be determined by the SEP; the *"doble plaza"* remained an important demand of and concession to the union.[18] While the Servicios Coordinados de Educación Pública (Coordinated Public Education Services, SCEP)[19] were now to be responsible for determining the number of teachers and support personnel required in the areas of their jurisdiction, this task remained in the hands of the union (de los Reyes 1986). In fact, the picture in the states was quite varied, reflecting local political conditions and the ability of the different actors to impose their will on the SEP administrative project. In the states where the dissident movement had consolidated itself, such as Oaxaca and Chiapas, the movement controlled the operative positions of supervisors and directors, whereas Vanguardia was able to make important inroads into the SCEPs (Reséndiz 1992:16). In other states Education Ministry bureaucrats and Vanguardia shared power within the SEP administrative structure; and in still others transitory forms of administration such as the USED (dominated by Education Ministry appointees) coexisted uneasily with the traditional chain of command involving federal directors, supervisors, and school directors. In this latter case the decentralization had not advanced at all (Reséndiz 1992:16).

In this way decentralization, like the deconcentration and the UPN project before it, remained a stalemated reform because of the union's persistent resistance to the government's policies and the latter's inability and unwillingness to confront union power head-on. This shift of power back toward the union leadership not only meant that the government's control over education administration in the states would remain limited, it also signaled an even more difficult and politically closed environment for the democratic locals that had managed to take hold in Oaxaca and Chiapas.

Oaxaca and Chiapas: Consequences of Legality

After the dissident movements occupied the formal structures of the union local, they began to function as officially recognized representatives of federal

---

were signed with twelve state governments during a "first phase" in July 1984. The most conflictive states—Oaxaca, Chiapas, Mexico State, and Hidalgo—were not considered in this first stage of decentralization. Two more agreements were signed in 1985, four in 1986, and twelve in 1987. The state of Mexico remained outside because of the objections of the SNTE (Martínez Assad and Ziccardi 1988:30–32).

18. Interview with former SEP official, Mexico City, September 22, 1987.

19. Between 1984 and 1987 the name of the state delegations changed once more as plans to decentralize advanced; the newest title was Servicios Coordinados de Educación Pública.

teachers from Oaxaca and Chiapas.[20] This legal status entitled the movement (now in its capacity as a union local) to process members' job-related requests and grievances, present demands through formal channels, and receive funds from the national executive committee. Legal status provided the movements in Oaxaca and Chiapas with the opportunity to meet many of the demands of their members, consolidate their organizations, and establish alternative union practices.

At the same time, legal status presented the Oaxaca and Chiapas movements with challenges and constraints different from those they faced as incipient movements. Most important, the regional movements' autonomy was circumscribed by national union officials, who retained the sole authority to call (and withhold) elections, controlled funding to the locals, and otherwise hindered local officials' handling of their responsibilities. In particular, the movements in both states were drawn into prolonged struggles for the renewal of their executive committees through local elections—struggles for the right, in effect, to retain legal status.

Several tensions inherent to the movements' legal status were never fully resolved. These included a persistent tension between the movements' need to mobilize to secure demands and the local leaders' need to maintain relations with authorities in order to function effectively as a union leadership. The movements also faced the challenge of trying to sustain the national teachers' movement and pursue broader goals while trying at the same time to survive as a formal organization and meet the demands of their members. Moreover, the demands that authorities placed on local leaders tended to adversely affect their relations with rank-and-file members, challenge movement strategies, and even threaten the democratic movements in these states. The following two sections examine both what these movements were able to achieve and the constraints they faced as a result of legal status.

Gains of the Legal Strategy

Legality gave movement representatives official authority to bargain. With legality the Oaxaca and Chiapas locals were thrown into the tasks of daily

20. For the Chiapas movement this period runs from the date of its successful electoral congress, in March 1981, to the decertification of its executive committee by the national committee in 1987. In the case of Oaxaca this period began in February 1982 and continued through 1989, when a new committee was finally recognized. In 1989 an electoral congress was also held in Chiapas and a new democratic executive committee was allowed to take office.

management and the handling of members' job-related demands (*gestoría*). Union committees could now appeal legally to the state offices of the SEP, the social security institute (Instituto de Seguridad y Servicios Sociales de los Trabajadores del Estado), and the state governor. This new legality and the capacity for handling member needs that went with it had important positive implications for the consolidation of the movement. The ability of the new democratic leadership to respond to long-standing member demands contrasted sharply with former practices by *charro* leaders and helped to secure the loyalty and support of the membership. Despite their legality, however, the regional movements continued to resort to familiar forms of mobilization in the face of intransigence on the part of government and union authorities. Important new gains were obtained, but they were obtained both by negotiating through official channels *and* by pressuring through marches, work stoppages, and building occupations. The persistent obstruction of these democratic locals' demands, therefore, also forced them to retain extralegal tactics and measures that were characteristic of opposition movements that lacked legal status.

In both Oaxaca and Chiapas the most immediate and daily concerns of the teachers came to displace wage and more political issues on the agenda of these locals. Attention to "social" demands—demands relating to benefits, social services, credits and loans, for example—represented efforts to address members' long-standing complaints that these issues had been resolved unfairly in the past. At the same time, economic demands had become more problematic. The difficulty with presenting and getting economic demands met (in particular, a direct increase in the base wage) was connected to the national union leadership's reticence to spearhead such demands and, consequently, to the scope of the actions required to pressure the leadership.[21] After 1982, furthermore, economic demands became increasingly difficult to win because of the onset of the economic crisis and the restrictive wage policy adopted by the de la Madrid administration.

In the beginning the Oaxaca and Chiapas locals were relatively successful in meeting the social needs of their members. Local committees were able to focus

---

21. The nature of the government agency involved in granting teachers' demands determined the way these demands were presented, the nature and size of collective activity that might accompany petitions, and the likelihood of obtaining a response. For example, economic demands were presented to the SEP, normally through the national executive committee of the SNTE. Job demands also had to be presented to the SEP, although some of these could be negotiated at the state level. Matters relating to pensioners and retirees, benefits, health services, credit, housing, and other forms of social assistance had to be negotiated through the national executive committee with the ISSSTE in Mexico City, although some of these issues could be negotiated with ISSSTE offices in the states (SNTE. Sección 22. 1982a).

on demands for improved social services and health clinics, and on more equitable distribution of loans, credit, and housing. In Chiapas the teachers' local worked together with other member organizations of the FSTSE in order to accelerate the process of decentralization of the ISSSTE, increase the number of subsidized stores in outlying regions, and obtain more fluid loan-processing arrangements that would benefit all federal and state employees (Peralta Esteva et al. 1985:15). After an initial series of protests and negotiations that brought national ISSSTE authorities to Chiapas, the number of doctors and support staff as well as the budget allocated to clinics and hospitals in the largest cities of Chiapas increased. In Oaxaca a similar focus on benefits and social services soon after legality generated discontent within the movement on the part of groups who felt that the Oaxaca local was concentrating too much effort on the ISSSTE issue and not enough on economic issues that could be shared by other regions.[22] This tension between the degree of attention paid to local versus national issues and demands was a constant in the lives of the democratic locals and was exacerbated by these locals' legal status and, consequently, their increased tendency to focus on local needs and demands.

The democratic locals' focus on resolving the problems of teachers coincided in several instances with SEP interests related to the administrative deconcentration and the expediting of services to SEP employees. In both states the local executive committees cooperated with the local SEP in finding ways to address the delayed payments problem. In Chiapas the local executive committee demanded that the SEP expand the number of disbursement offices located throughout the state in order to enable teachers to obtain their paychecks promptly. In Oaxaca the local played an important role in the reform of the paycheck delivery system.[23] In both cases the local committees' demands helped to accelerate the decentralization of services. The locals also pressed for the removal of a number of bureaucrats from the SEP delegation; in some instances these removals coincided with efforts at the central level SEP to reorganize its offices in the states.

The ability to negotiate and handle job-related issues was also very important for the democratic locals. Vanguardia Revolucionaria had based its power over union members on its control of these issues and hence of teachers' careers. As

---

22. *Avance* 1982a; *Educación Popular* 1982; SNTE. Sección 22. Comité Ejecutivo Seccional. 1982. See also ISSSTE. Delegación Estatal. Dirección General. 1982; and Maestros Democráticos de Base de las Delegaciones Sindicales . . . , "A los trabajadores de la educación: A los representantes democráticos," November 16, 1982.

23. SNTE-CNTE 1983, Peralta Esteva et al. 1985:19, Hernández Ruiz and Velázquez García 1983:16.

with some of the social demands, these job issues were negotiated at the state level through the SEP. Joint SEP-union committees in the states were reactivated in order to negotiate such matters as hiring and placement of new personnel, transfers to other schools, promotions, and other matters pertaining to the teachers' jobs and careers. The decisions about these personnel issues were no longer made by union officials or SEP bureaucrats alone but were placed in the hands of the teachers themselves, who devised a set of criteria to be applied in determining the distribution of job rights through democratic means. Rules to determine the granting of teacher requests for transfers, promotions, loans, credit, and even available housing were discussed, developed, and voted on in delegation assemblies and applied through the delegation executive committees (Peralta Esteva et al. 1985:20). School district supervisors and school directors were also promoted to these positions by vote of the delegations after consideration of the candidates' professional record, seniority, and participation in the movement. Previously, either professional record alone or, more often, personal connections determined who got these positions; the democratic local added the criteria of seniority and participation for supervisory and district appointments. Local SEP authorities typically were then pressured to recognize these "appointments" and to comply with these collectively determined standards when considering petitions in joint committees with the movement. In many cases they simply signed the official papers ratifying decisions already taken by the teachers.

The arbitrary power previously wielded by supervisors and other administrative personnel was therefore checked by a collective definition and formalization of procedures and norms that reflected members' sense of justice and of their rights as education workers.[24] According to teachers in the Chiapas highlands, speaking in 1983: "Before in Chiapas transfers were done by '*dedazo*' [decided unilaterally by administrators and supervisors]; the best positions were given to the friends of the supervisor, encouraging a whole system of corrupt practices. . . . Now we tell the supervisors what they're going to do; they simply sign the papers confirming the decisions on transfers, exchanges, new personnel, and

---

24. Susan Street's research in Chiapas bears this out: "In the case of the election of 30 new supervisors the nominees were elected in delegational assemblies. . . . Each supervisor needed *written approval of all the teachers* in the district. The lists of candidates for the entire state were sent back to the membership in order to ensure that there were no errors (to make sure someone who was 'unacceptable' had not gotten onto the list). All accusations had to be well-documented. Afterwords, in a *public* meeting, the 'points' [accumulated by each candidate] were summed up (according to the democratic version of the job grade [*escalafón*]) in order to decide democratically the assignment of supervisors to school districts" (Street 1992a:155; emphasis in original; my translation).

promotions taken by the membership in the assemblies."[25] Such developments led one movement leader in Chiapas to declare that "the SEP in Chiapas has lost its function as an employer" (Street 1992a:154).

The locals' relative success in this arena, as in the arena of social demands, enabled them to secure the confidence of rank-and-file teachers in their new committee leadership. Success provided an immediate measure of the effectiveness of the new union representatives. Democratic teachers' control over the assignment, transfer, and promotion of teachers also allowed them to limit the incursion of their vanguardista opponents into the schools, a factor crucial for the consolidation of the democratic movement at the base. Collective control over who worked as a teacher also helped to guard against corruption and abuses by local SEP officials and by union members, for whom unilateral control of teachers' careers could lead to a return to former practices—arbitrary hiring and firing, the sale of job placements, bribery, and sexual harassment—and to the construction of patronage networks around individual leaders and officials.

The early period of legality was also one in which teachers, after deliberation in workplace and delegation assemblies, expelled from the schools and the administration vanguardistas, so-called "opportunists," and people uncommitted to the movement. While these expulsions were primarily politically motivated, in time movement supporters also backed the expulsions with documentation that demonstrated corruption and poor job performance by these teachers, directors, and supervisors. In the course of doing so they also began to generate a consensus among themselves as to what the new rules of the game should be (Street 1992a:151; SNTE. Sección 7. 1984a). However, many of those who were expelled found jobs in the SEP delegation, from where they would be able to attack the movement at a later date. The significance of this is revealed in national union officials' persistent efforts to get vanguardistas into the SEP delegations in order to inhibit and even block the democratic locals' successful handling of members' job needs and demands. After 1985 in particular this would form part of the official strategy to weaken the movement by undermining the material basis of support for democratic local committee officials.

Legal status thus allowed the movement to operate as a formal union organization, engaged in the day-to-day management of the local. The successful resolution of demands helped to sustain the legitimacy of the new union representatives and consolidated loyalty and support for the organization,

---

25. Transcribed interviews with Coordinadora de Los Altos, Chiapas, p. 2.

strengthening it against the advances of vanguardistas, who in this period (1980–83) were still recovering from setbacks in their conflict with the government and the movement. Movement leaders and members also altered the ways in which everyday management had been handled in the past by democratizing decision making within the union organization. Moreover, SEP delegation practices—in a state of flux due to the deconcentration—adjusted to meet teacher demands in the immediate aftermath of legalization.[26]

The Struggle for Union Elections (1984–1988)

Under the increasingly adverse national political and economic context represented by the de la Madrid administration and the economic crisis, the democratic locals in Oaxaca and Chiapas were fast approaching the moment when they would have to appeal once again to national union officials in order to hold their local union elections. Under union statutes local executive committees were in place for three years, after which a new electoral congress had to be authorized and presided over by the national union leadership. This meant that the Chiapas local was scheduled to hold its congress in March 1984 and the Oaxaca local in February 1985. Although the movement in Chiapas was able to renew its local committee in 1984, when time came for a third electoral congress in March 1987, national union officials did what all had feared: they decertified the leadership of the Chiapas local. In Oaxaca, meanwhile, unionists were denied authorized elections for four years. The single largest issue for the CNTE in the second half of the 1980s, then, was the struggle for the *"congreso"*: securing authorized local elections so that the democratic committees could renew themselves, retain their legal status, and continue to resolve the problems and demands of their members.

Chiapas: From Renewal to Division

The months preceding March 1984 were filled with preparations for the renewal of the executive committee in Chiapas. As with the first democratic elections the teachers held a precongress on March 5, 6, and 7, during which they voted on the new committee and decided the specific measures to be taken in order to secure the smooth functioning of the congress. Delegates took special

---

26. For a more detailed analysis of changes in SEP practices and the role of the teachers' movement in democratizing administrative decisions in Chiapas see Street 1992a: chap. 4.

measures to rein in the executive committee leadership, which they saw as too autonomous and increasingly engaged in factional conflict for dominance of the committee. To this end the size of the committee was expanded from 13 to 60 members with the right to speak and vote (*voz y voto*). The committee was also to function by commissions (meaning that a several-member committee would fill a secretarial role instead of one official; the duties would thus be handled by teams). Delegates to the precongress also voted to allow former executive members to participate again as candidates to the new committee, yet they made all officers subject to recall.[27]

A multiple choice method—considered by many to be the most democratic—was used to select the 13 officers from among 280 registered candidates. From these 280, 60 with the most votes were subjected to another round of voting, from which 20 were selected and so on, until 13 candidates remained, and the one with the most votes from this group became secretary-general. In this particular instance the voting lasted seven hours (Hernández 1984:9). In both the 1982 Oaxaca congress and the Chiapas congress candidates were not explicitly linked to a particular office on the executive committee. Instead, offices were ranked and candidates occupied the position indicated by the number of votes they received in relation to other candidates. Those who opted for this method apparently thought this was the fairest way to proceed, although some delegates complained that in this way one could not always select the candidate who might be best suited to a particular office.

The committee that was finally chosen reflected a balance of the different political groups in the movement. In repudiation of what were perceived as behind the doors machinations to secure positions on the committee, delegates had placed in the secretary-general position an "independent": a man who had no known political ties nor following.

In the days surrounding the congress representatives of the national executive committee and Vanguardia had unleashed a full publicity campaign against the democratic movement. The substantial funding behind this effort was evident from the full page newspaper ads, radio announcements, and the increase in the number of people commissioned by the national union to work full time in the campaign.[28] On the day of the congress former SNTE secretary José Luis Andrade Ibarra held a meeting at the site of the precongress, but several thousand teachers gathered outside the building to ensure that the elections would not be interrupted. The congress itself was held only after late-night,

27. *Educador Socialista* 1984:8, Foweraker 1993:70.
28. *Educador Socialista* 1984, Hernández 1986a:70.

last-minute negotiations with the secretary-general of the local, and against the wishes of one of the national union committee members sent to preside over the event (another national official in favor of holding the congress won out) (Hernández 1984:10).

The congress was therefore held on March 9, 1984, in the presence of a national union representative, with 260 out of 265 delegates present. The list of candidates was approved quickly; by midday the congress was officially over. Outside, hundreds of teachers stood guard by the congress site in Tuxtla Gutiérrez, the state capital, and a statewide work stoppage was in effect throughout the days of the congress.

After the democratic electoral victory local vanguardistas went on the offensive. They sought out allies among city and state officials and penetrated the administration of the state SEP (especially the various branches of the Department of Regional Services), from where they would attempt to win over supporters by handling job-related requests submitted to their offices (SNTE. Sección 7. CES. 1984). Officials from the USED and ISSSTE began to deal with the vanguardistas, acting under pressure or from commitments with members of Vanguardia. In time it became more difficult for "democratic" members to obtain short-term loans, the SEP-union joint commissions no longer functioned, and USED administrators tried to reverse a number of earlier agreements they had made with the local concerning transfers, hiring, exchanges, and so forth. There was also a "general restriction in all services and benefits of the ISSSTE."[29]

After 1985 state and union officials' closure in response to movement demands became even more marked. With Miguel González Avelar as head of the Education Ministry the SNTE was able to make greater inroads into the state SEP delegations (Martínez Assad and Ziccardi 1988:37–38).[30] National union officials began their campaign to wear out the movement in Oaxaca by extending, then retracting, authorization for elections to renew the local executive committee. This went on over a period of four years. As a result, a committee that was to have remained in office for only three years, in accordance with union statutes, was forced to remain at the head of the local for seven. In this interim SEP and Interior Ministry officials displayed no real willingness to intervene to resolve the conflict.

The weakness of the CNTE during this period and the different timing of conflicts in Chiapas and Oaxaca also weakened these movements' resistance to

29. SNTE. Sección 7. 1984a; SNTE. Sección 7. CES. 1984:5.
30. For more detail see Chapter 3.

national union officials' attacks. By 1984 Chiapas and Oaxaca were practically all that was left of the CNTE. The vanguardistas' advances in the schools and delegations, the increase in administrative repression by the SEP, the meager wage advances, and the continuing economic crisis had begun to take their toll. Many rank-and-file teachers came to mistrust participation in the union and became disaffected from both Vanguardia and the CNTE (Equipo Pueblo 1984:2–3). The CNTE's efforts to form alliances with other popular sectors and to take the offensive with civic strikes in 1983 and 1984 also did not succeed in mobilizing additional member support; participation in the strikes was heavily debated, and one of the most important CNTE contingents, Chiapas, did not participate in 1983 (Hernández 1986b:68–69). Many disillusioned teacher activists began to work on other fronts. Some threw their efforts into the Asamblea Nacional Obrero Campesino Popular (National Worker Peasant Popular Assembly, ANOCP), a coalition of popular organizations formed in 1983; others worked more intensively in the peasant movement.[31]

Between October 1986 and March 1987 in Chiapas, as the date of new committee elections again drew near, teachers engaged in an intense period of mobilizations in demand of wage increases, authorization for the third electoral congress, and freedom for jailed teachers and peasant leaders. (In May of 1986 the governor had jailed several peasant leaders, a journalist, and three teachers, including the former secretary-general of Local 7, for protesting with corn farmers—including members of the official CNC—to support an increase in the government's guaranteed prices for corn [Hernández Aguilar 1986].) At the same time, vanguardistas gained strength within the USED, and its director took clear steps to repress the democratic movement. In February–March 1987, for example, the USED director fired more than 100 teachers, withheld the wages of another 1,800, and levied approximately fifty administrative sanctions per day against dissident teachers in the course of their sixty-two-day work stoppage (Campa 1988).

During this period teachers organized a permanent *plantón* in the main plaza of Tuxtla Gutiérrez and a "Dignity Camp" (*campamento de la dignidad*) in the atrium of the cathedral in downtown Mexico City. Teachers made their way from Chiapas to Mexico City on foot, in buses and trucks, and by hitching rides. They lived off the food, water, money, and medicines donated by the

---

31. The efforts of one of Local 7's leaders to involve the teachers' movement more in supporting local peasant organizations was heavily criticized by the state assembly in 1985, however, exemplifying the important internal differences over the role of the teachers' organizations in relations with other sectors. For more discussion on the relations between the teachers' movement and other popular organizations see Chapter 6.

communities they passed through. Medical teams from Oaxaca and the university in Puebla treated participants for heatstroke, sunburn, diarrhea, and blisters. Once in Mexico City teachers sported t-shirts reading "Visit Chiapas and enjoy its repression." Most protesters slept on the streets of the capital or inside the gate of the National Cathedral. Neighbors, students, unions, and popular organizations donated tents, food, water, and medical care. Flu, colds, and stomach problems were common, and the donated blankets and plastic sheets could barely keep out the cold and rain. During the day the teachers set out to speak at schools and subways, where they collected donations and informed Mexico City residents of the reasons for their protest, since the major news media tended to ignore them or portray them in a negative light.

In spite of these extensive efforts the teachers' demands were not met. On the day that Local 7's elections should have been held, exactly six years after the first democratic victory, the national executive committee of the SNTE decertified the Chiapas local executive committee, arguing that the local had "provoked division and confrontation within the union" (Campa 1988). News of the decertification shocked and demoralized teachers throughout the movement.

Protests and mobilizations of the movement continued for several weeks after the decertification, both in Chiapas and in Mexico City, and left one teacher dead, shot by gunmen in Tuxtla Gutiérrez on March 30, 1987.[32] Within a week, however, national union officials had installed an executive commission composed of eight vanguardistas and seven democratic movement members. The decertification of the executive committee and the negotiating commission's acceptance of a commission composed of vanguardistas and movement people provoked fierce debate within the Chiapas movement and deepened existing divisions. Two key factions within the movement—the trotskyists and the so-called "clasistas"—opposed the commission, as did much of the membership, who was prepared to continue to mobilize in repudiation of the national committee's maneuver. After further infighting over who would participate on the executive commission, forces linked to the incumbent leaders withdrew their candidates after they were charged by their political opponents with negotiating among themselves to retain their influence on the new commission. As a result, the two groups who had most vehemently opposed the commission were elected to sit on it as the movement representatives alongside the vanguardistas.

32. Celso Wenceslao López Díaz, twenty-nine years old, was shot by a local vanguardista, allegedly under the supervision of one of the union's top officials and a former secretary-general of the SNTE, José Luis Andrade Ibarra.

Divisions within the movement grew as members of Línea Proletaria who had been in power refused to recognize the authority of the commission and set about to reestablish the CCLs as a counterauthority. One immediate consequence of this arrangement was the existence of two leaderships within the movement. The other result was the disillusionment and apathy of the membership, expressed as desertion from the dissident ranks (Campa 1988). Many teachers stopped participating in movement activities and began to take their grievances to national executive committee representatives on the commission, who in turn were eager to drain the movement of supporters. The director of the USED, meanwhile, remained in his position and continued to exercise administrative repression against the teachers. He specifically blocked matters handled by the democratic representatives on the executive commission.

Such factional infighting in the Chiapas movement had alienated much of the membership and signaled to national union officials that they might be able to dismantle the eight-year-old dissident movement by capitalizing on these internal divisions. Two political groups in particular were important at the beginning of the Chiapas movement and remained in conflict throughout the 1981–87 period: the trotskyists, who were concentrated in the technical high schools and played a central role in the emergence of the movement in the north of the state, and members who emerged from the rural normal school Macumatzá in Tuxtla Gutiérrez, Chiapas, and were linked to Línea Proletaria, an organization with maoist roots and a history of successful grass-roots organizing in poor urban neighborhoods and some industrial unions throughout Mexico.[33]

Línea Proletaria members' close ties with the rank-and-file and their tendency not to identify themselves as part of a distinct political current helped them to win the majority of executive committee positions in Chiapas during the first democratic congress in 1981. Those linked to Línea Proletaria were apparently tolerated because they did not initially try to dominate the local leadership as a distinct group. The trotskyists were reportedly identified with more extremist, "all-or-nothing" positions and denounced for pursuing party interests. In a struggle to retain influence, members of the trotskyist group tried to disclose the links between the new leadership and Línea Proletaria.[34] Eventually both groups were "discovered" by the membership (SNTE. Sección 7. n.d.:33).

33. The trotskyists were linked to the Partido Revolucionario de los Trabajadores (Revolutionary Workers' Party, PRT), the Mexican branch of the Fourth International, formed in 1976.
34. Transcribed interviews with members of the Coordinadora del Centro, Chiapas, n.d., p. 5.

The trotskyists' early reputation as the ideologues of the movement was eventually usurped by Línea Proletaria. Members of Línea Proletaria soon acquired a reputation as the intellectuals of the movement "because they knew how to do the bulletins."[35] Eventually they also became known as the ones who did the more "comfortable" work—they remained in the city, stayed in hotels, and handled negotiations with the authorities—and were seen as increasingly divorced from the membership. Over time, differences between the secretary-general of the 1981–84 committee, Manuel Hernández, and the other executive committee members who belonged to Línea Proletaria grew, ostensibly over the issue of involvement with the membership. The secretary-general had a large following among the membership because his supporters were the ones who traveled to the remote regions of the state in order to preside over meetings and talk with the teachers.[36] He was also active in the independent peasant movement and frequently tried to bring the two movements closer together. The committee's conflict with the secretary-general may also have stemmed from the perception of other committee members that his growing personal popularity and power represented a threat to Línea Proletaria's hegemony in the leadership of the Chiapas movement. Hernández was criticized in June 1982 in the movement newspaper for his *caudillismo* (Campa 1988). In 1983 he formally split from Línea Proletaria, yet remained head of the union local. Thereafter he and his supporters became known as the "populists" because of their popular appeal and work with the rank-and-file.

Although everyone was aware of the presence of political factions in the state assembly and in the executive committee, any overt reference to these groups by their own members was interpreted as an attempt to impose group interests over the interests of the whole organization. Among the rank-and-file the perception of rampant political factionalism or of the dominance of group interests was demoralizing, yet members of the state assembly continually called for unity. When members of Línea Proletaria signed a document as Línea Proletaria in June 1983, it signaled their first public attempt as a group to secure their continued presence on the executive committee. This action cost Línea Proletaria support.[37] Evidence of the group's loss of legitimacy was seen in the 1984 elections for executive committee, in which a man with no political ties and no particular following was voted in as secretary-general. The outcome of

35. Ibid., p. 3.
36. Ibid., p. 4.
37. Ibid., p. 5.

this election was interpreted by many as member repudiation of political groups' efforts to dominate the leadership of the movement and their antidemocratic maneuvering for positions on the committee.[38]

After the election of the second executive committee in 1984, a third group composed mostly of younger activists began to emerge. This group, which included an array of political organizations of greater or lesser radicalism, was referred to as *"ultras"* (for "ultra-left") by those outside of it and *"clasistas"* by themselves. Up until this time their presence at the state assemblies had been limited.[39] Members from some of these currents admitted that they had been unsuccessful at advancing alternative proposals in the state assemblies because of a lack of coordination among them, the newness of their organizations, and their weak political and theoretical backgrounds. Most of their members, they argued, did not speak at assembly meetings and instead participated mostly as "activists" (COSDE 1987:14). Nonetheless, the *clasistas* acquired a greater resonance with the membership in the period surrounding what was to be the third local electoral congress in 1987. The increase in their status and influence was due largely to the membership's disillusionment with the infighting at the committee level, which had become quite public, as well as to the growing sense that the committee was selling out to the enemy at a time when renewed attacks on the movement by the SEP and union officials required greater resistance. By that time Línea Proletaria was widely viewed as a group that was willing to form alliances and negotiate deals with authorities at any cost to the movement in an effort to remain in power in the next election.[40] The lines were drawn between those accused of being *gobiernistas*—those who tried to contain the mobilizations in an effort to reestablish contacts with officials and who were identified with Línea Proletaria—and the "independents" or *clasistas*, who felt that mobilization should take priority over relations with officials (COSDE 1987:6–7).[41]

Oaxaca: *"Queremos Congreso"*

In Oaxaca the local executive committee was due to be renewed in February 1985, exactly three years after its democratic congress. During a period of four

38. Specifically, it was a response by the congress delegates to the discovery that members of Línea Proletaria, the "populists," and followers of the former finance secretary were trying to negotiate positions within the committee "behind the backs of the base" (Campa 1988).
39. Among these were the Corriente Democrática Magisterial, CODEMA; Corriente Sindical Democrática, COSDE; Unión de Trabajadores de la Educación, UTE; 27 de abril, and others.
40. Transcribed interviews with Coordinadora del Centro of Chiapas, p. 5.
41. For a more detailed account of the factional struggles within the Chiapas movement see Foweraker 1993: chap. 6.

months between December 1984 and March 1985 the executive committee in Oaxaca appealed to national union officials, the interior minister, and the governor for authorization of its electoral congress, but the union leadership conditioned authorization of the congress on being able to negotiate representation on the local committee. Meanwhile, the governor stated that he was trying to intervene with union officials on behalf of the movement, which led the union to accuse both the USED and the governor of being accomplices of the Oaxacan teachers and of tolerating repression against vanguardistas.

On February 9 the SNTE's national executive committee denied authorization for the Oaxaca congress, claiming a "lack of appropriate conditions."[42] In response, the movement escalated the mobilizations. A contingent of about 1,300 people began a march from Oaxaca to Mexico City (a distance of 545 kilometers) in protest of the delays. But the march was lifted before reaching the capital, after the negotiating team in Mexico City accepted a document (which officials from the SEP and the Ministry of the Interior signed as witnesses) that offered to grant authorization of the congress in exchange for the reinstatement of vanguardista teachers expelled in Oaxaca and for the establishment of national executive committee offices in the state.

This arrangement provoked serious internal dissent. It was felt that the negotiating commission had succumbed too soon, when the mobilizations had not yet reached their peak. Convinced that a deal had been negotiated with officials behind their backs, some members called for the removal of the secretary-general. Cooler heads prevailed, however, arguing that such divisiveness would play into the hands of their opponents.

Again, a congress date was set for April, and again it was postponed until June. Teachers held their assemblies to elect delegates for the precongress in June, but the election of a majority of more "radical" delegates led union officials to retract their authorization, after unsuccessful efforts to negotiate for representation on the executive committee.[43] In a letter announcing the decision on June 14, 1985, the national committee argued that actions promoted by diverse political currents within the movement had led to instability and the lack of guarantees for vanguardistas participating in the process.

42. *Meridiano 100*, Suplemento 1, Oaxaca, Oaxaca, April 16, 1985.
43. According to one document, the reason positions for Vanguardia on the committee were rejected by the membership was because such a concession would violate "the democratic electoral process which in Oaxaca does not permit anyone to occupy a position on the committee unless they have been elected by the membership. Second, Vanguardia will use one or more positions to form a beachhead or spurious government, to which it can give all its support, recognition, and legal authority to handle teachers' job-related matters, gradually taking over the executive committee" (Frente Magisterial Independiente Nacional 1985:6).

One interpretation of these events maintained that the secretary-general and secretary of organization of the executive committee had been promised elections "without conditions"—without vanguardista participation on the committee—if indeed they could secure a committee with a majority of moderate members. When in fact the assembly elections produced a majority of more radical delegates, the national committee retracted its authorization and the local committee leaders adopted a "radical" position in which they refused to negotiate with national union officials and instead sought continuation of the existing local committee (FMIN 1985:33). In any case, armed with the sole authority to convene local elections, national union officials appeared to be biding their time, waiting for the moment when the Oaxaca movement would be sufficiently weakened or divided for them to decertify the committee or gain some presence on it.

At the June 1985 state assembly, attended by both assembly representatives and recently selected congress delegates, the conflict with the leadership came to a head. There was an intense debate over how to proceed with respect to the congress, but in synthesis the response of the representatives present (and of one or two members of the executive committee) was to reject the "option" of negotiating representation on the executive committee and to retain the present committee, not because members had confidence in their leaders but because the movement faced a "critical situation" (FMIN 1985:26). The representatives resolved to resist the national executive committee by establishing a regional, state, and national plan of action that involved working to increase member participation in base-level organizations, improving relations with members of the community, setting out on information brigades throughout the country, and working closely with other members of the CNTE in an effort to break out of the isolation in which the Oaxaca movement found itself. Expanding member participation on the executive committee was also proposed. It was decided to do this with thirty-five people, five from each of the seven regions. Their job would be to write papers and political documents, organize and participate in brigades, handle transfers and other labor problems during summer vacation, develop petitions for the different sectors (teachers and parents) and levels, and keep alive the demands for the congress (FMIN 1985:23, 30). Significantly, the movement reacted to the pressure and attacks by authorities not by buttressing its bureaucratic aspects but by extending "horizontally" and developing its mobilizational capacity and democratic features.

The heated internal debate over the election issue reflected in part different understandings of what was at stake if the democratic locals in Oaxaca and Chiapas were to accept a congress "with conditions"—with vanguardista participation on the committee. One perspective held that a negotiated vanguardista participation would mean the end of the movement by providing opponents with a beachhead from which to take over the local (FMIN 1985:6). Compromising the movement's autonomy, then, implied compromising its ability to survive as well. Others believed there was little choice; to refuse the congress with conditions could provoke decertification by the national committee anyway. It was therefore necessary to compromise autonomy for the survival of the movement—of its legal-formal status. This had been the position of the Chiapas negotiating team in 1987, who saw accepting the commission with vanguardistas on it as the only way to keep from "falling into illegality" (COSDE 1987). Nonetheless, the majority of the members of the state assembly in Oaxaca were adamant in their refusal to accept a congress with conditions, even though authorization of the congress by national union officials hinged on this acceptance. To members, legal status was apparently not as important as the existence of the movement in fact, through the consolidation of its base organizations, horizontal alliances, and internal democracy. Success—survival as a movement—would depend on strengthening these "internal" factors in areas that the movement could control in order to stand up to national officials on an issue over which the movement controlled very little—the issue of whether or not it retained its formal status.

In early 1986 the electoral congress in Oaxaca was again set for January 27 and 28. The precongress began on January 26 and went on for over forty-eight hours. Delegates elected a representative from the Isthmus as secretary-general, along with a slate of representatives who were "close to the base"—whose movement credentials were strong. However, the national executive committee declared the selection of delegates invalid and canceled the congress.

Mobilizations were again planned in order to pressure union officials. The actions were extensive, very combative, and received solidarity from many sectors of the population, particularly impressing the residents of Mexico City.[44] Furthermore, the extent of member participation in these actions was remarkable given that the sole demand was a political one—union democracy. In contrast with actions at the beginning of the movement, these demonstrated a commitment to the issue of elections and revealed the way in which a political consciousness had developed over years of participation in the movement and the democratic local. The actions continued into March and included a

---

44. See Sindicato Nacional de Trabajadores de la Educación, Sección 22, Comisión de Información y Difusión and D-I-211 (Coalición de Promotores), 1986, *Ataca Oaxaca* (Mexico: Equipo Pueblo, Información Obrera, Leega); and Monsiváis 1987.

caravan-march of 2,000 teachers to Mexico City, an encampment before the offices of the SEP and SNTE in the capital, and hunger strikes in the main cathedral of Mexico City and in Oaxaca.

Teachers participated in these events at tremendous personal cost, most evident in the case of the hunger strikers, who literally risked their lives for the demands of their movement, but also in the case of the marchers and of others who remained at home but still supported the work stoppages and protest actions. Marchers were treated for blisters and gastrointestinal and respiratory illnesses along the way and returned to complete the walk to the capital. Mothers left children with relatives in order to participate. Participants did not know whether they would fall ill, suffer repression, or be docked wages for their support of the movement, yet their commitment was total. As one young hunger striker put it, "Many would have us believe that democracy is impossible in the SNTE. But as long as they don't kill us we will continue to believe the opposite" (Monsiváis 1987:179).

Teachers were forced to lift the strike on March 17, 1986, without a date for the elections, but also without having accepted national officials' terms for a mixed commission to prepare elections in which vanguardistas would have played a role. The mobilizations of 1986 showed that the strikes were no longer effective in securing movement demands in the face of union *and* government authorities' refusal to grant access. Although the actions had been impressive from the standpoint of their size, duration, and the unity expressed by the movement, they differed from past mobilizations in that a single political demand was being advanced. While other regional contingents extended their solidarity to the Oaxacan teachers, the demand for authorization of the Oaxacan electoral congress did not directly include them, and in any case other regions were too weak at the time for their support to have been decisive. The extensive participation by Oaxacan teachers and favorable public opinion, however, did enable the movement to avoid both decertification and the imposition of an executive committee with vanguardista participation.

After this period of mobilizations union officials stepped up their attacks. The USED in Oaxaca began to employ vanguardistas, who in turn tried to block the local executive committee's appeals to that office.[45] In May 1986 the national executive committee also cut off finances to the local, in spite of the fact that dues continued to be discounted from member paychecks.[46] Vanguard-

---

45. See "Carta de la CNTE a Bartlett" in *La Jornada*, October 23, 1987, p. 2. Also interviews with Oaxaca teachers and member of the local executive committee, Oaxaca, April 3, 1987.

46. Oaxacan teachers, no longer able to afford donations to the movement from their paychecks, began to participate in new forms of fundraising that were more personal in nature: bazaars and

istas were sent to work at schools, ignoring earlier SEP-union local agreements on criteria for transfers and hiring. Vanguardista takeovers of schools and the ensuing conflicts that emerged with democratic teachers and communities also served as a pretext for national union officials to deny authorization of electoral congresses.[47] As a result, movement resources were displaced to these frontlines of battle in the schools, and conflict with the USED increased. The SEP became more clearly defined as an enemy, acting in collusion with union officials. The resulting decline in the local committee's ability to resolve teachers' needs left members vulnerable to vanguardista offers to solve their problems. The movements were thus forced to fight opponents locally even though the causes of the movement's containment were national.

Violence, intimidation, and harassment of dissident members were further features of an official strategy to combat the movement. Some members of the CNTE placed the number of teachers killed or wounded over the course of the movement at one hundred in Oaxaca alone.[48] The often confusing circumstances and isolated locations of the killings make it impossible to determine exactly how many of these individuals had been targets of political violence due to their participation in union or peasant opposition activities, but conflicts with rural caciques or municipal presidents, often closely tied to or themselves vanguardistas, left many community activists and teachers dead.[49] Indigenous bilingual teachers, often leaders in peasant and community struggles with caciques, were frequent victims. Government attention to and punishment of these crimes was one of the movement's most consistent and unheeded demands. Other forms of collective and individual harassment, intimidation, and provocation were commonplace. The home of the secretary-general of the Oaxaca local was fired upon, and a member of the dissident movement in Chiapas was detained on a trumped-up murder charge and tortured by state police, to name just two of many examples.[50]

---

other kinds of sales, where teachers sold items they had made, film viewings, and collections from the public (*boteos*) (interview with high school teacher, Oaxaca, April 3, 1987).

47. Examples of the violence that sometimes erupted from placing vanguardistas in the schools can be seen in "El asesinato de un maestro en Oaxaca, denuncia la CNTE," in *La Jornada*, October 22, 1987. Also see examples in "La violencia charra," a pamphlet published jointly by Equipo Pueblo, Información Obrera, and the CNTE, 1988.

48. In 1989 the Mexican news agency Notimex reported that 150 union dissidents had been killed since the beginning of the movement (*Unomásuno*, April 24, 1989).

49. For cases of human rights abuses in rural Oaxaca and Chiapas see Amnesty International 1986, in particular the cases of Paulino Martínez Delia, bilingual teacher and leader of the Movement of Triqui Unification and Struggle (MULT), and Víctor Pineda Henestrosa, a primary schoolteacher and active member of the COCEI.

50. See Candelaria Rodríguez, "Denuncia la Sección VII del SNTE arbitraria detención de

The appointment of Heladio Ramírez López as governor of Oaxaca in December 1986 was believed to represent the government's interest in containing increasing social and political conflicts in that state through negotiation rather than repression. Ramírez was hailed by some sectors in Oaxaca as a reformer, and his indigenous ethnic background (he was a Mixteco) led some to suggest he would be more sympathetic to demands from popular organizations in the state.[51] Some leaders of the teachers' movement remained skeptical, however, noting in early 1987 that the governor had not even received them to hear their demands.[52] At the same time, the secretary-general of the teachers' local apparently appealed to the new governor in private, asking him to mediate in the teachers' conflict. This fueled suspicions among members about the secretary's contacts with officials and his efforts to demobilize the movement. By the end of 1987 the governor had intervened with President de la Madrid and President-elect Salinas on behalf of long-standing economic and social, but not political, demands of the movement.[53]

By 1987 teachers changed their tactics in an effort to conserve their energy and rebuild their relationship with the parents, which had been strained due to the strikes. Rather than repeat the large mobilizations of previous years, teachers were rotated into smaller *plantones* for three days at a time, allowing the majority of teachers to remain at work. Leaders worked hard to retain their access to the USED and to government officials. Still, the debate and negotiations over the Oaxaca local's elections continued through 1987 and 1988, revealing differences over how to interpret political opportunities to act and over each group's willingness to risk the loss of formal status. One group within the movement argued that the conjuncture of the economic crisis and upcoming presidential elections favored mobilizations and solidarity with other sectors battered by the crisis. According to this faction, a government-union strategy to decertify the movement should be resisted with large national mobilizations in Mexico City. Even if the national union leadership should decertify the local executive committee, however, the increasing organization and political

---

maestro," *La Jornada*, October 21, 1987; and Candelaria Rodríguez, "Aparece con huellas de golpes Luciano Hernández, del SNTE," *La Jornada*, October 22, 1987. On other cases of violence in Oaxaca see "Carta de la CNTE a Bartlett," *La Jornada*, 23 October 1987, p. 2. The pamphlet "La violencia charra" also lists various eye-witness accounts of intimidation, harassment, and conflict between vanguardistas and movement teachers.

51. Interview with advisor to Coalición de Promotores Indígenas, Oaxaca, June 14, 1990.
52. Interview with local executive committee member, Oaxaca, February 1987.
53. See "Mexicanos esforzados, llamó Heladio Ramírez a los coceístas ante MMH," *La Jornada*, October 16, 1987; "Se atenderán demandas de maestros de Oaxaca y Chiapas," *La Jornada*, October 17, 1987; and "Visos de solución al problema de los maestros de Oaxaca: Líderes," *La Jornada*, October 18, 1987.

consciousness of teachers were what really mattered in sustaining the movement (FMIN 1987).

Another point of view was reflected by the secretary-general of the local, who favored a committee that included members of Vanguardia because, he argued, they would be easier to deal with on the inside rather than as an outside enemy.[54] Still another perspective, which the Oaxaca movement eventually adopted, emphasized the importance of being able to handle member demands in order to maintain the legitimacy of union representatives and to strengthen the organizational development of the local.[55] This point led the group to argue that elections should not be the movement's only demand.[56] Rather, the most important issue was the removal of USED functionaries who blocked the committee's processing of members' requests and exercised administrative repression. Focusing the movement's demands and resources on this terrain was more likely to yield results, since the SEP could respond directly to the demands, and the state government could be used to pressure in this arena. In contrast, the demand for elections depended on a more obstinate national executive committee for response. Resolution of labor and administrative problems, the argument went, was the best way to consolidate the movement and keep the vanguardistas at bay.

The movement remained on the defensive throughout 1987; member disillusionment was reflected in the low turnout at the monthly state assemblies. The national committee's decertification of the democratic executive committee in neighboring Chiapas contributed to a growing sense of helplessness and isolation. In 1988 the Oaxaca movement again mobilized in Mexico City and Oaxaca in order to demand authorization of its congress, again with no results. Nonetheless, the Oaxaca movement remained unified between 1985–88, managing to avoid the divisive factionalism that had become public in the Chiapas leadership.

Although political factions also existed in the Oaxaca movement, these did not manage to overtake the movement in the way that they did in Chiapas. The political configuration of the executive committee (1982–89) in Oaxaca was quite varied. The secretary of organization, the second most important position in the committee, went to a man linked to the PRI. The secretary-general was not associated with any particular political party but was suspect to more radical members because of his prior relationship with the former local union boss, Ernesto Aguilar Flores, and because of his close relationship with

---

54. Interview with former secretary-general of Oaxaca local, Oaxaca, June 14, 1990.
55. See Movimiento Democrático Magisterial, *Praxis*, February 18, 1987.
56. This argument was echoed by groups within the Chiapas movement in 1986, who pointed to the isolation and failure of the Oaxaca movement during its mobilizations of March–April 1986.

the secretary of organization. At least two other members of the committee belonged to the Revolutionary Teachers' Movement, linked to the Unified Socialist Party of Mexico. The other members had no obvious links with political organizations, although assistants incorporated later included members from a range of more "radical" groups (UTE, Praxis, and others). As in Chiapas, each of the groups in the leadership had its own followers among delegation leaders and members of the state assembly. Leaders in Oaxaca rarely referred to their political affiliations, but they were identified politically in documents and during assemblies in attacks by different political currents on individuals in the leadership.

As with the Chiapas movement, in Oaxaca differences developed between a leadership defined as *gobiernista* and an activist membership in the state assemblies that favored mobilization, stronger cooperation with other members of the CNTE, and a stronger relationship with parents. During the period in which the Oaxaca local was fighting for its electoral congress, tensions between the secretary-general in particular and representatives in the state assembly were especially high. During these years—1985 to 1988—the secretary-general became increasingly isolated and ineffectual in state assemblies. Yet the state assembly refrained from removing him or renewing the executive committee outside of authorized elections because they feared that this action would provoke national union officials. In 1987 many members of the state assembly believed that the tensions between the secretary-general and the membership had been encouraged deliberately by union and government officials so that members would push for new elections during a period of weakness, when the movement was least able to mobilize supporters to ensure fair elections. An electoral congress at that time would have been vulnerable to manipulation by vanguardistas. In this context state assembly members tolerated the executive committee but continued to vote against the secretary-general on most issues.[57] Many dissatisfied members consequently viewed the secretary-general as *"un mal necesario"* (a necessary evil). Outside of the state assembly and urban areas, however, much of the rank-and-file membership continued to view the executive committee as a group to whom loyalty was owed.

Conclusion

The movement's goal of democratizing the union had become identified with a legal and institutional strategy of organizing to win union local elections. The

57. Interview with member of the state assembly, Oaxaca, April 1, 1987.

advantage of legal status was that those movements that were able to win their locals could exercise some authority with the state, especially at the local level. Legality enabled the regional movements to engage in the day-to-day management of union affairs and to make significant changes affecting the welfare of teachers. Legality also offered legitimacy in the public eye and some measure of protection from repression. Moreover, legal status ensured continuity; it provided some structural supports to the movement-organization even during periods of demobilization. This was key: other movements that lacked legal status floundered when mobilizations waned and lost support when they could not attend to the needs of members. These structural supports would prove crucial when the movement surged again, as in 1989 when Oaxaca and Chiapas would emerge to play key roles in the mobilizations. The significance that formal status held under these conditions helps to explain why the defense of legality became so important for these movements.

At the same time, legal status posed a dilemma for the democratic locals. This dilemma was a direct consequence of the movement's location within an oligarchic and centralized union whose leaders were hostile to the movement. Securing and maintaining legal status entailed securing authorization for elections from the national executive committee of the union. This implied at a minimum extended negotiations with union officials and an effort to involve government officials in mediation (especially the Interior Ministry). It also required a strong show of strength in the states through mobilization of the membership, with the support of the CNTE and other groups, if possible. Under these conditions the existence of national political openings for the success of the movement's mobilizational strategy was crucial.

At the state level the creation of SEP delegations after 1978 had given dissident locals greater autonomy in negotiating some issues. However, this autonomy was still conditioned by what happened at the central level between the state and union leadership. National union officials pressuring after 1983 succeeded in changing conditions in the states so that dissident locals found it more difficult to manage and gains were increasingly limited. In particular, the rollback of earlier SEP reforms and the increased presence of unionists hostile to the movement in the state SEP administration after 1985–86 acted as a special constraint. Changes in the movement's political environment and, especially, the narrowing of political space called into question the effectiveness of the movement's mobilization strategy, and placed strong pressure on movement leaders to negotiate and compromise without mobilizing their forces. At the same time, members of the state assembly within the democratic locals kept pressure on their leaders, forcing them to remain accountable to the membership in spite of the lack of elections. The membership fought the persistent threat of cooptation and demobilization by drawing attention to the need to deepen democracy within the organization.

The struggle for elections was also a battle to sustain the movement's autonomy. Despite the internal debate on this issue, the dominant position of the membership of both movements was to avoid a "composite committee" (of vanguardistas and movement members), and thus a threat to movement autonomy, even if this signaled a loss of the movement's *capacidad de gestoría* (ability to negotiate the demands of the movement through legal channels). This was a complicated position and a difficult one to sustain, yet Oaxaca managed to do so until 1989, while in Chiapas acceptance of the composite committee was a leadership decision that was not subjected to consultation and was harshly criticized by the membership. Thus the battle to sustain legal-formal status was simultaneously a struggle to maintain the autonomy of the movement.

In spite of the tremendous organizational advances of both the Oaxaca and Chiapas movements, the divisions in the Chiapas leadership eventually became strong enough that they severely weakened the movement before national union authorities, paving the way for the decertification of 1987. These factional struggles for domination of the movement leadership were present from the beginning of the movement but were kept in check for some time through the procedures devised by the movement: a reliance on consultation with the membership and an open airing of disagreements in the state assemblies. However, it was these factions' manipulation and violation of these procedures that ultimately produced such harmful consequences for the movement and turned this factionalism into a force that seriously undermined the leadership. Nonetheless, the internal democratization of the regional movement had had positive consequences, namely, the development of a membership that, while disappointed in its leaders, continued to "own" the movement. In this way representatives to the state assembly struggled to rein in leaders and to combat factional divisions in the leadership, and rank-and-file teachers took decisions to mobilize to defend the movement and continued to develop a democratic project in the schools and delegations. Moreover, the selection of a "third group" of more radical and independent teachers to the executive commission in 1987 reflected the actions of an activist and aware membership and the fact that new leaders had become available and had emerged over the course of the movement.

The efforts of union and government officials to hinder the democratic locals' daily management of union affairs had several consequences. One consequence was that movement resources were channeled primarily into securing and defending basic rights and survival. When the movements' formal status was challenged by the national executive committee during periods of electoral renewal, the struggle to sustain and defend that status became the movements' greatest priority, despite internal differences on this strategy. As a result, few resources could be devoted to moving beyond the union issue to developing alternative projects in other important areas, such as improving education services to the community. Instead, members were subjected to a prolonged campaign of *desgaste*—of attempts to wear down the movement by limiting its ability to handle teachers' professional and economic demands and by threatening its survival through the withdrawal of legal status.

The other consequence of union and government resistance to the democratic locals was the locals' need to maintain some of their movement characteristics in spite of legality: they continued to rely on the mobilization of their members (in combination with negotiation) in order to pressure elites to concede to their demands. Key internal differences revolved around the emphasis granted to negotiation versus mobilization, tactical differences that were heightened by internal political disputes in both Chiapas and Oaxaca. Nonetheless, to the extent that the movements relied on recurrent mobilization to press their demands, this focused attention in turn on the importance of member participation in the decisions of the union local. This emphasis on member participation after legality further helped to counter oligarchic tendencies in the movement's organization and helped to strengthen the accountability of leaders to the membership.

At the same time, because the locals faced such tremendous opposition, union life was not allowed to become routinized. Instead, members were engaged in a constant struggle for their rights and demands, which facilitated the maintenance of an oppositional collective identity among the membership and which tempered the likelihood of open revolts against the leadership in Oaxaca and, for some time, in Chiapas as well. The following chapter further explores the changes in organizational structure, decision making, participation, leadership, and strategy that characterized the "inner life" of the Chiapas and Oaxaca movements as they struggled to sustain their legal status throughout the 1980s.

6
Sustaining the Movement
Democracy as Survival Strategy

¡El maestro luchando también está enseñando!
The teacher, by fighting, is also teaching!
—Teachers' march chant

After winning official recognition from national union authorities, the democratic locals in Oaxaca and Chiapas were faced with the twin challenges of meeting the everyday needs of their members and sustaining the democratic teachers' movement, whose national presence had begun to diminish. Teachers became concerned with creating an organization that could continue to struggle for the democratization of the union and against the obstacles placed by government and union officials who opposed the movement. In Oaxaca and Chiapas teachers set about to democratize everyday practices in the schools, school districts, and union locals, thereby constructing a regional model of what the teachers' movement wanted to achieve at the national level. Democracy—understood as regular, meaningful rank-and-file participation in everyday decision making, and through this process the eventual transformation and politicization of teachers' attitudes and actions—was valued as both an end and a means. In the words of members of the CNTE:

> We cannot reduce the democratization of the SNTE to the fact that the instances of union government are occupied by democratically elected representatives. This is but one aspect of democratization, necessary but incomplete. We democratize when we construct mechanisms and instances for collective decision making; when we enable the membership to decide the direction of the movement; when we create the most representative and collective forms of leadership possible. (Hernández and Pérez Arce 1982:206)

This chapter explores some of the internal changes these movements undertook in the process of democratizing their organization, and examines how these changes helped the movements meet numerous internal and external challenges to organizational stability. As noted in Chapter 2, such challenges are common to most social movements and include strong organizational tendencies toward oligarchy, cooptation, and the loss of membership support, as well as repression and bureaucratic harassment by government and union authorities. This chapter examines in detail the democratic union locals' organization, including the mechanisms they devised to secure member participation and leadership accountability, the key strategies of those regional movements that obtained and sustained legal status, and how this process of democratization became a central component of the teachers' movement's struggle for survival.

Legal and Extralegal Organization

When they first emerged, the dissident movements in Chiapas and Oaxaca organized within the union locals, forming new organizational structures that in some instances paralleled those stipulated in the union's statutes. After the formal certification of the democratic local executive committees in these states, both regional movements further altered their organizational structures in ways that combined the functions of the "extralegal" components of the organization with those that were "legal," or statutory (Peralta Esteva et al. 1985:36).[1] At first, and in an effort to guard against decertification by national union officials, the political leadership of the locals was concentrated in these

---

1. Many of the new organizational structures that the movement created within the locals were not prohibited by union statutes but neither were they expressly stipulated in the statutes (Hernández 1988:4).

parallel structures. With time, however, the statutory components of the local's organization came to play a stronger leadership role, eventually combining the processing of members' everyday requests and demands (*gestoría*) with political direction.

Many of these organizational changes involved the democratization of the union local by broadening membership participation in decision making, ensuring representation for members in the smallest units of organization (the workplace and delegation), and restricting hierarchy and centralized decision making. Leaders saw democratic organization as a way to avoid factionalism and conflict, and thus as a way to create the unity so necessary to resisting government and *vanguardista* efforts to dismantle the movement.[2]

The levels of organization within the union local that were stipulated in the SNTE statutes included the following: the executive committee, which typically consisted of thirteen officers, including the secretary-general; the executive committee of the delegation, with five officers; and the plenary of delegation representatives, composed of delegation secretaries-general, who were to meet annually or when called by the local executive committee (Diagram 6.1). This organizational structure placed much of the burden of decision making on the

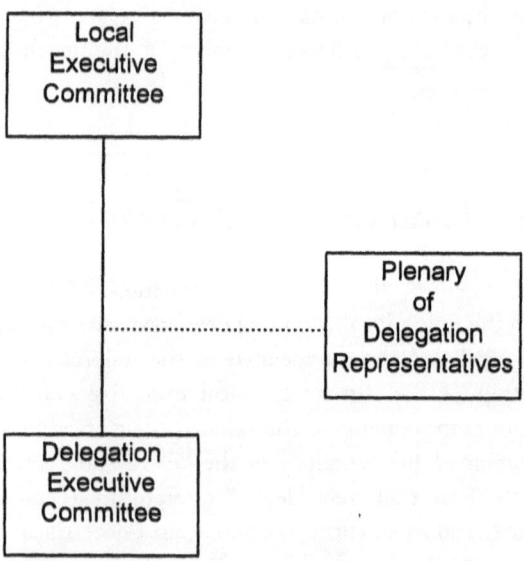

Diagram 6.1. Organizational structure of union local, SNTE

2. Interview with former executive committee member, Oaxaca, June 18, 1990.

executive committee of the local, which according to the statutes was also the only body that could authorize assemblies and elections at the delegation level. In practice, the plenary of delegation representatives met infrequently, and then often only to ratify the decisions already taken at the central executive level. In addition, union local elections were rarely fair electoral contests. Instead, local union bosses often handpicked the secretaries-general and electoral congresses were heavily manipulated. At best, union bosses respected various regional interests by alternating different groups' candidates in the leadership posts.

The movements in Chiapas and Oaxaca made several important changes in this organizational structure (Diagram 6.2). Both regional movements adopted the plenary of delegation representatives stipulated in the statutes and turned this institution into a more inclusive and more democratic representational organ with the primary decision-making responsibility in union local and movement affairs. This "State Assembly of Union Representatives" replaced the Chiapas movement's CCL and the Oaxaca movement's permanent assembly, although the new state assemblies contained many of the features of these earlier organizations.[3] The state assembly in both states became the "maximum organ of political leadership," the only body with the authority to legitimize a decision or agreement (SNTE. Sección 7. n.d.:21). In this way the state assembly replaced the local executive committee as the primary decision-making body. The assembly provided the directives, and members of the executive committee acted as "executors of the agreements of the membership before the different government branch offices."[4] Members of the state assembly also decided many strategic and tactical questions relating to the political development and struggles of the movement.

In order for the state assembly to play a central role in decision making leaders implemented three key changes that further distinguished this institution from its previous role. First, the state assembly met at least once a month, and more often if either the executive committee or a percentage of delegations felt it necessary. During mobilizations and periods of negotiations the state assembly

---

3. In Chiapas the state assembly was composed of three representatives per delegation—one representative from the executive committee and two noncommittee representatives from the base—or by two representatives per school or workplace that did not comprise a delegation (under forty members). (Elsewhere it is reported that the state assembly in Chiapas included three representatives per delegation and two per school—one base member and one union representative.) In Oaxaca one representative from the delegation executive committee and one from the delegation coordinadora, as well as representatives from regional and sector coordinadoras, attended the monthly state assembly.

4. Transcribed interviews with Comité Ejecutivo Seccional, Sección 7, n.d., p. 19.

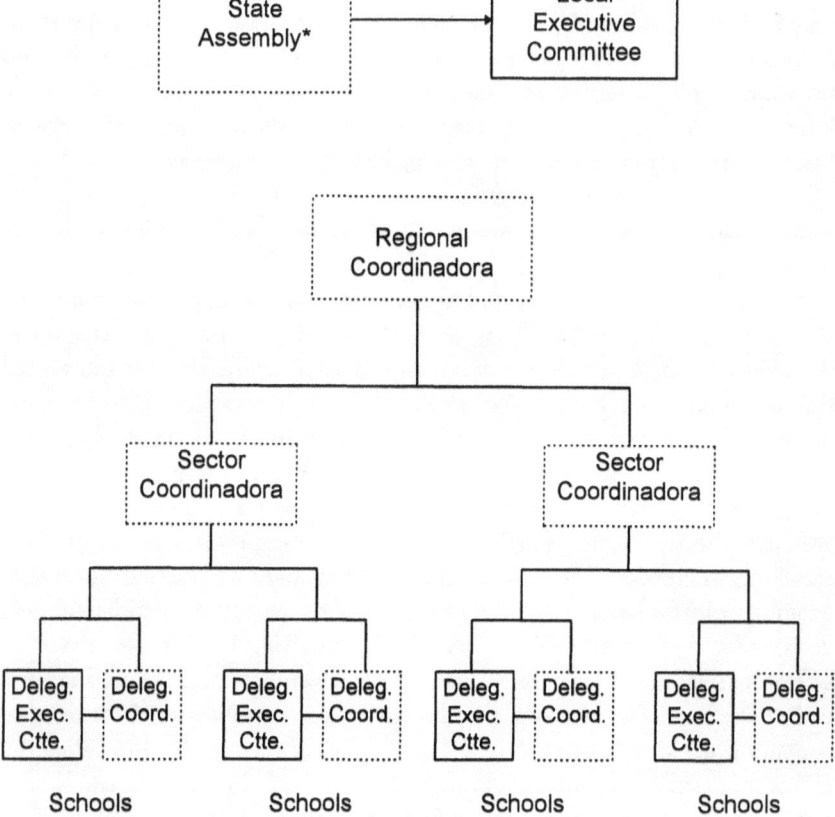

* The state assembly included representatives from each of the organizations shown.

.... = Non-statutory organizations
────────── = Statutory organizations

Diagram 6.2. Statutory and nonstatutory organizations in Local 22, Oaxaca, 1982–89

often met in "permanent session," and sometimes it met near the site of the negotiations so that negotiating commissions could confer more easily with the assembly. Second, the composition of the state assembly was expanded to include not just delegation secretaries but also representatives from nonstatutory "coordinadoras," in the case of Oaxaca, and rank-and-file delegation members, in the case of Chiapas.⁵ This meant that those granted decision-making authority included not just members of "official" levels of organization but also rank-and-file representatives from schools and workplaces or representatives from the parallel organizations. More important, the state assembly included people who could oversee what the elected delegation officials reported and decided in the assembly. Just as the state assembly could be expected to keep tabs on what local executive committee officers did, rank-and-file representatives and representatives from the coordinadoras in the state assembly could check the actions of delegation officers. The third important change in the state assembly had to do with the way decisions were made. State assembly representatives frequently returned to the rank-and-file membership—to delegation meetings, schools, and workplaces—to discuss the decisions before them in the state assembly and to register the opinions and the votes of the membership.

Not only did the centralized decision-making authority of the local executive committee change, but so too did the composition of the committee and the significance of committee positions (*secretarías*). For instance, executive committee members were voted into collective commissions rather than single-member offices. Formally, secretaries for each commission were named so as to adhere strictly to the stipulations of the union statutes and avoid legal challenges by the movement's political enemies.⁶ In practice, however, secretaries and commission members were equally responsible for the decisions and tasks of the commission. Moreover, all members of commissions or subcomisions were elected in the precongress and had equal responsibility before the membership (SNTE. Sección 7. 1984b). This arrangement distributed the work within the commissions and reduced the likelihood that individual members of the executive committee would be co-opted or renege on their duties. Other rank-and-file assistants were also incorporated to work on the commissions. These assistants were often drawn from among the younger, more politically radical and active members of the state assembly. Their inclusion in the tasks of the

---

5. The state assembly in Oaxaca included, in 1987, one representative from each of the *coordinadoras delegacionales* (458), one representative from each of the delegation executive committees (458), one representative from each *coordinadora de sector* (36), and all of the members from the *coordinadoras de región* (35). Also present at the state assembly were the members of the local executive committee and their assistants, which in 1987 totaled 63 people. (Interview with local executive committee member, Oaxaca, February 1987.) This figure was up 20 from 1985 (Equipo Pueblo 1985:8). See below for a description of the coordinadoras.

6. Commissions were also created in the delegation executive committees; in 1987 there were seven commissions at this level in Oaxaca.

commissions thus created an outlet for members who could potentially become part of a more disruptive internal opposition.

After the legalization of the executive committees in both states, members of the local created additional parallel organizations. Coordinadoras were formed at delegation, sector, and regional levels. In Oaxaca there was initially some tension over the formation of coordinadoras because of their informal status, and some members viewed the creation of these as a concession to groups within the movement who had been pushing for the formation of a CCL.[7] In Oaxaca the delegation coordinadoras were made up of five members elected by the school or workplace representatives gathered in a delegation assembly.[8] Members retained their position in the coordinadora for one year and could rotate into another position at that time during elections. The delegation coordinadora was given the specific task of carrying out political activities. Unlike the delegation committee, which mediated conflicts and handled requests for loans, transfers, and promotions, the coordinadora included a "political orientation" position to promote member participation, and educate and train members in democratic practice and union matters.

The coordinadoras undertook many of the activist tasks necessary to promote and sustain mobilizations and other collective activities. Besides the position of political orientation, members occupied positions in charge of press and propaganda and relations with the community and other delegations. Delegation coordinadoras also played a watchdog role that tended to set them apart from the executive committees. In some cases members of the coordinadoras even printed their own information bulletins for distribution to the delegation, underlining their separate but complementary functions.[9] In other instances the coordinadoras worked together with the executive committees, functioning like an expanded version of the executive committee. In some places, however, the coordinadoras did not function at all, or the same group of leaders moved among the coordinadora and committee positions year after year, forming "oligarchies" at the delegation level.[10] Still, the establishment of these parallel levels of organization within the delegation reflected the importance movement

---

7. SNTE. Sección 22. Comisión Ejecutiva. n.d.:28.
8. The delegation assembly consisted of the executive committee, members of the coordinadora, and school and workplace representatives (one per forty members). Offices in the executive committee included secretary-general, secretary of organization, finances, social assistance, youth and women. The delegation coordinadora contained the offices of organization, political orientation, press and propaganda, external relations, and finances (Equipo Pueblo 1985:8).
9. Personal communication with former movement activist, Oaxaca, November 15, 1987.
10. Interview with former executive committee member, Oaxaca, June 18, 1990.

leaders attributed to the political development of members, as well as their desire to create a minisystem of checks and balances that would hold officials elected to the statutory organizations in check. Another reason for the existence of these coordinadoras was tied more fundamentally to the issue of survival: if national union officials should decertify the executive committees of the dissident locals, it was believed that these parallel coordinadoras could then play a role as alternative delegation committees whose members would have the experience of political leadership and governance at the delegation level.

Other coordinadoras were formed in both Oaxaca and Chiapas after the electoral victories of the dissident movement in these locals. Regional and sector coordinadoras—intermediate-level organizations set up in order to identify the problems affecting a specific sector or region—assisted the executive committees in relaying information to regions and delegations and back to the state assembly and executive committee. In Oaxaca sector coordinadoras uniting several delegations were formed at the next level above the delegation. Representatives to these coordinadoras were named in sector assemblies attended by delegation coordinadoras and executive committees. The sector coordinadoras consisted of one representative from each of these bodies.[11] In some cases, however, sector assemblies also included the participation of rank-and-file teachers, and these could also be elected to the sector coordinadoras.

Regional coordinadoras were a response to the common problems faced by delegations in close regional proximity, and they helped to overcome the enormous communication and transportation difficulties within these states. In Oaxaca there were seven regional coordinadoras, each consisting of five members named in regional assemblies with the participation of one representative from each sector coordinadora. In Chiapas some regional coordinadoras were formed during the beginning of the movement, but these were developed further and more formally after the movement obtained legal status in 1981.[12] By 1987 there were ten regional coordinadoras in the state. Each contained between ten and forty delegations and had offices in the main municipalities of each region in the state.[13] Members of the regional coordinadoras were chosen in delegation assemblies from among volunteers who were most active in the movement.

The formation of these regional coordinadoras implied a decentralization of

11. Thirty-six sectors operated in Oaxaca in 1987.
12. The first regional coordinadoras were disbanded in Chiapas after the leadership of one of these tried to separate from the rest of the movement.
13. The union locals in Oaxaca and Chiapas divided the state into several distinct regions for organizational purposes, following accepted geographical and ethnic demarcations.

authority within the local: these regional offices negotiated loans, housing, payment problems, retirement, and related matters through the regional services departments of the SEP. In this way regional coordinadoras acted as branches of the executive committee and were able to resolve members' problems near their area of residence. The coordinadoras fulfilled an important political task, which was to respond directly to teachers' daily needs and complaints. Regional coordinadoras also carried out many functions of the executive committees at regional levels: they presided over assemblies when needed, analyzed documents, "oriented" the delegations, collected delegation opinions and synthesized them at the level of the regional coordinadora.[14] Through tighter control over activities in the region, these regional networks also made it easier to guard against the incursion of vanguardistas into the delegations (SNTE. Sección 7. n.d.:19). In sum, regional coordinadoras helped to secure greater cohesion at the rank-and-file level and made for a more efficient processing of grievances (Peralta Esteva et al. 1985:37). The proliferation of sector and regional coordinadoras also reflected the movements' greater attention to the professional needs of their members and the desire of movement leaders to distinguish themselves from the vanguardistas on this issue.

The organizational changes implemented by the teachers' movements in Oaxaca and Chiapas resolved several problems simultaneously. In the first place, the responsibility for making decisions was more widely shared, and there were more opportunities for members to participate in leadership positions because of the creation of the coordinadoras and the expansion of the state assemblies and the executive committees. This expanded organizational involvement, together with the presence of parallel organizations, provided insurance against the decertification of the union local leadership since practiced leaders and some form of organizational structure would be available to step in if the movement were to suddenly fall into illegality. Second, the political (mobilizational) and bureaucratic (*gestoría*) needs of the movement and the membership could be handled at the same time in this new expanded organizational structure; both "movement" and "union local" facets could be maintained and tended to. Finally, the organizational structure of the delegations and the composition of the state assembly provided for some vigilance over elected leaders, increasing the possibilities of achieving an accountable leadership in spite of the irregular occurrence of elections for the executive committees of the union locals.

---

14. Transcribed interviews with Comité Ejecutivo, Sección 7, n.d., p. 19.

Representation, Participation, and Accountability

Dissident teachers argued that under former local union governments members rarely participated in local decisions, member needs were not adequately represented by union leaders, and since elections were often manipulated, union leaders had little incentive to respond to the membership but looked instead to the union bosses who helped their careers. The dissident locals set about to change these practices by putting into effect those elements of the union statutes that were considered democratic and that had been neglected, and by creating new avenues for participation and new decision-making procedures where the statutes proved inadequate.

"Let the Membership Decide"

One of the key differences between former local union governments and the new dissident government was the latter's attention to rank-and-file opinion and decision making. The dissident locals institutionalized a process of "consultation with the membership" (*consulta a las bases*) that became the defining characteristic of the democratic teachers' movement. Many difficult decisions, particularly those that might divide the state assembly, were subjected to "*consulta*" as a way to reduce divisiveness, but also because members uniformly recognized the decisions reached in this way as the final word on a matter.

Both direct and representative forms of democracy were at work in the teachers' movements of Oaxaca and Chiapas. Even the representational form of decision making, however, relied heavily on the direct participation of rank-and-file members in the schools, work centers, and delegations.[15] Members elected workplace representatives to attend delegation assemblies, and they elected representatives from the delegation committees and coordinadoras to attend the state assembly, where the most important decisions affecting the local and the movement were taken. These representatives were often expected to report exactly what had been discussed and decided in delegation assemblies. The presence of rank-and-file members and of coordinadora representatives in

---

15. While representation in the coordinadoras recalled a pyramidal structure—sector and regional coordinadoras were selected in assemblies at the prior hierarchical level—representation in the state assembly was direct.

the state assembly further helped to ensure that the collective opinions and decisions of members were accurately reflected.

The method of decision making in the state assemblies of both locals was similar. State assembly delegates took the information and proposals that emerged during the assembly and presented them for review and consultation by the membership in the delegation assemblies. The rank-and-file representatives then took the proposals back to their workplaces, where they were discussed and where some agreement was reached and voted on. In order to ensure that base-level decisions and opinions were respected, school and workplace representatives had to carry with them to the next higher organizational level an *aval*—a document signed by all members of the workplace meeting, confirming who the representative was and what agreement had been reached. This was to guard against abuses of authority by elected representatives, as well as to prevent self-proclaimed "representatives" from attending and disrupting meetings. The agreement was then taken back to the delegation assembly, discussed and voted on, and this decision returned to the state assembly for final voting.[16] Thereafter, each delegation was expected to follow the decision reached by the state assembly.[17] In this way, according to one leader from Chiapas, "We are relieved from total responsibility in making a decision. . . . if they [the membership] make a mistake, it's their fault, but if they don't make a mistake, the victory is also theirs" (SNTE. Sección 7. n.d.:26).

Not every matter was given over to consultation, nor were all matters decided through the state assembly, but usually the most important matters were handled in this way. Decisions concerning whether or not to engage in an indefinite work stoppage, for instance, were typically turned over to the rank-and-file, while decisions to participate in one-day work stoppages were usually decided in the state assembly. Similarly, public announcements in the national press were sometimes approved in the state assembly, and other times they were handled within the executive committee. Decisions regarding whether to donate money or other forms of assistance were decided in the state assembly if the sum was small but discussed with the entire membership if the sum was large.[18] There were no hard and fast rules about what was subjected to *consulta*. Members of the state assembly could suggest turning any matter over, and a vote would decide how the issue was handled.

16. Equipo Pueblo 1985:9; SNTE. Sección 7. n.d.:26.
17. Transcribed unpublished interviews with the Coordinadora del Centro, Chiapas, n.d., pp. 6–7.
18. Interview with former executive committee member, Oaxaca, June 18, 1990.

During the state assembly itself, standard parliamentary procedure was followed. Meetings required a quorum; motions from the floor were seconded, then voted on, with usually a simple majority necessary to pass a vote, and usually everything that reached the state assembly was subjected to a vote. In one state assembly meeting I attended in Chiapas in 1985, motions from the floor were even taken to decide when to take a recess and how long the lunch break should be. In the middle of the night during another meeting members discussed what to do with a cow that had been donated by a peasant organization in solidarity. The seemingly endless suggestions from the floor only terminated after someone suggested that the cow be brought in to vote for herself!

Such practices often made these meetings tedious and long—fourteen or twenty-hour meetings were not unusual. Attendance was usually strictly monitored, with only certified representatives allowed to enter the meeting place and to vote, and frequently not permitted to leave until the meeting was over. Voting took place before everyone in the assembly, and even during the election of executive committee members in the precongresses and official congresses, delegates typically did not vote by secret ballot.[19]

The state assembly met at least once a month, and during mobilizations and work stoppages it met in permanent session. During these periods of conflict the permanent assembly often relocated to a site near the negotiating commission, which in turn met periodically with the assembly to discuss proposals and determine what course of action to take. Often it was deemed necessary to discuss matters at delegation and workplace levels, in which case state assembly representatives returned to their delegations to consult with members and reconvened as a state assembly at a later date. There were some differences between structures in the Oaxaca and Chiapas locals, but the process of consultation with the membership in delegation assemblies and workplace meetings was the same.

The movement's shift in emphasis to member participation in decision making—*"que la base decida"* (let the rank-and-file decide)—was supported by changes in the flow of information (bottom-up as well as top-down) and in the location of decision making. The latter was shifted to the most representative structures within the movement organization, from the local executive committee to the state assembly. The primacy of the state assembly over the executive committee in deciding guidelines for action, the decentralization of decision making to instances closer to the problem—at delegation, sector, and regional

---

19. The assembly could make the decision to vote by secret ballot if it so chose; the method of voting was often decided on each occasion.

levels—the existence of a parallel coordinadora within the delegation in charge of encouraging participation and checking abuses of power by committee members—all represented efforts to involve union members in decisions that affected them and all involved some degree of vigilance of elected union officials. Furthermore, in contrast with the period before 1979, the frequency of meetings allowed members to gain experience in discussing and resolving their own problems. As one leader from Chiapas noted, the monthly state, delegation, and workplace meetings meant that "meetings are not only held in order to decide on mobilizations, but especially to address concrete problems of interest to the members, which has turned the practice of discussion and decision making into a daily activity" (Peralta Esteva et al. 1985:38). It was this daily practice of discussion and decision making that was at the root of the new political consciousness movement leaders wanted to instill in union members.

Members were encouraged to participate directly in making decisions that affected them at their workplaces and to decide matters that were discussed at delegation and state assembly meetings. Crucial to determining how effective this participation was, however, was the degree to which members had access to full and accurate information central to the decision-making process. Access to information also revealed leaders' real commitment to rank-and-file participation. On this issue there was some disagreement among members of the executive committees. In Chiapas, local executive committee officers considered it their responsibility to "orient" and guide members, as well as to provide them with information (Peralta Esteva et al. 1985:37). According to a former leader in Chiapas, the role of the leadership was to orient members by presenting well-argued positions on a specific problem. These arguments were then presented to members in documents or in person through leaders' attendance at delegation assemblies. Instead of relying on members to develop their own positions on the spot, discussion during the assemblies would center on these arguments presented by the committee. As one leader admitted, "We don't hold anarchic assemblies where anything goes; we present some general guidelines that have been worked out before and on the basis of that the people decide what must be done" (SNTE. Sección 7. n.d.:26). Similarly, in Oaxaca an executive committee member admitted that consultations with the membership did not simply involve the transfer of raw information but rather consisted of pushing a particular point of view for the membership's consideration. The process of *consulta*, he said, was actually a process of *consulta-impulso*, of simultaneously gathering opinions and trying to persuade.[20]

20. Interview with former executive committee member, Oaxaca, June 18, 1990.

However democratic the methods adopted by the movement were, they were not perfect. Some teachers complained of what they called *asambleísmo*, the manipulation of the assembly to push forward certain positions. Clearly, the better-organized and more politicized groups had an advantage here, as did executive committee leaders. Informal groupings of teachers often met prior to key meetings to discuss their strategies for the assembly. As noted by less experienced activists, those who could talk, present ideas, and persuade others also had an advantage over those who were less practiced. Yet what is important is that, in spite of such practices, leaders and political groups did not always get what they wanted, and efforts to hide information or misrepresent what happened in negotiations sparked strong negative responses from the membership. Members of the state assemblies were not passive recipients of leaders' directives; rather, they were an increasingly active layer of mid-level movement cadres that continually questioned the leadership while trying to forge unity within the assembly.

Information and Decision Making

Since the executive committee had privileged access to information, especially in negotiations with state and union officials, how the committee transmitted that information to members was important. If leaders decided to withhold or manipulate the information, they could render the movement's representative organizations virtually irrelevant, especially in the absence of regular elections that would pressure leaders to remain accountable. Problems over this issue did arise. Conflicts between the executive committee and the state assembly typically arose over the issue of whether the committee had relayed all of its information to the state assembly, and whether in fact leaders had made direct commitments to officials in a way that bypassed the authority of the state assembly. These were perennial issues for both movements; the executive committees rarely went unchallenged in state assembly meetings.

Committee members apparently had no consistent position on how much information should be reported. In one instance a document from the union's national executive committee proposing a compromise on the 1987 electoral congress in Oaxaca prompted three different reactions from within the local executive committee. One response was to discuss the document among committee members only, another was to select the information to present to the membership, and a third was to present the entire document directly to the state assembly. In most cases, what was finally transmitted appeared to depend on the political sensitivity of the issue at hand, whatever agreement could be forged among committee members with different perspectives on this issue, and the fear of being discovered to have hid information from the membership. The executive committee thus acted as an important filter for the kind and quantity of information that passed to the membership, although the temptation of some members of the executive committee to hide information was restricted by the presence of other committee members and by members' strong rejection of such an action.

Members in the state assembly fundamentally mistrusted leaders on the executive committee, suspecting them not only of withholding information but also of negotiating with authorities behind their backs. These suspicions fueled a growing rift between state assembly members and the executive committee, and, in Oaxaca especially, representatives to the state assembly came to question much of what the secretary-general in particular reported. In the absence of formal elections in which the old committee would most certainly have been voted out, members of the Oaxacan movement were forced to resort to creative solutions to ensure that their leaders would remain accountable. Among these solutions was the decision in 1985 to expand the executive committee with rank-and-file assistants and to elect rank-and-file representatives to negotiating commissions alongside executive committee members. The presence of these additional members was intended to keep pressure on leaders to report what transpired in negotiating sessions. Since many assistants also came from opposing political currents, their participation on the committees was seen as another way to keep committee leaders in check. A similar response was adopted by delegates to the Chiapas congress in 1984, who decided to expand the size of the executive committee in order to secure greater accountability from their leaders.

Elections

Similarly creative approaches were adopted to handle local executive committee elections. In order to prevent national union officials from derailing the democratic process, local members elected congress delegates and the executive committee slate *prior* to the official elections, during a "precongress." The precongress was another instance of modifying the statutes to suit member needs. The precongress was the real congress and at the same time a rehearsal for the official congress that followed, where it would be important to maintain unity. As a result, factional conflicts and disagreements were aired during the precongresses, which often lasted through the night. In contrast, official congresses typically lasted only a few hours. Precongresses were also unpredictable. Some factions would try to influence the nominations and election of candidates while others would counter these efforts, and the voting could produce entirely different results from those expected. This would be the case during the 1984 elections in Chiapas, when members voted in a secretary-general who was not connected to the dominant political currents, and also in Oaxaca in 1985 and 1986, when a majority of "radical" delegates (those who rejected vanguardista participation on the committee) was elected, thereby causing the national executive committee of the union to retract its authorization of the congress.

At the precongress union members tried to secure the results of the official elections in the days before the congress so that no surprises would emerge during the congress itself. In Chiapas the precongress was initially opposed by some members who thought it antidemocratic, and national union officials obviously rejected this practice and tried to get the dissident locals to stop. But in the face of National Executive Committee efforts to sabotage delegation meetings and disrupt elections, the precongress offered the only possibility that the will of the majority of the delegates would be respected in a democratic congress.

National union officials used many tactics to control or upset local elections. Officials sometimes presided over electoral congresses whose location and time had not been disclosed to all delegates and that as a result might not have the majority of delegates present. During delegation assemblies to elect congress delegates, representatives from the national union—who were supposed to preside over elections—were known to not show up, invalidating the delegate selection, or they tore up official documents and staged violent interruptions of assemblies by hired thugs. Successful prior assemblies and congresses therefore required careful staging. In the few regions where these occurred with minimal disruption the dissidents had close to 100 percent of the delegates, maintained themselves unified in the course of the congress, and organized collective actions and work stoppages to watch for provocations in the city where the congress was being held.

Prior delegation assemblies were also held in order to select delegates to the precongress and the official congress. In delegation assemblies both "effective delegates" (voting delegates) and "fraternal delegates" (observers) were selected. Effective delegates were chosen in the proportion of one delegate per every one hundred members or group over forty, while two fraternal delegates per delegation were chosen. The task of the fraternal delegates was to watch over the voting delegates during the precongress to ensure that they voted in accordance with the wishes of the members they represented. At the official congresses fraternal delegates engaged in support activities outside the building where the congress was taking place.

The method of candidate selection varied from one precongress to the next, depending on what method the delegates present decided to employ. Members could choose from among several methods. They could advance names and vote directly for candidates for each position, they could put forward a list of three candidates, they could select slates of candidates, or they could use what they referred to as the "multiple choice" method. The first method was the one stipulated in the union statutes, but members decided it was antidemocratic. The second method was subject to manipulation by the presiding committee. The third, selecting slates, was considered too divisive. The multiple-choice method was the least divisive, the least subject to mediation by those who chaired the meeting, and the most inclusive.[21] Besides selecting the method of voting, delegates also decided whether incumbents could be reelected to committee positions or whether they should be barred. The discussion was renewed with each election, and sometimes different regional groups within the precongress would reach different decisions about the participation of incumbents. Delegates also selected—via majority vote—fellow delegates whose task was to count the number of votes during elections.

Ethnicity, Gender, and Participation

Member participation in the union local and the movement took a variety of forms. Rank-and-file members elected workplace representatives, delegation officials, and congress delegates. Anyone who could obtain the majority support of their colleagues could themselves become a representative or delegate. Vanguardistas were also able to participate if they followed the rules, and some members who were regarded as vanguardistas did in fact become congress delegates. However, informal obstacles to participation in leadership positions remained. These obstacles stemmed from ethnic, gender, and regional biases that existed even though they were not formally endorsed by the movement. For example, Indian bilingual teachers were unlikely to obtain the most important seats on the executive committee, and on the local executive

21. Ibid.

committee in Oaxaca even the secretariat for Indian affairs went to a non-Indian.

Indigenous Bilingual Teachers

By the time the dissident teachers' movement began in the late 1970s indigenous teachers in states such as Oaxaca had been mobilizing and organizing for years.[22] This level of experience was reflected in the indigenous teachers' willingness to join the emerging movement and to continue to protest and mobilize. Indigenous teachers were crucial in the brigade work that was done in the early months of the movement, and groups of indigenous teachers formed important contingents in the *plantones* and marches to Mexico City.

Throughout this time the organization of indigenous teachers (in Oaxaca) remained unified in the Coalición de Promotores, but somewhat isolated within the emerging CCL. Leadership positions were dominated by representatives from the central valleys (including Oaxaca city) and other regions, especially the Zapotec region of Juchitán. Teachers from the Mixe, Mixteco, and Triqui regions of the Sierra Juárez became the foot soldiers, but never the officers, of the emerging movement.

During the beginning of the movement in Oaxaca there was also some tension between the indigenous coalition and leaders of the CCL over the way in which the coalition would participate. Much of this had to do with the unique organizational and representational structure of indigenous bilingual teachers. When the movement began, members of indigenous education did not have a union delegation. But as a tactical measure, during the first movement congress bilingual teachers formed a delegation without dissolving their coalition. Representatives to the state assembly were not, strictly speaking, delegates or secretaries-general, as in the rest of the local's delegations, but rather were regional representatives, each area of a particular dialect constituting one region. As a result, the bilingual teachers' "fit" into the state assembly was problematic, since their representation was not strictly legal. Because of the size of the indigenous education sector (it was the largest level after primary education, and approximately one-third of the membership of the Oaxaca local was involved in indigenous education), it was potentially very powerful, and according to some participants there was concern within the local to contain its influence.

Representation of the Coalición within the union local decreased after the

22. See Chapter 4 for this background.

initiation of the movement. In 1980 the Coalición was represented within the state assembly by four voting members; later this representation was reduced to two voting members, although the executive committee at one point attempted to further reduce this representation to one nonvoting member.[23] In spite of the indigenous ethnic background of most teachers in the state, urbanized and more highly educated Zapotecs, Mixtecos, and mestizos in the teachers' movement tended to treat members of the indigenous teachers' coalition with a high degree of paternalism.

When asked about the staying power and "radical democracy" of much of the rank-and-file in the Oaxaca and Chiapas teachers' movements, many CNTE activists pointed to indigenous traditions of democratic self-government, responsibility to the community, and reciprocity as explanations for the strong presence of similar characteristics in the teachers' movement. In many Indian communities decisions were made collectively, and men rotated in their *cargo* as the authority of the community. These were hardship positions, since they were not remunerated, and the responsibilities often prevented community leaders from taking part in other forms of work. Leaders were therefore supported and provided for by other members of the community while they discharged their office. Indigenous teachers transferred this sense of responsibility and obligation to the community, as well as their consensus forms of decision making, to their union organization. Delegates and leaders in the Coalición accepted these positions as their *cargo*, often at great personal and economic cost, since compensation from the SEP was meager.[24]

The strong solidarity and willingness to participate shown by indigenous teachers also had their roots in traditions such as the *tequio* (communal work parties) in Oaxaca. In this sense, while for urban and mestizo teachers the *plantones*, community kitchens, and long marches that became commonplace within the movement were novel experiences, for indigenous teachers such activities conformed to long-standing traditions of commitment, reciprocity, and community sharing (Caballero 1990:2). Indigenous teachers also were more accustomed to physical hardship. In the Sierra of Oaxaca walking was often the only way to move between villages, and it was not unusual for teachers to walk ten hours straight to reach some form of public transportation into the cities. It was this form of communication that knit indigenous communities together during the early days of the teachers' movement, and this was also the way that teachers from the Sierra traveled for their monthly assembly meetings in Oaxaca.

23. Coalición de Promotores Indígenas de Oaxaca 1981.
24. Interview with advisor to the Coalición de Promotores Indígenas, Oaxaca, June 14, 1990.

The experiences and traditions of indigenous teachers and their communities found their way into the demands, organization, and tactics of the dissident teachers' movement. The presence of indigenous teachers in the movement reinforced the traditional animosities between region and center, between Indians and "Europeans," between poor and rich. Throughout the course of the teachers' movement the images of indigenous teachers protesting in the capital—marching down the Avenida Juárez in Mexico City, sleeping in the streets before national union headquarters—were especially powerful. In no other national union were the presence and influence of Mexico's various ethnic groups so visible.

In places like Oaxaca and Chiapas, however, ethnic identification was tied not only to different regions within these states but also to different villages within a similar ethnic region. Thus, one of the ways that the teachers' movement influenced indigenous teachers was by gradually forging an additional identity onto the ethnic-regional one. This additional identity was defined by teachers' professional membership. Movement leaders in Oaxaca identified the relatively new practice of meetings by professional "level" (high school, primary education, preschool) rather than region as a sign of progress and a move away from divisions based on regional identities.

Women in the Teachers' Movement

According to projections from the 1980 census, 57 percent of Mexico's teachers are women (Salinas Sánchez 1990:85).[25] This proportion varies by level and by region. For instance, in more economically developed regions, such as Mexico City and the state of Jalisco, the percentage of women rose to around 62 percent; in Local 9 of preschool and primary teachers in Mexico City the percentage of women was about 80 percent. In poorer states, such as Chiapas, there were more men than women in the profession (Salinas Sánchez 1990:85). In spite of this large presence of women in the union, the representation of women in leadership positions at both local and national levels has been highly disproportional in favor of men. Women have been concentrated at the preschool and primary school levels, while men have been concentrated in higher status jobs in secondary and higher education and in administrative and

---

25. A survey conducted by the union after 1989 reportedly showed an 80 percent female union membership. (Interview with researcher at the Universidad Pedagógica Nacional, Mexico City, June 28, 1990.)

union positions. Indian men rather than women also tend to dominate in the bilingual education field.

This stratification within the profession, as well as the number of women in it, may be due to the fact that for many years women were socially barred from universities and discouraged from entering other professions. Teaching thus became one of the most socially acceptable professions for young, single women (Galván 1985). Many young women then abandoned teaching after marriage, leaving male teachers to advance in the profession and dominate in leadership positions within the union. Women who became teachers did so for a variety of reasons, but several in particular stand out: they came from a family of teachers; their fathers chose the profession for their daughters; they could continue to teach while married; normal schools were generally cheaper than the university, so poor families often chose this option for economic reasons; the requirements for entering normal school were not as stringent as those for entering the university; teaching was viewed as a more "feminine" profession (Salinas Sánchez 1990:94–103). For poor families in particular, sending their daughters to normal school was an attractive option:

> For many parents, sending their daughters to the normal school was a more secure investment than sending them to the university. If they could get into the Nacional de Maestros they were assured a job in the Federal District and they could then obtain a scholarship or some form of material assistance. Besides, being a teacher was a job that could be shared with housework, and it took fewer years of study than any program in the university. (Salinas Sánchez 1990:98)

In recent years economic conditions and changing expectations concerning women's roles have led more women to retain their jobs in order to contribute to household income. Although significant difficulties remain, there is some indication that these changed conditions are also altering women's chances of seeking leadership positions within the union. Among the continuing difficulties, the most important is the woman's family obligations and the husband's objections to his spouse's union participation when it means less time spent on household activities. Child care and primary responsibility for meals and housework tie the female teacher to the home in ways that men have managed to avoid. Women's dual obligations to house and job become more evident in households where both husband and wife are teachers. In these cases the men were almost always the ones to attend union events. In instances where a woman's professional and union duties forced her to travel or attend meetings outside of normal working hours, tensions within the home would normally erupt. Outside of Mexico City, where union officers' duties often involved extensive travel throughout the state as well as to Mexico City, women were less able to perform in these roles.[26]

The presence of women in leadership positions in the CNTE generally mirrored that of the union as a whole. In fact, until recently women had perhaps been more visible in the leadership of the official union than they had been in the movement.[27] After Jonguitud's removal in 1989, a woman, Elba Esther Gordillo Morales, was selected to become secretary-general of the SNTE. Gordillo had held important positions in the union's national executive committee for many years and had been secretary-general of Local 36 in the state of Mexico. Women also came to play a much more central and visible leadership role in the mobilizations of 1989, especially in Mexico City, but also in old CNTE strongholds such as Oaxaca.

At the beginning of the Oaxacan movement the number of women in official leadership positions was very small relative to the proportion of female union members in the Oaxacan local, which was approximately half. The only woman on Oaxaca's first democratic executive committee was in charge of preschool affairs, an occupation filled mostly by female teachers. One woman from Oaxaca explained that in 1987 she had been nominated to head her delegation but declined because she felt that a female candidate would divide the delegation whereas a male candidate would not.[28] Later, however, this same woman became head of her delegation and went on to occupy a position on the executive committee in 1989.

The gender balance improved substantially on the second executive committee (1989–92) in Oaxaca, which had nine women on it. These women were also not restricted to traditional female roles but held a broad range of positions. Many of these women had been secretary-general of their delegations or had held some committee position at the delegation level prior to being elected to the executive committee. These contrasts in the composition of the Oaxacan executive committee between 1982 and 1989 offered encouraging evidence that attitudes about female leadership in the local had begun to change and that the movement itself had had an impact on women's participation.[29] Similarly, after

26. Ibid.
27. The head of Vanguardia, Carlos Jonguitud Barrios, had announced that the union needed to bolster the participation of women in the union (Cortina 1986:10). He himself oversaw the career development of Elba Esther Gordillo, who later became secretary-general of the national union.
28. Interview with high school teacher in Oaxaca, February 22, 1987.
29. For a study of women's participation in the movement in Oaxaca see Núñez Miranda 1990.

the mobilizations of 1989 in Mexico City, in which women were a visible political force, women occupied nearly half of the committee positions in Local 9 of preschool and primary teachers and several commissioned positions in Local 10, a male-dominated local of secondary and higher education instructors.

Women's traditional roles as housewives and mothers in addition to their professional careers nonetheless continued to create barriers to women's participation in leadership positions. Union officers and representatives had to travel a great deal and spent much of their time attending meetings, something that most women responsible for their homes as well as their jobs found difficult to do. Of the nine women on the executive committee in Oaxaca after 1989, all but one were either single, divorced, and/or had older children. The one woman on the committee who remained married and had younger children complained of tensions in her marriage as a result of her participation and stressed that her decision to accept a position on the committee had come at high personal cost.[30] In contrast, of the thirteen women on the executive committee of Local 9 in 1990, ten had partners and/or young children.[31]

Members also participated in direct collective actions—in marches, rallies, occupations, and strikes—or in the numerous support activities surrounding these mobilizations. Women were especially visible during these actions and almost always took charge of the cooking and child care, essential activities during mass mobilizations. Indeed, without these activities, it is unlikely that the movement's actions could succeed. Mobilizations always disrupted the daily lives of participants and their families. This disruption was even more pronounced for couples where both were teachers, since decisions had to be made regarding who would participate and who would take care of the children and household, tasks that often fell to the women. Even when women managed to participate in movement activities, they often left their children not with their husbands but with female relatives or friends. Mobilizations often provoked serious tensions in marriages (leading in many cases to separation and divorce), and in relationships between unmarried partners. Collective actions thrust people out of their routines and away from their spouses and partners, often giving rise to feelings of personal liberation as well as to destructive jealousies. During the marches and plaza occupations in Mexico City in 1989, one woman told me, "Many old relationships were destroyed and new ones formed."

The central participation of women in the collective actions of the movement nevertheless led many male colleagues to begin to reevaluate the ability of

---

30. Interview with local executive committee member, Oaxaca, June 16, 1990.
31. Interview with commissioned member of Local 10, Mexico City, June 28, 1990.

women to participate meaningfully in the movement, and, perhaps more slowly, it raised member awareness about inequalities in the home. In Oaxaca female teachers began to meet in 1987 to discuss issues that affected them as women and as movement participants, but they did so hesitantly, afraid to appear as though they might be acting divisively. Similarly, female committee members in Mexico City in 1990 did not discuss the particular problems that women might have as union activists but preferred to speak of movement issues in a nongendered way. "Feminism" was viewed negatively, even by many of the women in leadership positions, and several of the women active in leftist political organizations criticized discussion of women's issues as "petty-bourgeois deviationism."[32] It is nevertheless undeniable that by 1989 there was an increased awareness of women's special role and contribution to the teachers' movement among both male and female teachers. CNTE assemblies began to recognize the special problems affecting women for the first time in their meetings, and a special forum on women in the teachers' movement, held in Mexico City in May 1990, filled a large auditorium and drew both male and female speakers.

Well before women began to increase their role in the leadership of the movement, the strong participation of women in collective actions lent a distinctive flavor to these. Women were frequently the most combative participants in these actions, and stories abound on how the women of the movement shamed and embarrassed the (usually male) government and union officials. In one example of a building occupation in Oaxaca, teachers reportedly entered the SEP delegation offices and forced their way into the delegate's office. The women then kicked out all of the men except for the delegate and told him that since he always made them wait, he was going to have to wait for a change. They forced him to sit for hours while they knitted. When the delegate finally asked for permission to go to the bathroom, the women, in typical democratic fashion, formed a committee to take him there.

In another example from Tuxtla Gutiérrez, Chiapas, a local radio announcer known for his opposition to the teachers' movement used his radio program to advise young men to save money that evening by skipping the red light district and going instead to the central plaza, where dozens of female teachers were in the *plantón*, and where, the implication was, the women would "give it away" for free. When the radio announcer was spotted downtown later that evening, he was chased and caught by a group of women teachers, who then proceeded

32. Ibid.

to clip his hair with a scissors and tried to strip him of his clothing before he escaped.[33]

Participation and Collective Action

With the victory of the dissident movement in Oaxaca and Chiapas, teachers not only participated in mobilizations but also began to participate to a greater degree in discussions at their workplaces and delegations. These discussions ranged in topic—from what to do about an uncooperative colleague to pedagogical techniques to deciding whether to go on strike. A related and significant change brought about by the movement was the participation of teachers' delegations in determining the criteria for workers' promotions, transfers, and the distribution of loans, credit, and housing. Seniority, performance, and participation in the movement became standard criteria for promotion, in contrast with earlier times when contacts, favors, and money obtained what belonged to union members by right. As one leader put it, "Although it may seem difficult and utopian in a society such as ours, a serious process has been initiated, with membership consensus, in which friendship, *compadrazgo*, bribes, and blackmail are no longer the recourse for social promotion."[34]

In spite of the expanded opportunities for member participation in the activities and decisions of the local, levels of participation rose and fell throughout the course of the movement. Apathy and passivity among members would weaken the movement's ability to stand up to attacks. Partly in order to confront noninvolvement, most delegations incorporated participation in movement activities or union service as one of the criteria to be taken into account when deciding one's eligibility for benefits or mobility within the profession. For instance, teachers who requested transfers to other schools had to present evidence of their participation in the union, which normally consisted of a document signed by their former delegation committee, before they would be welcomed into the new delegation.[35] Requiring proof of participation before gaining entrance to work at a school was also a means to protect the movement from its opponents. By weeding out people who had not supported

33. Shaving an opponent's head and thus holding him up to public ridicule was a common practice for movement supporters in places like Chiapas, much to the dismay of some Mexico City intellectuals who condemned such practices as excessive and counterproductive (Monsiváis 1987:193–94).
34. Peralta Esteva et al. 1985:8; and SNTE. Sección 7. 1984a.
35. Transcribed interviews with Coordinadora del Centro, Chiapas, n.d., p. 9.

the movement, members of a delegation could control the promotion and transfer of workers who might later turn against the movement from a position of power. This requirement for benefits and mobility was decided by the members themselves in their delegations, and even though some were angered by it, they were forced to acknowledge that the decision to include it had been decided democratically and was for the good of the movement. In this way movement supporters provided individuals with incentives to participate in movement actions and discouraged free-riding.[36] Through political education and peer pressure, members were taught that all those who benefited from the mobilizations that secured wage increases or changes in social and working conditions should participate in these activities.[37]

"Democratic" Collective Identity

The democratization of the union locals in Oaxaca and Chiapas not only entailed structural and procedural changes that created new forms of participation, it also brought more intangible changes in member consciousness. These changes were brought about through teachers' participation in public spaces where they would "learn to speak in public, run meetings, analyze problems and their sources, write leaflets, and so forth" (Evans and Boyte 1992:192), and through the transformative power of participation in collective actions, such as the *plantones* in the central squares of Oaxaca City or Tuxtla Gutiérrez, or the marches and encampments in Mexico City. Through these actions, teachers changed the way they thought about their rights, the nature of authority, their ability to decide for themselves, and the ways in which they related to each other and to the rest of their community. A "democratic" collective identity was generated, part self-consciously and part accidentally, taking even the most activist movement leaders by surprise. As one teachers' movement activist and analyst wrote, "The teacher who belongs to the CNTE—who travels hundreds of kilometers in order to participate in a march or a *plantón*, who risks his job and more in a building occupation—is a new teacher" (Hernández 1988:5).

Several developments lend evidence to the existence of this "new teacher."

36. On the concept of the free-rider see Olson 1965.
37. In spite of these efforts, or perhaps even because of them, in 1990 committee members complained that some teachers had come to view their participation in movement activities as "payment" for the transfer or loan they had requested rather than as an act of conviction. Similarly, after ten years some people believed that the movement was there to defend them regardless of whether or not they met their work obligations. (Interview with executive committee member, Oaxaca, June 13, 1990.)

Gradually, over the course of a decade, the strong regional and ethnic identities that so marked the movement at its beginning came to coexist rather than compete with the teachers' broader collective identification as the "democratic teachers' movement," or even as part of the working class. Regional groups became less insular, and representation of professional levels became more important relative to regional representation on the committee. Constant participation in mobilizations especially changed social relations among teachers, between men and women, and between teachers and the community. Teachers reported feeling that they had been brought closer together over the years as a result of participating in movement actions. Many stereotypes were also broken in the course of working together for a common goal. Male teachers noted that seeing the women in the marches and the *plantones* had shamed them into fighting harder within the movement and taught them to respect their female colleagues. Women's participation in the movement challenged traditional assumptions about gender and family roles. Claims for teachers' rights and democracy in the workplace and union eventually extended to the domestic front (Núñez Miranda and Hernández Sibaja 1986).

The democratic collective identity that was forged out of the teachers' movement was in large part shaped by the movement's conflict with government and union enemies. The movement's democratic features in particular had been defined in relation to their opposite: the corruption, arbitrariness, and exclusion that characterized former union governments. Decisions imposed from above and the centralized appointment of past officials had been countered by organizational and procedural changes that broadened participation and encouraged pluralism and regular meetings and elections (at least within the local). As a teacher from Oaxaca put it, "People may not be very clear about what they're fighting for, but they're clear about being against Vanguardia, . . . against certain persons and practices considered corrupt, unjust, and despicable."[38] The existence of a visible enemy in Vanguardia Revolucionaria and this strong rejection of what Vanguardia represented helped to unify dissident teachers and, paradoxically, provided a guideline of correct behavior as well. This is not to say that at times Vanguardia's methods were not imitated. What is significant, however, is that the expectations and definitions of acceptable behavior in the movement had changed overwhelmingly, even if individual members and leaders did not always act "democratically." In the course of reorganizing and

---

38. Interview with high school teacher, Oaxaca, February 22, 1987.

democratizing the union locals the democratic teachers' movement had also constructed a moral code of conduct for union leaders and members.[39]

Community Organizing

One of the areas most affected by the new ways in which teachers identified themselves was their ties with the community. Several movement participants have noted that at the beginning of the movement teachers were reluctant to support other groups or to welcome peasants and workers into their mobilizations. Many teachers, particularly urban teachers, saw themselves as superior to other workers in status and education. Over time, and aided in particular by the economic crisis of the eighties, teachers became increasingly aware of the interests they shared with the workers, peasants, and parents who came out to support the movement during marches or school occupations. While the level of teachers' involvement with the community varied from place to place, a greater "class consciousness"—an awareness of shared conditions with other workers and a growing self-consciousness of the teacher as a worker—began to take shape among rank-and-file movement teachers. As a member of a coordinadora in the highlands of Chiapas (Los Altos) put it, "We feel that in this region it is no longer a union struggle, it has become a class struggle; the teachers are involved in working with the parents and the community in a variety of ways."[40]

During the eighties in both Chiapas and Oaxaca, teacher involvement with community projects and teacher solidarity with other popular organizations increased, although not at the pace nor to the extent that many movement activists would have liked. Teacher-community cooperation tended to be greater in rural areas, especially in Indian and campesino communities. This cooperation reflected a deeply rooted historical tradition of teacher-campesino alliances. Teachers' links to peasants during Cardenas's agrarian reform program in the thirties were echoed in the eighties, although now with the important difference that teacher-peasant alliances were often forged independently of and even against the government. Teachers' class origins and the lack of leftist parties in the peasant sector further reinforced this historical alliance (Hernández 1988:1). Teachers in the Chiapas highlands described some of the activities they had become involved in:

39. This code was partially represented in the "guiding principles" (*principios rectores*) developed in 1982 by the Oaxacan teachers' movement (see SNTE. Sección. 22 n.d.(g)).
40. Transcribed interviews with Coordinadora de Los Altos, Chiapas, n.d.

In some regions we are organizing committees with the parents in order to address their needs; in others, there has been the struggle for land; in still others, people are working to form cooperatives run by community members in order to harvest the forests and sell the wood. In San Cristóbal last year we drew up a joint petition combining the demands of fourteen communities. Some asked for roads, others for potable water, others for clinics, schools, and transportation, but we managed to narrow the list down to two demands that unified the communities: the construction of roads and the introduction of potable water.[41]

There were numerous cases of teacher involvement in community projects of this type. Generally, community members took the initiative, seeking out the assistance and guidance of teachers. Teachers played important advisory roles in establishing peasant cooperatives and regional marketing and supply networks, in democratizing peasant organizations (linking methods and strategies used in the teachers' movement with indigenous communal practices), and in mobilizing for local opposition candidates in municipal elections.[42]

The influence of the teachers' movement was felt beyond this direct participation of teachers in their communities. One analyst from Oaxaca noted that the teachers' movement had become the central axis of virtually every popular mobilization in Oaxaca in the 1980s, especially in urban areas. This phenomenon was particularly striking in view of the fact that political parties had had little success in mobilizing people.[43] The tactics of the teachers' movement had also been imitated by others: whereas prior to the movement occupation of the central plaza in Oaxaca had been unusual, it was now a regular practice for protesting groups. A former executive committee member in Oaxaca even attributed a freer local press and a broader democracy in traditional Indian communities to the movement's having set an example for the community.[44] Movement teachers also played a significant role in local municipal governments. In 1990 90 percent of the municipal presidents in the Mixtec region of Tlaxiaco were teachers, and 25 percent of the municipal leaders in the entire state of Oaxaca (which has 570 municipalities) were teachers.[45] The profound

41. Ibid.
42. See Hernández 1988:18–26 for more detail on these examples of teachers' involvement in community projects.
43. Interview with researcher from the Universidad Autónoma Benito Juárez, Oaxaca, June 18, 1990.
44. Interview with former executive committee member, Oaxaca, June 14, 1990.
45. Ibid.

impact that the teachers' movement had on communities in Oaxaca and Chiapas was discernible in other ways as well. Youngsters played "democráticos versus vanguardistas" and residents prayed for a favorable resolution to teachers' strikes in local churches. Teachers even influenced movements outside of their home states: Oaxacan teachers who had at one time been active in the dissident movement were instrumental in organizing Mixtec agricultural workers in California, Oregon, and Washington.

Natural Allies? Teachers and Parents

Teachers needed the support of parents in order for the movement to succeed. The teacher-parent relationship was a delicate one in many communities. Teachers' frequent strikes and work stoppages and their impact on the children and their parents strained relations between teachers and parents. Movement opponents used this delicate situation to drive a wedge between parents and teachers. Vanguardistas promoted antimovement parent associations, for example. In order to gain parental support, teachers had to engage in a process of political education—through actions more than words—that emphasized teachers' working-class status and that linked the disruptions of children's education to the government's unwillingness to invest in teachers and in education. This view of teachers and of education was a difficult one to promote in many rural communities, where education was seen as a privilege leading to social mobility. In this context striking teachers were seen as an obstacle to peasant children's success. As a movement leader from Hidalgo noted:

> The campesino typically sees education as an escape from his economic situation and an escape for his children from a situation of misery. So, when there are work stoppages or strikes, he feels that they are stealing from him the chance to evade his miserable state through education. For this reason we can't confront the people, and we must campaign and work with the parents so that they understand that we are not part of the service that the state provides for the peasants, but that we are workers just as they are, and that we therefore have the right to engage in forms of struggle.[46]

46. Ana Graciela Bedolla, "Entrevista a Roberto Meza," *Testimonios* 1987: 96.

In many areas teachers either succeeded in gaining the support of parents or the parent-teacher alliance had already existed historically. In other communities, however, the frequent strikes and work stoppages and the failure of teachers to return the favors poor families extended to them created tensions. Teachers tried to address this problem by holding class on weekends and during vacations to make up for lost time. Many teachers went without needed vacations after taking part in grueling marches or marathon meetings and encampments in Mexico City. However, by the end of the eighties many parents had become tired of what they saw as the "democratic" teachers' failure to perform in the classroom. Leaders in Oaxaca began to turn their attention to education—an area long neglected by the movement—out of concern for their own political survival as much as out of professional conviction.

Leadership

The possibility of co-optation, defection, or repression of movement leaders was lessened by decentralizing decision making and expanding opportunities for member participation within the movement.[47] The leadership of the movement was collective, diffuse, and inclusive. Members fought against the formation of personality cults around individual leaders, in contrast to many other popular movements and earlier teachers' movements where charismatic leaders or *caudillos* dominated.[48] A cohort of young teachers who had begun their careers and spent their adult years within the decade-long democratic movement also emerged to occupy leadership positions in delegations and coordinadoras. Often more radical than their leaders on the local executive committee, the younger members challenged leaders on the committees, participated in political organizations within the local, published bulletins expressing their views, were selected as delegates and representatives, and even participated on commissions to assist the executive committees. In this way new leaders were formed and old leaders were less able to consolidate a firm power base. The fact that channels for participation and opportunities to express dissent within the organization existed permitted the incorporation rather than the marginalization of young teachers. This was especially important given the influx of young teachers into

---

47. On organizational leadership vulnerability to these factors see Fox 1992a.

48. The 1950s teachers' movement in Mexico City was identified with the person of Othón Salazar. In contrast, the teachers' movement of the 1980s was typically referred to in the press by the organization's acronym, the CNTE, and members were not represented as followers of any one person or set of individuals.

the movement; the number of teachers more than doubled nationally between 1980 and 1988.

In both Oaxaca and Chiapas leaders on the executive committees faced external pressures that affected relations between the executive committee and the state assembly. Executive committee members' contacts with government and union officials, more regular and frequent after legalization, generated pressures that distanced leaders from members. Union and government officials often pressed leaders to accept compromise solutions without consulting the membership, yet any suspicion of "negotiated" compromises brought rejection from members in the state assembly. On several occasions actions recommended by local leaders were rejected by the state assembly, and actions not supported by committee members were carried out because members wanted to do so. Rank-and-file members participating in mobilizations were frequently willing to continue the actions after their leaders on negotiating teams were ready to pull back and accept a compromise. Moreover, although members were typically willing to accept partial responses to their demands in the interest of conserving the strength of the movement, members were unwilling to compromise on issues such as a vanguardista presence on the executive committee, something leaders were willing to do. In attempting to satisfy both the requirements imposed by officials and the expectations of union members, movement leaders were often in the contradictory position of having to appear radical to their membership and moderate to officials at the same time.

One of the principal divisions within the movement that emerged as a result of this tension was between "radical" and "moderate" groups or, as labeled by some political factions, between "*clasistas*" and "*gobiernistas*." Many groups perceived this as a split between union local officials (*gobiernistas*) and the membership in the state assembly (*clasistas*), but in fact members of both camps had their allies on the committee and in the state assembly. The main difference between these groups had to do with the emphasis placed on mobilizations as opposed to negotiations in pursuing the goals of the movement. *Gobiernistas* were seen to place too much faith in their contacts with officials (on negotiations without mobilizations) to obtain demands, and radicals or *clasistas* were skeptical of gains obtained without the mobilized pressure of the membership. *Gobiernistas* were viewed as having sacrificed the movement's independence by accepting the rules of the game as defined by government officials. A movement leader who consented to meet privately with a government official, allowed his expenses to be covered, and accepted to curtail the actions of his organization in exchange for satisfaction of the movement's demands was said to have accepted the government's rules of the game (FMIN 1985:35). Officials frequently insisted on negotiating with a single leader with whom they had established a relationship of this kind. According to one document, to be *gobiernista* meant to

> engage in politics that protected the government, that avoided challenging it . . . to brag about contacts with officials, saying that they respect us, that they will receive us at any moment, that they help us, etc., forgetting that all that is because of the movement and for the movement, and not for the *caudillos* nor due to their personal merit. (FMIN 1985:25)

Radicals or *clasistas*, on the other hand, saw the teachers' movement as a revolutionary force, believed in the actions of the "masses," and strongly distrusted people in official positions. Moderates tended to see radicals as simplistic and intransigent, and as people who rejected compromise in principle. Radicals could enjoy the luxury of being "revolutionary" precisely because they had little real leadership experience.

In reality, these were simplistic categories that obscured the nuances and overlap in both positions as well as the complexity of the tactical and strategic issues the movement faced. A more accurate depiction of the political positions among dissident teachers would be to portray these along a continuum according to the degree to which different groups favored negotiations over mobilizations. Yet even here positions could vary depending upon the specific circumstances. Oftentimes these labels were hurled about to strengthen a particular group's political position during factional conflicts and debates over strategy, and some teachers even claimed that the labels had been invented by government officials and *charros* to cause divisions within the movement.

Nonetheless, striking the "correct" balance between negotiation and mobilization was one of the principal tactical issues within the movement, and the tension between these two dimensions of movement bargaining was never fully resolved. It has been argued that people in the leadership of organizations tend to adopt more moderate positions,[49] but this seems less clear in the teachers' case. Leaders' attitudes regarding negotiations with officials and the role of mobilizations appeared to have more to do with the political ideologies of leaders than with the fact that they were on the executive committee. This is reflected in part by the fact that most of the "moderate" members of the 1982–89 executive committee in Oaxaca went on to positions in the state government and even the local PRI after they left the leadership of the

---

49. For example see Piven and Cloward 1979:xxii.

movement, and those leaders who had assumed more "radical" positions (i.e., who opposed vanguardista participation on the committee and who tended to support greater rank-and-file participation) stuck to a commitment they had made years earlier and returned to their "base," to the areas and schools they had worked in prior to participating in the leadership of the local. In other words, leaders started out with different interpretations of what was required to win demands and different notions regarding the final objectives of the movement. The various positions adopted by the political organizations and party factions that operated within the movement contributed to these differences of interpretation and ultimately of strategy.

As in Chiapas in 1987, members in Oaxaca expressed a preference for leaders who identified with "member interests" (*los intereses de la base*) in the precongresses of 1985 and 1986. Those who identified with member interests were those who appeared untainted by contacts with authorities—leaders in the movement who had not been co-opted and who were perhaps considered least likely to succumb to co-optation. In 1985 a majority of "radical" delegates had been chosen for the congress, and as a result national union officials refused to authorize elections. In 1986 the radical delegates again dominated at the precongress and selected a regional leader from Juchitán and member of the COCEI as secretary-general. Again national officials refused to authorize the congress, apparently due to the political orientation and affiliation of the elected secretary-general. During the 1989 elections a delegation leader active in opposition municipal politics and associated with one of the leftist political organizations was elected secretary-general, and the man who had been selected to head the local in previous elections but had been prevented from doing so was made secretary of organization. In this case the more charismatic and popular leader was deliberately selected to occupy a secondary role on the committee so as to obtain approval by national union authorities.

In both situations, after 1985 in Oaxaca and after the imposition of the executive commission in Chiapas, members expressed preferences not for candidates who necessarily lacked affiliation to political currents but for more "radical" leaders who were regarded as identifying closely with the membership. These candidates reflected political positions that were frequently opposed to those of previous executive committees. This choice of leadership also appeared to reflect a growing sense on the part of the membership that leaders were under constant risk of "selling out" the movement and must therefore be reined in and made to account for every action and decision. A document of one of the teachers' political organizations in Oaxaca reflected this sentiment in a reference to the selection of congress delegates (but that could just as easily have applied to committee members): "As long as there are doubts, it is better to have delegates who are a little bit inexperienced, but independent" (FMIN 1985:9).

Political Factions

Political factions—members of political parties and nonparty political currents—had an important presence and influence in the CNTE from the beginning. These groups ranged from the Revolutionary Teachers' Movement, linked to the Mexican Socialist Party in its various transformations, to far-left political groups such as the Unión de Trabajadores de la Educación (Union [Organization] of Education Workers, UTE), ostensibly pro-Albanian.[50] Since the larger of these groups often had the most developed political ideas and organizing experience, they influenced fundamental decisions affecting strategy, tactics, and demands. Many rank-and-file members were, however, generally suspicious of political parties and organizations because they believed political parties tended to use social movements for their own political and electoral purposes. As a result, members of political organizations typically did not identify themselves as such, and the forms that their influence in the movement took were usually more subtle.

Political organizations also saw themselves change as a result of the movement. Members of these groups had to propose initiatives that would earn the support of their colleagues, thus often defusing some of the more radical claims. Those groups that could not sustain support among the membership saw themselves steadily lose influence over the course the movement took. Still, divisions and conflicts within the movements were often linked to political factions competing for power. Much of the struggle over tactics, strategy, and elections was inextricably tied to political groups trying to influence the course of events, although members of these political groups usually strove to hide their factional interests behind some "collective interest" of the movement as a whole.

Most of the time the existence of political factions within the movement had a positive impact. The presence of many different political currents stimulated discussions, tended to preclude any one group from dominating completely in the leadership of the movement, and served the purpose of keeping vigilance

50. Many of these smaller leftist organizations defined themselves in terms of their support for various versions of communism, whether Chinese, Albanian, or Soviet. After the fall of communism in Eastern Europe and the Soviet Union, many of these groups lost their ideological raison d'etre and withered away.

over elected leaders.⁵¹ Political groups formed the basis of informal groupings where teachers could discuss and exchange ideas, write documents, and disseminate their positions among the membership. It is significant that in neither Oaxaca nor Chiapas did factional groups "leave" the movement; there were no formal schisms. Moreover, both the Oaxaca and Chiapas movements had constructed internal mechanisms intended to deal with factionalism: members of political groups had to represent sectors of the membership to be able to vote in the state assembly rather than speak as members of political currents; important decisions were to be turned over to consultation with the membership rather than decided in the executive committee. Yet teachers in Chiapas were ultimately unable to prevent the leadership from subsuming the interests of the movement to a factional competition for political dominance.⁵² This tendency may have been more developed in Chiapas because the existence of two strong factions—Línea Proletaria and the trotskyists—with members and allies of Línea Proletaria dominating the leadership, polarized this struggle. In Oaxaca, in contrast, no single group dominated the direction of the movement; multiple political groups and "independents" were represented on the committee and in the assembly. Thus, while in both the Chiapas and Oaxaca movements political factions were present, the conflicts within the Chiapas leadership were ultimately more damaging. Toward the end Chiapas showed the negative consequences of factionalism while Oaxaca appeared to demonstrate the more positive aspects.

Movement Strategies

Some of the most characteristic strategies of the dissident teachers' movement were initially defined by movement leaders from Chiapas linked to Línea Proletaria and then generalized to much of the rest of the movement through the CNTE. This was so even though members from Línea Proletaria were not

---

51. Although Gamson (1990) has shown that political factionalism in movement organizations almost always produced their downfall, Lipset, Trow, and Coleman (1956) and others have concluded that the existence of competing factions within union organizations can be important for organizational democracy, although the number of factions can affect stability.

52. Gamson (1990) has argued that factionalism tends to occur more in organizations that are decentralized and nonbureaucratic, which was certainly a characteristic of the teachers' movement. Yet it is also important to acknowledge that factionalism is common to "challenging groups." As Gamson recognizes, "it is in the nature of the beast" (p. 99). The key lies in the internal mechanisms groups construct to manage internal conflict.

dominant in other locals and even though important differences over strategies persisted. Nonetheless, leaders from the first successful regional teachers' movement played an important role in theorizing about strategy and disseminating this information within the movement. One reason for the apparent success of these strategies over others may have to do with the way in which ideology was subsumed under two elements of Línea Proletaria "praxis": the satisfaction of basic member needs as one of the goals of the movement, and an emphasis on finding and cultivating "organic" leaders from the membership. The success of Línea Proletaria's organizing efforts could be measured by the organization's strong presence not only in rural areas and poor urban communities but also in the labor sector (*Organización* n.d.: 20).[53] The association of a charismatic member of the Chiapas movement leadership with Línea Proletaria at the beginning of the movement also undoubtedly aided general acceptance of this group's way of "doing politics."

Like many leftist organizations that emerged in Mexico in the seventies, Línea Proletaria grew out of the 1968 student movement. An organization of maoist origins, Línea Proletaria's early work was in the countryside and in poor urban neighborhoods. After 1976 it began to work in the labor movement, where it made important gains in the telephone workers' union, among miners, and in auto unions.

Línea Proletaria represented a model of organization that was quite different from the marxist-leninist parties and political organizations that dotted the leftist political landscape in Mexico in the early seventies. Rejecting the leninist model of a vanguard party and the democratic centralism of the communists, Línea Proletaria was made up instead of small, loosely coordinated "brigades." Members of Línea Proletaria believed in the ability to transform society and to construct "popular power" from within capitalism. This was done by building "social bases of support" (*bases sociales de apoyo*) within different sectors of society. Following this strategy, members of the organization believed that the "apparatuses of the bourgeoisie" could be used by the proletariat to build popular power. Línea Proletaria also believed that the bourgeoisie was fragmented, not a homogeneous and monolithic bloc, and therefore the most appropriate strategy was to "neutralize" potential enemies by forming alliances with them while negotiating with the principal enemy. The organization also viewed

---

53. Also see Roxborough and Bizberg 1983 on Línea Proletaria's role in the miners' and metalworkers' union, and Harvey 1990 for a discussion of Línea Proletaria's role in peasant organizations in Chiapas.

official union leaders as a fraction of the dominant class with its own interests and consequently with the ability to come into conflict with other dominant class fractions. This strategy of dealing differentially with class enemies was labeled "the politics of two faces" (*la política de dos caras*). Línea Proletaria also opposed confrontation and insisted that compromises were part and parcel of the willingness to negotiate and did not imply defeat (*Organización* n.d.:18–20). On the issue of demands Línea Proletaria believed that economic demands served as a pretext for building organization and advancing toward strategic objectives. Members of the organization also believed in working *within* popular organizations and helping to bring out workers' needs and demands rather than "importing" theory or ideology from outside or imposing a political line from a party vanguard.

Thus, a relatively moderate and pragmatic strategy and program emerged from Línea Proletaria's vision of capitalism and society. Members of the organization would work within dominant institutions and organizations, and they would exploit conflicts among elites by seeking out alliances with some authorities and offering to negotiate in an effort to advance on specific demands, usually of an economic nature, that would unite members of the popular movement or organization. Instead of the revolutionary overthrow of the state, workers and campesinos would gradually learn to govern themselves so that the existence of numerous pockets of autonomous popular organizations and communities would eventually alter political, economic, and social relations of power in the country. Moreover, the decentralized, brigade method of organization, and Línea Proletaria's emphasis on supporting natural leaders from the community or union, often made it difficult to identify the organization as a distinct political entity.

The strategies of Línea Proletaria became a point of contention within the Chiapas teachers' organization and were harshly criticized by the other political currents operating within the CNTE. Línea Proletaria's "politics of two faces" was denounced by other sectors of the left as opportunism, used to justify alliances with union and government officials and attacks against sectors of the left that rejected these associations. Similarly, the organization's emphasis on the use of "bourgeois apparatuses," or official institutions and organizations, was criticized for its failure to distinguish between structures that could in fact be used and those that were inherently limited for the construction of popular power (*Organización* n.d.:21). In spite of these criticisms, the alternative positions of those who had initially called for the formation of an independent teachers' union, who believed in more confrontational tactics, and who wanted the CNTE to play a stronger ideological and leadership role in the movement were defeated in the course of debate during the early years of the CNTE.[54]

The following aspects of movement strategy were those over which there appeared to be the most agreement within the CNTE, and they came to embody a general philosophy or approach within the movement.[55] These were common elements of movement strategy disseminated to members in union education workshops. They especially guided the actions of the Chiapas and Oaxaca teachers' movements. Among these strategies or guidelines for strategic action were: (a) the use of both legality and "illegality"; (b) the combined use of mobilization and negotiation; (c) the avoidance of confrontation; (d) the limited definition of demands; and (e) the identification and use of political spaces and contradictions within the state.

(a) *The use of legality and "illegality," or "walking with both feet."* A union education pamphlet for teachers in the movement states:

> [Y]ou should learn to walk "WITH BOTH OF YOUR FEET" and not with just one. . . . We should learn to make broad use of legality but we should also create our own forms of organization and struggle, even though these may not be legal from the point of view of the *charro* statutes or from the point of view of the repressive government. (SNTE. Sección 7. 1983:16)

Movement leaders saw the use of these two strategies as interconnected—the "legal" and "illegal" were two aspects of the same process of moving toward movement goals.[56] The clearest expression of the use of this approach was evident in the organization of the movement, especially upon its emergence. The legal structures were the statutory or formally recognized instances of the union. To some these represented "bourgeois" legality, yet they were utilized

---

54. See Hernández and Pérez Arce 1982, and Salinas and Imaz 1984:127–30, for more on differences of strategy and debates among different organizations within the CNTE.
55. Many of these positions were laid out in other CNTE documents as well. An especially clear exposition can be found in the presentation to the II Forum of the CNTE by representatives of Delegation III-24 (INAH) of Local 11, "¡Unidos y Organizados Venceremos!" See Hernández and Pérez Arce 1982:39–48.
56. In fact, although movement members used the term "illegal," the organizational instances they developed and most of the tactics they adopted were not expressly prohibited by law or by union statutes, rather they were simply not legally sanctioned or officially recognized. A more accurate term would be "extralegal."

Sustaining the Movement 255

because it was only through possession of these instances that the movement could officially claim to represent its members and legally negotiate on their behalf. The instrumental consideration granted this bourgeois legality was reflected in the movement's willingness to construct alternative organizations that derived their legitimacy from the members who recognized and supported them rather than from union officials. "Real" power resided in these alternative organizations. Moreover, these alternative or parallel organizations functioned as a form of insurance against possible decertification by national union officials. As expressed in a document used by the movement in training union members:

> The correct thing to do is to reinforce the movement at the base. If they take away our executive committee, we will re-create the *Consejo Central de Lucha* and we will maintain the state assembly. If they decertify our delegation executive committees, we will rebuild our *comités de lucha*. . . . If they cease to recognize our legal organizations, we will continue with the illegal ones. We will never risk everything we have on the notion that we control the executive committee and on the erroneous assumption that if they decertify the [statutory] committee, the movement is lost. (SNTE. Sección 7. 1983:19)[57]

Legality and institutionality were important for the movement in other ways as well. The teachers' movement typically appealed to authorities through legal-bureaucratic and institutional channels before resorting to other measures. When the movement first emerged in various states, teachers had tried to get union officials to spearhead demands before using direct tactics, which ranged from ousting the official to bypassing him or her to appeal directly to higher union and government authorities. This approach had the effect of legitimizing the tactics that the movement would ultimately be forced to use in the face of authorities' refusal to negotiate with the movement. Legal appeals or petitions, however, were almost always accompanied by a simultaneous show of force. This typically involved the mobilization of movement participants and supporters in marches, encampments, open meetings, sit-ins, or building occupations, and included legal and illegal (or extralegal) actions, depending on the scope of the problem, the priority it had, and the target of the demands.

Another example of the movement's use of legality could be seen in leaders' efforts to secure agreements in writing from union and government officials.

57. While this idea of combining legal and extralegal organizations was central to the movement, reality was more complicated. Given the importance for the movement of its ability to resolve problems, the loss of legal status could be devastating (see Chapter 5).

This did not reflect a naive belief in the power of a legal contract but represented instead the possibility of fighting further on a terrain that officials could be forced to recognize as legitimate. Although many of these commitments were simply ignored by the authorities, at other times these signed agreements were what made significant concessions possible. Pressure could be more legitimately exerted against officials, and at the same time the legality of the demand functioned as an important organizing tool for the movement.

(b) *The combined use of mobilization and negotiation.* This was one of the movement's most important strategies, and it reflected the complementarity of the legal and illegal dimensions of the movement. Negotiation was a consequence of the condition of legality, though not exclusive to it, and mobilization was more a property of the illegal sphere—a product of the movement's marginality. Leaders' willingness to enter into negotiations and the central role of negotiation in the movement's strategy was rooted in a specific reading of state-popular movement relations in Mexico. Leaders believed that bargaining space did exist in Mexico, in contrast to Guatemala or El Salvador. This provided popular movements in Mexico with at least the *possibility* of winning political spaces through negotiations, unlike their Central American counterparts.[58] They also believed that negotiations did not happen without pressure, and agreements did not stick unless through the continued application of pressure via the mobilization of members and supporters. In this way mobilization was inextricably tied to the process of negotiation.

The need to mobilize as a key tactic in getting demands met arose when and because no other channels for handling grievances were available to the movement. In the absence of fair elections and legal channels for appeal people took to the streets. In this way mobilization has been a constant feature of practically all dissident movements in Mexico. Again, as expressed in a union education document:

> We start from the premise that the government, independently of whether or not it speaks of an opening, will in the beginning of a conflict always be closed to negotiation. . . . For this reason the first moment must be of mobilization, in order to open the way to negotiation. . . . And then in the middle of the negotiation we are going to announce other mobilizations in case the problem remains unsolved. . . . Negotiation itself has three moments: before, during, and after the

---

58. Transcribed interviews, Comité Ejecutivo, Sección 7, n.d., p. 23.

mobilization. . . . We negotiate with the strength that has been developed, and with that which will potentially be developed during the next mobilization. (SNTE. Sección 7. 1983:19)

Elsewhere this document states, "Gains are won through mobilization and not through the intelligence of the leader" (SNTE. Sección 7. 1983:23). The danger of not relying on mobilization—of accepting concessions or of negotiating without the full presence and participation of the membership in some type of action—left the resolution of problems and negotiation of demands entirely in the hands of the government and movement leaders. According to movement leaders, this increased the membership's dependence not only on its leaders but also on its "direct enemies, its class enemies" (SNTE. Sección 7. 1983:17). To the extent that leaders, even democratically elected ones, became "the negotiators" and acquired privileged access to authorities, the threat of cooptation of the leadership and of "decapitation" of the movement increased. This threat was especially pronounced where leadership accountability was weak or nonexistent and where the practice of participation in decision making had not been cultivated among the rank-and-file, so that new leaders could not emerge to challenge existing ones. Mobilization as part of the process of negotiation consequently functioned as another mechanism to ensure the accountability of movement leaders.

(c) *The avoidance of confrontation, or no "all-or-nothing" positions.*
This strategy was linked closely to the issue of how demands were defined. It was based on the idea that workers' struggles must proceed from their own interests, problems, and demands, and that periods of conflict must be structured around the winning of at least part of these demands, as opposed to adopting an absolute position of "all or nothing" in which compromise was rejected in principle. Political consciousness would develop out of workers' pursuit of their self-defined interests and should not be imposed by leaders with an ideology or vision:

> We consider a frontal confrontation [with the state] to be criminal, because when experienced or inexperienced leaders take the masses into direct confrontation with the government in cases where they do not have sufficient strength to resist the confrontation, [this] destroys the movement, the organization disappears, and the Mexican left continues to engage in defeat after defeat. . . . Construction of the workers' power must proceed from the workers themselves; no other force can supplant

the workers' power to make their own decisions and to define their own needs. (SNTE. Sección 7. n.d.:23)

According to a document produced by movement leaders in Chiapas, the movement had "learned" when to retreat during mobilizations as well as in negotiations, in order to conserve its strength and avoid exposing the movement to efforts to destroy it (Peralta Esteva et al. 1985:9). Encounters with repression were typically avoided in the belief that such repression would quickly discourage members from participating in future actions.[59] The trajectory of the movement was thus characterized by ebbs and flows, in which peak periods of mobilization followed by gains (*auges*) were followed in turn by tactical withdrawals (*repliegues*) and periods of relative calm in which the movement consolidated its gains and gathered strength for the next battle (*reflujos*).[60] According to movement leaders, the leadership had a special responsibility to recognize the correct moment at which the movement should withdraw:

> [T]he leadership must recognize the difficulties, study these carefully, and momentarily contain the movement. Not in order to keep [the movement] from advancing, but rather in order to advance in a zigzag, with greater caution. . . . This art of leadership, of conducting the movement in a zigzag fashion, is not possessed by *compañeros* who believe that the road to revolution is a broad avenue. They charge like bulls in the ring and suffer a similar fate. (SNTE. Sección 7. 1983:20)

Knowing when to retreat was therefore crucial in guiding the teachers' movement around potential repression. In a further effort to conserve the movement's capacity for mobilization, mobilizations were usually organized according to the nature of the demands and the channels through which grievances were typically presented. For example, ousting a particular school principal might only require the mobilization of teachers from that school, together with the parents of children who attended there. Similarly, the expulsion of a corrupt supervisor might require that an entire delegation mobilize. The demand of a wage increase, on the other hand, usually required mobilizing the entire union as well as other organizations. (SNTE. Sección 7. n.d.:23)

59. In contrast, some political currents within the CNTE held that repression built class consciousness by revealing the true repressive and antipopular nature of the state.
60. The *reflujo* was not always a product of victory but instead often reflected a weak or embattled organization on the defensive.

Another expression of the movement leaders' efforts to avoid confrontation or repression could be seen in their choice of moderate language in public pronouncements and documents. In these public statements the "usual expressions of the left, such as 'repressive bourgeois state,' are not found" (Peralta Esteva et al. 1985:9). Leaders suggested that these terms were counterproductive:[61]

> We do not say when we want to remove a *charro*, . . . "we want to oust him because he is a *charro*." Rather, we say we want to oust him because he is against the majority interests of the membership. . . . we do not mention revolution; we do not mention the objectives we hope to reach by ousting the *charro*. Why not? Because we know that the struggle to oust the *charro* would become more difficult then, because we would be converting that struggle into a political struggle. . . . better that we shorten that *charro's* path to defeat. (SNTE. Sección 7. n.d.:24)

And:

> The enemy is identified not through ideological denunciation but through practical evidence demonstrating that he is an obstacle to the resolution of the teachers' most heartfelt problems. (Hernández 1988:24)

This nonideological approach to dealing with the "enemies" of the movement often facilitated negotiations with authorities and made their demands for the replacement of teachers and school administrators more likely to be listened to. The use of moderate or nonideological language was also important in addressing the mistrust most movement participants felt toward political parties or ideological currents of the left, particularly in the first years of the movement. Most rank-and-file teachers tended to shy away from labels and actions that would identify their movement as "political." Labels followed, rather than preceded, members' awareness of the implications of their movement: "[T]he process itself led people to see when the problem ceased to be simply a syndical one, and became more a problem of class" (SNTE. Sección 7. n.d.:23). For many teachers there was also the cultural issue of how one customarily dealt with authority. For instance, one former executive committee member in

---

61. Members from other political currents suggested that confronting officials and calling them "*charros*" during negotiations or while sharing positions on an executive commission was a way of raising members' consciousness. This position was also expressed in the Chiapas movement during the period of the executive commission (Peralta Esteva et al. 1985:32–33).

Oaxaca recounted how many teachers were hesitant even to use the term "charro" when referring to the union officials they were about to throw out, seeing their use of this term as an indication of a lack of respect.

(d) *The limited definition of demands.* The leadership played a central role in orienting members in terms of what were attainable demands given "the balance of forces": "[W]e need to know what our enemies' strength is and what our own strength is, and from that we must determine our real chances of obtaining something" (SNTE. Sección 7. n.d.:22). According to leaders in Chiapas, presenting "unrealistic" demands that were unlikely to be met would cause disillusionment and dampen member's commitment to participate in the movement.[62] Similarly, broader, more political demands might invite repression or frighten off powerful allies. Instead, the construction of a movement (understood as the politicization of its members) should be built upon the pursuit of concrete goals and at least some attainable demands, not on political speeches.[63] Moreover, each "stage" of struggle should be defined in terms of one main objective, although other demands (e.g., 100 percent wage increase) might be articulated as well. Having a single, strongly articulated demand also facilitated alliances with other organizations in joint mobilizations (Hernández 1988:23).

(e) *The identification and use of political spaces and of contradictions within the state.* Movement documents and leaders stressed the importance of identifying the "political moment" in the following way:

> We should learn to judge the conjuncture: whether it is favorable or unfavorable; whether it is of long or short duration; in a word, our movement must learn to act scientifically as well as combatively—with a cool head and a burning heart. (SNTE. Sección 7. 1983:17)

> We understand that our enemy is the state. We also understand, however, the balance of forces, and at a given moment *we must know how to move within the state itself*, to take advantage of the conjunctures that exist within the state itself. This does not mean that we seek out alliances with the state, only that we search out the different conjunctures that present themselves (emphasis added).[64]

---

62. Transcribed interviews, Comité Ejecutivo Seccional, Sección 7, n.d., p. 21.
63. Ibid.
64. Transcribed interviews with Coordinadora del Centro, Chiapas, n.d., p. 9.

This "moving within the state" was one of the key ideas that identified Línea Proletaria's influence in the CNTE. It also demonstrates that leaders were aware of the possibility that political opportunities would emerge in their environment, and that they strove not only to take advantage of these but to create advantageous situations themselves through well-timed mobilizations and alliances. Due to the centrality of this idea for strategizing, emphasis was placed on analyses of the balance of forces in a given period in documents circulated for discussion at state assemblies and CNTE meetings. These analyses of the conjuncture (*de coyuntura*) were one of the principal tasks of the leadership in its efforts to orient the membership. They typically included an assessment of the movement's strengths and weaknesses, and those of its enemies, in order to set the context for any actions that might be carried out in that period. Courses of action and tactics were then based on perceptions of strategic openings or opportunities generated by periods of change (e.g., elections) or by conflicts and contradictions at the levels of national or state government, within the union, or between the union leadership and the government.[65]

These conjunctural analyses and leaders' efforts to orient the membership by them did not escape challenge during state assembly meetings. Different political currents often presented their own analyses of the period, with their own recommendations for action. Union representatives often engaged in fierce debate over whether or not the appropriate "conditions" existed for a work stoppage or demonstration. The abbreviated assessment *"Hay condiciones"* or *"No hay condiciones"* was frequently all the explanation needed to indicate why members had voted for or against a particular action. Groups within the CNTE also expressed intense disagreement over the nature of the state and its contradictions and over the practice of forming alliances with those in power (Salinas and Imaz 1984:129–30). Some groups rejected the notion that alliances could be developed with any group of union or government officials; others believed that movement leaders had mistakenly taken temporary conflicts between elites as indicative of more important "contradictions" between state fractions, leading the movement to underestimate the force of government opposition and the speed with which conflicts with national union officials could be mended. In spite of these criticisms and differences of interpretation,

---

65. The importance of such documents meant that the teachers generated an enormous amount of written communication. Flyers, pamphlets, and newspapers were produced by all of the political groups (not just the leadership) and members of delegations in efforts to persuade the membership of different positions and to pronounce themselves on matters of critical importance to the movement. These were handed out at meetings, in the schools, and in the mobilizations and actions of the movement, in a display of pluralist exchange as well as of political competition.

however, the practice of seeking out political spaces and of recognizing opportunities in which actions might be most likely to succeed was widely accepted and formed part of the ongoing discussion of movement strategies.

Conclusion

In spite of the relatively limited gains for the teachers' movement at a national level between 1983–89, considerable changes were taking place *within* the movements themselves, and consequently at a less visible level in Oaxaca and Chiapas. In particular, the *kind* of organization that movement members constructed prior to and following legal status was crucial for both the identity of the movement and for its ability to sustain itself in what turned out to be an increasingly hostile national and regional environment. Once they had conquered the union locals, movement members set out to expand and consolidate a democratic internal organization. Movement members sought to democratize their local organizations because democratization of the national union was one of the key goals of the CNTE, and the principal strategy for pursuing this goal was to win and democratize the union locals. Hence, organizational democracy was simultaneously a goal, a strategy, and a defining element of the teachers' movement's identity.

The kind of democratic organization that movement members constructed in each region, however, was a response to the particular needs of the movement and to the challenges the movements faced: the need for frequent mobilizations in order to pressure authorities; rank-and-file mistrust of political parties and political currents and, at the same time, the presence of a variety of these in the same movement; the need for representation of different in-state regional interests in the local organization; and the need to protect the movement and the union local against efforts to co-opt the leadership, to drain the movement of supporters, and to provoke fatal divisions within the movement.

Members of the teachers' movement in union locals in both Oaxaca and Chiapas changed the locals' internal organization to expand member participation in decision making and to restrict the centralization of power in the hands of union officials in the statutory organizations of the local. Members could participate directly in decisions that affected them through regular meetings in their workplaces and delegations and through changes in the flow of information and in decision making that lent priority to the grassroots. Significant decision-making autonomy was granted to intermediate levels of organization within the local, and decisions that primarily affected delegations, sectors, or regions were decided at these instances rather than at the level of the executive committee.

These organizational and procedural changes included creating mechanisms to ensure the accountability of elected leaders, even in those cases where elections were not possible, such as at the executive committee level. The participation of rank-and-file representatives and members from the coordinadoras in the state assembly, and the participation of noncommittee members in negotiating teams and as assistants to executive commissions, provided direct links between rank-and-file members and elected local union officials. The coordinadoras at the delegation level also provided a role for members who engaged in the more political tasks of the movement and who could keep committee officers in check. Other ways of ensuring accountability from elected representatives included the system of *avales* (documents signed by delegations confirming the election of the representative and/or the agreement reached), and the presence of fraternal delegates as observers along with voting delegates at the precongresses. Finally, one of the most important changes was to grant the more representative state assembly the primary role in making decisions affecting the local.

Many of the new forms of participation that emerged within the movement functioned as defenses against movement enemies. Decision making at workplace and delegation levels protected the movement by engaging members at the most basic organizational level of the local and by enlisting member support against abuses of power and arbitrary changes in schools and school districts. Member engagement, as well as their requirement that teachers seeking to move within the system have proof of participation in movement or union activities, protected the schools against efforts by vanguardistas to infiltrate school districts and positions of power within the administration. (Although this protection was effective for a time, the local's inability in the second half of the 1980s to control vanguardista presence in the SEP delegations eventually turned the schools and delegations into centers of conflict.) Finally, the precongresses and prior delegation assemblies were among the clearest examples of defensive measures taken by the movement to protect its decision-making autonomy during elections to renew the executive committee.

A key resource of the movement was its mobilizational capacity, even after legality. Sustaining this mobilizational capacity was aided by instilling in members a sense of "ownership" of the movement, which was accomplished by expanding member participation in decision making, by creating mechanisms to make union local leaders more accountable in spite of the absence of authorized elections, and in the course of the mobilizations themselves. Incorporating the membership into the decision making regarding whether and when they would engage in mobilizations helped to ensure that these would realize their full potential. The movement's mobilization was also fed, however, by the continued resistance of government and union officials to grant the demands of the union locals. This treatment of the movement helped to foster a sense of group solidarity that in turn was crucial for internal cohesion. But another critical factor in helping sustain the movement's mobilizational capacity was the important, if fragile, protection afforded by the legal status of the Oaxaca and Chiapas movements. This meant that even though there might be an ebbing of the movement's ability to engage in mobilizations, its formal organization could continue to reside within the framework of the union local. At the same time, protection against the effects of decertification resided in the movement's simultaneous concern with sustaining the array of parallel, extralegal organizational instances that would not be directly affected by the withdrawal of legal status.

With the movement, schools and work centers, union locals, and mobilizations functioned as "schools for democracy" for the membership. The relative autonomy members experienced in these areas, together with the politicization produced over the course of their struggle, provided members with the "free spaces" they needed for the generation of new, public skills. The new procedures and organization developed by the movements, the increased participation in collective actions, and the constant struggle with government and union officials had an important though almost intangible effect on members of the teachers' movement—an increased political consciousness and the formation of a democratic collective identity among members. This increased political consciousness was reflected in a number of areas: in the increased participation of women in leadership positions within the movement; in the emergence of new leaders; in the mistrust members felt toward officials and their own leaders; in the selection with time of more radical union leaders; in members' increasing willingness to mobilize for political and not just economic demands; and in the increased participation of movement teachers in community organizing and other popular movements. These indicators of change reflected subtle yet nonetheless important transformations in attitudes and ways of thinking that could in turn translate into altered behavior in the classroom, in local and national elections, and in future actions within the teachers' union.

The dissident teachers' movement struggled to democratize the national teachers' union by constructing a democratic movement. Where members of the movement could have chosen to centralize decision making and to smother internal dissent for the sake of unity in the face of their enemies, they chose instead to broaden participation, decentralize decision making, and actively challenge the authority of their leaders. Although there were certainly costs to internal democracy—the slowness with which decisions were made, the time and energy required by frequent meetings, the inexperience of new leaders, the competition for power among factions, and even, at times, the tactical errors of the majority—these were outweighed by the longer-term benefits of democratic organization: the strengthening of a grass-roots defense against the movement's enemies through a sense of "ownership" of the movement by its members, the facilitation of mobilization, the reduced likelihood of co-optation, the generation of new leaders, the creation of political consciousness, and the expansion of horizontal alliances. Democracy, cumbersome and difficult to sustain at times, was seen as the only means to democratize the union. More important, democracy proved to be a functional strategy for the movement's survival.

7
Resurgence of National Mobilization

¡Primero fue La Quina, ahora Jonguitud!
First La Quina, now Jonguitud!
—Teachers' chant during 1989 mobilizations

Throughout most of the 1980s the general refusal of government and union officials to respond to the demands of the teachers' movements—especially their requests for elections—appeared to signal the effective containment of the movement. At the end of the decade, however, a new shift in the political environment would provide a broader political opening than the one that assisted the emergence of the movement ten years earlier. In early 1989 conflict between President Salinas and traditional labor bosses—a tension that would run throughout Salinas's term but which was symbolized by the arrest of the head of the oil workers' union—would coincide with a period of general political uncertainty in the aftermath of the 1988 presidential elections, as well as with elections at national and local levels within the teachers' union. This shift of events, and the subsequent mobilization and gains of the teachers' movement, offer the clearest evidence of the difference that changes in the political environment make for popular movements, especially those situated within established institutions. At the same time, the new environment for teachers and for popular movements in general after 1989 generated a new set of challenges for the movements and introduced a new ambivalence in the relationship between popular movements and democratization in Mexico.

National Mobilization and Political Opening: 1988–1989

It took another national political opening and national-level mobilization for the Oaxaca and Chiapas movements to break through the paralysis in which they found themselves. This new opportunity appeared in 1989, after an eventful nine months that included controversial presidential elections in July 1988, Carlos Salinas de Gortari's assumption of office in December, attacks on the head of the oil workers' union in January 1989, and a conflictive national congress in the SNTE in February. This succession of events formed the backdrop to what would be the largest teachers' protest in the history of the SNTE, culminating in the fall from power of Carlos Jonguitud Barrios on April 23, 1989.

From the perspective of the labor movement Carlos Salinas de Gortari was perhaps the most unpopular of the six "precandidates" of the ruling PRI that were announced prior to the 1988 presidential elections. As minister of programming and the budget under de la Madrid he was widely viewed as responsible for the austerity measures that had so devastated labor during the 1980s. Nonetheless, the SNTE quickly jumped onto Salinas's campaign bandwagon, pledging its members' commitment to the presidential campaign (in the form of eight million votes), and reiterating its perennial request for the top position in the Education Ministry. But the highly controversial July 1988 presidential elections revealed vast differences in voting behavior between union members and their leaders when many union members voted for opposition candidate Cuauhtémoc Cárdenas. Even official union leaders divided over support for the PRI candidate; in an unprecedented move oil union leader Joaquín Hernández Galicia ("La Quina") told his union's members to vote for Cárdenas.

The opposition accused the PRI of imposing its candidate through electoral fraud (in official results Salinas won a little over 51 percent of the vote). The elections left a trail of electoral protests and a government with little public support. For Mexico City residents in particular, the success of opposition candidate Cuauhtémoc Cárdenas's presidential campaign (the *cardenistas* won the capital) provided a needed boost to popular organizing efforts throughout the city and further eroded the authority of the Salinas administration.

Salinas assumed office in December 1988 speaking of economic and political "modernization." In an apparent move to make good on his word, one of Salinas's first actions upon assuming office was the dramatic arrest of the leader of the Mexican oil workers' union in January 1989. The oil workers' union was recognized as one of the country's most corrupt and powerful labor unions and had long been regarded as untouchable. At the same time, the oil leaders' animosity toward Salinas was well known.[1] Even so, Salinas's action took many by surprise. Some hailed it as a courageous and necessary act that demonstrated the kind of strong leadership Salinas would provide during his term. Others condemned the arrest as a violation of union autonomy and expressed concern over the government's use of the armed forces in a labor matter, which was reminiscent of the interventions by the government in the *charrazos* of the 1940s and 1950s. Opposition and labor groups were divided, many finding it hard to defend La Quina but finding the government's means reprehensible. While many in labor were not likely to view this action as an indication of government support for union democracy, they did interpret it as a sign from Salinas that traditional labor bosses were no longer inviolable. The executive's new attitude rekindled old demands for union democracy in a number of unions, including the teachers' union.

Like other workers, the teachers were further affected by continuing economic deprivation. Real wages had fallen dramatically since 1982.[2] The wage erosion had spread discontent to locals throughout the country. Stirrings of discontent among other public sector workers began anew in December of 1988, when the government attempted to eliminate the traditional six-year bonus it granted to its employees at the end of each presidential administration. At the same time, Locals 9, 10, and 11—representing secondary, preschool, and primary schoolteachers in Mexico City as well as technical, manual, and administrative workers in dependencies of the SEP throughout the country—began to mobilize on behalf of wage increases and in preparation to select

---

1. This animosity between Salinas and the leadership of the oil workers' union stemmed from Salinas's efforts, as minister of programming and the budget, to limit the union's control over a substantial proportion of PEMEX contracts (Middlebrook 1995:415, n. 3). On the political dimensions of the conflict between Salinas and the leadership of the oil workers' union see also Collier 1992:137.

2. Real wages for primary schoolteachers had fallen about 63 percent between 1982 and 1989 (Guzmán Ortiz and Vela Glez 1989:47). In early 1989 preschool teachers were making less than 300,000 pesos (U.S.$130) a month, and the average primary schoolteacher base wage was 317,000 pesos (U.S.$138) a month (dollar amounts are in 1989 dollars).

delegates to their local congresses and to the SNTE national congress that was to be held in February 1989.

Teachers' union officials reverted to their traditional methods of manipulating local assemblies throughout the country and of obstructing the opposition in the selection of delegates to its national congress.[3] Leaderships were imposed in the congresses of Locals 10 and 11. For members of union locals throughout the country the union leadership's handling of the national congress was the last straw. Congress delegates were flown or bused to the distant city of Chetumal, Quintana Roo, a site selected so as to hinder dissidents' attempts to attend the congress. In any case, union officials had already exercised careful control over the selection of congress delegates, which resulted in the complete absence of dissident delegates from the national congress.[4] The discontent generated by these maneuvers and by Jonguitud's tight control over who obtained key positions in the union leadership revealed dissension even among former allies of the union boss.

These factors converged in early 1989 to produce one of the largest demonstrations of teacher dissent in the history of the SNTE. Newspapers reported that 500,000 union members joined the work stoppages scheduled in April 1989, more than half of the country's largest union.[5] The dissident movement encompassed far more than the traditional opposition—it included rank-and-file members who had never participated in the movement, as well as disgruntled former supporters of Jonguitud.[6] The center of the dissent was Mexico City, where the union's largest locals were located, and all three locals were involved in the protests.[7] The participation of these locals was significant in several respects. They had taken part in only a limited way during the teachers' mobilizations a decade earlier. Local 9 of primary and preschool teachers had also always represented the stronghold of the SNTE leadership (Jonguitud had been secretary-general of the local). The fact that the Mexico City locals were

---

3. Among the techniques used in 1989 was stacking the congresses at the last minute with "fraternal delegates" who would vote in the vanguardista leaders. See *La Jornada*, February 10, 1989, p. 6.

4. This was in stark contrast to the national SNTE congress held three years earlier in 1986 in Tepic, Nayarit, which 169 dissident delegates attended. This disparity in the number of dissidents attending reflected the stronger efforts by leaders of the union to keep dissidents out rather than the actual scope and intensity of member discontent, which was evidently greater in 1989 than in 1986.

5. *La Jornada*, April 18, 1989, p. 1.

6. The dissident movement also drew school directors and supervisors (with traditionally close links to Vanguardia) who joined dissident ranks once their own union leaders' positions became unstable.

7. The total number of members represented by these locals was approximately 250,000.

now the center of teacher dissent reflected the disintegration of that power base and of Vanguardia's control.[8]

Mexico City in 1989 was also a changed place in contrast to the 1979–81 period of teacher mobilization. The 1985 earthquakes had increased public wariness of government and given rise to a number of new urban popular movement organizations in the capital (Bennett 1992; Ramírez Saiz 1990). The years following the earthquake had seen Mexico City shaken by two important popular movements: the march of Oaxaca's teachers in the spring of 1986, and the rise of a new student movement, the Consejo Estudiantil Universitario (CEU), during 1986–87. In the presidential elections of July 1988 Mexico City residents came out in strong support of Cuauhtémoc Cárdenas. By the time the teachers' mobilizations began again in early 1989, support for the teachers' protests was tremendous, far surpassing anything seen a decade earlier.

Teachers from throughout the country engaged in work stoppages, marches, hunger strikes, and *plantones* in Mexico City and in regional capitals from February to May 1989. Teachers formed organizational committees, spoke at schools, unions, and in public spaces, organized fund-raising events (parties, bake sales, raffles), and collected donations for the strike fund.[9] They prepared study guides for their students for the period during which classes would be canceled. Schools and workplaces remained important centers of activity; teachers were supposed to check in daily and use these sites as a base for strike-related activities. In this way teachers also hoped to avoid being charged with abandoning their jobs, an administrative allegation used by officials to fire dissident teachers during work stoppages.

New regional contingents continued to join the movement. The Education Ministry, headed by Manuel Bartlett Díaz, condemned the actions, called for teachers to return to work, and emphasized the harm they were causing to the nation's schoolchildren. On April 13 the government offered a combination of wage and benefits increases (10 percent increase in the base wage and increases in various other categories that totaled an increase of 18 percent, according to

---

8. The decline of support for Vanguardia among members of Local 9 was in part due to the decline in the number of members represented by this local in the years of Vanguardia's tenure at the leadership of the union. In contrast, Locals 10 and 11 increased their membership. Local 10 had always been more closely linked to former leaders of the union than to Jonguitud, and the delegations joined in Local 11 were generally more autonomous and dominated by the CNTE. The dissident base of support in this period was also overwhelmingly formed by young teachers who did not identify with the old political factions that dominated the union leadership (Arnaut Salgado 1989a).

9. One of the most lucrative events at one school bazaar was "Pin the Tail on Jonguitud," a creative adaptation of the well-known school child's game "pin the tail on the donkey."

the SEP), but teachers scoffed at the meager increase and held out for both a higher wage increase (the public demand was 100 percent) and union democracy, meaning, for the first time in the history of the movement, a call for new *national* union elections and the removal of the leadership recently ratified in the February congress, as well as the resolution of the political demands of a number of union locals.[10] Teachers seemed convinced that economic issues were tied to the issue of union democracy: the current leaders had to be removed and fair elections instated if such dramatic wage deterioration were to be avoided in the future.[11]

On April 17 locals in Mexico City, Oaxaca, Chiapas, Valle de México, and several other places began an indefinite national work stoppage, which was supported by numerous other contingents throughout the country with demonstrations and twenty-four and forty-eight hour work stoppages. Negotiations between SNTE leaders and a large commission dominated by the CNTE continued, but progress was slow and SNTE leaders appeared to stall in spite of SEP pressure to reach an agreement. On April 22 the Federal Conciliation and Arbitration Board issued an order to the national executive committee to hold another congress for Local 9, and also ordered protesters back to work within twenty-four hours, an order that protesting teachers ignored. The demonstrations and shows of support continued. A number of universities struck in solidarity, and students from the National Autonomous University of Mexico spread out throughout the city to collect money, food, and clothing for the striking teachers.

Finally, on April 23, 1989, Carlos Jonguitud Barrios emerged from a meeting with President Salinas and announced his resignation from his positions in Vanguardia and the SNTE. The next day the secretary-general of the union, Refugio Araujo del Angel, was also forced to step down from his position in the union after a late-night meeting in the Interior Ministry, during which the conditions of leadership transition within the union were no doubt hammered out. Araujo's successor, Elba Esther Gordillo, was present at the meeting and

---

10. The increase in benefits was later adjusted to 15 percent, for a total wage and benefits increase of 25 percent. The wage increases were to be in effect after May 15, National Day of the Teacher, a date on which the government traditionally declared some kind of increase for teachers. Moreover, this figure reflected a gross increase. The net increase after taxes, union dues, payments for insurance, and so forth would be much lower. After this increase a primary schoolteacher's take-home salary would reach 469,565 pesos a month (about U.S.$195 in 1989 dollars). This announcement thus carried a much reduced impact for teachers.

11. Interviews with rank-and-file teachers as portrayed in the 1989 video produced by Información Obrera, "Escuela por escuela."

emerged in the early morning to be ratified by a hastily convened meeting of union local secretaries-general called by the interior minister.[12]

Rank-and-file teachers were jubilant at the news of Jonguitud's resignation but rejected Gordillo's appointment as antidemocratic. Gordillo was considered to be cut of the same cloth as Jonguitud, and many dissidents believed she was linked to the assassination of Misael Núñez Acosta, a prominent CNTE leader from the Valle de México who was slain in 1981. Demonstrations continued. Three hundred thousand protestors filled the Zócalo (Mexico City's enormous central square) the day after Jonguitud's removal in what became a celebration as well as a protest.

Gordillo's political base within the union was weak, however, and many factions within the union saw this as an opportunity to gain a foothold. The new secretary-general's appointment appeared to be contingent upon her negotiating the dissident movement's political demands and successfully dismantling the vanguardista network. She quickly removed several Jonguitud loyalists and followers of Araujo from their positions at the head of the SCEPs in the states, and Jonguitud's network began to unravel in San Luis Potosí, a state that he had governed (Campa 1989). Gordillo also moved quickly in negotiations with the democratic contingents, agreeing to authorize elections in those locals where the democratic movement had been the strongest: Oaxaca, Chiapas, and among primary and preschool teachers in Mexico City, Local 9. When the dissident negotiating commission tried to hold out for the demands of contingents that had joined the protests later, it was pressed by the Interior Ministry to accept the terms extended to them by Gordillo. In some of these other locals (and in the rest of Mexico City) dissidents gained representation on temporary executive commissions and obtained commitments to review the results of earlier electoral congresses and to schedule future elections.[13]

---

12. The Salinas government had placed a former protégé of Jonguitud's in the leadership of the union. Gordillo had had a long career within the union, first as a union local leader in the state of Mexico, then in the national executive committee of the union. She had been bypassed twice for the position of secretary-general, which had recently increased the friction between her and her former mentor. Gordillo had also been on the national committee of the PRI and a federal congressional deputy and was recognized as a political ally of Salinas and particularly of Manuel Camacho, at the time a close Salinas aide and regent of Mexico City. She was in fact serving as a Federal District delegate at the time she was called to head the union.

13. The national executive committee had committed itself to holding an electoral congress in Chiapas (Local 7) on June 15–16, 1989. In Local 9 the national executive committee agreed to the formation of an executive commission made up of half national executive committee loyalists and half dissidents that would prepare for the electoral congress to be held July 17–18. Local 10 also obtained an executive commission divided equally between national executive committee loyalists and dissidents, with the presidency appointed by the national executive committee. Dissidents in

The resurgence of conflict within the union thrust the movements in Oaxaca and Chiapas back into action alongside the teachers from Mexico City and numerous other regions. In Oaxaca the movement had changed its tack in early 1989 and had voted in a new executive committee without an authorized congress. To avoid legal challenges, the "old" executive committee and the new were merged. After the 1989 mobilization the Oaxaca movement was able to ratify its formerly elected committee in an authorized congress on May 12, 1989, over which Elba Esther Gordillo herself presided. Federalized teachers in Chiapas and primary schoolteachers in Mexico City were also able to establish new executive committees, the first in June and the latter in July.

Conditions had changed for the better, but the Oaxaca and Chiapas locals now faced new challenges as well. The new Oaxaca committee turned its immediate attention to local matters: it wanted to get Gordillo to follow through on agreements to repair the union building and the teachers' hotels in Oaxaca and Puerto Escondido and to build a central supply store for union members. The Oaxaca local also faced challenges by former vanguardistas (*and* democratic members) whose paychecks had been suspended because, according to democratic local officials, they had not been going to work. At a national level the Oaxaca and Chiapas teachers also continued to support other locals as these pressured for their electoral congresses, and they lent support to administrative, technical, and manual employees who were still fighting for a wage increase, having been left out of the earlier round of increases extended to teachers. The locals also turned their attention to the forthcoming national union congress at the end of January 1990, in which the CNTE wanted to press for changes in the union statutes, and to their commitment with parents of the communities where they worked. Here teachers began to address the issue of

---

Local 11 were to receive ten new positions in a restructured executive committee and some response to their economic demands (the 25 percent increase did not affect technical, administrative, and manual employees of the SEP). In Oaxaca (Local 22) a previously elected committee took possession and was officially recognized on May 12, 1989. Local 36 of Valle de México was the only one of the six original dissident contingents not to receive a favorable response to its demands. Later, Locals 11, 10, and 9 (Mexico City) would also run into problems in getting the national executive committee to comply in good faith with the agreements. Other contingents that joined the protests later with demands for electoral congresses were: Aguascalientes, Baja California, Hidalgo, Local 40 of Chiapas (state teachers), Veracruz, Michoacán, Zacatecas, Yucatán, Guerrero, Guanajuato, Jalisco, Sonora, Morelos, Puebla, and the state of México. Michoacán and Guerrero both held electoral congresses in the fall, but the procedures and results were contested in each case. Four of these contingents were included in discussions over a so-called "third package," but the core contingents lifted the work stoppage before concrete solutions to these demands were obtained. See Enrique Garay, "Menos de 500 mil pesos, el sueldo mensual del maestro," *La Jornada*, May 20, 1989, p. 8.

an "alternative education" that would counteract the government's proposed "curriculum modernization" and that would be rooted in local traditions, democratic practices, and teachers' experiences.[14]

After 1989 the locals also found that they had greater access to the SEP than before. One leader from Oaxaca put it simply: "Now they receive us, before they didn't."[15] In Oaxaca the local continued to face resistance, however. Relations with the state governor's office became more strained as the governor became a more powerful force in the state both because of the impending decentralization of education and also because of the federal Programa Nacional de Solidaridad (National Solidarity Program, PRONASOL) funds that were being channeled through the governor's office in Oaxaca to create "model" schools, bypassing the union local.[16] This issue was all the more sensitive because several former members of the Oaxacan teachers' local executive committee had gone to work for the governor, and one had moved to the state committee of the PRI. The new executive committee was convinced meanwhile that national union officials and the state governor were intent on spurring divisions within the local and forcing a call for new elections that would bring in leaders more sympathetic to the state government and the national executive committee.[17]

Meanwhile, the changes within the national leadership of the union ushered in a period of closer relations between the SNTE and the Salinas government. Gordillo was also initially more open to the dissidents but acted in order to stabilize the organization and to build her own support base. To this end she offered members of the CNTE positions on the national executive committee and tried to extract commitments of support in private negotiations with dissident leaders. Those who did not respond to her overtures were marginalized in the competition for power that ensued. Further countering perceptions anyone might have had of the new leadership as committed to internal democracy, Gordillo assured regional SNTE leaders during a meeting in Coahuila in May 1989: "Let's not speak anymore of Vanguardia, but let there be no misunderstanding, we cannot abandon a political current. . . . What we have to do is change strategies, change our name, but those of us who are and

14. Interview with local executive committee member, Oaxaca, June 18, 1990. For a discussion of alternative education before this date see CNTE, 1984, and *Cuadernos Educativos* No. 1, 1985. After 1989 the Oaxaca local initiated an alternative education project based on community and teacher participation; see the local's newspaper, *Alternativa*, and the magazines *Educación . . . ?* and *Educación Alternativa*, both from Oaxaca.
15. Interview with local executive committee member, Oaxaca, June 13, 1990.
16. Ibid.
17. Interviews with local executive committee members, Oaxaca, June 18, 1990.

have been will continue and we're not leaving. . . . [a willingness to engage in dialogue] does not mean we will give up power" (Campa 1989:9).

Gordillo nonetheless stood up to old factions of vanguardistas who were trying to build their own bases of support within the union, and to those who opposed advances by the democratic movement. Vanguardia was officially disbanded, and in its place Gordillo announced a new "broad front" (*frente amplio*) that would incorporate the various currents found within the union. Her style of leadership reflected that of the Salinas administration toward popular movements during his term: while Gordillo displayed a greater willingness to negotiate with contingents outside of the leadership's traditional sectors of support, negotiations would proceed on her (and the government's) own terms. This proved to be a very divisive strategy for the CNTE, whose contingents were forced to take a position on whether or not to negotiate with Gordillo and on whether or not to accept the offers of participation she extended. The CNTE not only divided over this issue but was unable to act in a unified manner in subsequent mobilizations. In addition the movement experienced a natural decline in participation due to the extensive nature and intensity of the spring 1989 mobilizations. In time Gordillo was able to consolidate her hold over the union leadership in a way that made the support of the once powerful dissident movement no longer as important.

For much of the 1980s the rapprochement between union and government officials served to limit the advances of the dissident teachers' movement. However, the political opening in 1989 was in many ways even broader than the one that assisted the dissident movement's emergence ten years earlier. Whereas the political opening in 1979–81 was largely due to conflict between the government and the SNTE, the political opening during 1989 emerged from a combination of conjunctural "opportunities." First, there was a national period of transition that affected the country as a whole and Mexico City in particular, as well as the teachers' union—the teachers' immediate environment. Highly controversial presidential elections had just been held. Leadership turnovers were also occurring in many union locals and in the national union (including local assemblies for delegate selection). Second, state-union conflict was also present, but this time both more broadly expressed than in 1979–81 and more directly situated between the president and the "corporatist" union leadership. Traditional labor bosses immediately came into conflict with the president's new "modernizing" project for the country, and this greatly weakened their position.

The teachers' movement, led by the CNTE, had scored a tremendous victory. By the strength of its mobilizations it had led the government to intervene in removing the head of Vanguardia Revolucionaria. Nonetheless, in removing Jonguitud the government also moved to gain effective control over a union and a sector that had yet to face many changes, including the decentralization of education, which remained a government objective. The Salinas administration therefore succeeded in breaking the control of Jonguitud Barrios and an already weakened Vanguardia Revolucionaria over the union, capitalizing on the mobilizations of the ten-year-old democratic movement and the discontent of regional union leaders who were former vanguardistas. The government's renewed influence over the leadership of the union would eventually enable it to move forward in its plans for a decentralized educational system, a move that had been blocked for years under the former union leaders.

While the movement was able to make important gains during this period of conflict, the new circumstances that emerged in government-SNTE relations and the SNTE leadership's reaction to the internal opposition created a set of challenges for which many in the movement were unprepared. The mobilizations of 1989 and the fall of Jonguitud marked the end of an especially conflictive chapter in the teachers' union but opened another of more subtle and complex challenges. Among these, the democratic locals faced the problem of how to distinguish themselves clearly from the new national leadership of the union and how to sustain unity within the movement in the absence of a clear common enemy, Vanguardia Revolucionaria. Leaders acknowledged that confrontation with Vanguardia had unified the movement, focusing member discontent with movement leaders on an external threat.[18] It would be far more difficult to rally members around a program of alternative education than it had been to rally them around wage demands or even issues of union democracy in the past. Equally important, the subsequent accommodation between the government and the union, together with the increased opportunities for the opposition to participate in the governance of the union, altered the structure of opportunities for the movement at both national and regional levels.

Changes in the Mexican Political Environment: Implications for the Teachers' Movement

Much of the argument presented in this book relates to the situation of a social movement that emerges within a relatively closed environment. Such an

---

18. Ibid., June 14 and 18, 1990.

environment shapes the tactics and strategies of social movements in particular ways. In this case it was essential that the movement sustain the capacity to mobilize its members around its key demands. The need for regular mobilization in turn shaped the kind of organization the movement developed; I have argued that it gave democracy a central place in the movement's organization. After the teachers' protests in 1989 their political and economic environment changed significantly, although these changes still occurred in the context of an authoritarian regime. The changes were in part the result of the success of the movement's strategy, in part the result of successful state efforts to channel and contain a process that threatened to escape its control. The end result was relatively greater openness to some currents within the CNTE, and a relatively greater influence of these currents on the national union leadership. This changed environment presented new challenges to the teachers' movement. At the same time, the degree of incorporation of the movement into the mainstream of the union and the divisions that emerged within the CNTE raised questions about the continued viability of the teachers' movement as an autonomous social movement.

Although full attention to the new conditions and new issues teachers faced after 1989 is beyond the scope of this book, it is important to consider here what happened after 1989 if only because this period represented a strikingly new environment for the teachers' movement, and therefore demonstrates how changes in political context so alter a movement's tactical, strategic, and organizational options.

The CNTE had much to do with the ouster of Jonguitud in April 1989. It spearheaded the protests and represented the most coherent and articulate voice of opposition among a heterogeneous mass that included former allies of Jonguitud and apolitical but disillusioned union members as well as solid CNTE supporters. It had little to say about who would replace him, however, or the means used to install the new secretary-general of the union. The greater openness toward some sectors within the CNTE came after Elba Esther Gordillo had been imposed, and amounted to efforts to assuage the most consolidated democratic factions of the union (Oaxaca and Chiapas) and some of those that had emerged as the strongest in the recent protests (Local 9 and, to a lesser extent, Locals 10 and 11 in Mexico City). It was in these few months after the fall of Jonguitud that the CNTE's influence could have been the strongest, but it was during this period that internal divisions sharpened, with the aid of government authorities and the new union officials.

The divisions became apparent before Jonguitud's fall, when latecomer contingents joined the protests in 1989 and pressed for CNTE leaders to negotiate the "entire package" of demands with union and government officials. CNTE negotiators, uncertain where the protests would lead and pressured by Interior Ministry officials, were unwilling to sacrifice the likelihood of gaining strong concessions for the possibility of expanding the circle of beneficiaries. These differences developed into marked tensions between newer, in some ways more radical, contingents (and younger leaders) and the veteran activists of the CNTE (Hernández 1989b). The tendency of some leaders (and of the media) to highlight personal accomplishments rather than collective ones in the course of the protests and negotiations fueled this growing animosity toward some members of the CNTE. For their part many CNTE leaders felt they had to take advantage of a historic opportunity to expand their participation and influence in the union, and could not afford to allow the explosion of demands on the part of new contingents to ruin this opportunity.

Union and government officials exploited these divisions. Gordillo quickly and personally acted to grant the political demands of the more consolidated dissident locals and blocked those where the dissidents were more radical or very vocal but in the minority. At the same time, she extended invitations to some CNTE leaders who had been key in the negotiations to participate on the national executive committee of the union.[19] The question of whether or not to participate in the official structures of union governance, alongside one's enemies, had always been a divisive issue for the teachers' movement. During a SNTE congress in early 1990 differences on this issue came to light when some CNTE locals decided to allow their representatives to accept positions on the national executive committee while others refused. In addition, a previously agreed-upon plan to walk out when Gordillo's ratification as secretary-general came up was foiled when some contingents left the floor early, leaving a very weak CNTE representation in the assembly. This much-criticized move revealed a CNTE fraught with internal divisions.

Nonetheless, the influence of some CNTE factions on the national union leadership became greater than ever before. What emerged after 1989 were in fact multiple CNTEs, with one of these closer to Gordillo than were any of the former vanguardistas. To what extent did the movement's participation in the union change conditions within the union and its relations with the state? To what extent did these changes correspond to the CNTE's earlier goals as a movement?

Soon after her appointment as interim secretary-general of the SNTE, Gordillo called for the formation of a "broad front" (*frente amplio*) within the

19. Interview with CNTE leader, Local 10, Mexico City, June 27, 1990.

union, consisting of various political currents that had existed within the union, often at odds with each other. The notion of the *frente amplio* was that these currents would now have similar status within the union, in circumstances where before the CNTE had been excluded from full participation. This change reflected a pragmatic decision on the part of a union leader who did not have broad-based support within the union, and who certainly did not have it from all of the formerly vanguardista currents. The decision also reflected the fact that segments of the powerful CNTE were willing to grant the new secretary-general conditional support against former jonguitudista factions who were preparing for a struggle for control of the union. As part of the *frente amplio* idea, Vanguardia Revolucionaria was also officially abolished. No longer would unionists sing the Vanguardia anthem nor would the Vanguardia emblem appear on union documents.

CNTE members enjoyed full participation in the union's first congress after the 1989 mobilizations. They reportedly impressed former vanguardistas with their experience, their ability to maneuver positions through the assembly, and their proposals. Many of these were incorporated into the documents and resolutions of the 1990 congress. It was also especially important for Gordillo that the SNTE be able to demonstrate to the Salinas government that it could generate new ideas, "modernize" itself, and do so while incorporating the strongest elements of the opposition.[20] The union was especially vulnerable given the recent shake-up in the leadership, the demonstrated strength of the dissidents, and the impending decentralization of education. Moreover, the Salinas government's dramatic arrest of the leader of the oil workers' union in early 1989 left union leaders little doubt that the government would be willing to intervene again in other "official" unions.

Several important reforms were adopted that reflected the demands of the CNTE for greater democracy in the union. Among them, voting would be done by secret ballot, and the statutory clause that called for union members' massive affiliation to the PRI would be dropped. The union also established its independence and autonomy from political parties and the state in its statutes' "Declaration of Principles" (SNTE 1992). The SNTE thus became the first major union since the 1970s to formally disconnect itself from the PRI. In practice the secretary-general was still very much tied to the party and to the president's circle, but the formal disaffiliation reflected both the powerful presence of different currents within the union *and* a more widespread tendency

---

20. Interview with advisor to Elba Esther Gordillo, Mexico City, June 26, 1992.

under Salinas for labor unions to loosen their ties with the party while strengthening them with the executive.[21]

These changes within the union reflected at least in part the successful efforts of the dissident teachers' movement. Like all popular movement gains in Mexico, however, there was another side to this success. The changes also reflected the government's ability to adapt to new circumstances in ways that permitted it to retain the upper hand, which is not to deny that popular pressure continued to play a role. The more open environment within the union altered conditions for the CNTE in fundamental ways. For one, it no longer made sense to speak of *the* CNTE, or at least to speak of it in terms of its early constituents. There was a segment of the movement that still felt disenfranchised, that had rejected its former leaders, and that won little after 1989, either because it was not strong enough to do so at a regional level and/or because it rejected the strategy of collaboration with the union leadership that some CNTE leaders favored.

The greater openness within the union also altered the strategic and tactical choices of the opposition. Where one sector of the CNTE felt that the time had come to switch from resistance and street mobilizations to negotiation, policymaking, and administration—because the doors had opened—another fell back on old tactics: denunciations, demonstrations, and attacks on other members of the erstwhile opposition. Numerous articles and statements by those in the former faction pointed to the inability of the "radical" factions to recognize the change in terrain and the need to switch tactics.[22] One prominent leader, denounced by the radical faction of the CNTE for his participation in the national executive committee of the union, complained that some CNTE members saw the union movement as an instrument of revolutionary transformation, when in fact, he argued, it could not be more than an instrument of reform.[23] Nonetheless, many CNTE members continued to denounce and reject this commitment to reform rather than radical transformation of the system displayed by several key CNTE leaders.

It was not only the greater openness within the union that made mobilizations less effective but the fact that after the 1989 protests the government responded to the dissidents' economic demands. Teachers in 1989, 1990, and 1991 received bigger wage increases than most other sectors, and while this did not

---

21. This move by the union in 1991 followed a change in PRI requirements for affiliation, determined during the 1990 PRI National Assembly, permitting individual affiliation as opposed to affiliation through mass organizations.
22. See Hernández 1989b and 1992, Cano et al. 1992.
23. Interview with CNTE leader, Local 10, Mexico City, June 27, 1990.

make up for thirteen years of real wage decline, it defused much of the protests and made it harder to justify mobilizing for economic demands. When some dissident sectors called for mobilizations in the fall of 1989 to protest inattention to the political demands of some of the locals, the lack of support stood in stark contrast to the outpouring of solidarity months earlier. Exhaustion, parents' protests, and emerging internal divisions over strategy plagued the dissident efforts. Some CNTE leaders and potential supporters found it more difficult to understand and support demonstrations in this new environment.

One of the earliest strengths of the CNTE was the outward demonstration of unity between rank-and-file members and leaders that was most evident during mass actions (rallies, marches), when both leaders and members were excluded by a common enemy. After 1989 the common enemy was less clearly defined, the exclusion more selective and in some ways more subtle. This situation magnified a problem that had always existed beneath the surface of the movement—the tensions and potential for conflict between members and leaders, and especially the former's mistrust of leaders who had frequent contact with authorities. The functions and tasks of leaders and members had become more separate: leaders talked, negotiated, and spoke to the press; members felt most a part of the movement when they fought to defend it in marches, *plantones*, and hunger strikes. The reduced importance of the latter activities not only increased the distance between leaders and rank-and-file members, it also raised the question of whether what was left could any longer be accurately described as a social movement. The CNTE had joined the institution; it had become several currents within a union that now formally acknowledged its heterogeneous membership, and thus something quite different from what it was before.

For those locals that managed to obtain official recognition of their democratically elected leaderships in 1989 (Oaxaca, Chiapas, Local 9 of Mexico City), greater openness at the national level of the union should have permitted these locals to devote their energies to education, community organizing and participation, and deepening democratic decision making. To some degree this did happen. Many leaders saw a stronger commitment to improving the service they provided to the community as a way to distinguish the democratic movement from the new national leadership of the union, and thus as a way to maintain a distinct collective identity that would continue to feed the movement. Yet greater openness also brought with it greater factionalism among democratic forces at the regional level as well as in the national CNTE. One of the Oaxaca local's leaders acknowledged as much when she told me in 1990, in response to rumors that Gordillo was trying to force new elections in order to push out the newly elected Oaxacan leaders, that all the union leadership had to do was to stop attacking them and they would fall apart into different fighting factions and probably disintegrate entirely.[24]

The commitment to leadership rotation favored by some regional movements also hurt the continuity of local union projects. The movement in Oaxaca had had an executive committee leadership that lasted well beyond the statutory limit of three years. After 1989 the committee was again renewed every three years, and the membership often chose to bar former leaders from reelection. In Oaxaca some former executive committee members obeyed their earlier promise to "return to the base"—to return to their original schools and workplaces and reintegrate themselves into the membership. Others used their union experience as dissidents to do what their enemies used to do—accept positions in government or the party. One former leader of the Oaxaca local confessed that after eight years at the head of one of the most important contingents of the CNTE, he simply couldn't see himself quietly going back to his rural primary school teaching job.[25] In other regions some former dissident leaders became close advisors to Gordillo, others threw themselves into work for the PRD and became federal congressional deputies for the opposition. This mobility of the old leadership left room for new leaders to take their places in the union locals, but new leaders also brought their inexperience, which often left them unprepared to bargain in the new political climate.

The irony of the CNTE's integration into the SNTE was that, while it reflected the existence of a greater and perhaps unprecedented degree of democracy within the union, the SNTE's relationship with the government was not dramatically altered. Admittedly, there were important modifications. Under the leadership of Gordillo the union altered its profile from that of a union led by "dinosaurs" to a more vigorous, "modern," and presumably independent union. It moved quickly to join other unions that, with the blessing of President Salinas, began to press for a "new" form of unionism in Mexico under the guise of the FESEBES (Federation of Goods and Services Unions).[26] Gordillo herself even updated her personal image, surrounded herself with intellectual advisors, and organized a series of international conferences focusing on the state of unionism in Latin America.

24. Interview with local executive committee member, Oaxaca, June 18, 1990.
25. Interview with former local executive committee leader, Oaxaca, June 14, 1990.
26. The FESEBES was formed in 1990 by the telephone workers' union, the Mexican Electrical Workers (Sindicato Mexicano de Electricistas, SME), the airline pilots' and flight attendants' associations, tramway workers, and manual workers from the cinematography industry. After 1992 it was joined by the Volkswagen workers' union. The SNTE was an ally but not a formal member of the federation.

Nonetheless, the SNTE also became more closely tied to the Salinas administration and represented less of an obstacle to projected government reforms than it had under Jonguitud's leadership. This situation was the result of several developments: the manner in which the new union leader was installed, which made her dependent on the government; the divisions within the CNTE, which acted to undermine its influence; and the Salinas government's efforts to restructure the regime's relationship with key trade unions and with the party, which encouraged the existence of more "independent" unions as long as these did not challenge the government's economic and policy reforms. Not only had the context changed for teachers and for their union but the overall political environment for popular movements in the opposition had also changed significantly.

Popular Movements and the New Political Environment Under Salinas

Analysts have struggled to characterize the Salinas administration's relations with social actors to determine what elements corresponded to decidedly new forms of mediation between state and society and which constituted merely a "repackaging" of the traditional populism, clientelism, and corporatism of the past.[27] Part of the difficulty is due to the different ways in which diverse sectors—labor unions, urban popular movements, rural organizations, and opposition parties—were handled by the administration and the diversity of positions groups within each of these sectors adopted.

If one had to generalize about each of these sectors, one could argue that labor unions faced a relatively greater degree of exclusion from regime participation under the Salinas administration than in the past; urban popular movements—at least some of them—established a tie with the administration that enabled them to expand their local base; independent rural organizations likewise found a sympathetic ear in the government for demands concerned with agricultural production but not for land distribution claims; opposition parties on the right found a willingness to negotiate and expanded their presence in state governments; left parties encountered repression, electoral fraud, and exclusion. In general, those organizations that had for decades

27. See the collection of essays in Cook, Middlebrook, and Molinar Horcasitas 1994, and Harvey 1993.

formed the central pillars of the PRI and the regime—the CTM, the CNOP, and the CNC—lost status and preferential access to government in the early years of the administration in favor of more independent organizations that had risen in the 1970s and 1980s.[28]

It is important to point out, however, that within this broad category of "new" social organizations, only a few were able to establish access to the new government. Within labor these included those unions that were willing to cooperate in the administration's drive to raise productivity and increase labor flexibility, usually by limiting wages and benefits and granting employers greater prerogatives. Also favored were those rural organizations that had proven their technical ability in agricultural cooperatives and marketing networks. Among urban popular movements those that received privileged status entered into agreements (*convenios*) with the federal government for services for their communities and distanced themselves from the opposition Party of the Democratic Revolution. All of these "new interlocutors" were willing to negotiate with the Salinas administration, were nonideological and pragmatic in their political alliances and strategies, and had relatively strong social bases.[29]

The possibility that some independent popular organizations would be able to secure access to government and meet some of their demands limited the opportunities available to organizations that had made their mark through mass mobilization and denunciation. It isolated the more radical as well as the more principled organizations, limited their resources, and weakened their ability to get results for their members.[30] If the Salinas government's aim was to divide popular movements and weaken their ties to the PRD in the wake of the 1988 presidential elections, then it appeared to have succeeded. The positions that many popular movements adopted under the Salinas government were especially controversial given that 1988 had seemed to promise the possibility of greater national unity among opposition groups in Mexico.

The requirements for popular movement "success" also changed. The "coor-

---

28. For fuller development of the discussion presented here see Cook, Middlebrook, and Molinar Horcasitas 1994:28–40.

29. On the relationship between the Salinas administration and rural organizations see Fox 1994c; on urban popular movements under Salinas see Haber 1994; on labor unions see La Botz 1992, de la Garza Toledo 1994, and Cook 1995.

30. This was illustrated quite clearly in the case of the Comité de Defensa Popular (CDP) of Durango, an urban popular movement that signed a *convenio* with the government, split from the PRD, and formed its own well-funded political party, the Partido del Trabajo. The contrasting case is represented by the Asamblea de Barrios, whose loyalty to the PRD and commitment to a national political strategy cost it access to state resources and ultimately led to a decline in its membership (Haber 1994).

dinadora" model of social organization—consisting of regional autonomy, diffuse collective leadership, strong emphasis on mobilization, and political autonomy from parties and government—proved to be less effective in this new climate. Instead, organizations with a clearly defined (and more centralized), politically pragmatic leadership experienced in negotiating with authorities and willing to form tactical alliances fared best. It also helped to have considerable flexibility while negotiating, which meant some insulation from membership claims and from the possibility of removal or turnover. For urban popular organizations these conditions were often satisfied by the presence of charismatic leaders who spent most of their careers tied to the organization; in some key unions (telephone workers) leaders found ways to remain at the head of their organizations by altering union statutes forbidding reelection. The very conditions that gave strength to the teachers' movement during its struggle within a closed environment—reliance on mobilization, rank-and-file vigilance, and demands for accountability—became to many popular movement leaders in the early 1990s encumbrances to be shrugged off. Mobilizational capacity was no longer as important as a personal relationship with key government officials. One of the consequences of this shift in tactics and strategy was the demobilization of popular movements.

Another characteristic of the recent period that further undermined the coordinadora model of popular organization was the renewed importance that elections acquired as an arena of conflict and mobilization. Popular mobilizations around elections gathered force among mostly middle-class and conservative PAN supporters in the north of the country during the mid-1980s. With the presidential elections of 1988 and Cárdenas's candidacy, the left—which had generally been stronger in popular movements than in political parties—also became centrally involved in election struggles.

Elections presented many complications for popular movements. Voting appealed to individuals in their role as citizens rather than to the collective interests of popular organizations. In the mid-1980s many popular movement activists perceived this shift of the arena of conflict and mobilization away from labor and popular movements (except for urban popular movements) toward a citizenwide movement for electoral democracy, and noted the limited role popular organizations could play in this as long as they insisted on autonomy from political parties. With Cárdenas's presidential run in 1988 some organizations abandoned this position and threw their support behind the candidate, while others (such as the CNTE) sustained its position of not pronouncing itself in support of a party or coalition, but neither would it interfere with the individual party militancy of its members. After 1988 the tensions that emerged between the PRD leadership and many of the popular organizations that had joined the party reflected, among other things, the latter's fundamental need to meet the material demands of their members, and thus their need to cultivate a relationship with the state, versus the party's need to distance itself from the government and to preserve its distinct political identity (Haber 1994). Overall, while popular movements played an important role in the coalition that forged the National Democratic Front and, later, the PRD, the shift in focus from sectoral/organizational struggles for material gains and representation to elections displaced popular movements as the "social subjects" of the period in favor of citizenship and territorial struggles. The Salinas administration's acknowledgment of this shift was reflected in the government's efforts to restructure the PRI in ways that diminished the role of corporate interests in favor of individual/territorial ones (Cook, Middlebrook, and Molinar 1994:24).

In the aftermath of 1988 the Salinas administration was surprisingly effective at dividing popular movements and undermining the political opposition of the left. Its efforts to "restructure" state-society relations had the effect of isolating popular organizations from each other and shifting attention away from a national program and debate over democracy—such as existed around 1988—to more localized and regional struggles in which organizational survival often became the chief concern. This disarticulation of popular movements at the national level, and the successful reseparation of popular movements from electoral issues, decreased the likelihood that they would play a role in any national movement for democracy and, at least initially, appeared to lessen the possibility that such a move would occur around the 1994 presidential elections. Moreover, the approval of the North American Free Trade Agreement by the United States Congress in November 1993, and the announcement of the PRI's presidential candidate that same month, appeared to signal the administration's successful consolidation of economic reforms and the stability of the presidential succession process, the keystone of the authoritarian political system.

Multiple developments during 1994 altered this perception, however. The uprising of armed indigenous peasants in Chiapas in January 1994 threw into sharp relief both the shortcomings of the government's economic reforms and the limitations of the incremental electoral reform—in lieu of more complete democratization—pursued by the regime. The uprising was the jolt that was needed to reactivate citizen's groups and renew calls for democracy in a country that seemed to have "changed to remain the same." The uprising also provided a political opening to the left PRD, which became central to discussions of further electoral reform. The government's confidence was shattered: the assassination of the PRI presidential candidate in March 1994, the Chiapas uprising, the heightened international attention to Mexican domestic politics as an outgrowth of NAFTA, all in the months prior to what promised to be a well-watched and potentially controversial presidential election in August, revealed deep divisions and tensions within the government and the party.

The final year of the Salinas administration also revealed further development of a tendency that started in the 1980s: the increased importance of struggles over issues of citizenship, of the rights to have one's vote respected, to demand accountability from leaders, to receive accurate information from government and the media, to receive protection from arbitrary action by the state. Although such issues were part of the struggle of many popular movements over the course of the 1970s and 1980s, the difference in the 1990s was that the struggle for such rights was beginning to occur outside of political parties and outside of popular organizations as well. The appearance of citizen watchdog groups, such as the Civic Alliance, which coordinated thousands of domestic and foreign poll watchers on election day in 1994, best reflects this novel development.

Moreover, in spite of efforts to generate new allies and to distance itself from and reshape its relations with some of the traditional mass organizations, the Salinas administration had not fully succeeded in separating itself from its old bases of electoral support, such as labor, nor had it succeeded in consolidating new bases of support from among other sectors of society. Its efforts to reorganize the popular sector of the party failed, as did its efforts to empower a new sector of the labor movement. And although the political opposition remained disorganized (especially the left), it could not be said toward the end of Salinas's term that the changes in state-society relations had found institutional expression—neither in the traditional sense of incorporation in the party nor in a commitment to procedural democracy. Although some independent popular organizations had closer ties to the state than before, this did not mean that the relationship would necessarily continue with another president. These ties were based on a more personalistic and pragmatic set of alliances than on ideology or historic loyalty to the regime. In this way societal organizations had become more *ideologically* autonomous from the state, and hence *potentially* a free-floating political resource. Political elites could not be assured of the support of these "new" organizations, and had undermined the material and ideological bases of support by traditional allies. Such groups, then, might be just as likely to throw their support behind an opposition party should a viable political alternative emerge.

Additional developments that have come to light in the 1990s promise to both alter the context for future social movements and the nature and range of the resources at their disposal. First, the debate surrounding NAFTA produced interesting and "unintended" consequences: the formation of a number of cross-border alliances and contacts among popular organizations, citizens' groups, and labor unions, and an increased awareness of and interest in developments in Mexico on the part of such groups in the United States and Canada. This development has heightened international scrutiny of the Mexican government's handling of the Chiapas uprising, its investigations into the political assassinations of 1993–94, labor rights, and elections. More important, it has made available to groups in Mexican civil society international allies for their domestic struggles. Second, the rapid increase in the number of nongovernmental organizations in Mexico during the 1980s and 1990s also increases the range of allies and of resources (including international resources and contacts) available to social movements and other groups and provides a nongovernment outlet of employment for middle-class professionals. Finally, the media (especially print and radio) has become much more important recently in transmitting critical information to the public. Although it is still criticized (particularly television) for heavily favoring the government, a number of newspapers and radio programs have emerged that offer far more independent analysis, increasing the possibilities for a much more informed citizenry and for the rapid diffusion of events. Nowhere has the relevance of the media emerged more clearly than in the case of the Chiapas rebels, and in particular of one of its leaders, subcommander Marcos, whose international and domestic image was shaped and sustained through newspaper and radio reports from the mountains of Chiapas, as well as through the internet.

In late 1994–early 1995 Mexico was wracked by political scandal and by economic crisis. The strong showing by the PRI in the August 1994 elections, bolstered by a record voter turnout and relatively limited incidence of electoral fraud, was quickly overshadowed by the assassination of the PRI's secretary-general in September 1994 and the devaluation of the peso in December. The economic crisis and political uncertainty that have come in the wake of these events raise new questions about the future direction of the Mexican regime. Yet what is virtually certain is that the "citizens" generated and shaped by the social movements of the 1970s, 1980s, and 1990s will play a central role in the ongoing struggle for a democratic regime in Mexico.

Conclusion

The popular mobilization surrounding the 1988 presidential elections and the subsequent political realignments in state-popular sector relations under the Salinas administration again altered national political conditions for popular movements in Mexico. Because of the decade-long experience of the CNTE and a series of events specific to the teachers' union, the national teachers' movement was in a unique position to press forward on a range of demands in 1989. The events of 1989, accompanied by the Salinas administration's greater general openness to selected popular movements in the wake of 1988, secured for the teachers' movement a greater degree of institutional access than ever before. As this chapter demonstrated, access brought to the surface earlier tensions and divisions in the movement, highlighted the need for a more centralized coordination of demands and strategy, and undermined the effectiveness of a strategy of mobilization and denunciation. It called into question the political goals of the movement: Was it enough, finally, to democratize the union, or should the movement also adopt a political stance on the democratization of the country? Did participation in the national committees and councils of the SNTE jeopardize the movement's ability to pursue this larger goal as well? Further administrative and organizational changes slated for the education system, such as the decentralization of public education, would also dramatically alter conditions for the movement. In all likelihood decentralization would consolidate the division of the national movement into regional movements active only at the state level.

Other popular movements would also be affected by changes in the way that the Salinas administration related to them: by its efforts to single out certain popular organizations to grant their demands in exchange for demobilization and distance from the PRD, by its placement of officials more willing to negotiate with popular movements into key agency positions, by its simultaneous efforts to close off access for more "intransigent" or "radical" movements. These state actions were accompanied by the effort to move away from traditional bases of social support—the official labor movement and other corporate groups—and to seek out new allies and new social bases among business, the middle class, new sectors of labor, small farmers, the urban poor, and segments of the unorganized poor.[31] Moreover, the increasing number of conflicts surrounding elections—at municipal, state, and, perhaps again, national levels—have made the electoral arena a likely one for action by broad popular coalitions and by citizens' groups, with important implications for the future of Mexican democracy. Although the political future of the regime remains uncertain, the continuing challenge for popular groups and citizens' organizations will be to generate and seize the opportunities to open further the boundaries of the authoritarian regime.

31. The latter in particular has been the target of the National Solidarity Program, a controversial but much-publicized antipoverty program initiated by the Salinas administration. For a critical evaluation see Dresser 1991, and Cornelius, Craig, and Fox 1994.

8
Conclusion

Social movements are movements for change. At some point, then, their study prompts us to ask how successful they have been and what difference they make. The first part of this chapter summarizes and assesses the impact of the teachers' movement on several areas: the union, educational policy, the teachers' work environment, and social and political changes in Mexico. The second part of the chapter summarizes the central argument and the findings presented in the preceding chapters, and the final section presents an assessment of the contributions of this study for the comparative study of social movements.

The Mexican Teachers' Movement: Assessing the Impact

Throughout this book I have referred to the teachers' movement as a successful social movement because it persisted, against opposition, for at least a decade within an official union. Compared to other dissident or democratic movements within unions in Mexico, this was a significant achievement. It also makes sense, however, to ask what impact a movement had on its environment in order to determine its significance for social or political change. How one studies and conceptualizes the effects of social movements is a matter of ongoing debate; many discussions of movement effects have viewed these in narrow terms, as in "external" effects only (Rucht 1992). I do not plan on elaborating on this discussion here but will take as a starting point Claus Offe's (1987:94) outline of three dimensions by which a movement's success can be assessed: political, procedural, and substantive. For Offe political success comes when recognition and support are granted by institutional actors; procedural success entails changes in the mode of decision making; substantive success refers to decisions made by political elites that conform to the demands of a social movement. These types of success can be expanded to include not only responses by elites but also positive actions by the movement that affect other nonelite actors and that help to change the balance of power between social actors and the state. By Offe's measure as well as by this more expanded notion, the teachers' movement was able to effect significant changes in several areas.

The changes the movement was able to effect in the political arena stand out. Among these were the state's, and eventually also the national union leadership's, recognition of the CNTE as the interlocutor for a large force of dissident teachers; the leading role of the CNTE in the formation of several popular coalitions and fronts during the 1980s; the participation of CNTE activists in other popular struggles, especially in rural areas; the undermining of the clientelistic network of Vanguardia Revolucionaria within the union and of union locals' relations with PRI officials—a change that had direct bearing on the important area of corporatist state-labor relations. Ultimately, this change in the balance of forces within the teachers' union helped to bring in a new leadership in 1989 and expanded the participation of the CNTE in the union's top councils and committees.

In places such as Oaxaca and Chiapas, where the movement became most consolidated, democratic union locals were able to effect significant changes in the procedural arena as well (many of these were described in Chapter 5). Even with important constraints, these locals were able to govern themselves in ways that differed from previous local committees and from locals in the rest of the country. Members departed from the union's statutes or added to them in creative ways in selecting their leaders, in regulating meetings, and in deciding a host of issues. Relations with SEP officials in the states were changed so that the union locals not only had a say in administrative matters, but the norms they imposed on SEP officials were based on collective decisions by teachers in the movement. Changing the way decisions were made also changed the substance of these decisions: there was an effort to distribute benefits according to a set of objective criteria agreed to by members; hiring and promotions were to be dealt with in a similar manner. These reforms nonetheless amounted to temporary changes in practices and norms rather than official changes in procedure. Such changes could be implemented only as long as there was a movement able to mobilize to defend them or tolerance for such practices at the national level. What the 1989 protests permitted finally was reform of the union statutes, some of it in directions supported and originally practiced by the democratic movement (SNTE 1990, 1992).

In the substantive arena the teachers' movement was able to force national union officials to grant official status to some CNTE locals, it was able to extract wage concessions from the government, and it was able to get officials to meet various of their national and regional demands at different times. In one obvious area, however—education and education policy—relatively little change could be recorded, in part because the movement did not strongly direct its efforts in this direction. From the beginning the CNTE focused on union democracy and on economic and professional issues, not on educational change, though at times this matter found its place alongside demands for wages and democracy. Part of the reason for this was that movement leaders believed that changes in education practice and content could not be discussed until teachers received better wages, were allowed to conduct their professional lives in a democratic manner, and the government increased the funds allotted to education. The relative lack of attention to pedagogical and curriculum issues, however, did take its toll on the movement by straining the relationship with parents, especially more middle-class and urban parents. Many movement leaders noted this strain, and in Oaxaca and Chiapas the locals undertook efforts to forge an "alternative" education for students, one that was more in touch with local conditions and incorporated the community better. In the end, though, only a limited number of teachers and certain sectors, such as indigenous bilingual teachers, became involved in alternative educational programs. On many issues of educational policy and administration, the CNTE's position did not differ significantly from that of the national executive committee of the union.

An additional yardstick that can be used to measure a movement's success is whether the movement has managed to accomplish its own publicly stated goals. Insofar as one of the goals of the movement was democratization of the union, the impact of the movement was significant, if incomplete. The democratization of the locals in Oaxaca and Chiapas over the course of the 1980s, the elevation of union democracy as a national demand in 1989, and

Conclusion 293

the expansion of the movement to new arenas within the union were successes by any measure. Moreover, the greater initial influence of the CNTE in the union and its more formal participation in its governing structures (although heavily debated within the movement) were consistent with its goals of expanding its influence in the union. Insofar as the goals of the movement included dominating the union or radically transforming its orientation and relationship to the state, the movement was less successful, at least as of the early 1990s. Here, however, disagreement among the various strategic and political currents within the movement has made it difficult to clearly identify the movement's ultimate objectives. For the dominant position within the CNTE incremental gains were a sign of success, as was, of course, "mere" survival. Recognition by authorities, autonomy, resistance, and the construction of a distinct identity were all signs of progress. Expanding the movement's influence in the union and obtaining greater positions of power were consistent with this incremental strategy. For others, however, nothing short of radical social transformation could qualify as success. Without this, whatever other accomplishments the movement had managed were ephemeral. Moreover, accepting positions of power in the union, and accepting to act as a reformist movement whose project of transformation was limited to the union rather than extended beyond to politics and society, seriously undermined the movement's ability to pursue a larger transformative project. These distinctly different interpretations of the movement's goals, always present to some extent in the movement, became even more pronounced after 1989.

Another measure of a movement's ability to effect change can be examined by looking at its "internal effects" (Rucht 1992): its benefits for members, the extent to which membership commitment to the movement grows, the stability of the movement organization, the extent to which unity is forged around strategies and goals. Chapters 5 and 6 largely focused on these kinds of internal effects, and in many ways it was the movement's gains in this terrain that were most significant. In Chapter 6 I also elaborated on the connection between the construction of a collective identity and actual and potential social change by looking at how the practices of resistance and democratic organization altered members' relations with their communities and with their leaders and how they affected other popular struggles and even family members. What is important here is that the *experience* of participants remains; whether the opportunity to act on this experience reappears is a separate question. But the experience at least makes the recurrence of protest more likely "when the environment shifts again" (Alvarez and Escobar 1992:325).

Did the teachers' movement have an impact on political liberalization in

Mexico? Against the high hopes of many social movement analysts who began to study social movements in the 1980s, most now note that the impact of social movements on regime change and political democratization remains unclear, limited, or indirect. Movement struggles over material demands, recognition, and representation did not by themselves create the broad coalitions that eventually preceded transitions to democracy in most authoritarian regimes, although "the resurrection of civil society" was an important element in the dynamic that led to regime transitions (O'Donnell, Schmitter, and Whitehead 1986). What makes movement impact on the political system even more uncertain is the fragmentation and sense of exclusion experienced by many movements under the new democratic regimes. In particular, the return of political parties has posed new and complicated challenges for many movements, while, at the same time, material demands and economic issues remain important and unresolved, especially in countries undergoing extensive economic reform. Touted instead is movements' impact in the social arena, in the "democratization of civil society." It is through incremental, cumulative changes in civil society that movements exert influence over the liberalization or democratization of the regime. For instance, the experience of movement participation often generates new expectations and demands for participation in the political system among those who had always been marginalized: popular movements create potential "citizens" where before there had been clients or masses.

The teachers' movement in Mexico has played this role in civil society through the "deep democratization" undertaken by some of its contingents and through the example it set for others by its struggles for union democracy. Yet, the popular pressures for democracy in Mexico that I outlined in Chapters 1 and 7 are not the result of one movement but reflect the cumulative impact of multiple, often localized, movements over a period of years, in spite of periodic setbacks and the continued but increasingly limited co-optative capacity of the Mexican regime.[1] It would be difficult to understand the Mexican regime's many liberalization measures without the pressure created by multiple autonomous movements, whose very presence challenged the corporatist and authoritarian character of the regime. The catalytic effect on democratic reform that the Chiapas uprising initially had is only the most extreme example of this dynamic of the liberalization process in Mexico.[2]

---

1. For similar portrayals of the development of popular movements in Mexico see Bennett 1992 and Foweraker 1989.
2. See Fox 1994a and Cook, Middlebrook, and Molinar Horcasitas 1994:26-27.

At the same time, there is a lingering tension between popular movements that seek material demands and recognition and even spaces over which they exert autonomous control, and the construction of a broader coalition necessary for a democratic transition. The period of the Salinas administration best exemplified this tension, when several independent movements gained increased benefits and recognition but also withdrew from participation in the coalition headed by Cárdenas. The effects of this period, while temporary perhaps, nonetheless signaled both the persistent capacity of the regime (and of the president) to selectively reward and repress its challengers, and the ambivalent relationship of many popular social movements toward democracy. It is not simply that popular movements don't care about democracy (although some undoubtedly do not), but that they are not always able or willing to pay the costs to their organization and their members that involvement in a broader national coalition for democracy may entail.[3] It is only when such costs are lowered that participation becomes more attractive, as when Cuauhtémoc Cárdenas first emerged as an opposition candidate in 1988 and many believed he had a chance of defeating the PRI candidate. Such calculations are made in the context of a constantly changing political environment.

Emergence and Survival of the Mexican Teachers' Movement: Revisiting the Argument

The fundamental challenge that the rise of the democratic teachers' movement posed for observers of Mexican politics and popular movements was to understand how a grass-roots, oppositional movement for union democracy could emerge, survive, and later expand in one of Mexico's most traditional official unions? Dissent and insurgency in Mexico were not in themselves new, but the extent of the insurgency, the movement's legal conquests, and its survival were unparalleled in the labor arena. The institutional and political context of an "official" union posed special constraints for dissident movements, and the Mexican authoritarian regime's characteristic response to movements that threatened corporatist structures and relations—co-optation, coercion, and repression—represented an additional challenge.

---

3. A telling example was the case of the Comité de Defensa Popular of Durango, which argued that "pursuing electoral democracy was an ineffective strategy not worth the costs and lost privileges of pursuing a more 'cooperative' relationship with the Salinas administration" (Haber 1994:299).

Given this context of government and official union leadership opposition to dissident movements, the successful emergence of such movements cannot be understood solely in terms of the existence of discontent or their ability to mobilize internal resources. Changes in the political environment of movements and, in particular, the existence of political openings play a central role in explaining the emergence of social movements in all contexts, but are especially key to understanding how movements emerge in the closed political contexts generally represented by authoritarian regimes. In the case of the teachers' movement this political opening or political opportunity came in the form of an important conflict at the national level between major actors in the teachers' immediate environment. This conflict centered on the implementation of a key administrative reform among whose objectives it was to weaken the influence and autonomy of the leadership of the teachers' union. Unlike past tensions between union and government officials, this conflict had consequences for teachers throughout the country and was played out in the states as well as at the national level. The extent of discontent that came to exist within the union, together with the tensions between union leaders and the government, was a reflection of the "unstable equilibrium" that has characterized relations between the Mexican regime and "official" Mexican unions. The case also illustrated the ways in which economic constraints and policy redirections can further undermine the equilibrium, generating strategic opportunities for dissident movements.

Although state-union conflict in this case created the context and opportunity for the emergence of the movement, the appearance of various regional movements depended as well on regional openings and on the internal resources that the movements could command. At a minimum regional movements relied on the existence of a core group of leaders with activist experience, and on the existence of widespread discontent based not only on shared national grievances—wage increases, cost-of-living adjustments, timely payment of salaries—but on local conditions and events: divisions within the union local, leaders' unwillingness to spearhead demands, the death of a teacher, a barricaded union building. The context of regional movements emerging throughout the country also created the opportunity for new contingents to appear. However, when the national political opening passed, not all of the regional movements were able to survive. Those that did had the broadest base of support in their regions and an elaborate network of grass-roots organization. They also proceeded cautiously, combined mobilization with negotiation, were careful not to over-politicize their demands, pursued a more "legalistic" strategy, and avoided explicit identification with political parties and currents. Theirs was an incremental struggle to "legalize their strength," meet the needs and demands of their members, and to democratize their union. Yet the "failure" of other regional movements was not simply a matter of greater organizational weakness or more confrontational positions, although these were clearly factors. These movements also contended with stronger regional opposition and greater violence, proof of the harsh resistance to dissident movements and of the authoritarian environments they faced in spite of periodic and temporary openings.

The teachers' movement was in some ways unique among popular social movements in that one of its central goals was obtaining legal status as recognized locals within the union, and two regional contingents managed to win this status. In other contexts achieving this kind of legal status might be the end of the story, a sign that the movement had "succeeded" by achieving institutional participation. Yet in the hostile environment of the union, reinforced by an alliance with the state, the movements' legal conquests were fragile because they were constantly under attack. These movements did not simply represent a case of co-optation by the system nor did they become just another union local; they continued to represent a threat to the union leadership and the system because of their emphasis on democratization and their continued support for a mass movement that would transform the nature of the union and of its relationship to the regime.

Once "inside" the union the movement had to contend with the rules and political constraints of the "official" union structure. Their political and institutional environment included a national union that retained exclusive authority to recognize the local leadership, call elections, and issue funds; and a government that had once again turned to the teachers' union for political support and that had been powerless to implement a reform according to its original goals and design. This was a regime that, in spite of periodic support of competing currents in order to maintain a degree of control over union leaderships, remained committed to supporting its official unions and to the basic structural outlines of a corporatist political regime.

In spite of the enormous constraints posed by the two regional movements' legal status, legality was important for the social movement in several respects. Legal status gave the movements some breathing room—a relatively "free space" in which to expand and consolidate the democratic organization of the regional movement and of the union local to create a new kind of democratic and responsive unionism inside the most traditional and antidemocratic of unions. Because the movements lived out their legality under continued threats to their survival, however, they did not become "institutionalized," nor "bureaucratized," nor allowed to operate under what might be considered normal or routine conditions for unions elsewhere. Instead, these union locals had to remain social movements as well: they had to continue to build their grass-roots networks, strengthen their mobilizational capacity, blend negotiations with the mobilized pressure of the membership, and learn to "move within the state."

Legal status, therefore, did not ensure the movements' stability nor endurance. Faced with the arbitrariness of the national union leadership and the limited autonomy of union locals, the movements in Oaxaca and Chiapas had to continue to draw creatively on their internal resources in order to survive. I have argued throughout this book that the internal organization of the movements under legal status provides the best expression of the ways in which the movements addressed fundamental challenges to organizational stability that emerged as a result of continued attacks. These attacks were especially prevalent in the mid-1980s, after the renewed alliance between the government and Education Ministry and renewed efforts by union leaders to take back the union locals. The movements in Oaxaca and Chiapas did not simply occupy the union structures that existed before, they chose to change the organizational structure of the locals in order to better fight their enemies. The threat of co-optation and the problem of lack of accountability were battled by expanding more intermediate levels of organization and of decision making, by increasing vigilance of elected leaders through parallel coordinadoras and elected rank-and-file assistants on negotiating commissions, and by the role of the state assembly, which not only took on a central role in decision making for the movement and local but kept strong reins on the executive committee. The problem of the potential loss of member support was combated by responding to and working to represent member demands, by changing practices and behavior within the union so as to respect teachers' rights, by expanding political education, by involving rank-and-file members in decision making in schools and workplaces and delegations, by determining collectively to reward movement participation in the distribution of benefits, promotions, and transfer requests, by relying centrally on the mobilization of the membership to defend the movement.

The democratization of the movement and of the way that the union locals operated was therefore fundamental to the movements' need to counteract strong external challenges to the movements' survival and tendencies to undermine it from within. Although in Chiapas the factionalism that was present in all movements greatly debilitated that movement's ability to defend its legal status, the existence of the movement over the years and its rootedness in the experiences of rank-and-file members made possible the continuity of the movement throughout the period of the executive commission after 1987 until new elections in 1989. The "deepening" experience of the movement was a direct result of its democratization and could be seen in the changed relationship between leaders and rank-and-file members, in increased distrust of "officials," greater commitment to popular sector allies, increased participation of women, the generation of new leaders, and experimentation with developing "democratic" and alternative forms of education.

These developments were perhaps the most important and lasting consequences of the movement's democratization as a survival strategy. They represented the acquisition of skills and experiences that prove vital to sustaining democracy in society or, in the case of Mexico's incomplete democratic transition, they offer the possibility of a continued struggle for citizenship rights. They also demonstrate that it is possible to organize democratically within authoritarian environments. Moreover, the democratic organization of the movement was crucial to the pursuit of its larger goal of union democracy and union autonomy from the state and political parties. This was a movement in which the quest for member benefits was not divorced from the means— democratic organization and representation. The challenge for the movement resided not so much in gaining new advantages for its members as in *surviving* as an *oppositional movement* in order to continue to change the environment. This was the meaning behind the Oaxaca movement's long struggle to gain authorization for democratic elections: whereas the membership could have resolved many of its material problems by accepting Vanguardia's conditions for elections (i.e., vanguardista participation on the committee), it opted to hold out.[4] Preserving the autonomy of the movement was crucial because it meant the future opportunity to define and meet member needs and the chance to revive and extend the national movement. Thus, what was at stake here was not so much institutional linkage, but linkage as much as possible *on their own terms*.

Political Process and Social Movements in Authoritarian Regimes

To what extent are the features that characterized the teachers' movement's development found in other social movements in authoritarian regimes? What

---

4. Teachers in Chiapas had also expressed an interest in resisting through mobilizations after the decertification of the leadership in 1987; it was their leadership that submitted to vanguardista control over the executive commission against the wishes of the assembly (see Chapter 5).

does the case of the Mexican teachers tell us about dimensions of movements under authoritarianism? Although it is not possible to generalize from the case of the teachers' movement to all movements in closed conditions, the discussion in this section is intended to suggest in a preliminary fashion possible similarities and differences among movements under authoritarian conditions along the following dimensions: political opportunities in the movement's environment, strategies and tactics, organization, and what happens to movements when environments become more open.[5]

Political Opportunities

Under what conditions are strategic opportunities for movement mobilization generated under authoritarian regimes? In Chapter 2 I suggested that the conditions outlined for authoritarian regimes may be broadly similar to those that appear in democratic regimes: elite tolerance (institutional access), instability of political (electoral) alignments, influential allies, and conflict or disunity among elites. Yet I also suggested that such opportunities in authoritarian regimes are likely to be rare and short-lived, and that authoritarian governments are more likely to use repression against a movement. A higher occurrence of such opportunities in democratic regimes, however, does not automatically mean that more social movements are likely to emerge in these contexts. Democratic regimes may be more able to absorb protest movements, thus channeling them toward becoming pressure groups. Authoritarian regimes, on the other hand, may both inspire greater opposition (increasing the potential for protest movements to emerge) and be incapable of incorporating or institutionalizing movements that do emerge, thus prolonging their lives as social movements.[6] Eisinger's findings remain relevant: "[P]rotest is often necessary to communicate discontent in a closed system," whereas "discontent . . . may be expressed more easily through conventional political strategies in an open system" (Eisinger 1973:25).

In the Mexican case I have suggested that elite tolerance for independent movements was present for a brief time under the Echeverría (1970–76)

---

5. More systematic comparison would be an important task for future research; it is beyond the scope of this chapter, however. Comparison is made more difficult given the paucity of case studies that have been conducted from the political process perspective in Latin America.

6. Of course, the higher likelihood that movements in authoritarian regimes will face repression means that not many movements will be able to survive under such conditions. Repression can, however, reinforce commitment to protest movements (see Tarrow 1994:92–93).

administration, when the period of democratic opening acted as a protective umbrella for the emergence of some movements. Elite tolerance (at the presidential level) has not been a significant factor since then, but tolerance by elites (state governors, SEP delegates) at regional levels (that is, not directly aiding, but neither engaging in active repression) may have helped the movement in some states. Elite tolerance may also have been a factor in the expansion of other kinds of movements in other authoritarian regimes. In the case of women's movements in authoritarian Brazil, for example, the regime allowed women to organize while still actively repressing other sectors of civil society: "Viewing women as intrinsically 'apolitical,' military rulers appear to have believed women's groups posed lesser threats to national security" (Alvarez 1990:262). Similarly, in Argentina the human rights movement was not destroyed under authoritarian rule because it was composed of ordinary citizens "who were politically marginal—but economically secure and socially legitimate" (Brysk 1994:2).

While many authoritarian regimes are characterized by the lack of elections, in the Mexican case political jockeying around the presidential succession may have granted certain strategic advantages to groups that chose to mobilize in this period. In the case of the teachers this preelectoral period during 1982 played both ways: initially, the interbureaucratic competition may have increased the chances for protesting teachers of getting authorities to the negotiating table. After a point, however, the proximity of presidential elections dictated that the government forge some kind of accommodation with the national leaders of the teachers' union, which in turn narrowed the political space available to the movement. The 1988 elections may have been an exception in that they represented a more conventional example of the role of unstable electoral alignments in favoring movement mobilization. The controversy surrounding these elections not only emboldened popular protest but they contributed to the uncertainty and fluidity of politics in the months following the elections, a factor that served as an important backdrop to the teachers' mobilizations of 1989.

Influential external allies, a third variable in the political opportunity structure, was not a significant factor for the teachers' movement. This is not to say that the solidarity of other groups—parents, trade unions, other popular movements, and an occasionally favorable press—were not important. But significant elite allies at the national level (politicians, businessmen, funding agencies, political parties, the church, even other sectors of the labor bureaucracy) were largely missing during the teachers' mobilizations in the 1970s and 1980s. Although some well-placed individuals expressed sympathy for aspects of the teachers' protests at some times, by and large elites were united in their interest in containing the dissident movement. The favorable actions of some government officials, as I explained in Chapter 3, does not mean that we should consider these individuals allies of the movement (as indeed the movement did not). Instead, such actions reflected political expediency in the course of trying to contain both the movement and the power of the national union leadership. The fact that the movement was not dependent on elite or institutional allies for finances or other resources also meant that the movement was not subject to the kinds of pressures and constraints such allies may impose on movement strategy and tactics (Lipsky 1968, McAdam 1982, Schwartz and Paul 1992).

Lower-class allies, on the other hand, may provide solidarity, food, shelter, and money without exacting the kinds of commitments from the movement that can prove divisive, beyond an implicit commitment to reciprocity.[7] The solidarity and basic material resources provided by key groups, such as parents, peasants, students, and other trade unions was crucial, especially during the periods of intense mobilization of the movement. Nonetheless, at a national and more political level the teachers' movement's more formal alliances with other popular sectors, reflected in several multisectoral coalitions formed in the early 1980s, were short-lived and had a limited impact on each contingent's ability to make gains. At a regional level, however, the impact of popular alliances might be greater, and elite allies (church, business groups, state government officials, other public employees, universities, media) were more likely to be available and significant for the movement.

In other countries, such as Brazil, Chile, and Argentina, influential allies were key for movements emerging in those authoritarian regimes: for Brazilian rural trade unions a range of allies were important in helping to found and sustain the unions, including Church laity and priests, lawyers, party militants, public functionaries, and others; in Chile the Catholic Church was the primary source of external assistance to popular organizations; for the human rights movement of Argentina it was the international human rights regime; in Brazil and Chile political parties and groups of the left, operating underground, also provided critical resources to the women's movement and to some urban communities during military rule.[8] As noted in Chapter 7, the late 1980s and 1990s have seen the increase of new potential allies and the emergence of new resources: domestic and international nongovernmental organizations,

---

7. Given the relative strength and influence of the teachers' movement, especially at the regional level, its support of other popular struggles was significant. This was particularly so in the case of peasant movements, as discussed in Chapter 6.

8. Maybury-Lewis 1994, Oxhorn 1994:752, Brysk 1994, Alvarez 1990, Schneider 1995.

international funding agencies, counterparts and solidarity groups in North America and Europe, more critical media, and technological developments that facilitate communication (fax, internet). These are likely to change the context for future movements.

The successful emergence and mobilization of social movements may also be the "unintended consequence" of some other process: disunity among elites, conflict among powerful authorities in the immediate environment of the movement, a state-initiated reform or government policy. The emergence of the teachers' movement was a case of conflict among authorities that was exacerbated by a government policy (the deconcentration) and manifested itself at both national and regional levels. In the Mexican countryside a government food distribution program for the rural poor helped to spur mobilization of autonomous peasant organizations under the López Portillo administration (Fox 1992b).[9] In the case of the expansion of the Brazilian rural trade union movement the facilitating factor was the military dictatorship's easing of the restrictions for forming rural trade unions and its extension of health and pension benefits to the countryside; the opportunity was then seized by some organizers to create "progressive" trade unions (Maybury-Lewis 1994). Thus the introduction of new policies and reforms (even by hostile governments) can produce unintended consequences in the form of popular mobilization.[10]

Social movement studies have tended to focus on periods of widespread mobilization and change, such as the 1960s and 1970s, or on the periods immediately preceding regime transitions in Latin America and Eastern Europe. Yet the political process approach should also be able to tell us what conditions are propitious for "individual" social movements to emerge in nonexceptional situations—under "everyday conditions" in authoritarian regimes, as in the long years of the Brazilian dictatorship or the stable authoritarianism of Mexico in the 1970s and 1980s. This calls for a more intermediate or sectoral appreciation for the appearance of political spaces. As I noted in Chapter 2, attention to the level at which opportunities appear (and the breadth or narrowness of political space) can signal the nature and extent of the advantages that movements may gain and the alliances they may form.[11]

---

9. The mobilization spurred by the implementation of the Sistema Alimentario Mexicano (SAM) analyzed by Fox is also an example of the existence of external allies, in this case, democratic state reformists in charge of the program (Fox 1992b).

10. Under Salinas antipoverty programs under the auspices of the National Solidarity Program may have had similar effects in certain cases. See Cornelius, Craig, and Fox 1994.

11. A movement's ability to interpret such political openings also needs more research. Here the role of leadership, ideology, and strategy in recognizing spaces seems important.

Movement Tactics and Strategy

Although conditions for movements vary in different kinds of states and within different sectors, a more closed political environment is likely to produce distinct pressures on a movement to define its strategy in a particular way and to adopt certain tactics and eschew others. In the case of the Mexican teachers' movement a generally moderate and legalistic approach characterized the more successful regional contingents of the movement, as discussed in Chapters 4 and 6. The features of this approach included a willingness to negotiate, a nonconfrontational strategy (including moderate and nonpolitical language), an appeal to widely shared and "legitimate" demands (such as economic and professional demands), the choice to operate within the union in seeking to win union locals rather than going outside the union, the effort to secure legal agreements (written authorization for union elections, agreements with the SEP) in spite of the recognition that these were often not enforced. A legal strategy broadened the appeal of the movement and diminished the chances of open repression by lowering the threat to the regime. A legal strategy uncovered the hypocrisy of the union leadership and of the government when they ignored agreements, elevating the legitimacy of the teachers' struggle. A more moderate and legal strategy also reflected the recognition that the balance of forces (in the union, in the country) did not favor a frontal attack on power.

Yet a legal strategy also rendered the movement vulnerable to the manipulations of government officials and the arbitrariness of union leaders' actions. "Moving within the state" and moving within the legal and institutional structure of the union meant moving about in an environment that was hostile to their efforts, among laws and statutes that were stacked against dissident movements. In this way the movement's capacity to mobilize became crucial: mobilization was often what forced government and union leaders to the negotiating table, and mobilization is what limited the chances that the outcome would be co-optation of the movement. Important here also was the movement's emphasis on "extralegality," on "walking with both feet" in pursuit of its goals. As noted in Chapter 6, this meant moving within and outside of the statutes and the law: setting up parallel organizations within the union local, using only those statutes that served the movement, imposing their own norms on education administrators, holding elections before national union officials arrived to preside over them.

Elsewhere in Latin America, legalistic (and moderate) approaches were also important for movements that operated under authoritarian regimes. In Argentina human rights protesters defended "traditional, legitimate values like the right to life, the rule of law, and the sanctity of the family"—their key resource was legitimacy (Brysk 1994:2). In Brazil a legal strategy and nonconfrontational approach were central components of those "progressive" rural trade unions that survived. As Maybury-Lewis writes:

> Union people understood that excessive provocation of rural elites and the authorities, given the power relations in the countryside, would likely hurt them and set back their organization drive. They were not about to provoke reactions to which they could not respond. They learned the value of respecting the law. Indeed, the unionists became champions of the law, pushing for enforcement of legislation on the books ostensibly to protect their rights. (1994:73)

The degree to which movements could employ mobilization in pursuit of their goals appeared to vary considerably. As noted, mobilization was a central feature of the teachers' movement in Mexico, although it was less effective in obtaining important advantages from the state during the more closed period of the mid-1980s. For the teachers mobilization was not only easier to carry out under the "soft authoritarianism" of the Mexican regime but it also made sense given the large size of the movement and the nature of the teachers' struggle. Since the teachers were engaged in a battle over representation in the union, showing their strength by mobilizing large numbers in marches, rallies, or work stoppages was an important and logical tactic. Other kinds of movements, such as human rights movements, rely on other forms of protest to achieve their objectives. Moreover, in countries where demonstrations, rallies, and occupations are more difficult to carry out due to more open repression, other forms of protest may play a similar role to that of larger mobilizations: they force authorities to notice the protesting group, make negotiation possible, attract supporters or allies, and/or generate solidarity among participants.[12] In any case, for movements that wished to survive, repressive conditions typically called not for more radical and confrontational tactics (although perhaps for more innovative tactics) nor for escalation but for scaling back, for waiting for better conditions, for "advancing in a zigzag."

---

12. See, for example, the expressive and symbolic protest of the mothers and grandmothers of the Plaza de Mayo in Argentina (Brysk 1994).

Movement Organization

The organization a movement adopts can be the function of a number of factors: ideology, size, objectives, the requirements for mobilization and for communication within the movement, the need for representation of diverse interests, the need for and frequency of negotiation, whether a formal apparatus exists that the movement may occupy, the nature of external attacks on the movement, and so forth. One key question is how the openness or closed nature of the environment of a movement affects the type of organization it constructs. For trade union movements in particular the organizational structure of the movement may be relatively straightforward and follow the established outlines of the given structure. Yet even in this case, as shown by the teachers' movement, the given structure can be molded and adapted to serve the movement's purposes. For Mexican teachers the particular democratic organization they adopted responded to their effort to contain political party domination and factionalism, their need to engage in recurrent mobilization, and their goals of transforming internal practices and democratizing the union. In the face of external threats of co-optation or demobilization the membership fought back with additional amendments to their organizational structure and internal procedures, as I detailed in Chapters 4, 5, and 6. The movement's need for recurrent mobilization, in particular, and the persistent need to measure its strength via collective actions, led the organization to adopt its distinctive mechanisms of consultation with the rank-and-file membership.

Relatively few studies of Latin American social movements have paid close attention to the internal practices and organizational forms movements have adopted, making it difficult to draw comparisons. The presumption from the new social movements literature is that these tend to be more democratic, favoring nonhierarchical internal organization, rotating or collective leadership, and consensus forms of decision making. Yet it appears that from a preliminary review of other cases the nonhierarchical and participatory forms of organization often assumed in the new social movements literature are not that common.[13] Brysk points to the centralism, personalism, and hierarchy that was present in

---

13. The new social movements literature has tended to present nonhierarchical and informal forms of decision making within movements as a sign of grass-roots democracy rather than formal organization such as that found in the teachers' movement. Yet informality and lack of hierarchy are no guarantee that the collective will of the membership is being expressed. The teachers' firm attention to procedure and checks and balances was intended to ensure, as much as possible, that "informal" methods of decision making did not mean that minority decisions would be imposed upon majorities.

Conclusion   307

the most effective human rights organizations in Argentina (1994:160). Chinchilla refers to the vanguardism (elitism, top-down leadership style, membership as the depository of the wisdom of the leadership) that was strong among organizations of the women's movement in Peru (Vargas 1988, cited in Chinchilla 1992:48). In Mexico, too, organizational forms vary. According to Rubin, the COCEI in Oaxaca "continues to favor leadership-based forms of organizing and decision making, with mass participation focusing on consultation, mobilization, and neighborhood solidarity rather than on explicit procedures of representation or collaborative decision making" (1990:264). This would also characterize the organization and decision-making style of urban popular movements such as the Comité de Defensa Popular of Durango or Tierra y Libertad of Monterrey, whose leadership, moreover, was highly personalistic.

A key question that needs more comparative research is how different kinds of movement organizations address common challenges. These challenges were discussed in detail in Chapter 2, and include such problems as how to sustain membership commitment, how to avoid co-optation, how to prevent oligarchy, how to maintain group solidarity, among others. Although this kind of query has been difficult to find in studies of Latin American social movements, some such mechanisms to manage these tensions must be in place in those movements that persist. For instance, Schneider points out that among the *poblaciones* where communist influence was strong, efforts by the Party to exert hegemonic control over the neighborhood councils led leaders to lose contact with their base, which weakened the movement's ability to maintain a constant level of resistance. Yet when leaders maintained a more open, democratic relationship with the membership, division was less likely and resistance more effective (Schneider 1995:209–10). While in rural Brazil, meanwhile, the incorporation of the rank-and-file in all levels of the union organization was rare, it was considered a central component of those unions that were pushing for a more autonomous and combative organization (Maybury-Lewis 1994:195).

Greater attention needs to be paid to the relationship between the environment, internal organization, and movement goals, strategies, and tactics. Such an inquiry would lead to a better understanding of what features of a movement are most successful in a particular political environment. In the case of the teachers' movement, for example, recurrent mobilization was an important component of the movement's ability to negotiate effectively with authorities. The ability to mobilize frequently over time implied the existence of certain conditions in the movement's internal organization—especially some kind of democratic decision-making process that would enable movement leaders to determine what it was possible to do at any given moment but that would also impart a sense of "ownership" to members, strengthening group solidarity and member commitment to the movement. At the same time, a closed environment—even after legality was won—meant that the movement lived in an extended "mobilizational phase"—with implications for internal organization. In this way an assumption present in some of the social movement literature, that social movement organizations will move from mobilization to institutionalization, and consequently to greater centralization and bureaucracy, appears to make greater sense in relatively open political systems that are more capable of absorbing protest movements than in those systems that continue to exclude protest groups.[14] Insofar as persistent mobilization also demands more democratic internal decision-making processes or more accountable leadership, this suggests the somewhat paradoxical development that authoritarian environments may actually stimulate internal democracy within some protest movements.[15] Of course, it is not only tactical requirements that may spur democratization. As noted in Chapters 2 and 6, authoritarian rule can help to generate group solidarity (collective identity) because it functions as a unifying target for the movement. If what is opposed are authoritarian *practices*, then this opposition may lend further support to the construction of internal democratic practices within the movement organization.

Moving from Closed to Open Environments

Many observers of social movements in Latin America have noted the impact that moving from an authoritarian regime to a formal democracy has for movements. Although, as noted above, the actions of movements prior to the end of an authoritarian regime are an important element in the dynamics of democratic transition, the outcomes for movements are more uncertain. In writing on Brazil, Maybury-Lewis noted that the return of party competition and formal democracy in Brazil meant that unionists no longer had to contend with changes in authoritarian state structures but with changes in the whole political system. The new tasks in this environment would consist of "alliance building and party politics." While "the opening of the political system, the

---

14. See Piven and Cloward 1979 for a discussion of the "progression" of movements in North America. The authors suggest that less bureaucratic forms of organization are likely when a movement is in an earlier, mobilizational phase.
15. Oxhorn (1995) develops a similar argument in his study of shantytown movements under authoritarian rule in Chile.

reemergence of political parties, and the competition among allies made new possibilities available to local unionists . . . the openings complicated the prospects for unionists schooled in the institutional setting of corporatist dictatorship" (1994:197, 206). Brysk explains that with the establishment of democratic institutions in Argentina, "the human rights movement assumed a much less visible and more reactive role." The human rights movement, she notes, "arose in a political environment in which bargaining was impossible, but the new democratic environment rewarded the logic of bargaining more than persuasion" (Brysk 1994:156, 20). This also had an impact on the nature of leadership: "[T]he human rights movement's emergence and persistence under authoritarian rule required determined, charismatic, and single-minded leadership, which often proved inappropriate to consolidation-era democratic politics" (Brysk 1994:20). And Schneider describes the impact of the return of formal democracy for the shantytown organizations that had been so active in resisting the Pinochet regime: "[T]he structure of incentives in the new democracy undermined traditional collective identities and dispositions" (1995:200). In an effort to avoid confrontational politics, party leaders and government elites also gave up reliance on popular mobilization: "[T]he governing parties no longer needed grassroots activists," which led many of them to feel "abandoned and betrayed by the new democracy" (Schneider 1995:201).

In the case of the teachers' movement in Mexico increased institutional access under authoritarian rule appeared to have had a similar divisive and demobilizing effect on the movement, at least initially. As I outlined in Chapter 7, the new opening in the environment of teachers permitted the movement to occupy more of the union, but it also raised questions concerning the future direction of the movement and placed more emphasis on effective bargaining relationships than on mobilized pressure. Other popular movements and trade unions under the Salinas administration faced similar challenges when the government opened access to some movements and marginalized others.[16] This illustrates that it is not only the return of formal democracy and of competitive party politics that can dramatically change the shape of the environment for

---

16. Yet the end of the Salinas term saw the emergence of one of the most important movements in many years, the Zapatista National Liberation Army. This movement differed in important ways from previous popular movements. It was a movement composed of the most marginalized of Mexicans, it was armed, and it gave voice to both local demands and more absolute national values that remained unfulfilled. As Bishop Samuel Ruiz of San Cristóbal de las Casas, Chiapas, said, "They don't want to seize power. This is something new. They want to create a democratic process that all Mexicans take part in. They want recognition of Indigenous culture, history, autonomy" (cited in Weinberg 1994:7).

movements; shifting degrees of openness and closure within the formal outlines of an authoritarian regime may have similar, if perhaps less stable, effects.[17]

More open environments, and in particular the reemergence of political parties and a competitive electoral system, may affect social movements accustomed to authoritarian rule in several ways. First, it means that there may be some institutional access for movements where before there was none, either through political parties or direct access to or participation in local government.[18] The possibility of access implies in many cases a strategic reorientation of the movement, and the relatively greater importance of bargaining and of the ability to develop proposals than of mobilization and denunciation. Such a reorientation, together with the loss of the "clear enemy" in the form of the authoritarian regime, is likely to encourage internal divisions and weaken member support.[19] The return of parties may also mean the abandonment and isolation of the movement, a loss of its erstwhile allies, and a general decline in its importance for civil society and vis-à-vis the political arena, as in the case of Chilean shantytowns and the human rights movement in Argentina.[20] Taken together such conditions signal the need for a reevaluation of the movement's "ethos." Those leaders who have invested their identities in a particular mode of operation, however, may be hard-pressed to change, giving rise to internal

---

17. Under the Zedillo administration, for instance, it may well be that protest mobilization will be more effective than under the Salinas administration. The political crises of the regime (the Chiapas uprising, political assassinations), the economic crisis following the December 1994 devaluation, the perception of Zedillo as a weak president, the more public divisions in the ruling party, and the fact that democratization remains an unfinished project combine to increase the opportunities for protest and mobilizational tactics. In the early months of the administration several examples have already emerged. One of the most important of these has been the middle-class farmers'/debtors' movement known as "El Barzón" (see Rodríguez and Torres 1994).

18. Oxhorn notes, for example, that in spite of the general decline in citizen movements, some urban popular movements in Chile may be able to increase their influence over the neighborhood councils, which now enjoy institutionalized access to the state through new, more powerful local governments (1994:756). In Mexico heightened electoral competition at municipal and state levels may also help to increase movements' access to government (Fox and Hernández 1992).

19. As noted earlier, such changes in the external environment are likely to alter the internal pressures for particular types of movement organization. Thus, the oligarchy and centralization that many observers have ascribed to movement organizations in advanced democracies may well be a feature or tendency, not of social movements *per se*, but of some movements in relatively more open societies, or of movements whose need to resort to membership participation in collective actions is less frequent or pressing. The experience of the teachers' movement, for instance, suggests the troubling possibility that the democratic internal organization of sections of the movement has become less "functional" in a climate where the need for frequent mobilization has been reduced. In a context where formal institutional participation and regular bargaining is the norm, the conditions may be more propitious for oligarchy and bureaucratization.

20. Such conditions of isolation may be temporary, however, as movements and parties establish new forms of connection after transitions (see Alvarez and Escobar 1992:324, Oxhorn 1994).

Conclusion

debates over the direction and leadership of the movement. As one rural trade union leader from Brazil remarked, "We learn the rules and they change them. This slows us down" (Maybury-Lewis 1994:171).

Several additional developments that have accompanied democratic transitions in Latin America make it difficult to determine clearly whether the experience of movements is due strictly to the change in political context or whether economic changes have been decisive. The transitions to democracy have been carried out in many cases under conditions of economic crisis and in the midst of a reorientation of national economies in a more neoliberal direction, with important implications for poor people's movements. Unfavorable economic conditions therefore often combined with disillusionment—that which follows the realization that democracy does not necessarily mean improved material circumstances nor greater inclusion in the political process for popular movements (Oxhorn 1994:753–54). In addition, the broader political consensus surrounding such market reforms in many countries generally has also meant an increased role for more conservative parties, a declining role for the left, a greater interest on the part of government elites in not alienating businessmen, and an expanded role for the private sector in policy decisions. This generally more conservative climate has tended to marginalize the demands of popular movements for improved conditions and material gains, not to mention their political demands of greater participation and more equitable distribution. The key issue is not that the social movements that emerged during the 1980s should survive at all costs in new democracies but, as many others have noted, the issue is how demands for equity and greater social participation exemplified by the movements of the 1980s can be incorporated into consolidating democracies.

This focus on the changing political environments of movements and the effects of these changes on movement strategies, organization, and demands further weakens the notion, as Alvarez and Escobar note (1992:324), that "successful" movements necessarily move through a linear progression of strategies, from "quotidian resistance to transformational projects." Instead, movements tend to adapt—or not—to a changing environment that itself does not offer a linear progression of opportunities. In this context successful movements advance and retreat in accordance with what the environment will permit, engaging in a range of tactics simultaneously. Moreover, different authoritarian and democratic regimes reflect various degrees of openness and closure. Thus, while formal democracies and authoritarian regimes do generally present different sets of political and institutional constraints and parameters for movement actions, individual movements will experience these constraints differently, depending on their immediate political environments, their institutional location, and the nature of their organization and demands. While it may not be possible nor even desirable, therefore, to construct a "general theory" of movement behavior in authoritarian contexts, future comparative research may be able to uncover patterns in the relationships between environment, organization, strategy, and so forth that would greatly expand our understanding of movements' constraints and possibilities in a variety of contexts. At stake is not only a more comprehensive understanding of movement dynamics under different conditions but a more profound knowledge of what it takes for the relatively powerless to improve their lives and change their surroundings.

Appendixes

Appendix A

SNTE Leaders, Education Ministers, and Interior Ministers, 1976–1994

SNTE Secretary-General	Education Minister	Interior Minister
Carlos Jonguitud Barrios, 1974–77	Porfirio Muñóz Ledo, 1976–77	Jesús Reyes Heroles, 1976–79
José Luis Andrade Ibarra, 1977–80	Fernando Solana Morales, 1977–82	Enrique Olivares Santana, 1979–82
Ramón Martínez Martín, 1980–83	Jesús Reyes Heroles, 1982–85	Manuel Bartlett Díaz, 1982–88
Alberto Miranda Castro, 1983–86	Miguel González Avelar, 1985–88	Fernando Gutiérrez Barrios, 1988–92
Antonio Jaimes Aguilar, 1986–89	Manuel Bartlett Díaz, 1988–92	Patrocinio González Garrido, 1992–94 (Jan.)
José Refugio Araujo del Angel, 1989 (Feb.–April)	Ernesto Zedillo Ponce de León, 1992–93	Jorge Carpizo MacGregor, 1994 (Jan.–Dec.)
Elba Esther Gordillo Morales, 1989–95	Fernando Solana Morales, 1993–94	

Appendix B
Chronology of the Democratic Teachers' Movement

1977

December: Muñóz Ledo resigns as minister of education; Solana Morales is appointed in his place.

1978

March: Deconcentration decreed by government.

August: Creation of National Pedagogical University decreed.

1979

June–October: Movement originates in Chiapas and Tabasco. Strike in Chiapas.

December: Coordinadora Nacional de Trabajadores de la Educación is formed.

1980

January–February: SNTE congress; Martínez Martín becomes secretary-general.

March–April: Movement emerges in Morelos; Consejo Central de Lucha formed.

May–November: Movements emerge in Oaxaca, Guerrero, Hidalgo, and the Valle de México.

June: "Great march" of dissident teachers in Mexico City. Executive commission set up in Oaxaca. Morelos movement meets to decertify executive committee.

November: Morelos, Chiapas, and Guerrero stage sit-in and march in Mexico City. Executive commissions formed in Chiapas and Morelos. Valle holds "mass" congress, not recognized by union officials.

December: Hidalgo holds mass congress.

1981

January: Misael Núñez Acosta, Valle leader, assassinated.

February: CNTE march with Valle, Hidalgo, Guerrero, and Morelos contingents. SEP and SNTE proposal to expand committees with dissident representation accepted by Valle, Hidalgo, and Guerrero movements.

March: Congress held in Chiapas; democratic committee wins.

March–April: Spurious congress held in Morelos. Movement begins hunger strike and protests. Movement elects new committee in central plaza in April. Dissident members eventually accept positions on commissions in executive committee.

October: Valle movement takes over Federal Offices of Primary Education in the state of Mexico to protest lack of response to demands.

December: Ezequiel Reyes Carrillo, Valle leader, abducted.

1982

February: Ambush and shoot-out at CCL march in Hidalgo, two killed. Congress held in Oaxaca, democratic committee wins. National Council expels dissident members on Hidalgo and Valle committees. Council also demands and obtains removal of Fernando Elías Calles, director of delegations and chief negotiator of SEP.

March: During a CNTE march in Mexico City Valle contingent occupies union bulding to force union officials to negotiate.

April: Agreements with national union leadership to hold congresses for Hidalgo, Morelos, and Valle in September.

September: Parallel elections held in Hidalgo, executive committee imposed. Morelos congress held, new committee not recognized and previous year's committee remains. Executive committee imposed on Valle de México local.

December: De la Madrid becomes president; Reyes Heroles is minister of education; minster of interior is Bartlett Díaz. General Castellanos becomes governor of Chiapas.

1983

January–February: SNTE congress held; Miranda Castro becomes secretary-general. CNTE obtains five positions on national executive committee. Government's decentralization plans attacked by union leadership.

May: CNTE marchers beaten by thugs from Vanguardia during May 1 parade.

June: Strike wave called by CTM and independent unions, in which CNTE participates.

July: Escuela Normal Superior main campus in Mexico City closed.

August: Agreement on decentralization reached by SNTE and SEP.

October: Civic strike organized by ANOCP; CNTE one of the organizers. Vanguardistas take over local building in Oaxaca, occupiers forced out after two days. Comité Institucional organized by vanguardistas in Oaxaca.

1984

March: Chiapas elections held, democratic committee renewed.

October: Another civic strike held, participation weak.

1985

February: Oaxaca due for new elections but authorization refused. March to Mexico City begun, then lifted when national union committee agrees to hold elections in April, then June.

March: Reyes Heroles dies. González Avelar appointed minister of education.

June: Preparations for Oaxaca congress begun; event called off by union officials.

1986

January–March: Oaxaca congress date set. Precongress held but congress canceled by national committee. Extensive protests follow, without results.

February: SNTE congress held; Jaimes Aguilar becomes secretary-general.

February–April: Oaxaca teachers continue mobilizations in demand of congress. Caravan-march to Mexico City.

May: Teachers' movement and peasant leaders jailed for participating in peasant protests in Chiapas.

June: Oaxaca teachers hold precongress, authorization again denied.

December: Heladio Ramírez López becomes governor of Oaxaca.

1987

March–April: Chiapas committee decertified by National Council of SNTE. Executive commission with some national committee appointees formed. A movement teacher, Celso Wenceslao López, shot and killed during protests. Protests and mobilizations continue through April.

1988

July: Presidential elections held; results contested by opposition parties.

December: Salinas ratified by electoral congress as Mexico's president. Bartlett becomes education minister; Gutiérrez Barrios becomes interior minister.

1989

January: "La Quina," head of oil workers' union, is arrested by government using military.

February: SNTE congress held. Refugio Araujo becomes secretary-general amid much discontent. Oaxaca teachers decide to hold elections without authorization. They elect new committee and merge it with old until legal ratification can be obtained.

March–June: Mobilizations in numerous locals throughout the country, protesting wages and lack of union democracy. Massive mobilizations in Mexico City. In April Jonguitud Barrios and Refugio Araujo step down. Elba Esther Gordillo replaces Araujo as secretary-general. In May Oaxaca ratifies previously elected committee. Chiapas and Local 9 (primary schoolteachers) of Mexico City also hold elections and select democratic committees in June and July. Executive commissions are set up in several locals, including Guerrero, Michoacán, and Local 10 (secondary and higher education) of Mexico City.

Bibliography

Secondary Sources

Aboites, Hugo. 1984. "El salario del educador en México (1925–1982)." *Coyoacán*, no. 16, pp. 69–95.

———. 1986. "Sesenta años del salario del educador (1925–1985)." *México: Los salarios de la crisis*. Cuadernos Obreros del Centro de Documentación y Estudios Sindicales del Trabajo, A.C.

Aguayo Quezada, Sergio. 1987. "Chiapas: Las amenazas a la seguridad nacional." El Colegio de México. Unpublished paper.

Aguirre M., Alberto. 1994. "Zedillo y su estilo impositivo en la SEP: Se peleó con el magisterio, con los historiadores y con el ejército." *Proceso*, no. 909 (April 4): 14–15.

Alcalá Rivera, María del Rocío, and Claudia Edith Martínez Martínez. 1984. "Proceso político generada de la lucha magisterial (1972–1981)." Tesis de licenciatura, Universidad Autónoma Metropolitana-Azcapotzalco, Mexico City.

Alcocer V., Jorge. 1994. "Party System and Political Transition in Mexico: A Pragmatic Approach." In *The Politics of Economic Restructuring: State-Society Relations and Regime Change in Mexico*, edited by Maria Lorena Cook, Kevin J. Middlebrook, and Juan Molinar Horcasitas. U.S.-Mexico Contemporary Perspectives Series, 7. La Jolla: Center for U.S.-Mexican Studies, University of California, San Diego.

Alonso, Antonio. 1972. *El movimiento ferrocarrilero en México, 1958–59*. Mexico City: Ediciones Era.

Alvarado, Arturo, ed. 1987. *Electoral Patterns and Perspectives in Mexico*. La Jolla: Center for U.S.-Mexican Studies, University of California, San Diego.

Alvarez, Alejandro. 1987. *La crisis global del capitalismo en México, 1968/1985*. Mexico City: Ediciones Era.

Alvarez, Sonia E. 1990. *Engendering Democracy in Brazil: Women's Movements in Transition Politics*. Princeton, N.J.: Princeton University Press.

Alvarez, Sonia E., and Arturo Escobar. 1992. "Conclusion: Theoretical and Political Horizons of Change in Contemporary Latin American Social Movements." In *The Making of Social Movements in Latin America: Identity, Strategy, Democracy*, edited by Arturo Escobar and Sonia E. Alvarez. Boulder, Colo.: Westview Press.

Amnistía Internacional. 1986. *México: Los derechos humanos en zonas rurales*. London: Amnesty International Publications.

Anderson, Bo, and James D. Cockroft. 1972. "Control and Cooptation in Mexican Politics." In *Dependence and Underdevelopment: Latin America's Political Economy*,

edited by James D. Cockroft, André Gunder Frank, and Dale L. Johnson. Garden City, N.J.: Doubleday.
Angell, Alan. 1980. "Peruvian Labour and the Military Government Since 1968." University of London, Institute of Latin American Studies, Working Paper No. 3.
Anguiano, Arturo. 1975. *El estado y la política obrera del cardenismo*. Mexico City: Ediciones Era.
Arnaut Salgado, Alberto. 1986. "Comentarios a la ponencia de la Lic. Yolanda de los Reyes." In *Descentralización y democracia en México*, edited by Blanca Torres. Mexico City: El Colegio de México.
———. 1989a. "La evolución de los grupos hegemónicos en el SNTE." Unpublished manuscript.
———. 1989b. "Los supervisores entre la SEP y el SNTE." Unpublished manuscript.
Arriaga, María de la Luz. 1981. "El magisterio en lucha." *Cuadernos Políticos*, no. 27: 79–101.
Bailey, John. 1994. "Centralism and Political Change in Mexico: The Case of National Solidarity." In *Transforming State-Society Relations in Mexico: The National Solidarity Strategy*, edited by Wayne A. Cornelius, Ann L. Craig, and Jonathan Fox. U.S.-Mexico Contemporary Perspectives Series, 6. La Jolla: Center for U.S.-Mexican Studies, University of California, San Diego.
Balboa, Juan, and Sergio Antonio Reyes. 1988. " 'No creo en el derecho de la sangre,' dice Patrocinio . . . pero cómo lo ha ayudado." *Proceso*, no. 586 (January 25): 24, 27.
Barrera, Manuel, and J. Samuel Valenzuela. 1986. "The Development of Labor Movement Opposition to the Military Regime." In *Military Rule in Chile: Dictatorship and Oppositions*, edited by J. Samuel Valenzuela and Arturo Valenzuela. Baltimore: The Johns Hopkins University Press.
Basáñez, Miguel E., and Víctor Raúl Martínez V., eds. 1987. *La composición del poder: Oaxaca 1968–1984*. Mexico City: Universidad Nacional Autónoma de México and Instituto Nacional de Administración Pública.
Basurto, Jorge. 1983. *En el régimen de Echeverría: Rebelión e independencia*. La clase obrera en la historia de México No. 14. Mexico City: Siglo XXI.
Benjamin, Thomas. 1989. *A Rich Land, A Poor People: Politics and Society in Modern Chiapas*. Albuquerque: University of New Mexico Press.
Bennett, Vivienne. 1992. "The Evolution of Urban Popular Movements in Mexico Between 1968 and 1988." In *The Making of Social Movements in Latin America: Identity, Strategy, Democracy*, edited by Arturo Escobar and Sonia E. Alvarez. Boulder, Colo.: Westview Press.
Berger, Suzanne D. 1979. "Politics and Antipolitics in Western Europe in the Seventies." *Daedalus* (Winter): 27–50.
———. 1981. *Organizing Interests in Western Europe: Pluralism, Corporatism, and the Transformation of Politics*. Cambridge: Cambridge University Press.
Bizberg, Ilán. 1983. "Las perspectivas de la oposición sindical en México." *Foro Internacional* 23, no. 4: 331–58.
———. 1984. "Política laboral y acción sindical en México (1976–1982)." *Foro Internacional* 25, no. 2: 166–89.
Boschi, Renato. 1984. "On Social Movements and Democratization: Theoretical Issues." Stanford-Berkeley Occasional Papers in Latin American Studies No. 9.

Britton, John A. 1979. "Teacher Unionization and the Corporate State in Mexico, 1931–1945." *Hispanic American Historical Review* 59, no. 4: 674–90.
Brockett, Charles D. 1991. "The Structure of Political Opportunities and Peasant Mobilization in Central America." *Comparative Politics* 23 (April): 253–74.
Brysk, Alison. 1994. *The Politics of Human Rights in Argentina: Protest, Change, and Democratization.* Stanford, Calif.: Stanford University Press.
Burdick, John. 1992. "Rethinking the Study of Social Movements: The Case of Christian Base Communities in Urban Brazil." In *The Making of Social Movements in Latin America: Identity, Strategy, Democracy,* edited by Arturo Escobar and Sonia E. Alvarez. Boulder, Colo.: Westview Press.
Bustamante, René, et al. 1984. *Oaxaca una lucha reciente: 1960–1983.* 2d ed. Mexico City: Ediciones Nueva Sociología.
Caballero, Juan Julián. 1990. "Lo indio en el movimiento magisterial democrático." *Alternativa* 1, no. 4 (May).
Calderón, Fernando, Alejandro Piscitelli, and José Luis Reyna. 1992. "Social Movements: Actors, Theories, Expectations." In *The Making of Social Movements in Latin America: Identity, Strategy, Democracy,* edited by Arturo Escobar and Sonia E. Alvarez. Boulder, Colo.: Westview Press.
Calva, José Luis. 1993. *El modelo neoliberal mexicano: Costos, vulnerabilidad, alternativas.* Mexico City: Fontamara and Friedrich Ebert Stiftung.
Camacho, Manuel. 1984. *El futuro inmediato.* La clase obrera en la historia de México No. 15. Mexico City: Siglo XXI.
Camp, Roderic. 1980. "Reclutamiento político y cambio en el México de los setentas." *Foro Internacional* 20, no. 3: 463–83.
———. 1995. *Mexican Political Biographies, 1935–1993.* 3d ed. Austin: University of Texas Press.
Campa, Homero. 1988. "Dividida en grupos y corrientes, la disidencia magisterial de Chiapas se destruye en pugnas internas." *Proceso,* no. 586 (January 25): 25–26.
———. 1989. "Funcionarios y dirigentes adictos a Jonguitud, sustituidos o marginados." *Proceso,* no. 658 (June 12): 6–10.
Canel, Eduardo. 1992. "Democratization and the Decline of Urban Social Movements in Uruguay: A Political-Institutional Account." In *The Making of Social Movements in Latin America: Identity, Strategy, Democracy,* edited by Arturo Escobar and Sonia E. Alvarez. Boulder, Colo.: Westview Press.
Cano, Arturo, René Bejarano, Luis Hernández, Jesús Martín del Campo, Julio Moguel, Andrés Nájera, Carlos Rojo, Gisela Salinas, Etelvina Sandoval. 1992. *La Coordinadora: La Coordinadora Nacional de Trabajadores de la Educación, su presente y sus retos.* Mexico City: Hojas Ediciones.
Carr, Barry. 1991. "Labor and the Political Left in Mexico." In *Unions, Workers, and the State in Mexico,* edited by Kevin J. Middlebrook. La Jolla: Center for U.S.-Mexican Studies, University of California, San Diego.
Carrillo, Teresa. 1990. "Women and Independent Unionism in the Garment Industry." In *Popular Movements and Political Change in Mexico,* edited by Joe Foweraker and Ann L. Craig. Boulder, Colo.: Lynne Rienner.
Casar, María Amparo. 1982. "El proyecto del movimiento obrero organizado en la LI legislatura." *Estudios Políticos* 1, no. 1 (October–December): 33–45.

Casar, María Amparo, and Carlos Márquez. 1983. "La política de salarios mínimos legales: 1934–1982." *Economía Mexicana*, no. 5: 221–59.
Cevallos, Diego. 1995. "Media Demonstrates Partiality in Chiapan Conflict" (InterPress Service). *Mexico NewsPak* 3, no. 8 (May 8–21, 1995).
Chassen de López, Francie R. 1977. *Lombardo Toledano y el movimiento obrero mexicano (1917/1940)*. Mexico City: Extemporáneos.
Chinchilla, Norma Stoltz. 1992. "Marxism, Feminism, and the Struggle for Democracy in Latin America." In *The Making of Social Movements in Latin America: Identity, Strategy, Democracy*, edited by Arturo Escobar and Sonia E. Alvarez. Boulder, Colo.: Westview Press.
Coleman, John R. 1956. "The Compulsive Pressures of Democracy in Unionism." *American Journal of Sociology* 61, no. 6: 519–26.
Coleman, Kenneth M., and Charles L. Davis. 1983. "Preemptive Reform and the Mexican Working Class." *Latin American Research Review* 18, no. 1: 3–31.
Collier, David, ed. 1979. *The New Authoritarianism in Latin America*. Princeton, N.J.: Princeton University Press.
Collier, David, and Ruth Berins Collier. 1977. "Who Does What, to Whom, and How: Toward a Comparative Analysis of Latin American Corporatism." In *Authoritarianism and Corporatism in Latin America*, edited by James M. Malloy. Pittsburgh: University of Pittsburgh Press.
Collier, Ruth Berins. 1982. "Popular Sector Incorporation and Political Supremacy: Regime Evolution in Brazil and Mexico." In *Brazil and Mexico: Patterns in Late Development*, edited by Sylvia Ann Hewlett and Richard S. Weinert. Philadelphia: Institute for the Study of Human Issues.
———. 1992. *The Contradictory Alliance: State-Labor Relations and Regime Change in Mexico*. Research Series No. 83. Berkeley: International and Area Studies, University of California, Berkeley.
Collier, Ruth Berins, and David Collier. 1979. "Inducements Versus Constraints: Disaggregating 'Corporatism.'" *American Political Science Review* 73, no. 4: 967–86.
———. 1991. *Shaping the Political Arena: Critical Junctures, the Labor Movement, and Regime Dynamics in Latin America*. Princeton, N.J.: Princeton University Press.
Colmenares, Ismael, Miguel Angel Gallo, Francisco González, Luis Hernández, eds. 1985. *Cien años de lucha de clases en México (1876–1976)*. 2 vols. Mexico City: Quinto Sol.
Comisión Federal Electoral. 1977–79. *Reforma Política*. 3 vols. Mexico City: Comisión Federal Electoral.
Contreras, Gabriela, and Herón Escobar, eds. 1987. *Empezar de nuevo: Por la transformación democrática de la UNAM*. Mexico City: Equipo Pueblo/Praxis.
Cook, Maria Lorena. 1990a. "Organizing Dissent: The Politics of Opposition in the Mexican Teachers' Union." Ph.D. dissertation, Department of Political Science, University of California, Berkeley.
———. 1990b. "Organizing Opposition in the Teachers' Movement in Oaxaca." In *Popular Movements and Political Change in Mexico*, edited by Joe Foweraker and Ann L. Craig. Boulder, Colo.: Lynne Rienner.
———. 1991. "Restructuring and Democracy in Mexico: Twenty Years of Trade Union

Strategies, 1970–1990." Paper presented at the International Congress of the Latin American Studies Association, April 4–6, Washington, D.C.
———. 1995. "Mexican State-Labor Relations and the Political Implications of Free Trade." *Latin American Perspectives* 22, no. 1 (Winter): 77–94.
Cook, Maria Lorena, Kevin J. Middlebrook, and Juan Molinar Horcasitas. 1994. "The Politics of Economic Restructuring in Mexico: Actors, Sequencing, and Coalition Change." In *The Politics of Economic Restructuring: State-Society Relations and Regime Change in Mexico*, edited by Maria Lorena Cook, Kevin J. Middlebrook, and Juan Molinar Horcasitas. U.S.-Mexico Contemporary Perspectives Series, 7. La Jolla: Center for U.S.-Mexican Studies, University of California, San Diego.
———, eds. 1994. *The Politics of Economic Restructuring: State-Society Relations and Regime Change in Mexico*. U.S.-Mexico Contemporary Perspectives Series, 7. La Jolla: Center for U.S.-Mexican Studies, University of California, San Diego.
Coordinadora Nacional de Trabajadores de la Educación (CNTE)/Información Obrera. 1981. "Misael Núñez Acosta: Biografía de una lucha, relato de una infamia." Pamphlet.
Córdova, Arnaldo. 1974. *La política de masas del cardenismo*. Mexico City: Ediciones Era.
Cornelius, Wayne A., Ann L. Craig, and Jonathan Fox, eds. 1994. *Transforming State-Society Relations in Mexico: The National Solidarity Strategy*. U.S.-Mexico Contemporary Perspectives Series, 6. La Jolla: Center for U.S.-Mexican Studies, University of California, San Diego.
Cornelius, Wayne A., Judith Gentleman, and Peter H. Smith, eds. 1989. *Mexico's Alternative Political Futures*. Monograph Series 30. La Jolla: Center for U.S.-Mexican Studies, University of California, San Diego.
Cortina, Regina. 1985. "Power, Gender, and Education: Unionized Teachers in Mexico City." Ph.D. dissertation, Department of Education, Stanford University.
———. 1986. "Family Life and the Subordination of Women in the Teaching Profession: The Case of Mexico City." Michigan State University, Women in International Development Working Paper No. 128.
Costain, Anne N. 1992. *Inviting Women's Rebellion: A Political Process Interpretation of the Women's Movement*. Baltimore and London: The Johns Hopkins University Press.
Craig, Ann L. 1990. "Institutional Context and Popular Strategies." In *Popular Movements and Political Change in Mexico*, edited by Joe Foweraker and Ann L. Craig. Boulder, Colo.: Lynne Rienner.
Cruz C., José Antonio. 1982. "Absalón Castellanos y terratenientes: Un análisis coyuntural." Thesis, Universidad Autónoma de Chiapas, México.
Cuadernos Educativos. 1985. No. 1. Mexico City: Aguirre y Beltrán.
Cuéllar Vázquez, Angélica. 1986. *Una rebelión dependiente: La tendencia democrática frente al estado mexicano*. Mexico City: Terra Nova.
Davies, James. 1962. "Toward a Theory of Revolution." *American Sociological Review* 27, no. 1 (February): 5–19.
Davis, Charles L., and Kenneth M. Coleman. 1986. "Labor and the State: Union Incorporation and Working Class Politicization in Latin America." *Comparative Political Studies* 18, no. 4: 395–417.
Davis, Diane E. 1989. "Review of Susan Eckstein, ed., *Power and Popular Protest: Latin American Social Movements*." *Journal of Interamerican Studies and World Affairs* 31, no. 4 (Winter): 225–34.

———. 1994. *Urban Leviathan: Mexico City in the Twentieth Century*. Philadelphia: Temple University Press.
de la Garza Toledo, Enrique. 1982. "Estructura organizativa y democracia en el SNTE." *Información Obrera* 1 (Summer): 37–46.
———. 1991. "Independent Trade Unionism in Mexico: Past Developments and Future Perspectives." In *Unions, Workers, and the State in Mexico*, edited by Kevin J. Middlebrook. La Jolla: Center for U.S.-Mexican Studies, University of California, San Diego.
———. 1994. "The Restructuring of State-Labor Relations in Mexico." In *The Politics of Economic Restructuring: State-Society Relations and Regime Change in Mexico*, edited by Maria Lorena Cook, Kevin J. Middlebrook, and Juan Molinar Horcasitas. U.S.-Mexico Contemporary Perspectives Series, 7. La Jolla: Center for U.S.-Mexican Studies, University of California, San Diego.
de la Garza, Enrique, León Tomás Ejea, and Luis Fernando Macás. 1986. *El otro movimiento estudiantil*. Mexico City: A Pleno Sol/ Extemporáneos.
de los Reyes, Yolanda. 1986. "Descentralización de la educación." In *Descentralización y democracia en México*, edited by Blanca Torres. Mexico City: El Colegio de México.
Dresser, Denise. 1991. *Neopopulist Solutions to Neoliberal Problems: Mexico's National Solidarity Program*. La Jolla: Center for U.S.-Mexican Studies, University of California, San Diego.
Duke, Benjamin C. 1973. *Japan's Militant Teachers: A History of the Left-Wing Teachers' Movement*. Honolulu: The University Press of Hawaii.
Durand Ponte, Víctor Manuel. 1991. "The Confederation of Mexican Workers, the Labor Congress, and the Crisis of Mexico's Social Pact." In *Unions, Workers, and the State in Mexico*, edited by Kevin J. Middlebrook. La Jolla: Center for U.S.-Mexican Studies, University of California, San Diego.
———, ed. 1984. *Las derrotas obreras, 1946–1952*. Mexico City: Instituto de Investigaciones Sociales, Universidad Nacional Autónoma de México.
Eckstein, Susan, ed. 1989. *Power and Popular Protest: Latin American Social Movements*. Berkeley and Los Angeles: University of California Press.
Edelstein, J. David, and Malcolm Warner. 1976. *Comparative Union Democracy: Organization and Opposition in British and American Unions*. New York: Wiley.
———. 1977. "Research Areas in National Union Democracy." *Industrial Relations* 16, no. 2 (May): 186–98.
Eisinger, Peter K. 1973. "The Conditions of Protest Behavior in American Cities." *American Political Science Review* 67, no. 1 (March): 11–28.
Equipo Pueblo. 1984. "Balance de la CNTE." 6(118/119).
———. 1985. "Organización y democracia sindical." Folleto No. 2. Mexico City: Ediciones Pueblo.
———. 1986. "Oaxaca: Los maestros en lucha contínua." Mexico City: Equipo Pueblo.
Equipo Pueblo, CNTE, and Información Obrera. 1988. "La violencia charra." (Series: Historias del sindicalismo mexicano 10). Mexico City: Pueblo, CNTE, Información Obrera.
Escobar, Arturo. 1992. "Culture, Economics, and Politics in Latin American Social Movements Theory and Research." In *The Making of Social Movements in Latin*

America: Identity, Strategy, and Democracy, edited by Arturo Escobar and Sonia E. Alvarez. Boulder, Colo.: Westview Press.
Escobar, Arturo, and Sonia E. Alvarez, eds. 1992. *The Making of Social Movements in Latin America: Identity, Strategy, and Democracy*. Boulder, Colo.: Westview Press.
Espinosa, José Antonio. 1982. "Los maestros de los maestros: Las dirigencias sindicales en la historia del SNTE." *Historias*, no. 1.
Estados Unidos Mexicanos. Presidencia de la República. 1989. "Carlos Salinas de Gortari: Primer informe de gobierno." Mexico City: Presidencia de la República.
Evans, Sara M., and Harry C. Boyte. 1992. *Free Spaces: The Sources of Democratic Change in America*. 2d ed. Chicago and London: University of Chicago Press.
Fernández Dorado, Rubelio. 1982. *El auge magisterial de marzo de 1982*. N.p.
Foweraker, Joe. 1989. "Popular Movements and the Transformation of the System." In *Mexico's Alternative Political Futures*, edited by Wayne A. Cornelius, Judith Gentleman, and Peter H. Smith. Monograph Series 30. La Jolla: Center for U.S.-Mexican Studies, University of California, San Diego.
———. 1993. *Popular Mobilization in Mexico: The Teachers' Movement, 1977–87*. Cambridge: Cambridge University Press.
Foweraker, Joe, and Ann L. Craig, eds. 1990. *Popular Movements and Political Change in Mexico*. Boulder, Colo.: Lynne Rienner.
Fox, Jonathan. 1992a. "Democratic Rural Development: Leadership Accountability in Regional Peasant Organizations." *Development and Change* 23, no. 2 (April): 1–36.
———. 1992b. *The Politics of Food in Mexico: State Power and Popular Mobilization*. Ithaca, N.Y.: Cornell University Press.
———. 1994a. "The Challenge of Democracy: Rebellion as Catalyst." *Akwe:kon Journal* (Summer): 13–19.
———. 1994b. "The Difficult Transition from Clientelism to Citizenship: Lessons from Mexico." *World Politics* 46, no. 2 (January): 151–84.
———. 1994c. "Political Change in Mexico's New Peasant Economy." In *The Politics of Economic Restructuring: State-Society Relations and Regime Change in Mexico*, edited by Maria Lorena Cook, Kevin J. Middlebrook, and Juan Molinar Horcasitas. U.S.-Mexico Contemporary Perspectives Series, 7. La Jolla: Center for U.S.-Mexican Studies, University of California, San Diego.
Fox, Jonathan, and Gustavo Gordillo. 1989. "Between State and Market: The Campesinos' Quest for Autonomy." In *Mexico's Alternative Political Futures*, edited by Wayne A. Cornelius, Judith Gentleman, and Peter H. Smith. Monograph Series 30. La Jolla: Center for U.S.-Mexican Studies, University of California, San Diego.
Fox, Jonathan, and Luis Hernández. 1992. "Mexico's Difficult Democracy: Grassroots Movements, NGOs, and Local Government." *Alternatives* 17, no. 2 (April).
French, John D. 1992. *The Brazilian Workers' ABC: Class Conflict and Alliances in Modern São Paulo*. Chapel Hill: The University of North Carolina Press.
Fuentes Molinar, Olac. 1983. *Educación y política en México*. Mexico City: Nueva Imagen.
Galván, Luz Elena. 1983. "Política de descentralización educativa: La opinión de los maestros democráticos." In *Notas sobre las políticas del estado mexicano hoy*.

Cuadernos de la Casa Chata, no. 87. Mexico City: Centro de Investigaciones y Estudios Superiores en Antropología Social.

———. 1985. *Los maestros y la educación pública en México*. Mexico City: Centro de Investigaciones y Estudios Superiores en Antropología Social and SEP/Cultura.

Gamson, William. 1990. *The Strategy of Social Protest*. 2d ed. Belmont, Calif.: Wadsworth Publishing Co.

Garrido, Luis Javier. 1989. "The Crisis of Presidencialismo." In *Mexico's Alternative Political Futures*, edited by Wayne A. Cornelius, Judith Gentleman, and Peter H. Smith. Monograph Series 30. La Jolla: Center for U.S.-Mexican Studies, University of California, San Diego.

Gómez Tagle, Silvia. 1980. *Insurgencia y democracia en los sindicatos electricistas*. Mexico City: El Colegio de México.

Gómez Tagle, Silvia, and Marcelo Miquet. 1976. "Integración o democracia sindical: El caso de los electricistas." In *Tres estudios sobre el movimiento obrero en México*, edited by José Luis Reyna, Francisco Zapata, Marcelo Miquet Fleury, and Silvia Gómez Tagle. Mexico City: El Colegio de México.

González Paredes, Guadalupe, and David Turner. 1990. "Education in the Largest City in the World: Mexico." In *Education in Central America and the Caribbean*, edited by Colin Brock and Donald Clarkson. London and New York: Routledge.

González Ruiz, José Enrique. 1985. "Proyectos educativos: Crisis oficial, crisis de alternativas." *El Día* (Suplemento especial de XXIII aniversario). June.

Gouldner, Alvin W. 1955. "Metaphysical Pathos and the Theory of Bureaucracy." *American Political Science Review* 49, no. 2: 496–507.

Greaves, Patricia. 1980. "Las Relaciones SEP-SNTE." In *Simposio sobre el Magisterio Nacional*. Vol. 1. Cuadernos de la Casa Chata, no. 29. Mexico City: Centro de Investigaciones y Estudios Superiores en Antropología Social.

Greenfield, Gerald M., and Sheldon L. Maram, eds. 1987. *Latin American Labor Organizations*. New York: Greenwood Press.

Guevara Niebla, Gilberto, ed. 1985. *La educación socialista en México (1934–1945)*. Mexico City: SEP/El Caballito.

Gurr, Ted. 1970. *Why Men Rebel*. Princeton, N.J.: Princeton University Press.

Guzmán Ortiz, Eduardo, and Joaquín H. Vela Glez. 1989. "Maestros 1989: Crisis, democracia, y más salario." *El Cotidiano* 6, no. 30: 44–49.

Haber, Paul Lawrence. 1994. "The Art and Implications of Political Restructuring in Mexico: The Case of Urban Popular Movements." In *The Politics of Economic Restructuring: State-Society Relations and Regime Change in Mexico*, edited by Maria Lorena Cook, Kevin J. Middlebrook, and Juan Molinar Horcasitas. Contemporary Perspectives Series, 7. La Jolla: Center for U.S.-Mexican Studies, University of California, San Diego.

———. 1996. "Identity and Political Process: Recent Trends in the Study of Latin American Social Movements." *Latin American Research Review* 31, no. 1: 171–88.

Harvey, Neil. 1990. "Peasant Strategies and Corporatism in Chiapas." In *Popular Movements and Political Change in Mexico*, edited by Joe Foweraker and Ann L. Craig. La Jolla: Center for U.S.-Mexican Studies, University of California, San Diego.

———. 1994. "Rebellion in Chiapas: Rural Reforms, Campesino Radicalism, and the

Limits to Salinismo." Transformation of Rural Mexico Series No. 5. La Jolla: Center for U.S.-Mexican Studies, University of California, San Diego.
———, ed. 1993. *Mexico: Dilemmas of Transition.* London: The Institute of Latin American Studies, University of London and British Academic Press.
Hellman, Judith Adler. 1992. "The Study of New Social Movements in Latin America and the Question of Autonomy." In *The Making of Social Movements in Latin America: Identity, Strategy, Democracy,* edited by Arturo Escobar and Sonia E. Alvarez. Boulder, Colo.: Westview Press.
Hemingway, John. 1978. *Conflict and Democracy: Studies in Trade Union Government.* Oxford: Clarendon Press.
Hernández, Luis. 1982. "Sobre el grupo Vanguardia Revolucionaria." *Información Obrera* 1 (Summer): 47–51.
———. 1983. "La fuerza ambivalente de la CNTE para el estado." *Punto* 1, no. 41.
———. 1984. "Vanguardia va a la lona: Crónica del congreso sindical del magisterio chiapaneco." *Folletos de Educación Sindical,* no. 15.
———. 1985a. "Y el cerco se rompe. CNTE, un balance." *Información Obrera,* no. 58: 25–26.
———. 1985b. "Marzo, mes de los chiapanecos." *Información Obrera,* no. 56: 9–14.
———. 1985c. "Un paro con mayúsculas: El inicio del paro magisterial chiapaneco." *Información Obrera,* no. 55: 1–6.
———. 1986a. "Los maestros de la CNTE: La disputa del futuro." *Fin de Siglo,* no. 8: 23–27.
———. 1986b. "The SNTE and the Teachers' Movement, 1982–1984." In *The Mexican Left, the Popular Movements, and the Politics of Austerity,* edited by Barry Carr and Ricardo Anzaldúa Montoya. Monograph Series 18. La Jolla: Center for U.S.-Mexican Studies, University of California, San Diego.
———. 1988. "La construcción social de la autonomía: Maestros y autogestión." Presented at the Forum on Social Movements and Self-Determination, Oaxtepec, Morelos, Mexico.
———. 1989a. "Maestros: Jaque al rey." *El Cotidiano* 6, no. 28 (March–April): 30–35.
———. 1989b. "Maestros: Del gambito de dama al jaque mate." *El Cotidiano* 6, no. 30 (July–August): 55–58.
———. 1992. "SNTE: La transición difícil." *El Cotidiano* 8, no. 51 (November–December): 54–59; 70.
———, ed. 1981. *Las luchas magisteriales, 1979/1981 (Documentos I).* Mexico City: Editorial Macehual.
Hernández, Luis, and Francisco Pérez Arce, eds. 1982. *Las luchas magisteriales, 1979/1981 (Documentos II).* Mexico City: Macehual.
Hernández Aguilar, Jorge Enrique. 1986. "En nombre del maíz." Mexico City: Equipo Pueblo.
Hernández Ruiz, Samael, and Rodrigo Velázquez García. 1983. *Los servicios educativos federales en Oaxaca, 1974–1982.* Oaxaca: Secretaría de Educación Pública.
Hernández S., Ricardo. 1987. *La Coordinadora Nacional del Movimiento Urbano Popular CONAMUP, su historia 1980–1986.* Mexico City: Equipo Pueblo.
Hobsbawm, E. J. 1974. "Peasant Land Occupations." *Past and Present* 62 (February): 120–52.

Información Obrera. 1989. "Escuela por escuela." Video.
Instituto Nacional de Antropología e Historia (INAH). Delegación-III-24. 1982. "Balance. La quinta oleada del movimiento magisterial." *Folleto de Educación Sindical* No. 10.
Inter-American Development Bank. 1988. *Economic and Social Progress in Latin America. 1988 Report. Special Section: Science and Technology.* Washington, D.C.: Inter-American Development Bank.
———. 1989. *Economic and Social Progress in Latin America. 1989 Report. Special Section: Savings, Investment, and Growth.* Washington, D.C.: Inter-American Development Bank.
Jelín, Elizabeth, ed. 1990. *Women and Social Change in Latin America.* London and N.J.: Zed Books in association with United Nations Research Insititute for Social Development.
Jenkins, J. Craig, and Charles Perrow. 1977. "Insurgency of the Powerless: Farm Worker Movements (1946–1972)." *American Sociological Review* 42 (April): 249–68.
Jessop, Bob. 1982. *The Capitalist State.* New York: New York University Press.
Katzenstein, Mary Fainsod, and Carol McClurg Mueller, eds. 1987. *The Women's Movements of the United States and Western Europe; Consciousness, Political Opportunity, and Public Policy.* Philadelphia: Temple University Press.
Keck, Margaret E. 1989. "The New Unionism in the Brazilian Transition." In *Democratizing Brazil: Problems of Transition and Consolidation,* edited by Alfred Stepan. Oxford: Oxford University Press.
———. 1992. *The Workers' Party and Democratization in Brazil.* New Haven: Yale University Press.
Keeler, John T. S. 1981. "Corporatism and Official Union Hegemony: The Case of French Agricultural Syndicalism." In *Organizing Interests in Western Europe: Pluralism, Corporatism, and the Transformation of Politics,* edited by Suzanne D. Berger. Cambridge: Cambridge University Press.
Kitschelt, Herbert P. 1986. "Political Opportunity Structures and Political Protest: Anti-Nuclear Movements in Four Democracies." *British Journal of Political Science* 16, pt. 1 (January): 57–85.
Klandermans, Bert. 1989. *International Social Movement Research,* vol. 2, *Organizing for Change: Social Movement Organizations in Europe and the United States.* Greenwich, Conn.: JAI Press.
Klandermans, Bert, and Sidney Tarrow. 1988. "Mobilization into Social Movements: Synthesizing European and American Approaches." In *International Social Movement Research,* vol. 1, *From Structure to Action: Comparing Social Movement Research Across Cultures,* edited by Hanspeter Kriesi and Sidney Tarrow. Greenwich, Conn.: JAI Press.
Knight, Alan. 1990. "Historical Continuities in Social Movements." In *Popular Movements and Political Change in Mexico,* edited by Joe Foweraker and Ann L. Craig. La Jolla: Center for U.S.-Mexican Studies, University of California, San Diego.
Kornhauser, William. 1959. *The Politics of Mass Society.* Glencoe, Ill.: The Free Press.
Kovacs, Karen. 1983. "La planeación educativa en México: La Universidad Pedagógica Nacional (UPN)." *Estudios Sociológicos* 1, no. 2: 263–92.
———. 1990. "Intervención estatal y transformación del régimen político: El caso de

la Universidad Pedagógica Nacional." Ph.D. dissertation, Centro de Estudios Sociológicos, El Colegio de México.
La Botz, Dan. 1992. *Mask of Democracy: Labor Suppression in Mexico Today.* Boston: South End Press.
Latapí, Pablo. 1980. *Análisis de un sexenio de educación en México, 1970–1976.* Mexico City: Nueva Imagen.
Levy, Daniel, and Gabriel Székely. 1985. *Estabilidad y Cambio: Paradojas del sistema político mexicano.* Mexico City: Centro de Estudios Internacionales, El Colegio de México.
Lipset, Seymour Martin, Martin Trow, and James Coleman. 1956. *Union Democracy.* Garden City, N.Y.: Anchor Books.
Lipsky, Michael. 1968. "Protest as a Political Resource." *American Political Science Review* 62, no. 4: 1,144–58.
Loaeza, Soledad. 1994. "Political Liberalization and Uncertainty in Mexico." In *The Politics of Economic Restructuring: State-Society Relations and Regime Change in Mexico,* edited by Maria Lorena Cook, Kevin J. Middlebrook, and Juan Molinar Horcasitas. U.S.-Mexico Contemporary Perspectives Series, 7. La Jolla: Center for U.S.-Mexican Studies, University of California, San Diego.
López Monjardín, Adriana. 1986. *La lucha por los ayuntamientos, una utopía viable.* Mexico City: Siglo XXI and Universidad Nacional Autónoma de México.
Loyo Brambila, Aurora. 1979. *El movimiento magisterial de 1958 en México.* Mexico City: Ediciones Era.
Luna Jurado, Rogelio. 1977. "Los maestros y la democracia sindical." *Cuadernos Políticos,* no. 14: 73–103.
Lustig, Nora. 1992. *Mexico: The Remaking of an Economy.* Washington, D.C.: The Brookings Institution.
MacRae, Edward. 1992. "Homosexual Identities in Transitional Brazilian Politics." In *The Making of Social Movements in Latin America: Identity, Strategy, Democracy,* edited by Arturo Escobar and Sonia E. Alvarez. Boulder, Colo.: Westview Press.
Mainwaring, Scott. 1985. "Grass Roots Popular Movements and the Struggle for Democracy: Nova Iguaçu, 1974–1985." The Helen Kellogg Institute for International Studies, Working Paper No. 52, University of Notre Dame.
———. 1987. "Urban Popular Movements, Identity, and Democratization in Brazil." *Comparative Political Studies* 20, no. 2: 131–59.
———. 1988. "Political Parties and Democratization in Brazil and the Southern Cone." *Comparative Politics* 21, no. 1: 97–117.
Mainwaring, Scott, and Eduardo Viola. 1984. "New Social Movements, Political Culture, and Democracy: Brazil and Argentina in the 1980s." *Telos* 61 (Fall): 17–52.
Malloy, James M., ed. 1977. *Authoritarianism and Corporatism in Latin America.* Pittsburgh: University of Pittsburgh Press.
Martin, Roderick. 1968. "Union Democracy: An Explanatory Framework." *Sociology* 2, no. 2: 205–20.
———. 1971. "Edelstein, Warner, and Cooke on 'Union Democracy' (Critical Note)." *Sociology* 5, no. 2: 243–44.
Martínez Assad, Carlos, ed. 1985. *Municipios en Conflicto.* Mexico City: Universidad Nacional Autónoma de México and G. V. Editores.

Martínez Assad, Carlos, and Alicia Ziccardi. 1988. "La descentralización de las políticas públicas en México." Seminar on "Descentralización del Estado, Requerimientos y Políticas en la Crisis," Centro de Estudios Urbanos y Regionales, Buenos Aires, November 9–11.

Martínez Vásquez, Víctor Raúl. 1990. *Movimiento popular y política en Oaxaca: 1968–1986*. Mexico City: Consejo Nacional para la Cultura y las Artes.

Maybury-Lewis, Biorn. 1994. *The Politics of the Possible: The Brazilian Rural Workers' Trade Union Movement, 1964–1985*. Philadelphia: Temple University Press.

Maza, Enrique. 1992. "En los libros de texto se resalta lo que se quiere para justificar el proyecto salinista." *Proceso*, no. 827 (September 7): 6–12.

McAdam, Doug. 1982. *Political Process and the Development of Black Insurgency, 1930–1970*. The University of Chicago Press.

McCarthy, John D., and Mayer N. Zald. 1977. "Resource Mobilization and Social Movements: A Partial Theory." *American Journal of Sociology* 82, no. 6: 1,212–41.

McGinn, Noel, Guillermo Orozco, and Susan Street. 1983. *La asignación de recursos económicos en la educación pública en México: Un proceso técnico en un contexto político*. Mexico City: Fundación Barros Sierra.

McNall, Scott G. 1987. "Thinking about Social Class: Structure, Organization, and Consciousness." In *Recapturing Marxism: An Appraisal of Recent Trends in Sociological Theory*, edited by Rhonda F. Levine and Jerry Lembcke. New York: Praeger.

Melucci, Alberto. 1989. *Nomads of the Present: Social Movements and Individual Needs in Contemporary Society*. Philadelphia: Temple University Press.

Meyer, Lorenzo. 1977. "Historical Roots of the Authoritarian State in Mexico." In *Authoritarianism in Mexico*, edited by José Luis Reyna and Richard S. Weinert. Inter-American Politics Series, vol. 2. Philadelphia: Institute for the Study of Human Issues.

———. 1989. "Democratization of the PRI: Mission Impossible?" In *Mexico's Alternative Political Futures*, edited by Wayne A. Cornelius, Judith Gentleman, and Peter H. Smith. Monograph Series 30. La Jolla: Center for U.S.-Mexican Studies, University of California, San Diego.

Michels, Robert. 1959. *Political Parties: A Sociological Study of the Oligarchical Tendencies of Modern Democracy*. New York: Dover Publications.

Middlebrook, Kevin J. 1986. "Political Liberalization in an Authoritarian Regime: The Case of Mexico." In *Transitions from Authoritarian Rule: Latin America*, edited by Guillermo O'Donnell, Philippe C. Schmitter, and Laurence Whitehead. Baltimore and London: The Johns Hopkins University Press.

———. 1989. "Union Democratization in the Mexican Automobile Industry: A Reappraisal." *Latin American Research Review* 24, no. 2: 69–93.

———. 1995. *The Paradox of Revolution: Labor, the State, and Authoritarianism in Mexico*. Baltimore and London: The Johns Hopkins University Press.

Miller, Marjorie. 1989. "Dissident Mexico Teachers Go On Strike for 100% Raise and 'Union Democracy.'" *Los Angeles Times* (San Diego County Edition). April 18, 1989.

Miranda López, Francisco. 1992. "Descentralización educativa y modernización del Estado." *Revista Mexicana de Sociología* 54, no. 2: 19–44.

Moguel, Julio. 1987. *Los caminos de la izquierda*. Mexico City: Juan Pablos Editor.

Monsiváis, Carlos. 1987. *Entrada libre: Crónicas de la sociedad que se organiza.* Mexico City: Ediciones Era.
Morales-Gómez, Daniel A., and Carlos A. Torres. 1990. *The State, Corporatist Politics, and Educational Policy-Making in Mexico (1970–1988).* New York: Praeger.
Morris, Aldon, and Cedric Herring. 1987. "Theory and Research in Social Movements: A Critical Review." In *Annual Review of Political Science*, edited by Samuel Long. Vol. 2. Norwood, N.J.: Ablex Publishing Corporation.
Movimiento Revolucionario del Magisterio. 1981a. "Balance de la insurgencia magisterial (Ponencias al III Foro de la CNTE, abril de 1981)." (Educación democrática No. 13.) Mexico City: Ediciones Movimiento.
———. 1981b. "Las corrientes sindicales y la insurgencia en el SNTE." (Educación democrática No. 14.) Mexico City: Ediciones Movimiento.
———. 1981c. "Los estatutos del SNTE y la lucha de los trabajadores de la educación." (Educación democrática No. 12.) Mexico City: Ediciones Movimiento.
———. 1985. "¿Unificación o descentralización educativa?" (Educación democrática No. 17.) Mexico City: Ediciones Movimiento.
Munck, Gerardo L. 1990. "Identity and Ambiguity in Democratic Struggles." In *Popular Movements and Political Change in Mexico*, edited by Joe Foweraker and Ann L. Craig. Boulder, Colo.: Lynne Rienner.
Munck, Ronaldo. 1989. *Latin America: The Transition to Democracy.* London and N.J.: Zed Books.
Murphy, Arthur D., and Alex Stepick. 1991. *Social Inequality in Oaxaca: A History of Resistance and Change.* Philadelphia: Temple University Press.
Noriega Chávez, Blanca Margarita. 1992. *Crisis y descentralización educativa en México, 1982–1988.* Informe de Investigación 2. Mexico City: Universidad Pedagógica Nacional.
Núñez Miranda, Concepción Silvia. 1990. "Maestras Oaxaqueñas: Movimiento magisterial, vida cotidiana y democracia, 1980–1989." Tesis de Licenciatura en Sociología, Facultad de Ciencias Políticas y Sociales, Universidad Nacional Autónoma de México.
Núñez Miranda, Concepción Silvia, and Blanca A. Hernández Sibaja. 1986. "La maestra y su vida cotidiana." Presented at VI National Forum: State, Crisis, and Education. Instituto Tecnológico Agropecuario de Oaxaca, Oaxaca. October 16–18.
Oberschall, Anthony. 1973. *Social Conflict and Social Movements.* Englewood Cliffs, N.J.: Prentice-Hall.
O'Donnell, Guillermo A. 1977. "Corporatism and the Question of the State." In *Authoritarianism and Corporatism in Latin America*, edited by James M. Malloy. Pittsburgh: University of Pittsburgh Press.
O'Donnell, Guillermo, and Philippe C. Schmitter. 1986. *Transitions from Authoritarian Rule: Tentative Conclusions About Uncertain Democracies.* Baltimore and London: The Johns Hopkins University Press.
O'Donnell, Guillermo, Philippe C. Schmitter, and Laurence Whitehead, eds. 1986. *Transitions from Authoritarian Rule in Latin America and Southern Europe.* Baltimore and London: The Johns Hopkins University Press.
Offe, Claus. 1981. "The Attribution of Public Status to Interest Groups: Observations

on the West German Case." In *Organizing Interests in Western Europe: Pluralism, Corporatism, and the Transformation of Politics*, edited by Suzanne D. Berger. Cambridge: Cambridge University Press.

———. 1987. "Challenging the Boundaries of Institutional Politics: Social Movements Since the 1960s." In *Changing Boundaries of the Political*, edited by Charles S. Maier. Cambridge: Cambridge University Press.

Offe, Claus, and Helmut Wiesenthal. 1980. "Two Logics of Collective Action: Theoretical Notes on Social Class and Organizational Form." In *Political Power and Social Theory*. Vol. 1. Greenwich, Conn.: JAI Press.

Olson, Mancur. 1965. *The Logic of Collective Action: Public Goods and the Theory of Groups*. Cambridge, Mass.: Harvard University Press.

Ontiveros Balcázar, Manuel. 1986. *MRM: 30 años de lucha contra el sindicalismo domesticado (1956–1957)*. Mexico City: Ediciones Movimiento.

———. 1992. *Historia del MRM, 1958–1961: El presidente aplastó a la Sección 9 democrática*. Mexico City: Editorial Pueblo Nuevo.

Organización. N.d. "Informe: Línea Proletaria." Photocopy.

Oxhorn, Philip. 1994. "Understanding Political Change After Authoritarian Rule: The Popular Sectors and Chile's New Democratic Regime." *Journal of Latin American Studies* 26: 737–59.

———. 1995. *Organizing Civil Society: The Popular Sectors and the Struggle for Democracy in Chile*. University Park, Penn.: The Pennsylvania State University Press.

Peláez, Gerardo. 1980. *Insurgencia magisterial*. Mexico City: Edisa.

———. 1984a. *Historia del Sindicato Nacional de Trabajadores de la Educación*. Mexico City: Ediciones de Cultura Popular.

———. 1984b. *Las luchas magisteriales de 1956–1960*. Mexico City: Ediciones de Cultura Popular.

Peralta Esteva, Julio, Librado Santiago Constantino, and Rafael Arellanes Caballero. 1985. "Radiografía y diagnóstico de un proceso sindical: El movimiento magisterial chiapaneco." Presented at the Seminar on Latin American Perspectives, South-Southeast Regional Meeting, Oaxaca, Mexico.

Pérez Arce, Francisco. 1988. *A muchas voces. Testimonios de la lucha magisterial*. Mexico City: Praxis, Información Obrera, Universidad Autónoma de Sinaloa.

———. 1990. "The Enduring Union Struggle for Legality and Democracy." In *Popular Movements and Political Change in Mexico*, edited by Joe Foweraker and Ann L. Craig. Boulder, Colo.: Lynne Rienner.

Pérez Arce, Francisco, Enrique de la Garza, and Luis Hernández. 1982. "Del SNTE a la CNTE: La lucha por la democracia sindical en el magisterio mexicano." *Información Obrera*, no. 1: 23–78.

Pescador, José Angel, and Carlos Alberto Torres. 1985. *Poder político y educación en México*. Mexico City: UTEHA.

Piven, Frances Fox, and Richard A. Cloward. 1979. *Poor People's Movements: Why They Succeed, How They Fail*. New York: Vintage Books.

Pizzorno, Alessandro. 1978. "Political Exchange and Collective Identity in Industrial Conflict." In *The Resurgence of Class Conflict in Western Europe Since 1968*, vol. 2, *Comparative Analyses*, edited by Colin Crouch and Alessandro Pizzorno. New York: Holmes and Meier.

Poniatowska, Elena. 1971. *La Noche de Tlatelolco.* Mexico City: Ediciones Era.
Pozzi, Pablo A. 1988. "Argentina 1976–1982: Labour Leadership and Military Government." *Journal of Latin American Studies* 20, no. 1: 111–38.
Prawda, Juan. 1984. *Teoría y praxis de la planeación educativa en México.* Mexico City: Grijalbo.
Prieto, Ana María. 1986. "Mexico's National Coordinadoras in a Context of Economic Crisis." In *The Mexican Left, the Popular Movements, and the Politics of Austerity,* edited by Barry Carr and Ricardo Anzaldúa Montoya. Monograph Series 18. La Jolla: Center for U.S.-Mexican Studies, University of California, San Diego.
Punto Crítico. 1983. "SNTE, ejemplo de corporativismo," and "La descentralización educativa." Pamphlet.
———. N.d. "La hora de los maestros." (Articles published between May and November 1980 in *Punto Crítico* on the teachers' struggle.) Pamphlet.
Purcell, Susan Kaufman. 1977. "The Future of the Mexican System." In *Authoritarianism in Mexico,* edited by José Luis Reyna and Richard S. Weinert. Inter-American Politics Series, vol. 2. Philadelphia: Institute for the Study of Human Issues.
Purcell, Susan Kaufman, and John F. H. Purcell. 1980. "State and Society in Mexico: Must a Stable Polity be Institutionalized?" *World Politics* 32, no. 2: 194–227.
Raby, David L. 1974. *Educación y revolución social en México (1921–1940).* Mexico City: Secretaría de Educación Pública (Sep-Setentas 141).
Ramírez Saiz, Juan Manuel. 1990. "Urban Struggles and Their Political Consequences." In *Popular Movements and Political Change in Mexico,* edited by Joe Foweraker and Ann L. Craig. Boulder, Colo.: Lynne Rienner.
Reséndiz García, Ramón. 1992. "Reforma educativa y conflicto interburocrático en México, 1978–1988." *Revista Mexicana de Sociología* 54, no. 2 (April–June): 3–18.
Reyna, José Luis. 1977. "Redefining the Authoritarian Regime." In *Authoritarianism in Mexico,* edited by José Luis Reyna and Richard S. Weinert. Inter-American Politics Series, vol. 2. Philadelphia: Institute for the Study of Human Issues.
———. 1979. "El movimiento obrero en una situación de crisis: México 1976–78." *Foro Internacional* 19, no. 3.
Reyna, José Luis, and Richard S. Weinert, eds. 1977. *Authoritarianism in Mexico.* Inter-American Politics Series, vol. 2. Philadelphia: Institute for the Study of Human Issues.
Rodríguez, Guadalupe, and Gabriel Torres. 1994. "El Barzón y COMAGRO: La construcción social de las políticas neoliberales de México y las estrategias de cambio de los agroproductores." *Espiral* 1, no. 1 (September): 129–76.
Rodríguez, Victoria E. 1987. "The Politics of Decentralization in Mexico: Divergent Outcomes of Policy Implementation." Ph.D. dissertation, Department of Political Science, University of California, Berkeley.
———. N.d. *Decentralization in Mexico: From Reforma Municipal to Solidaridad to Nuevo Federalismo.* Boulder, Colo.: Westview Press, forthcoming.
Rodríguez Victoria E., and Peter M. Ward, eds. 1995. *Opposition Government in Mexico.* Albuquerque: University of New Mexico Press.
Rodríguez Araujo, Octavio. 1979. *La reforma política y los partidos en México.* Mexico City: Siglo XXI.
Romero M., Miguel Angel, and Luis Méndez. 1989. "SNTE, CNTE, y modernización educativa." *El Cotidiano* 6, no. 28 (March–April): 40–43.

Rosenthal, Naomi, and Michael Schwartz. 1989. "Spontaneity and Democracy in Social Movements." In *International Social Movement Research*, vol. 2, *Organizing for Change: Social Movement Organizations in Europe and the United States*, edited by Bert Klandermans. Greenwich, Conn.: JAI Press.

Roxborough, Ian. 1984. *Unions and Politics in Mexico: The Case of the Automobile Industry*. London: Cambridge University Press.

———. 1986. "The Mexican Charrazo of 1948: Latin American Labor from World War to Cold War." Helen Kellogg Institute for International Studies, Working Paper No. 77, University of Notre Dame.

Roxborough, Ian, and Ilán Bizberg. 1983. "Union Locals in Mexico: The 'New Unionism' in Steel and Automobiles." *Journal of Latin American Studies* 15, no. 1: 117–35.

Rubin, Jeffrey W. 1987. "State Policies, Leftist Oppositions, and Municipal Elections: The Case of the COCEI in Juchitán." In *Electoral Patterns and Perspectives in Mexico*, edited by Arturo Alvarado. Monograph Series 22. La Jolla: Center for U.S.-Mexican Studies, University of California, San Diego.

———. 1990. "Popular Mobilization and the Myth of State Corporatism." In *Popular Movements and Political Change in Mexico*, edited by Joe Foweraker and Ann L. Craig. Boulder, Colo.: Lynne Rienner.

Rucht, Dieter. 1992. "Studying the Effects of Social Movements: Conceptualization and Problems." Paper presented at the ECPR Joint Meetings, Workshop on "Studying the Effects of Social Movements," Limerick, Ireland, March 30–April 4.

Sabel, Charles F. 1981. "The Internal Politics of Trade Unions." In *Organizing Interests in Western Europe: Pluralism, Corporatism, and the Transformation of Politics*, edited by Suzanne D. Berger. Cambridge: Cambridge University Press.

Salinas Alvarez, Samuel, and Carlos Imaz Gispert. 1984. *Maestros y estado*. 2 vols. Mexico City: Línea.

Salinas Sánchez, Gisela Victoria. 1990. "Mujer y maestra: Una aproximación antropológica a las maestras de educación primaria." Tesis de Licenciatura en Antropología Social, Escuela Nacional de Antropología e Historia, México.

Sandoval Flores, Etelvina. 1985. "Los maestros y su sindicato: Relaciones y procesos cotidianos." Masters thesis, Centro de Investigación y Estudios Avanzados, Departamento de Investigaciones Educativas, Instituto Politécnico Nacional, México.

———. 1986. "Los maestros y su sindicato: Relaciones y procesos cotidianos." *Cuadernos de investigación educativa*, no. 10. Departamento de Investigaciones Educativas, Instituto Politécnico Nacional, México.

San Juan, Carlos. 1983. "Movilización y frentes obreros (1970–1983)." Presented at Seminar on Social Movements, Mexico.

———. 1984. "El dilema de la historia obrera reciente: Revolución pasiva y acumulación de fuerzas en 1970–1982." *Historias*, no. 5.

Santibáñez Orozco, Porfirio. 1982. "Oaxaca: La crisis de 1977." In *Sociedad y política en Oaxaca, 1980: 15 estudios de caso*, edited by Raúl Benítez Zenteno. Oaxaca: Universidad Autónoma Benito Juárez de Oaxaca.

Schmitter, Philippe C. 1974. "Still the Century of Corporatism?" *The Review of Politics* 36, no. 1 (January): 85–131.

Schneider, Cathy. 1992. "Radical Opposition Parties and Squatters Movements in Pinochet's Chile." In *The Making of Social Movements in Latin America: Identity, Strategy, Democracy*, edited by Arturo Escobar and Sonia E. Alvarez. Boulder, Colo.: Westview Press.

———. 1995. *Shantytown Protest in Pinochet's Chile*. Philadelphia: Temple University Press.

Schwartz, Michael, and Shuva Paul. 1992. "Resource Mobilization versus the Mobilization of People: Why Consensus Movements Cannot Be Instruments of Social Change." In *Frontiers in Social Movement Theory*, edited by Aldon D. Morris and Carol McClurg Mueller. New Haven and London: Yale University Press.

Scott, James C. 1985. *Weapons of the Weak: Everyday Forms of Peasant Resistance*. New Haven and London: Yale University Press.

Secretaría de Educación Pública (SEP). 1983a. *Memoria 1976–1982*, vol. 1, *Política educativa*. Mexico City: Secretaría de Educación Pública.

———. 1983b. *Memoria 1976–1982*, vol. 2, *Delegaciones estatales*. Mexico City: Secretaría de Educación Pública.

Segovia, Rafael. 1975. *La politización del niño mexicano*. Mexico City: Centro de Estudios Internacionales, El Colegio de México.

Shorter, Edward, and Charles Tilly. 1974. *Strikes in France, 1830–1968*. Cambridge: Cambridge University Press.

Sikkink, Kathryn. 1993. "Human Rights, Principled Issue Networks, and Sovereignty in Latin America." *International Organization* 47, no. 3: 411–41.

Sindicato Nacional de Trabajadores de la Educación (SNTE). Sección 22. Comisión de Información y Difusión, and D-I-211 (Coalición de Promotores). 1986. *Ataca Oaxaca*. Mexico City: Equipo Pueblo, Información Obrera, Leega.

Slater, David, ed. 1985. *New Social Movements and the State in Latin America*. Amsterdam: CEDLA.

Smith, Peter H. 1979. *Labyrinths of Power, Political Recruitment in Twentieth-Century Mexico*. Princeton, N.J.: Princeton University Press.

Solana, Fernando. 1982. *Tan lejos como llegue la educación*. Mexico City: Fondo de Cultura Económica.

Stepan, Alfred. 1978. *The State and Society: Peru in Comparative Perspective*. Princeton, N.J.: Princeton University Press.

Stephens, Evelyne Huber. 1983. "The Peruvian Military Government, Labor Mobilization, and the Political Strength of the Left." *Latin American Research Review* 18, no. 2: 57–93.

Stevens, Evelyn P. 1974. *Protest and Response in Mexico*. Cambridge, Mass.: The MIT Press.

Street, Susan. 1983. "Burocracia y educación: Hacia un análisis político de la desconcentración administrativa en la Secretaría de Educación Pública (SEP)." *Estudios Sociológicos* 1, no. 2: 239–62.

———. 1984. "Los distintos proyectos para la transformación del aparato burocrático de la SEP." *Perfiles Educativos*, no. 7: 14–29.

———. 1990. "La dimensión educativa de la educación política: El movimiento magisterial chiapaneco." In *De las aulas a las calles*, edited by Gisela Salinas and Arturo Cano. Mexico City: Información Obrera/Equipo Pueblo.

———. 1992a. *Maestros en Movimiento: Transformaciones en la burocracia estatal (1978–1982)*. Mexico City: Ediciones de la Casa Chata, Centro de Investigaciones y Estudios Superiores en Antropología Social.

———. 1992b. "El SNTE y la política educativa, 1970–1990." *Revista Mexicana de Sociología* 54, no. 2: 45–72.

———. 1994. "La cultura política del movimiento magisterial chiapaneco." In *Cultura política y educación cívica*, edited by Jorge Alonso. Mexico City: Miguel Angel Porrúa and Centro de Investigaciones Interdisciplinarias en Humandades, Universidad Nacional Autónoma de México.

Taibo II, Paco Ignacio. 1984. "Paciencia y acabamos con el charrismo. CNTE vs SNTE (Entrevista exclusiva con Luis Hernández [CNTE])." *Cambio*, nos. 1–4 (October 1981/September 1982).

Tamayo, Jaime. 1990. "Neoliberalism Encounters *Neocardenismo*." In *Popular Movements and Political Change in Mexico*, edited by Joe Foweraker and Ann L. Craig. Boulder, Colo.: Lynne Rienner.

Tarrow, Sidney. 1983. *Struggling to Reform: Social Movements and Policy Change During Cycles of Protest*. Western Societies Program Occasional Paper 15. Ithaca, N.Y.: Center for International Studies, Cornell University.

———. 1988. "National Politics and Collective Action: Recent Theory and Research in Western Europe and the United States." *Annual Review of Sociology* 14: 421–40.

———. 1989a. *Democracy and Disorder: Protest and Politics in Italy, 1965–1975*. Oxford: Oxford University Press.

———. 1989b. *Stuggle, Politics, and Reform: Collective Action, Social Movements, and Cycles of Protest*. Western Societies Program Occasional Paper 21. Ithaca, N.Y.: Center for International Studies, Cornell University.

———. 1991. " 'Aiming at a Moving Target': Social Science and the Recent Rebellions in Eastern Europe." *PS: Political Science and Politics* 24, no. 1 (March): 12–20.

———. 1994. *Power in Movement: Social Movements, Collective Action, and Politics*. Cambridge Studies in Comparative Politics. Cambridge: Cambridge University Press.

Terrazas, Ana Cecilia. 1993. "Los sexenios de Díaz Ordaz, Echeverría, López Portillo, de la Madrid y Salinas, inexistentes en los textos gratuitos de Historia." *Proceso*, no. 875 (August 16): 18–21.

Testimonios, no. 3. ("CNTE"). 1987. Mexico City: CNTE, EDIPSA, Cuadernos Educativos.

Thompson, Mark, and Ian Roxborough. 1982. "Union Elections and Democracy in Mexico: A Comparative Perspective." *British Journal of Industrial Relations* 20, no. 2 (July): 201–17.

Thorup, Cathryn L. 1991. "The Politics of Free Trade and the Dynamics of Cross-Border Coalitions in U.S.-Mexican Relations." *Columbia Journal of World Business* 26, no. 2 (Summer): 12–26.

Tilak, Jandhyala B. G. 1989. "The Recession and Public Investment in Education in Latin America." *Journal of Interamerican Studies and World Affairs* 31, nos. 1–2 (Spring–Summer 1989): 125–46.

Tilly, Charles. 1978. *From Mobilization to Revolution*. Englewood Cliffs, N.J.: Prentice-Hall.

———. 1984. "Social Movements and National Politics." In *State-Making and Social Movements: Essays in History and Theory*, edited by Charles Bright and Susan Harding. Ann Arbor: University of Michigan Press.
Touraine, Alain. 1981. *The Voice and the Eye: An Analysis of Social Movements*. Cambridge: Cambridge University Press.
———. 1985. "An Introduction to the Study of Social Movements." *Social Research* 52: 749–87.
Trejo Delarbre, Raúl. 1978. "El movimiento de los electricistas democráticos (1972–1978)." *Cuadernos Políticos*, no. 18.
———. 1984. "Historia del movimiento obrero en México, 1860–1982." In *Historia del movimiento obrero en América Latina*, edited by Pablo González Casanova. Vol. 1. Mexico City: Siglo XXI.
———. 1990. *Crónica del sindicalismo en México (1976–1988)*. Mexico City: Siglo XXI.
Treviño Carrillo, Ana Helena. 1984. "El movimiento magisterial en México: El caso de Morelos (1980–1981)." Masters thesis, Facultad Latinoamericana de Ciencias Sociales, Mexico City.
Valdéz Vega, María Eugenia. 1986. "Participación de los maestros de primaria del Distrito Federal en la insurgencia magisterial de 1979–1983." Masters thesis, Facultad Latinoamericana de Ciencias Sociales, Mexico City.
Valenzuela, J. Samuel. 1989. "Labor Movements in Transitions to Democracy: A Framework for Analysis." *Comparative Politics* 21 (July): 445–72.
Vargas, Virginia. 1988. "The Feminist Movement in Peru: Inventory and Perspectives." In *Women's Struggles and Strategies*, edited by Saskia Wierings. Brookfield, Vt.: Gower.
———. 1989. *El aporte de la rebeldía de las mujeres*. Lima, Peru: Ediciones Flora Tristán.
Vaughan, Mary Kay. 1982. *The State, Education, and Social Class in Mexico, 1880–1928*. DeKalb, Ill.: Northern Illinois University Press.
Weinberg, Bill. 1994. "Zapata Lives On: A Report from San Cristóbal." *Akwe:kon Journal* (Summer): 5–12.
Whitehead, Laurence. 1994. "Prospects for a 'Transition' from Authoritarian Rule in Mexico." In *The Politics of Economic Restructuring: State-Society Relations and Regime Change in Mexico*, edited by Maria Lorena Cook, Kevin J. Middlebrook, and Juan Molinar Horcasitas. U.S.-Mexico Contemporary Perspectives Series, 7. La Jolla: Center for U.S.-Mexican Studies, University of California, San Diego.
Wolfe, Joel D. 1985. *Workers, Participation, and Democracy: Internal Politics in the British Union Movement*. Westport, Conn.: Greenwood Press.
Yescas Martínez, Isidoro, and Gloria Zafra. 1985. *La insurgencia magisterial en Oaxaca, 1980*. Oaxaca, Mexico: Universidad Autónoma Benito Juárez.
Zald, Mayer N., and John D. McCarthy, eds. 1979. *The Dynamics of Social Movements: Resource Mobilization, Social Control, and Tactics*. Cambridge, Mass.: Winthrop.
Zapata, Francisco. 1987. *Relaciones laborales y negociación colectiva en el sector público mexicano*. Documentos de Trabajo. Mexico City: Centro de Estudios Sociológicos, El Colegio de México.
Zazueta, César, and Ricardo de la Peña. 1983. "El sindicalismo y la nueva administración." *Revista A* (Universidad Autónoma Metropolitana-Azcapotzalco) 4, no. 9: 105–27.

———. 1984. *La estructura del Congreso del Trabajo*. Mexico City: Fondo de Cultura Económica.
Zermeño, Sergio. 1978. *México: Una democracia utópica*. Mexico City: Siglo XXI.

Primary Sources

Alternativa. 1990. (Organo Informativo de la Comisión Ejecutiva de la Sección XXII del SNTE.) Newspaper.
Avance. 1982a. "Asamblea Estatal." Suplemento 3. November 27.
———. 1982b. (Vehículo de comunicación gráfica del movimiento democrático de los trabajadores de la educación realizado en la Sección 22 del SNTE.) "Información a la Asamblea Estatal." October 23.
Caminemos. 1987. Vol. 5, no. 18 (October).
Claridad. Sección 36. Consejo Central de Lucha Magisterial del Valle de México "Profr. Misael Núñez Acosta."
CNTE (Coordinadora Nacional de Trabajadores de la Educación). 1980. "Proyecto de programa y plataforma de acción para discusión de la conferencia nacional de septiembre." August.
———. 1984. *III Foro Nacional de Educación Alternativa*, no. 4.
Coalición de Promotores Indígenas de Oaxaca. 1981. "Boletín informativo." Mimeo.
CODEMA, OM-27, UTE, COSDE (Oaxaca-Chiapas). 1987. "Boletín informativo I: Las principales luchas en los últimos 90 días." April.
Comité Ejecutivo Seccional. Sección 7. N.d. Transcribed interviews.
Consejo Central de Lucha, Chiapas. N.d. Transcribed interviews.
Consejo Central de Lucha del Magisterio de Guerrero. Sección XIV, SNTE. 1985. "Juicio político a 'Vanguardia Revolucionaria.' " Pamphlet.
Consejo Central de Lucha del Magisterio Hidalguense. N.d. "Documento de análisis y discusión sobre la línea político sindical." Photocopy.
———. N.d. Pamphlet.
Consejo Central de Lucha Magisterial Morelense. 1981. "El movimiento magisterial morelense: Una experiencia de lucha." Pamphlet.
Consejo Central de Lucha "Misael Núñez Acosta." 1982. "Balance del movimiento magisterial del Valle de México." Pamphlet.
Coordinadora de los Altos, Chiapas. N.d. Transcribed interviews.
Coordinadora del Centro, Chiapas. N.d. Transcribed interviews.
COSDE (Corriente Sindical Democrática). 1987. "Resistencia magisterial en Chiapas." July.
Educación . . . ? 1990. No. 1. Published by the Coalición de Maestros y Promotores Bilingües del Estado de Oaxaca.
Educación Alternativa. 1990. Quarterly publication of Local 22 of the SNTE, Oaxaca, Oaxaca.
Educación Popular. 1982. (Organo de información y educación política de la Unión de Trabajadores de la Educación.) Suplemento 57. November 6.
Educador Socialista. 1984. (Organo político del Frente Magisterial Independiente Nacional.) "Informe sobre el VIII Congreso (2º Democrático) de la Sección 7 de Chiapas." March 15.

Espacios. 1983–1984. Nos. 1–3. Mexico.
Estados Unidos Mexicanos. Secretaría de Hacienda y Crédito Público. Dirección General de Egresos. Subdirección de Estudios y Planeación Presupuestal. 1976. "Sobresueldos: Cuotas máximas congeladas." Photocopy.
Frente Magisterial Independiente Nacional (FMIN). 1985. "Gobiernismo y disidencia en Oaxaca." Mimeo.
———. 1987. "A la Asamblea Nacional de la CNTE." Tuxtepec, Oaxaca. January 17.
Hora Cero. 1980–1984. Oaxaca, Oaxaca. Newspaper.
ISSSTE (Instituto de Seguridad y Servicios Sociales de los Trabajadores del Estado). Delegación Estatal. Dirección General. 1982. "Respuesta de la Dirección General del ISSSTE/Delegación Estatal en Oaxaca al Secretario General y de Acción de la Sección 22." Oaxaca, Oaxaca. November 26. Letter.
Maestros Democráticos de Base de las Delegaciones Sindicales . . . (Oaxaca). 1982. "A los trabajadores de la educación: A los representantes democráticos." November 16.
Magisterio. Publicación del Sindicato Nacional de Trabajadores de la Educación. Vol. 14, no. 142 (March 1974).
———. Publicación del Sindicato Nacional de Trabajadores de la Educación. Vol. 15, no. 146 (September 1974).
Meridiano 100. 1985. "El nuevo magisterio." Suplemento 1. Oaxaca, Oaxaca. April 16. Newspaper.
Movimiento Democrático Magisterial. 1987. *Praxis.* February 18.
Notifrente Magisterial. 1983. June.
Organización Revolucionaria de los Trabajadores de la Educación (ORTE). 1982. "XII Congreso Extraordinario de la Sección XXII de los Trabajadores de la Educación en Oaxaca (febrero de 1982)." *Cuadernos Políticos* 1 (July).
Praxis. 1982. (Organo Informativo del Movimiento Democrático Magisterial del Istmo. Istmo de Tehuantepec, Oaxaca.) May 6.
SEP (Secretaría de Educación Pública). Delegación General. 1981. Letter to members of the Comisión Ejecutiva of Sección 22, SNTE (oficio no. 191/81). June 8.
———. Delegación General. 1983. "Respuesta de la Delegación General de la SEP al Secretario General de la Sección XXII, Oaxaca (oficio no. 157/83)." May 11. Mimeo.
———. Subsecretaría de Planeación Educativa. 1982–87. "Cronología de los principales acontecimientos del sector educativo de la presente administración." Vol. 1 (1982–85), Vol. 2 (1986), Vol. 3 (1987). Unpublished.
———. N.d. "Memoria del programa para el diseño e implantación del sistema desconcentrado de pagos al personal de la Secretaría de Educación Pública, 1980–1982." Internal document.
SNTE (Sindicato Nacional de Trabajadores de la Educación). 1990. "Documentos rectores para la jornada nacional de información." February.
———. 1992. *Estatutos.*
———. Sección 7. 1983. "El nuevo sindicalismo y las luchas de la CNTE." (Curso de orientación sindical noviembre 9–diciembre 5). Mimeo.
———. Sección 7. Comité Ejecutivo Seccional. 1984. "En una nueva etapa de lucha. . . ." September.

———. Sección 7. 1984a. "La profundización de la democracia sindical." Mimeo.
———. Sección 7. 1984b. "Resolutivos del VIII Congreso Seccional Ordinario." March 5–9. Mimeo.
———. Sección 7. N.d. "CNTE. Organización y democracia sindical." Folleto 1. Ediciones Pueblo. Pamphlet.
———. Sección 22. 1982a. "Jerarquización de ponencias del XII congreso de la Sección 22 del SNTE." April 21.
———. Sección 22. 1982b. "Reseña del primer congreso democrático de la Sección 22 del SNTE." June.
———. Sección 22. 1983a. "Acuerdos, pronunciamientos y balance de la Asamblea Estatal del día 4 de junio de 1983 celebrada en el auditorio de la Sección XXII." June 4.
———. Sección 22. 1983b. "Ponencias que el Comité Ejecutivo de la Sección 22 del SNTE pone a consideración de las bases magisteriales, para ser presentadas en el XIII Congreso Nacional Ordinario del SNTE." February.
———. Sección 22. 1987a. "Acuerdos y pronunciamientos de la Asamblea Estatal del 16 de enero de 1987, realizada en la ciudad de Tuxtepec, Oaxaca."
———. Sección 22. 1987b. "Asamblea Estatal: Orden del día." November 14.
———. Sección 22. 1987c. "Resolutivos de la Asamblea Nacional Representativa de la CNTE realizada en Oaxaca, Oax. 26 Sept. de 1987."
———. Sección 22. 1987d. "Resolutivos emanados de la Asamblea Nacional Representativa de la CNTE, en Tuxtepec, Oax., el día 17 de enero de 1987."
———. Sección 22. N.d.(a). "Coordinadoras de lucha delegacional, sector y región." Oaxaca. Mimeo.
———. Sección 22. N.d.(b). "Declaración de principios." Mimeo.
———. Sección 22. N.d.(c). "Finalidades de los principios rectores del movimiento." Mimeo.
———. Sección 22. N.d.(d). "Guión de sugerencias para presidir una asamblea delegacional." Mimeo.
———. Sección 22. N.d.(e). "Planteamientos que hace el Comité Ejecutivo de la Sección 22 del SNTE de Oaxaca, Oax., exigiendo su pronta solución."
———. Sección 22. N.d.(f). "Ponencias que presentan los trabajadores de la educación de la Sección XXII del SNTE, del estado de Oaxaca, ante el XIII Congreso Nacional Extraordinario."
———. Sección 22. N.d.(g). "Principios rectores del movimiento magisterial oaxaqueño apoyados en la Asamblea Estatal del día 6 de febrero 1982 en Puerto Escondido, Oaxaca, que rigen el movimiento sindical democrático estatal." Mimeo.
———. Sección 22. N.d.(h). "Reglamento General de Asambleas." Mimeo.
———. Sección 22. N.d.(i). "Relación de maestros vanguardistas que no trabajan." Mimeo.
———. Sección 22. N.d.(j). "La Secretaría de Organización Política y Sindical informa acontecimientos realizados el 27 de mayo fecha en que se efectuó el paro de labores a nivel nacional."
———. Sección 22. Comisión Ejecutiva. 1981. "Respuesta al Delegado General de la SEP en Oaxaca (oficio no. 897)." March 26. Letter.

———. Sección 22. Comisión Ejecutiva. N.d. "Anteproyecto de la convocatoria para la realización del XII Congreso Extraordinario."
———. Sección 22. Comité Ejecutivo Seccional. 1982. "A los trabajadores de la FSTSE. . . ." November 8.
———. Sección 22. Comité Ejecutivo Seccional. 1983. "Acuerdos y pronunciamientos de la Asamblea Estatal del día 16 de abril de 1983." April 19.
———. Sección 22. Comité Ejecutivo Seccional. N.d. "Actividades que viene realizando Vanguardia en el estado." Mimeo.
SNTE-CNTE. Secciones 40, 7, y 22. 1983. "Primera asamblea de representantes sindicales delegacionales y de centros de trabajo de los trabajadores de la educación de Oaxaca y Chiapas." Matías Romero, Oaxaca. October 22–23. Mimeo.
Unión de Trabajadores de la Educación (UTE). 1983. "Del Congreso Nacional del SNTE al paro de 27 de mayo." *Educación Popular* (Suplemento 67). June 4.
———. 1987. "Ante la política criminal de 'Vanguardia Revolucionaria' y sus aliados la unidad y movilización de las bases." *Educación Popular* (Suplemento 117). November 14.

Index

Agricultural-Technical School movement (ETA), 109, 113
Aguilar Flores, Ernesto, 118, 120, 212
Alemán, Miguel, 63, 64
allies, of social movements, 43, 49, 52, 301–3
 elite, 43, 52, 301–2
 lower-class, 43, 52, 302
Alvarez, Sonia E., 57, 311
Amnesty International, 143
Andrade Ibarra, José Luis, 116, 199, 201 n. 32
ANOCP (Asamblea Nacional Obrero Campesino Popular), 200
Araujo del Angel, Refugio, 271
Argentina
 authoritarianism, 13, 309
 democratic transition, 309, 310
 human rights movement, 301, 302, 305, 305 n. 12, 307, 309, 310
Ariel Bárcenas, Víctor, 113
Arnaut Salgado, Alberto, 71
Asamblea Nacional Obrero Campesino Popular (ANOCP), 200
assassinations, 131–32, 272
authoritarianism
 conditions for protest movements, 40–44, 300–303
 elements missing from, 14–15
 function of elections, 42
 in Latin America, 12, 13–14, 56, 309
 in Mexico, 11–14, 42–43
 political opportunities in, 300–303
 social movements under, 4–9, 10–11, 14–15, 58, 299–312
autonomy, of union locals, 48 n. 39, 127–42, 148–50
 increased by deconcentration, 93
 lack of, 80, 192
 from political parties, 147–48, 259, 279–80, 285
 struggle for, 135–37

avales, 226
Avila Camacho, Manuel, 62, 63
Ayala, Darío, 132

Bartlett Díaz, Manuel, 270
bilingual teachers. See indigenous teachers
Bloque Reivindicador, 126
Boyte, Harry C., 54
Brazil
 authoritarianism, 13
 democratic transition, 308–9, 311
 labor unions, 171 n. 119, 302, 303, 305, 307, 308–9
 women's movement, 301, 302
brigades, of teachers, 160–61, 160 n. 104
Brysk, Alison, 306–7, 309

Cabañas, Lucio, 108 n. 7, 113
Camacho, Manuel, 272 n. 12
camarillas, 45, 45 n. 33
Cárdenas, Cuauhtémoc, 19, 267, 268, 270, 285, 295
Cárdenas, Lázaro, 62
Castellanos Domínguez, Absalón, 155, 188–89
Catholic Church, 43
 support for social movements, 113, 302
CCL. See Consejo Central de Lucha
CCLMM (Consejo Central de Lucha del Magisterio Morelense), 124, 125, 128–29. See also Morelos union local
CCLMVM (Consejo Central de Lucha Magisterial del Valle de México), 126, 126 n. 48, 129–30. See also Valle de México union local
CED (comité ejecutivo delegacional), 160, 218, 221 n. 6
CEN (Comité Ejecutivo Nacional). See National Executive Committee

Central Council of Struggle of Morelos Teachers. *See* CCLMM
Central Council of Teachers' Struggle of the Valley of Mexico. *See* CCLMVM
CES (comité ejecutivo seccional). *See* local executive committee
CEU (Consejo Estudiantil Universitario), 270
charrismo, 95, 108 n. 6, 165, 259–60, 259 n. 61
Chávez Orozco, Luis, 63, 64, 65
Chiapas
  agricultural technical schools (ETA), 109, 113
  economic development, 113 n. 20, 115, 189
  ethnic groups, 235
  federal policy on, 188–89
  governors, 154–55, 188–89
  indigenous teachers, 110–11
  peasant-teacher alliances, 243–44
  peasant uprising, 20, 286–87, 288, 309 n. 16
  violence in, 155, 157, 189, 200, 201, 210
Chiapas union local (7)
  accomplishments, 194, 195–96, 281
  alternative education, 292
  brigades, 160–61
  congresses, 135–37, 137 n. 69, 157, 198–201, 204, 204 n. 38, 272 n. 13
  Consejo Central de Lucha (CCL), 116, 116 n. 23, 117, 135–37, 158–60, 158 n. 103
  consultation with members, 228
  coordinadoras, 223
  decertification, 201
  delegation executive committees (CEDs), 160
  demands, 115–17, 116 n. 23
  efforts for local autonomy, 135–37, 192
  elections, 135, 136–37, 197–201, 204
  executive commission, 135, 135 n. 67, 201–2, 207
  executive committees, 140, 163, 189–90, 198, 201, 221–22, 228, 230, 273
  formation of CNTE, 114–18
  influence in other regions, 162, 251–52
  internal conflicts, 163, 201–4
  leadership, 113, 163, 166, 170
  legal status, 183–84, 192–93, 192 n. 20
  Línea Proletaria in, 163, 202–4, 251–54, 253
  negotiations on elections, 129
  organizational structure, 158–60, 219–24, 298
  participation in national protests, 121, 144

paycheck delivery, 194–95
political factions, 163, 251
precongresses, 136, 198
relations with national union, 192
relations with other locals, 149
relations with state governors, 155
relations with state SEP administration, 93, 191, 199
secretaries-general, 198, 203, 204
state assembly, 219–21, 219 n. 3
strategies, 127, 149, 162, 170, 207
strikes, 115–17, 126, 271
supporters, 170
survival of democratic movement, 298–99
trotskyists, 201, 202, 202 n. 33, 203, 251
vanguardista resistance, 135–36, 189–90, 198–201
violence against members, 157, 201, 201 n. 32, 210
Chihuahua union local, 109–10
Chile
  authoritarianism, 13
  democratic transition, 309
  social movements, 302, 310, 310 n. 18
Chinchilla, Norma Stoltz, 307
Christian base communities, 113
citizenship rights
  under authoritarian regimes, 14
  watchdog groups, 20, 287
Cloward, Richard A., 41, 42, 49
CNC (Confederación Nacional Campesina), 62, 284
CNOP (Confederación Nacional de Organizaciones Populares), 2, 9 n. 14, 284
CNPA (Coordinadora Nacional "Plan de Ayala"), 17, 84, 148
CNTE (Coordinadora Nacional de Trabajadores de la Educación). *See also regional union locals*
  accomplishments, 3–4, 193–96, 291–95
  allies, 302
  autonomy from political parties, 147–48, 259, 285
  autonomy of locals, 48 n. 39, 127–42, 148–50
  avoidance of confrontations, 257–60
  brigades, 160–61, 160 n. 104
  clasista faction, 247–48
  compared to earlier protests, 69–70
  consultation with membership, 225–26, 227–29

Index

coordination of locals, 131, 145–47, 149
daily management activities (*gestoría*), 193–97, 215, 218, 224, 240–41
decision-making in, 24, 161–68, 219–21, 225–29, 263–64
decision to work within SNTE, 148, 165
decline of national movement, 114, 134, 139–40, 145, 200
demands, 83, 95, 169–70, 257–60
documents, 261, 261 n. 65
education workshops, 254
effect of state-SNTE conflicts, 102–4, 275–76
election procedures, 230–32
emergence of, 17, 84, 113–18, 145–47, 168–69, 295–97
factors in survival, 169–73, 296–99
formal-legal status, 128, 183–84, 213, 254–56, 281–82, 297–98
fundraising, 209 n. 46
gobiernista faction, 166, 212, 247–48
human rights issues, 143
impact on individuals, 241–43
importance of internal democracy for survival, 55, 214–15, 218, 299
inclusionary coalitions in, 170
influence of locals on each other, 126, 162, 251–52
information access, 228, 229–30
internal divisions, 163, 166–67, 214, 230–31, 247–50, 261, 277–78, 280, 281–82, 293
lack of elite support, 301–2
leadership, 158, 161–68, 232–33, 246–50, 259–60, 278
local SNTE officials in, 170
mass support, 170–71
membership, 3, 3 n. 5, 240–41, 241 n. 37
mobilizational cycles, 150, 153, 305
national protests, 121, 129, 131, 132–33, 140, 144, 187, 201
objectives, 292–93
organizational structure, 148–50, 150 n. 90, 158–62, 217–24, 254–55, 298, 306, 306 n. 13
party affiliations of members, 147 n. 87
political analyses, 261
political impact, 20–21, 23–24, 291
political organizations' roles in, 147–48, 250–51

political space for, 60–61, 105–6, 169, 260–62, 275–77, 296, 300–301
procedural success, 291–92
protest traditions, 108–9, 110–13
reaction to SEP reforms, 94–95
relations with government, 100, 143–44, 144, 150–56, 184, 186, 209, 247–48, 302
relations with state SEP administration, 100 n. 74
representatives on national executive committee, 188, 188 n. 12, 278
in Salinas administration, 268–73, 274, 275–76, 277–78
sexual harassment policies, 79
songs, 74 n. 29
strategies, 95, 127–28, 147, 166–67, 169–73, 251–62, 304–5
tactics, 120, 171, 247–49
teacher training issues, 88
voting procedures, 147, 227
women in, 237–38, 242
Coalición de Promotores, 111, 233–35
Coalición Obrero Campesino Estudiantil del Istmo. *See* COCEI
Coalición Obrero Campesino Estudiantil de Oaxaca. *See* COCEO
COCEI (Coalición Obrero Campesino Estudiantil del Istmo), 18, 112, 160, 307
COCEO (Coalición Obrero Campesino Estudiantil de Oaxaca), 112
Coleman, James, 55
comité ejecutivo delegacional (CED), 160, 218, 221 n. 6
Comité Ejecutivo Nacional (CEN). *See* National Executive Committee
comité ejecutivo seccional (CES). *See* local executive committee
comités de lucha, 158
 in Oaxaca, 119
 in Valle de México, 126
 voting power within CNTE, 147
comités municipales de lucha, 159
Communist party, 17–18. *See also* PSUM
 CNTE members and, 161
 MRM and, 67, 69
 organization, 307
 relations with unions, 62, 63
CONAMUP (Coordinadora Nacional del Movimiento Urbano Popular), 17, 84, 148
Confederación de Trabajadores de México (CTM), 17, 18, 59, 62, 100, 284

Confederación Nacional Campesina (CNC), 62, 284
Confederación Nacional de Organizaciones Populares (CNOP), 2, 9 n. 14, 284
Confederación Regional Obrera Mexicana (CROM), 62
Confederation of Mexican Workers (CTM), 17, 18, 59, 62, 100, 284
confrontation, avoidance of, 257–60
Congreso del Trabajo (CT), 2, 17, 18
congresses, union. *See also* precongresses
  candidate selection, 141
  Chiapas local, 135–37, 137 n. 69, 157, 198–201, 204, 204 n. 38, 272 n. 13
  delegate selection, 231–32
  fraternal delegates, 231–32
  held without dissidents, 137
  Hidalgo, 131
  mass, 130, 130 n. 57, 131
  Morelos, 137–38
  national, 97, 188, 269, 269 n. 4, 273, 278, 279
  Oaxaca, 138–39, 139 n. 73, 140–42, 157, 273
  postponed, 205–9, 249
congress, Mexican
  labor representatives in, 18
  SNTE candidates, 71
Consejo Central de Lucha (CCL), 158–59
  Chiapas union local, 116, 116 n. 23, 117, 135–37, 158–60, 158 n. 103
  effectiveness, 161
  Hidalgo, 130–31
Consejo Central de Lucha del Magisterio Morelense. *See* CCLMM
Consejo Central de Lucha Magisterial del Valle de México. *See* CCLMVM
Consejo Estudiantil Universitario (CEU), 270
Consejo Regional del Norte, 126
Consejo Regional Sindical Magisterial de la Montaña de Guerrero, 123–24
Coordinadora Nacional del Movimiento Urbano Popular (CONAMUP), 17, 84, 148
Coordinadora Nacional de Trabajadores de la Educación. *See* CNTE
Coordinadora Nacional "Plan de Ayala" (CNPA), 17, 84, 148
coordinadoras
  in CNTE organization, 222–24, 225–26
  effectiveness, 285

  formation of, 17–18
  organizational model, 19, 148, 150 n. 90
  regional, 223–24
  rural, 17, 84
  sector, 223
  strategies, 18
  urban, 84, 148
Coordinated Public Education Service (SCEP), 191
corporatism, 32–34, 33 n. 16
corruption
  doble plazas, 76, 76 n. 34, 157, 191
  in SNTE, 76, 79
  CROM (Confederación Regional Obrera Mexicana), 62
  CT (Congreso del Trabajo), 2, 17, 18
  CTM (Confederación de Trabajadores de México), 17, 18, 59, 62, 100, 284
cycles of protest, 107 n. 2, 172, 172 n. 121

decentralization, of SEP, 86 n. 53, 185–86, 191
decision-making processes
  of CNTE, 161–68, 219–21, 225–29, 263–64
  of social movements, 52
deconcentration, of SEP, 86–87, 86 n. 53, 88–89, 89 n. 58
  consequences, 90–94, 96, 103, 152
  implementation, 92, 194
  as threat to SNTE power, 90, 118–19
delegation assemblies, 222, 222 n. 8, 225, 231
delegation executive committees (CEDs), 160, 218, 221 n. 6
democracy. *See also* union democracy
  indigenous traditions, 234
  in schools, 216
  in social movements, 53–56, 57, 58, 299, 307–8
  social movements in, 40
  transition in Latin America, 56–57, 308–12
democratic movement. *See* CNTE
Democratic Teachers of Morelos (MDM), 124
Díaz Ordaz, Gustavo, 71
dissident movements. *See* CNTE; social movements
doble plazas, 76, 76 n. 34, 157, 191
Dorantes, Isidoro, 132

Echeverría Alvarez, Luis
  education policy, 89 n. 58
  political reforms, 73 n. 27
  relations with labor, 73, 75, 83

Index

response to student movement, 15, 71 n. 24
at SEP, 75
Education Ministry. *See* SEP
education policy
  alternative, 274, 292
  conflicts over, 81, 88–89, 99, 185–87
  deconcentration, 86–87, 86 n. 53, 88–96, 89 n. 58, 103, 118–19
  lack of CNTE attention to, 292
education system. *See also* SEP
  budget cuts, 82–83, 82 n. 47, 185 n. 3
  growth of, 70–71, 71 n. 23, 75–76, 83 n. 48
  indigenous education, 110–12, 112 n. 17
  levels, 187 n. 8
  reforms, 85–95
  telesecundarias, 109, 109 n. 10
Eisinger, Peter K., 4, 37–38, 300
elections
  in authoritarian regimes, 42
  fraud in, 19, 267
  as political opportunities, 42–43, 301
  presidential (1988), 19, 267–68, 285
  presidential (1994), 20, 286–87, 288
  presidential, 42–43, 301
  role of social movements, 285–86
elections, union. *See also* congresses; precongresses
  authorization of local, 140–42, 272 n. 13
  Chiapas, 135, 136–37, 197–201, 204
  CNTE, 230–32
  efforts to hold, 116 n. 23, 121, 128, 129, 192, 197–201, 205–9, 273, 299
  Local 9 (Mexico City), 68
  Morelos, 135, 137
  Oaxaca, 140–42, 199–200, 205–9, 249, 273, 299
  postponed, 205–9
  SNTE efforts to control, 231
  SNTE locals, 219, 221
electoral reforms, 15–16, 17, 20, 84, 105
Elías Calles, Fernando, 99, 144, 151
Escobar, Arturo, 57, 311
Escuela Normal Superior, 184
Escuela Técnica Agropecuaria (ETA), 109, 113
ETA (Escuela Técnica Agropecuaria), 109, 113
ethnicity. *See* indigenous teachers
Evans, Sara M., 54
executive committees. *See* delegation executive committees; local executive committees; National Executive Committee

Federación de Sindicatos de Trabajadores al Servicio del Estado (FSTSE), 2, 194
Federal Conciliation and Arbitration Board, 72, 75, 271
Federal Labor Law (LFT), 80
Federal Law of Public Service Workers (LFTSE), 81
Federation of Goods and Services Unions (FESEBES), 282, 282 n. 26
Federation of Public Service Workers' Unions (FSTSE), 2, 194
feminism, 239. *See also* women
FESEBES (Federation of Goods and Services Unions), 282, 282 n. 26
Figueroa, Rubén, 124, 133, 156
FNOC (Frente Nacional de Organizaciones y Ciudadanos), 9 n. 14
fraternal delegates, 231–32
free spaces, 158
Frente Nacional de Organizaciones y Ciudadanos (FNOC), 9 n. 14
Frente Reivindicador de Trabajadores de la Educación en Chiapas. *See* FRTECH
Front for the Demands of Education Workers in Chiapas. *See* FRTECH
FRTECH (Frente Reivindicador de Trabajadores de la Educación en Chiapas), 189–90
FSTSE (Federación de Sindicatos de Trabajadores al Servicio del Estado), 2, 194

gestoría, 193–97, 215, 218, 224, 240–41
González Avelar, Miguel, 190, 199
González Blanco, Salomón, 155
Gordillo Morales, Elba Esther
  appointment as secretary-general, 271–72
  "broad front," 275, 278–79
  career, 237, 272 n. 12
  conflicts with SEP, 100 n. 73
  on Vanguardia, 274–75
  opposition to, 126, 272
  political activities, 272 n. 12
  relations with dissidents, 272, 273, 274, 275, 277, 278–80, 282
  supported by Jonguitud, 237 n. 27
government. *See* Interior Ministry; Mexico; SEP; state-labor relations
group solidarity, 50–52, 58
Guerrero
  economic development, 113 n. 20
  governors, 124, 133, 156

indigenous teachers, 110–11, 123–24
social movements, 113
Guerrero union local
  brigades, 160–61
  democracy in, 123–24
  emergence of dissident movement, 117, 123–24, 169
  executive committees, 98, 131, 188 n. 11
  indigenous teachers, 123–24
  internal divisions, 161, 168
  negotiations with national union, 132, 133–34, 144–45
  organizational structure, 161, 168
  participation in national protests, 121, 131, 132–33, 144
  SEP reaction to, 144
  sit-ins, 124, 132–33
  strategies, 168 n. 117
  strikes, 133
  supporters, 167
  violence against members, 156, 157
Gutiérrez Barrios, Fernando, 122

Henríquez Guzmán, Miguel, 65
Hernández Galicia, Joaquín ("La Quina"), 267, 268
Hernández, Manuel, 203
Hidalgo
  class divisions, 156–57
  economic development, 113 n. 20
  indigenous education, 110–11
  peasants, 245
  rural normal schools, 156–57
  social movements, 113
  state government, 155–56
Hidalgo union local
  Consejo Central de Lucha (CCL), 130–31, 134–35
  demands, 127, 131
  emergence of dissident movement, 127, 169
  executive committees, 98, 99, 131, 134–35, 144–45
  ideological purity, 164–67
  mass congress, 131
  negotiations with national union, 133–34, 144–45
  organization, 167–68
  participation in national protests, 121, 131, 132–33, 144
  press coverage, 130

SEP reaction to, 130, 144
  strategies, 127, 164, 167
  strikes, 131
  supporters, 167
  tactics, 164
  timing in protest cycle, 172
  vanguardistas, 143
  violence against members, 143, 157
hospitals, teachers' protests over service of, 124–25, 125 n. 40, 126
human rights
  in Argentina, 301, 302, 305, 305 n. 12, 307, 309, 310
  violations, 143, 189

IIISEO (Instituto de Investigación e Integración Social del Estado de Oaxaca), 111
independent unions, 82, 83, 84, 112
indigenous teachers, 110–12
  as community leaders, 110, 233
  demands in Guerrero, 123–24
  role in dissident movement, 124, 232–35
  as SEP employees, 111, 111 n. 15
  status, 110, 112 n. 17
  violence against, 209
  women, 236
INI (Instituto Nacional Indigenista), 111
Institute of Social Security and Services for State Employees. See ISSSTE
institutional access, by social movements, 40–41, 40 n. 28, 309, 310, 310 n. 18
Institutional Revolutionary Party. See PRI
Instituto de Investigación e Integración Social del Estado de Oaxaca (IIISEO), 111
Instituto de Seguridad y Servicios Sociales de los Trabajadores del Estado. See ISSSTE
Instituto Nacional Indigenista (INI), 111
Interior Ministry
  intervention in teacher protests, 98, 121–22, 130, 137, 138, 144, 151–52
  ministers, 315
ISSSTE (Instituto de Seguridad y Servicios Sociales de los Trabajadores del Estado)
  decentralization, 194
  hospitals, 124–25, 125 n. 40, 126
  responsibilities, 81, 152
  Vanguardia and, 199
Isthmus of Tehuantepec
  COCEI (Coalición Obrero Campesino Estudiantil del Istmo), 18, 112, 160, 307

Index

precongress participants, 141
teacher protests, 118, 120

Jenkins, J. Craig, 38, 49
Jiménez Cantú, Jorge, 155
Jiménez Ruiz, Eliseo, 154
Jonguitud Barrios, Carlos
  conflicts with government officials, 137 n. 69, 152, 154
  downfall, 3, 267, 271, 277
  as governor, 98 n. 71, 152
  influence in SNTE, 3, 72, 73–74, 76–77, 269
  National Vigilance Committee, 72, 72 n. 25
  as SNTE secretary general, 73–74, 76–77, 237 n. 27
  Vanguardia Revolucionaria, 73–75

Kitschelt, Herbert P., 38

Labor Congress (CT), 2, 17, 18
labor regulations, for public sector workers, 80–82
labor unions. *See also* SNTE; state-labor relations
  in Brazil, 171 n. 119, 302, 303, 305, 307, 308–9
  charrismo, 95, 108 n. 6
  demands for independence and democracy, 16–18
  dissidents within, 36–37
  electrical workers', 17
  history, 62–63
  independent, 82, 83, 84, 112
  in Latin America, 13 n. 22
  leadership, 34–36, 34 n. 20, 285
  Línea Proletaria in, 252
  in 1970s, 83
  in 1980s, 18, 19, 185, 267–68, 282, 282 n. 26, 283, 284
  official, 9–11, 35, 59–61, 83
  oil workers, 268, 268 n. 1
  organizational structures, 306
  political factions in, 251 n. 51
  public employee, 80–82, 83
  reforms in 1960s, 70 n. 22
  regulation of, 81–82
  support for PRI candidates, 267
  unrest in 1950s, 69
  within PRI, 9–11, 33, 34
Latin America
  authoritarianism, 12, 13–14, 56, 309

  democratic transitions, 56–57, 308–12
  labor movement, 13 n. 22
  social movements, 28–29, 47 n. 37, 54, 56–57, 302, 308–12
León Bejarano, Armando, 155
Ley Federal de los Trabajadores al Servicio del Estado. *See* LFTSE
Ley Federal del Trabajo. *See* LFT
LFT (Ley Federal del Trabajo), 80–81
LFTSE (Ley Federal de los Trabajadores al Servicio del Estado), 81
Línea Proletaria, 113
  in Chiapas local leadership, 113, 163, 202–4, 251, 253
  criticism of, 253–54
  influence, 163, 251–54, 261
  in Oaxaca, 141
  organization, 252
  origins, 252
  strategies, 252–53
Lipset, Seymour Martin, 55
Lipsky, Michael, 49
Local 9 (Mexico City)
  dissident movement (1950s), 66–70, 69 n. 19
  dissidents in, 99
  elections, 68
  executive commission, 272 n. 13
  executive committee, 273, 281
  Jonguitud as leader, 72, 269
  mobilization in late 1980s, 268–71
  Vanguardia in, 270 n. 8
  women in leadership, 238, 239
Local 10 (Mexico City), 270 n. 8
  executive commission, 272 n. 13
  mobilization in late 1980s, 268–71
  women in leadership, 238
Local 11 (Mexico City)
  executive committees, 188 n. 11, 272 n. 13
  mobilization in late 1980s, 268–71, 270 n. 8
  strategies, 149
local executive committees, 218
  assistants, 221–22
  Chiapas, 140, 163, 189–90, 198, 201, 221–22, 228, 230, 273
  collective commissions, 221–22
  conflicts with state assemblies, 229, 230, 247–48
  decertified, 201
  dissidents expelled, 99, 144
  efforts to hold democratic elections, 121, 128, 129

expanded, 144–45, 165, 166, 198, 230
Guerrero, 98, 131, 188 n. 11
Hidalgo, 98, 99, 131, 134–35, 144–45
information provided to members, 228, 229–30
Local 9 (Mexico City), 273, 281
Local 11 (Mexico City), 188 n. 11, 272 n. 13
Mexico State, 98, 99
Morelos, 137–38, 144–45, 166
negotiations on expansion, 98, 144–45
negotiations with national union, 121–22, 132, 133–34
Oaxaca, 120, 141, 162, 205 n. 43, 211–12, 221–22, 228, 237, 272 n. 13, 273–74, 282
officially recognized, 131
powers, 219
struggle for control of, 127–42
Valle de México, 131, 144–45, 165, 166
women in, 237
Lombardo Toledano, Vicente, 22 n. 42, 62, 63, 64–65, 64 n. 11
López Díaz, Celso Wenceslao, 201 n. 32
López Mateos, Adolfo, 70 n. 22
López Portillo, José, 82–96, 87, 98

de la Madrid Hurtado, Miguel, 100, 184–85, 188, 189, 190
Maestros Democráticos de Morelos (MDM), 124
Mainwaring, Scott, 56
Maldonado Robles, Fernando, 118, 119, 120
Martínez Martín, Ramón, 98–99, 98 n. 71, 99, 125
 and dissidents, 128, 128 n. 51
 as senator, 144
Martínez Noriega, Pedro, 163
mass congresses, 130, 130 n. 57, 131
Maybury-Lewis, Biorn, 305, 308–9
McAdam, Doug, 30, 49–50
MDM (Maestros Democráticos de Morelos), 124
Méndez Arceo, Sergio, 113
Mexican Academy of Human Rights, 189
Mexican Regional Labor Confederation (CROM), 62
Mexico. *See also* state-labor relations
 authoritarianism in, 11–14
 corporatism, 32–34, 33 n. 16
 economy, 16, 18, 82–84, 105, 115, 185
 electoral reforms, 15–16, 17, 20, 84

federal government reaction to teacher protests, 151–56
oil boom, 18, 83–84, 84 n. 51, 105, 115
political liberalization, 15–21
political opportunities, 300–301
repression of popular movements, 13
social movements, 15–21, 112–13, 283–88, 289, 294–95, 309
student movement, 15, 16, 71, 71 n. 24, 107–8, 270
Mexico City. *See also* Local 9; Local 10; Local 11
 Escuela Normal Superior, 184
 Oaxaca teachers' protests in, 121–22, 126
 teachers' protests in, 129, 133, 140, 144, 201
 urban popular movements, 19, 84
 Vanguardia in locals, 157
Mexico State
 economic development, 113 n. 20
 governors, 155
 social movements, 113
Mexico State union locals, 125 n. 42. *See also* Valle de México
 emergence of dissident movement, 125–27
 executive committees, 98, 99
Meza, Roberto, 113
Michels, Robert, 48–49
Ministry of Programming and the Budget (SPP), 81
Ministry of Public Education. *See* SEP
Miranda Castro, Alberto, 186 n. 6, 187
mobilization
 capacity, 50–52, 305
 combined with negotiation, 256–57, 258
 cycles, 150, 153
 declining support for, 281
 group solidarity and, 50–52, 263–64
 national, 121, 129, 131, 132–33, 140, 144, 187, 201, 268–71
Morelos
 economic development, 113 n. 20
 governors, 155
 social movements, 113
Morelos union local
 congresses, 137–38
 demands, 128–29, 142
 elections, 135, 137
 emergence of dissident movement, 124–25
 executive commission, 128
 executive committees, 137–38, 144–45, 166

Index   353

ideological purity, 164–67
internal divisions, 142–43
march to Mexico City, 129
negotiations on elections, 128, 129
organization, 167–68
protests, 121, 143, 144
SEP reaction to, 144
strategies, 127, 164, 165, 166–67
strikes, 128–29, 129 n. 53
supporters, 167, 170
tactics, 164
Vanguardia in, 138, 156
violence against members, 143, 157
Movimiento Revolucionario del Magisterio. See MRM
MRM (Movimiento Revolucionario del Magisterio), 67, 68, 69–70, 110
alliance with other unions, 69
in Oaxaca, 112–13, 141, 212
response to student movement, 71 n. 24
strategy, 74–75
Munck, Gerardo L., 57
Muñóz Ledo, Porfirio, 87 n. 54

NAFTA (North American Free Trade Agreement), 20, 286, 288
National Action Party (PAN), 19, 20, 285
National Confederation of Popular Organizations (CNOP), 2, 9 n. 14, 284
National Coordinating Committee of Education Workers. See CNTE
National Coordinating Committee of the Urban Popular Movement (CONAMUP), 17, 84, 148
National Executive Committee (CEN)
dissidents as members, 188, 188 n. 12, 278
negotiations with locals, 133–34
reaction to dissidents, 156, 231
National Front of Organizations and Citizens (FNOC), 9 n. 14
National Institute for Indigenous Affairs (INI), 111
National Peasant Confederation (CNC), 62, 284
National Pedagogical University (UPN), 86, 87–88
National "Plan of Ayala" Coordinating Committee (CNPA), 17, 84, 148
National Solidarity Program (PRONASOL), 274, 289 n. 31, 303 n. 10

National Union of Education Workers. See SNTE
National Vigilance Committee, 72, 72 n. 25
National Worker Peasant Popular Assembly (ANOCP), 200
new social movements approach, 28–29, 54
normal schools, 186, 186 n. 7, 236
graduates, 87 n. 56
protests in, 108, 109, 109 n. 8
rural, 108, 108 n. 7, 113, 157
North American Free Trade Agreement (NAFTA), 20, 286, 288
Núñez Acosta, Misael, 131–32, 272

Oaxaca
deconcentration of SEP in, 92 n. 62, 118–19
economic development, 113 n. 20
ethnic groups, 235
governors, 154, 190, 205, 210, 274
indigenous teachers, 110, 111–12
municipal governments, 244
popular organizations, 18, 112–13, 244
PRI, 118
SEP delegates, 120
USED, 208–9
Oaxaca union local (22)
accomplishments, 194, 281, 299
alternative education, 274, 292
brigades, 160–61, 160 n. 104
CNTE affiliation, 162 n. 106
comités de lucha, 119
congresses, 138–39, 139 n. 73, 140–42, 157, 273
congresses postponed, 205–9, 249
consultation with members, 228
coordinadoras, 222, 223
delegation assemblies, 222, 222 n. 8
delegation executive committees (CEDs), 221 n. 6
demands, 120–21
elections, 140–42, 199–200, 205–9, 249, 273, 299
emergence of dissident movement, 95, 115, 118–23
executive commission, 120–21, 122, 138–39, 139 n. 73, 162 n. 105
executive committees, 120, 141, 162, 205 n. 43, 211–12, 221–22, 228, 237, 272 n. 13, 273–74, 282
fundraising, 209 n. 46

guiding principles, 243 n. 39
indigenous teachers in, 233–35
influence in local SEP, 191
internal divisions, 162, 162 n. 106, 205, 207, 210–11, 212, 281–82
leadership, 119, 120, 163, 166, 212, 237, 248–50, 281–82
leadership accountability, 230
legal status, 183–84, 192–93, 192 n. 20
negotiations with national union, 122, 205–9
newspaper coverage, 118 n. 29
organizational structure, 160, 162, 219–24, 298
participation in national protests, 144
paycheck delivery, 194–95
permanent assembly, 160
political factions, 212, 251
precongresses, 140–42, 207, 249
protest background of leaders, 108–9
protests in Mexico City, 121–22, 126
relations with governor, 274
relations with national union, 192, 199–200, 299
relations with parents, 210, 273–74
relations with state SEP administration, 93
secretaries-general, 209–10, 211, 212, 249
state assembly, 219–21, 219 n. 3, 221 n. 5, 230
strategies, 127, 170, 206, 210–11
strikes, 119–20, 271
supporters, 170, 208
tactics, 120, 138–39
timing in protest cycle, 172
Vanguardia in, 138, 156, 156 n. 95, 190, 205 n. 43, 208–9
violence against members, 157, 209–10
women in, 237, 239
Workers' Day march (1980), 119
Offe, Claus, 35, 291
Olivares Santana, Enrique, 71, 97, 97 n. 70
Olmos Sánchez, Carlos, 72
organization
 ability to mobilize, 50–52, 305
 democracy, 53–56, 58, 299
 forms, 46, 53
 parallel, 158–59, 217–18, 222–24, 255
 political constraints on form, 306–8
 relationship to strategies and tactics, 52

Palma, Pedro, 143
PAN (Partido Acción Nacional), 19, 20, 285

parents, dissident teachers' relations with, 210, 243, 245–46, 273–74, 292
Partido Acción Nacional (PAN), 19, 20, 285
Partido Popular, 65
Partido Revolucionario Institucional. *See* PRI
Partido Revolucionario de los Trabajadores (PRT), 113
Partido de la Revolución Democrática (PRD), 19–20, 284, 286
Partido de la Revolución Mexicana (PRM), 63
Partido Socialista Unificado de México (PSUM), 18, 161, 212
Partido del Trabajo, 284 n. 30
Party of the Democratic Revolution (PRD), 19–20, 284, 286
Party of the Mexican Revolution (PRM), 63
Paul, Shuva, 55
peasant organizations, 113, 303
 Coalición Obrero Campesino Estudiantil del Istmo (COCEI), 18, 112, 160, 307
 Coalición Obrero Campesino Estudiantil de Oaxaca (COCEO), 112
 Confederación Nacional Campesina (CNC), 62, 284
 Coordinadora Nacional "Plan de Ayala" (CNPA), 17, 84, 148
 links with CNTE, 203, 243–44
 relations with government, 283, 284
peasants
 alliances with teachers, 243–44
 Chiapas uprising, 20, 286–87, 288, 309 n. 16
 view of education, 245
Perrow, Charles, 38, 49
Peru
 authoritarianism, 13
 teachers, 21
 women's movement, 307
Pescador, José Angel, 185
Piven, Frances Fox, 41, 42, 49
Pizzorno, Alessandro, 35
plenary of delegation representatives, 218, 219
political environment. *See also* authoritarianism; political space
 changes after 1989, 275–77
 changes in 1980s, 184–85
 conditions for protest movements, 40–44
 democratic transitions, 56–57, 308–12
 elections, 42–43, 301
 elite conflict, 43–44, 45–46
 external allies, 43, 49, 52, 301–3
 immediate, 39, 43–44, 106, 296
 impact on organizational forms, 306–8

Index

national level, 39
opportunities, 38–40, 42–43, 300–303
of social movements, 29–30, 37–40, 308–12
political parties. *See also specific parties*
affiliations of CNTE members, 147 n. 87
autonomy of CNTE from, 147–48, 259, 285
autonomy of SNTE from, 279–80
autonomy of social movements from, 47–48, 47 n. 37, 48 n. 41
in democratic transitions, 310
leftist, 17–20, 105, 283, 285
rightist, 283
political process approach, 5–6, 29–31, 303
political space, 39–40, 39 n. 26
for dissident teachers, 60–61, 105–6, 169, 260–62, 275–77, 296, 300–301
identifying and using, 260–62
state-labor conflict, 45–46, 296
popular movements. *See* social movements
PRD (Partido de la Revolución Democrática), 19–20, 284, 286
precongresses, 221, 230–32
Chiapas, 136, 198
Oaxaca, 140–42, 207, 249
press coverage
of dissident teachers, 118 n. 29, 130, 201
independent, 288
PRI (Partido Revolucionario Institucional). *See also* elections
dominance, 11
education ministers as presidential candidates, 100 n. 73, 190
history, 33 n. 15
in Oaxaca, 118
official unions in, 9–11, 33, 34
relationship with SNTE, 141, 144, 279–80
restructuring of, 10 n. 17, 280 n. 21, 286
scandals, 288
sectors, 2, 33, 33 n. 15, 284
SNTE role in, 2, 9 n. 14, 23, 71
SNTE support of, 64, 65, 71, 76, 267
PRM (Partido de la Revolución Mexicana), 63
Programa Nacional de Solidaridad. *See* PRONASOL
promotores. *See* indigenous teachers
PRONASOL (Programa Nacional de Solidaridad), 274, 289 n. 31, 303 n. 10
protest
cycles of, 107 n. 2, 172, 172 n. 121
traditions of, 107–13
protest movements. *See* social movements

PRT (Partido Revolucionario de los Trabajadores), 113
PSUM (Partido Socialista Unificado de México), 18, 161, 212
public sector workers, 80–82, 83
Puebla, indigenous education, 110–11
"La Quina." *See* Hernández Galicia, Joaquín

Ramírez López, Heladio, 210
repression. *See also* violence
of popular movements in Mexico, 13, 71 n. 24
of teachers in 1950s, 68–69, 70
resource-mobilization approach, 27–28
Revolutionary Teachers' Movement. *See* MRM
Revolutionary Workers Party (PRT), 113
Reyes Carrillo, Ezequiel, 143, 143 n. 84
Reyes Heroles, Jésus, 184, 187, 190
Reyna, José Luis, 13
Robles Martínez, Jesús, 64, 66, 69 n. 20, 71
Rosenthal, Naomi, 54–55
Rubin, Jeffrey W., 307
Ruíz Cortines, Adolfo, 65, 67
rural normal schools, 108, 108 n. 7, 113, 157
rural organizations. *See* peasant organizations

Sabines Gutiérrez, Juan, 137 n. 69, 154–55
Salazar Ramírez, Othón, 67, 68, 70
Salinas administration
compulsory education, 187 n. 8
labor relations, 267, 268, 268 n. 1, 275, 287
National Solidarity Program (PRONASOL), 274, 289 n. 31, 303 n. 10
political reforms, 10 n. 17, 12, 20
SNTE relations with, 3, 10 n. 17, 267, 271–72, 274, 276, 279–80, 283
social movements and, 20, 283–88, 289, 295, 309
Salinas de Gortari, Carlos, 3, 20, 271–72
Sánchez, Enrique W., 66, 69 n. 20
Sánchez Vite, Manuel, 67, 69 n. 20, 98
SCEP (Servicios Coordinados de Educación Publica), 191
Schmitter, Philippe, 32
Schneider, Cathy, 307, 309
school directors, 78, 269 n. 6
schools. *See also* education system
democracy in, 216
Schwartz, Michael, 54–55
Secretaría de Educación Pública. *See* SEP
Secretaría de Programación y Presupuesto (SPP), 81

356   Index

SEP (Secretaría de Educación Pública). *See also* SEP-SNTE relations
- administrative reforms, 93–94
- administrative structure, 89–90, 89 n. 60
- corruption, 76
- decentralization, 86 n. 53, 185–86, 191
- deconcentration, 86–87, 86 n. 53, 88–96, 89 n. 58, 103, 118–19, 194
- employment conditions, 81
- importance in teachers' lives, 77
- indigenous teachers, 111, 111 n. 15
- influence of CNTE, 93–94, 191
- management, 94, 94 n. 68
- ministers, 315
- paycheck delivery, 93–94, 95, 95 n. 69, 118, 194–95
- political appointments, 81, 81 n. 43
- relations with CNTE, 100, 121–23, 152–53
- relations with rank-and-file teachers, 93–94
- responses to dissidents' demands, 121–23, 270–71, 280–81
- state delegates, 92, 92 n. 64, 120, 144
- state level, 78–79, 89–90, 100 n. 74, 191, 199
- technocratic faction, 85–89, 87 n. 54, n. 56, 90–92

SEP-SNTE relations
- conflicts, 82–96, 88 n. 57, 98–100, 102–4, 118–19
- conflicts as political space for dissidents, 60–61
- conflicts over education policy, 81, 88–89, 99, 185–87, 186–87
- deconcentration, 86–87, 88–96, 92 n. 62, 99, 118–19
- effects of dissident movement, 96–100, 282–83
- influence on dissident movement, 102–4, 275–76
- rapprochements, 100–101, 144, 184, 190–91
- sources of conflicts, 85–96
- union influence over administrative positions, 79, 79 n. 40, 80, 90, 96, 190, 191
- union's power in, 75–76, 92–93

Servicios Coordinados de Educación Publica (SCEP), 191

sexual harassment, 79

Sindicato Nacional de Trabajadores de la Educación. *See* SNTE

SNTE (Sindicato Nacional de Trabajadores de la Educación). *See also* SEP-SNTE relations; Vanguardia Revolucionaria; *and regional union locals*
- centralization of power in, 80
- commercial ventures, 76 n. 35
- corruption, 76, 79
- coup of 1972, 71–73, 73 n. 28, 74, 75
- democratic reforms, 279–80
- dissident representatives on national executive committee, 188, 188 n. 12, 278
- dues, 78 n. 38
- early dissidents, 66–70, 109–10
- factional conflicts, 61, 63–66, 67–68, 69 n. 20, 71–73, 97
- finances, 80, 80 n. 41
- government offices held by leaders, 23, 65–66, 71, 99, 144, 151
- government support of, 75–76
- history, 59–73
- impact of CNTE, 96–99
- importance in teachers' lives, 77, 79–80
- Jonguitud's power in, 3, 72, 73–74, 76–77, 269
- leaders, 315
- linked with local politicians, 156–57
- local leadership conflicts, 67, 67 n. 12
- local officials and CNTE, 70, 131, 156–57
- locals, 2 n. 2, 80
- male dominance of leadership, 23
- members as PRI candidates, 76, 78
- membership, 2, 2 n. 3
- national congresses, 97, 269, 269 n. 4, 273, 278, 279
- National Vigilance Committee, 72, 72 n. 25
- negotiations on elections, 121, 129, 205–9, 299
- negotiations on local executive committees, 98, 121, 122, 129, 133–34, 136, 144-45
- as official union, 59–61
- paycheck delivery issue, 95, 118
- political independence, 279–80
- positions on education policy, 81, 88–89, 99
- reaction to dissidents, 79–80, 99, 122 n. 35, 144, 156, 188
- relations with CNTE, 149, 150–51, 189–90, 197, 198–201, 231–32, 269
- relations with PRI, 2, 9 n. 14, 23, 64, 65, 66, 71, 76, 100, 279
- response to Chiapas strike, 115–17
- Salinas government and, 3, 10 n. 17, 267, 271–72, 274, 276, 279–80, 283

telesecundarias teachers, 109
women in leadership, 23, 23 n. 44, 235–38
women members, 23, 235 n. 25
Social Integration and Research Institute of Oaxaca (IIISEO), 111
social movements. *See also* peasant organizations; urban popular movements
  in authoritarian environments, 4–9, 10–11, 14–15, 40–44, 58, 299–312
  autonomy from political parties, 47–48, 47 n. 37, 48 n. 41
  decision-making processes, 52
  in democracies, 40
  democratic organization of, 53–56, 57, 58, 299, 307–8
  democratic transitions and, 56–57, 308–12
  economic conditions for, 311
  effectiveness, 285
  elite tolerance of, 40–42, 300–301
  external allies, 43, 49, 52, 301–3
  external pressures, 49–50
  growth of, 18–19, 19 n. 38
  institutional access, 40–41, 40 n. 28, 309, 310, 310 n. 18
  internal tensions, 49
  in Latin America, 28–29, 47 n. 37, 54, 56–57, 302
  leadership accountability, 51, 51 n. 44
  member participation, 51–52
  in Mexico, 15–21, 112–13, 283–88, 289, 294–95, 309
  moderate strategies, 304–5
  new social movements approach, 28–29, 54
  organizational forms, 46, 50–52, 150 n. 90, 306–8
  political environment, 29–30, 37–40, 283–88, 308–12
  political factions in, 251 n. 51
  political impact, 56–58, 294–95
  political process approach, 5–6, 29–31, 303
  predecessors of CNTE, 110–13
  regional, 18–19
  repression in Mexico, 13
  resource-mobilization approach, 27–28
  role in elections, 285–86
  successful, 47–48, 56–58, 291
  support of Catholic Church, 113, 302
  survival, 6–9, 46, 48–50
  in Western Europe, 56
Solana Morales, Fernando, 87 n. 54, 89, 90, 92, 98, 100, 121

SPP (Secretaría de Programación y Presupuesto), 81
State Assembly of Union Representatives, 219–21, 219 n. 3, 221 n. 5, 225–28, 225 n. 15
  conflicts with executive committees, 229, 230, 247–48
  indigenous teachers in, 233–34
state governors. *See also specific states*
  reactions to dissident teachers, 153–56
  role in education system, 92 n. 63, 186, 274
state-labor relations. *See also* SEP-SNTE relations
  conflict, 45–46, 275–76
  independent unions, 83–84
  in Mexico, 9–10, 32, 34–37, 59–60, 62–63, 63 n. 7, 83–84, 97
  opportunities for dissidents, 275–76, 296
strategies
  Chiapas local, 127, 149, 162, 170, 207
  CNTE, 127–28, 147, 166–67, 169–73, 251–62, 304
  coordinadoras, 18
  Guerrero local, 168 n. 117
  Hidalgo local, 127, 164, 167
  internal democracy as, 55, 214–15, 299
  Línea Proletaria, 252–53
  moderate, 304–5
  Morelos local, 127, 164, 165, 166–67
  Oaxaca local, 127, 170, 206, 210–11
  to obtain control of union locals, 127–28
  relationship to organizational form, 52
  Valle de México local, 127, 164, 173
Street, Susan, 95
strikes
  in Chiapas, 115–17, 126
  in Guerrero, 133
  in Hidalgo, 131
  in Mexico City, 68–69
  in Morelos, 128–29, 129 n. 53
  national, 121, 131, 144, 269, 271
  in Oaxaca, 119–20
  restrictions on, 80
  at universities, 271
  in Valle de México, 130
student movements
  influence on dissident teachers, 108–9
  of 1968, 15, 16, 107–8, 112
  in rural normal schools, 108, 109, 109 n. 8
  SNTE reaction, 71, 71 n. 24

student organizations
  Coalición Obrero Campesino Estudiantil del Istmo (COCEI), 18, 112, 160, 307
  Coalición Obrero Campesino Estudiantil de Oaxaca (COCEO), 112
supervisors, 78, 79, 269 n. 6

Tabasco union local, 117
tactics
  CNTE, 120, 171, 247–49
  disagreements among dissidents, 120, 247–49
  relationship to organizational form, 52
  of union locals, 120, 138–39, 164
Tarrow, Sidney, 38
teachers. *See also* indigenous teachers; wages
  attraction of profession, 77–78
  class origins, 22, 77–78, 87 n. 56, 108
  community activism, 200, 243–45
  discontent, 105
  emigration, 185
  increased numbers of, 71 n. 23, 75–76, 83 n. 48, 247
  job assignments, 76, 76 n. 34, 89, 191, 195–96, 240–41
  in municipal governments, 244
  relations with parents, 210, 243, 245–46, 273–74, 292
  role in society, 21–22
  SNTE members, 78 n. 38
  social mobility of, 77–78, 110
  supervisors, 78, 79, 269 n. 6
  women, 23, 68, 77–78, 235–37
  young, 246–47, 270 n. 8
teachers' movement. *See* CNTE
teacher training
  conflicts over, 86
  Escuela Normal Superior, 184
  normal schools, 87 n. 56, 108, 108 n. 7, 109 n. 8, 113, 157, 186, 186 n. 7, 236
  Universidad Pedagógica Nacional (UPN), 86, 87–88
telesecundarias, 109, 109 n. 10
Torres Bodet, Jaime, 63
Torres, Carlos Alberto, 185
trade unions. *See* labor unions; SNTE
trotskyists, 201, 202, 202 n. 33, 203, 251
Trow, Martin, 55
Tuxtla Gutiérrez (Chiapas), 136, 199, 201, 239–40

Unidades de Servicios Educativos a Descentralizar. *See* USED

Unified Socialist Party of Mexico (PSUM), 18, 161, 212
union democracy
  collective identity and, 241–43
  consultation with membership, 225–26, 227–29
  demands for, 16–18, 123–24, 271
  failings, 229
  impact outside union, 24, 244–45, 293–94, 299
  job assignments and promotions, 195–96, 240–41
  in SNTE locals, 109–10, 216–17, 225–28, 279–80, 292–93
  strategies of CNTE, 127–28, 169–70, 214–15, 217–18, 299, 306
  studies of, 55
Unión de Trabajadores de la Educación (UTE), 204 n. 39, 250
Union of Education Workers (UTE), 204 n. 39, 250
unions. *See* labor unions; SNTE
United Farm Workers, 38
United States
  agricultural workers organized in, 245
  elections, 42
Units of Educational Services to be Decentralized. *See* USED
Universidad Pedagógica Nacional (UPN), 86, 87–88
UPN (Universidad Pedagógica Nacional), 86, 87–88
urban popular movements
  Chile, 310 n. 18
  Coordinadora Nacional del Movimiento Urbano Popular (CONAMUP), 17, 84, 148
  effectiveness, 285
  Mexico City, 19, 84
  organizational structures, 307
  relations with government, 283, 284, 284 n. 30
USED (Unidades de Servicios Educativos a Descentralizar), 190
  Chiapas, 199, 200–201, 202
  Oaxaca, 208–9
UTE (Unión de Trabajadores de la Educación), 204 n. 39, 250

Valle de México union local (36)
  assassination of Núñez Acosta, 131–32, 272

Index

demands, 126–27, 129–30, 142
emergence of dissident movement, 125–27
executive committees, 131, 134, 144–45, 165, 166
ideological purity, 164–67
mass congress, 130
negotiations with national union, 133–34, 144–45, 272 n. 13
organizational structure, 161, 167–68
participation in national protests, 121, 131, 132–33, 144
relations with state governors, 155
SEP reaction to, 144
strategies, 127, 164, 173
strikes, 130, 271
supporters, 134, 167, 170
tactics, 142, 143, 164
timing in protest cycle, 172
Vanguardia in, 157
Vanguardia Revolucionaria, 73–75
anthem, 74, 74 n. 29
in Chiapas, 135–36, 189–90, 198–201
as congress delegates, 232
criticized by dissidents, 98 n. 72
declining support, 270, 270 n. 8
disbanded, 275, 276, 279
efforts to co-opt dissident supporters, 138, 157
efforts to strengthen, 145
as enemy, 242
Gordillo's view of, 274–75
in Hidalgo, 143
members expelled from jobs, 196–97
in Mexico City, 157
in Morelos, 138, 156
in Oaxaca, 138, 156, 156 n. 95, 190, 205 n. 43, 208–9
parent associations, 245
power, 76, 77, 80, 191, 195
protests on paycheck delays, 95
in Valle de México, 157
violence of, 132, 172
weakness, 171–72
Vasconcelos, José, 110
Vásquez Colmenares, Pedro, 140, 154, 190
Vázquez, Genaro, 113
de la Vega Domínguez, Jorge, 155
Véjar Vásquez, Octavio, 62–63

Veracruz, indigenous education, 110–11
Vindicative Bloc, 126
Viola, Eduardo, 56
violence
abductions and torture, 143, 157, 157 n. 101
assassination of Núñez Acosta, 131–32, 272
attacks on dissidents, 68–69, 99, 201
in Chiapas, 155, 189, 200, 201, 201 n. 32, 210
in delegation assemblies, 231
in Guerrero, 156, 157
in Hidalgo, 143, 157
linked to class conflicts, 157, 189, 209
linked to vanguardista strength, 132, 172
in Morelos, 143, 157
in Oaxaca, 157, 209–10

wages, teachers'
in 1940s and 1950s, 68 n. 15
CNTE demands, 83, 98, 115–17, 121–23, 280–81
decline in 1970s, 82–83, 82 n. 46
decline in 1980s, 185, 268
increases, 121–23, 129, 270–71, 271 n. 10, 280–81
women
in CNTE leadership, 237–38, 239
contribution to CNTE, 238–40, 242
dissidents, 235–40
household duties, 236–37, 238, 239
movement of, in Latin America, 301, 302, 307
sexual harassment, 79
in SNTE leadership, 23, 23 n. 44, 235–38
SNTE members, 23, 235 n. 25
teachers, 23, 68, 77–78, 235–37
Worker-Peasant-Student Coalition of Oaxaca (COCEO), 112
Worker-Peasant-Student Coalition of the Isthmus (COCEI), 18, 112, 160, 307

Yáñez, Agustín, 71

Zapatista National Liberation Army, 20, 309 n. 16
Zaragosa, Odón, 143
Zárate Aquino, Manuel, 154
Zedillo Ponce de Leon, Ernesto, 100 n. 73, 310 n. 17

www.ingramcontent.com/pod-product-compliance
Lightning Source LLC
Chambersburg PA
CBHW031542300426
44111CB00006BA/150